Paths of Desire
Images of Exploration and Mapping in Canadian Women's Writing

Marlene Goldman

Previous studies on exploration and mapping images in literature have concentrated on the issue of anticolonialism. Few critics have traced the influence of postmodern and feminist theories on writings by Canadian women authors. In this study of the experimental works of five writers, Marlene Goldman posits intriguing connections between the act of map-making, postmodern theory, and female identity.

Goldman examines images of exploration and mapping in the works of Audrey Thomas, Susan Swan, Daphne Marlatt, Aritha van Herk, and Jane Urquhart. These authors use the images both to portray women's positions within traditional discourse and to chart alternative representations of female identity. What emerges is a series of feminist, subversive tactics: challenges to a particular discourse, such as romantic narrative; parodic appropriation and mimicry; attempts to construct a female-centred frame of reference; and full-blown, violent efforts to destroy the narrative frame altogether. Goldman's close readings of individual texts are interwoven with related discussions of contemporary theory.

For the first time these writers' works are considered together and receive the critical attention they deserve. Paths of Desire establishes the importance of feminist images of exploration and map-making in the Canadian literary tradition.

MARLENE GOLDMAN is an assistant professor in the Department of English at the University of Toronto.

THEORY/CULTURE

General Editors:
Linda Hutcheon, Gary Leonard, Jill Matus,
Janet Paterson, and Paul Perron

MARLENE GOLDMAN

Paths of Desire:
Images of Exploration
and Mapping in Canadian
Women's Writing

UNIVERSITY OF TORONTO PRESS
Toronto Buffalo London

© University of Toronto Press Incorporated 1997
Toronto Buffalo London
Printed in Canada

ISBN 0-8020-0986-7 (cloth)
ISBN 0-8020-7944-X (paper)

∞

Printed on acid-free paper

PR
9188
.G65
1997
oct.1999

Canadian Cataloguing in Publication Data

Goldman, Marlene, 1963–
  Paths of desire : images of exploration and mapping
in Canadian women's writing

(Theory/culture)
Includes bibliographical references and index.
ISBN 0-8020-0986-7 (bound)   ISBN 0-8020-7944-X (pbk.)

1. Canadian fiction (English) – Women authors – History
and criticism.*   2. Canadian fiction (English) – 20th
century – History and criticism.*   3. Women in literature.
I. Title.   II. Series.

PS8191.W65G64 1997   C813'.5409352042   C96-932108-2
PR9192.6.W6G64 1997

'The Infant Giantess' and 'The Kentucky Giant's Hymeneal' are reproduced by
permission of Susan Swan.

This book has been published with the help of a grant from the Humanities and Social
Sciences Federation of Canada, using funds provided by the Social Sciences and
Humanities Research Council of Canada.

University of Toronto Press acknowledges the assistance to its publishing program of the
Canada Council and the Ontario Arts Council.

Contents

Acknowledgments

This project could not have been undertaken or seen to completion without the help and encouragement of friends and family. I owe thanks to Bob Goldman, Elizabeth Jones, Ann Baranowski, Malcolm Woodland, Dominic Jenkins, Teresa Heffernan, Francois Lachance, and Laura Hancu for their enduring emotional and intellectual support. Thanks are also due to Heather Murray and Rosemary Sullivan, who read earlier drafts of the manuscript. The editors at the University of Toronto Press were also very helpful, and I wish to thank Joan Bulger for her unflagging cheerfulness and Judy Williams for her thoughtful suggestions and editorial comments. My greatest debt for direction and guidance is to Linda Hutcheon, who gave me the courage to take risks and transformed the often daunting process of writing this book into a wonderful adventure.

PATHS OF DESIRE

1

Introduction

[I]f an explorer should come back and bring word of other sexes looking through the branches of other trees at other skies, nothing would be of greater service to humanity ... (Woolf, *Room*, 84)

I began a foray into contemporary Canadian fiction to determine if and how women writers were responding to the statement made by Virginia Woolf that, in literature, the linguistic terrain is obscured by the 'dominance of the ... [male] "I"' (*Room*, 96). Woolf implies that it is futile and perhaps even dangerous for women to attempt to map themselves onto the existing linguistic landscape because '[n]othing will grow there' (96). Her insights, which represent language as a precarious ideological space for women, have been recently reformulated in the light of poststructuralist theory. Teresa de Lauretis also refers to language as a 'terrain' which is 'populated with the intentions of others' (*Alice*, 2), and she echoes Woolf when she asks, 'how does one write or speak as a woman?' (10).

When I turned to contemporary Canadian fiction, it struck me that many women writers are actively struggling with the problem of representing female subjectivity within the linguistic terrain. Quite a few writers, in keeping with Woolf's analogy, draw comparisons between the plotting of language and the mapping of the geographical terrain, and invoke images of exploration and cartography to signal their interest in recoding traditional representations of female identity. In the past, critics have noted that women writers are obsessed with the problem of 'character formation' and 'the difficulty of maintaining ontological security' (Stan Fogel qtd. in Hutcheon, *Canadian*, 5). While it may be 'a commonplace of metafiction to use maps that record roads as images of linear narrative' (Hutcheon, *Canadian*, 130), in the case of Canadian women's fictions, I would suggest that these images reflect a particular concern to explore the possibility of transforming inherited cultural and literary maps that have charted the terrain of female identity.

In Audrey Thomas's *Intertidal Life*, the narrator, Alice Hoyle, remarks that women must assume the roles of explorers and cartographers if they hope to change established notions of female identity:

> I read about ... this whole male world of the age of exploration and I see that women are going to have to get out there and do the same thing. ... [W]hat's happening to men and women today is just as exciting and terrifying as the discovery that the earth was round, not flat. ... But we all need new maps, new instruments to try and fix our new positions. ... (170–1)

Many of the novels in this study feature characters like Alice Hoyle, writers on journeys or quests who self-consciously adopt images of map-making and exploration because they themselves are engaged in creating fictions that portray women embarked on voyages of discovery. This type of mirroring or *mise en abyme* serves to emphasize the importance of map-making and its relationship to the writing process, clarifying that the 'new maps' and 'new instruments' will ultimately be forged within the domain of language, and that women's 'new positions' must be fixed within specific discourses. By 'discourse' I refer to what Catherine Belsey describes as a 'domain of language-use, a particular way of talking (and writing and thinking). A discourse involves certain shared assumptions which appear in the formulations that characterize it' (Belsey, 5). All of the fictions in this study posit a link between a subversive engagement with established discourses and attempts to disrupt the configuration of gender within society at large.

This subversive project is by no means straightforward, as Coral Ann Howells points out in her valuable study of Canadian women's fiction, because attempts at revising traditional discourses are problematized by the knowledge that 'self-definition can take place only within the very traditions that are being questioned' (*Private*, 3). This paradoxical situation, common to postmodern texts, raises a serious concern: Are Canadian women writers adopting traditional narrative structures ostensibly for the purposes of questioning these structures, while, in fact, leaving the basic elements and underlying ideologies intact? As far as Howells is concerned, the answer is yes. She implies that these fictions are governed by a conservative attitude; as she says, they seek shifts 'of emphasis rather than revolution' (186).

Where Howells sees shifts of emphasis, I see subversion. Although the pitfalls of simply reproducing existing ideologies remain a persistent danger in the fictions treated in this study, the nature of the texts' self-conscious and parodic appropriation of traditional narratives precludes the replication of these structures and their ideological underpinnings. As Linda Hutcheon asserts:

> Parody – or intertextuality in general – plays an important role in much women's fiction

today, as it seeks a feminine space while still acknowledging ... the power of the (male /
'universal') space in which it cannot avoid, to some extent, operating. *This enforced complicity does not diminish the impact of its protest*, but it does set up the conditions within which
it will exist. (*Canadian*, 110; my emphasis)

In order to appreciate the impact of the protests launched by these fictions –
protests that move beyond the conservative gesture of mimicry – it is crucial to
consider the extent to which many of the novels advocate a radical reshaping of
the map-making process which, in some cases, means abandoning traditional
maps and map-making altogether. I mean 'mapping' literally: the production of 'a
representation of the earth's surface or a part of it, its physical and political features, etc., or of the heavens, delineated on a flat surface of paper or other material, each point in the drawing corresponding to a geographical or celestial position
according to a definite scale or projection' (*OED*). However, I am even more concerned with the term's more figurative sense, which includes maps that take the
form of narrative accounts – maps that provide 'a circumstantial account of a state
of things' (*OED*).

In Canada, the current practice of reformulating the discursive maps that have
generated images of female subjectivity must be seen in the light of texts written
previously – texts that first put into question the prevailing nineteenth-century
discourses that accompanied the shift from predominantly agrarian societies to
industrial capitalism and divided domains of experience according to sex, encouraging men to become heroic explorers, while defining women as the Angels in the
House who kept the home fires burning.[1] One novel that instigates this disruption
is Ethel Wilson's *The Swamp Angel* (1954), a story that opens with a woman
preparing supper for her husband, eating dinner, and then retreating to the
kitchen supposedly to wash the dishes. Instead of cleaning up, however, she folds
her apron, escapes through the kitchen door into the night, and begins a journey
through the wilds of British Columbia.

Like Wilson's fiction, the novels by Margaret Laurence similarly challenged the
legitimacy of a literary tradition that only had room for male heroes and explorers.
In the novel *A Bird in the House* (1963), the narrator, Vanessa, writes a story featuring two famous coureurs-de-bois and a woman she names Marie. Vanessa runs
into trouble when she tries to get Marie 'out of her unpromising life.' She realizes
that the men 'wouldn't give [Marie] ... a second glance'; this fact depresses her
·and she does not want to finish the story. As she says, 'What was the use, if she
couldn't get out except by ruses which clearly wouldn't happen in real life?' (178).
The insistence that what is written must be possible in real life implies that women were not writing solely for amusement, but in order to furnish themselves with
stories, which, like maps, could serve as guides to lead them out of unheroic, un-

promising lives. In accordance with these early fictions, many of the novels examined in this study reflect a belief in the power of fictions to forge escape routes for women.

Focusing on the intersection between women and fiction, as it does, this study has implications for critics of women's literature and feminist narrative strategies. Yet, in the light of the fact that the texts under consideration emphasize relationships between cartographic and gender inscription, it should also appeal to a more general audience concerned with the discursive construction of Canada and critiques of this representation. In an attempt to address a wide variety of readers who may not all be conversant in literary theory, the study offers close readings of individual texts interwoven with related discussions of contemporary theory. The study steers away from established authors such as Atwood, Laurence, Munro, and Gallant, to name a few, whose fictions also rely on metaphors of map-making and cartography to portray women's place in patriarchal society. The decision to focus on lesser-known authors stems from a belief that there are now many other innovative women writers whose fictions deserve critical attention.

As Robert Lecker points out in his book *Making It Real: The Canonization of English-Canadian Literature* (1995), for the most part, Canadian critics have championed a mimetic orthodoxy that privileges authors working in the realist mode (34–46). According to Lecker, this bias toward realist fiction helps to explain why experimental writers have received little critical or popular recognition. He goes on to cite two influential critics, David Stouck and W.J. Keith, who, in their accounts of Canadian literature, ignore the contributions of non-realist writers. Stouck defends his decision to overlook these writers on the grounds that they supposedly 'have found their models and sources of inspiration outside the country' (27). In his survey of Canadian literary history entitled *Canadian Literature in English* (1985), Keith likewise dismisses the contributions of accomplished experimental writers, arguing that they fail 'to display a coherent, unifying vision' (172).

In an attempt to balance the critical favour showered on traditional writers who rely on the conventions of representational realism, this study focuses on the works of experimental women writers who trouble realist, conservative assumptions. The contemporary texts which form the basis of this study include Audrey Thomas's *Intertidal Life*; Susan Swan's *The Biggest Modern Woman of the World*; Daphne Marlatt's *Ana Historic*; Aritha van Herk's *Judith, The Tent Peg, No Fixed Address*, and *Places Far from Ellesmere*; and Jane Urquhart's *The Whirlpool*. These works were chosen because each posits intriguing connections between female identity, language, and the act of map-making. More precisely, each relies on the figures of mapping and exploration to portray both women's position within a set of traditional discourses and attempts to chart alternative representations of female identity. The second feature that the novels have in common relates to their unorthodox treatment of traditional narrative strategies. All of the works listed above compose narratives that draw on a variety of genres, and they often weave traces of other – usually traditional, canonical – texts into their narratives for the purposes of parodic appropriation. One effect of this blurring of genre boundaries, in combination with the insistence on intertextuality, is the disruption of the ability to make clear-cut distinctions about what is fact and what is fiction, what is original or authentic and what is imitation. This type of confusion serves to underscore the 'constructedness' of meaning itself. In the hands of women writers, this confusion becomes a tactic for subversion because, by problematizing the nature of 'fact,' the texts strategically call into question the supposedly historical and factual discourses that have defined what it means to be female.

Although the novels display a common concern with map-making, they nevertheless demonstrate striking differences in their approaches to traditional discourses, and they offer widely divergent methods of challenging these discourses. In many ways, what emerges in this study is a series of tactics of subversion. Tactics range from the most basic attempt to arrest the workings of a particular discourse, such as the narrative of romance (a strategy which is adopted in *Intertidal Life*), to the use of parodic appropriation and mimicry (in Swan's text), to attempts to move beyond a masculine frame of reference by constructing a female-centred one (in Daphne Marlatt's *Ana Historic*), to full-blown, violent efforts to destroy the narrative frame altogether, so as to move beyond recognizable, established forms of representation (in van Herk's most recent fictions). In some cases, as in Urquhart's novel, many of these tactics are combined, allowing readers to evaluate the pros and cons of each strategy.

Admittedly, my interest in the issues of orientation and disorientation has ensured some element of commonality among the texts. In the context of a study of the images of exploration and map-making in the works of Canadian women writers, there is a strong temptation to link the search for personal identity depicted in the texts with the national problem regarding identity. While I do highlight this link, for the most part, I am following the lead of the texts which self-reflexively draw attention to the connections between gender identity and national identity, and emphasize the deployment of narrative strategies that consistently undermine traditional literary structures. The presence of these shared features indicates that, over and above any act of selection, these works seem to have been informed by a set of related historical and literary discourses. Given that these writers are or have become Canadian, it seems probable that the ongoing discussions of national identity have played a part in their tendency to contest established representations of female identity using images of exploration and mapping.

In this country, a number of famous (some would say infamous) critical studies have posited links between questions concerning national identity and problems of spatial orientation. In *Survival: A Thematic Guide to Canadian Literature* (1972), a book which became Canada's 'most popular and most influential work of literary criticism' (see McCombs, 7), Margaret Atwood forges a direct connection between Canadian identity and the practices of exploring and map-making. According to Atwood, in this country, when you've gone through 'a thin topsoil of immediate ancestors, what you hit will not be Richard the Third or the American or French Revolutions; it will probably be either a Settler or an Explorer' (112–13). Her representation of Canada's literary tradition, based as it is on a European legacy of settlers and explorers and an over-arching 'victim-survival' thesis, has angered several critics who view her perspective as Eurocentric and her thematic schema as monolithic and reductive.[2] Frank Davey criticized Atwood for over-emphasizing writers whose works fit her model and simply ignoring other fictions that might contradict her views (Davey, 'Atwood,' 83–4). Whether or not Atwood's thesis provides an empirically accurate picture of the development of literature in Canada (and I do not think it does), her study has proved to be a compelling fiction – a myth, if you like. As Robert Lecker suggests, Davey can argue all he likes that the book was of 'limited use to educators,' but the fact remains that it outsold all other critical books on Canadian literature combined (87). Owing to *Survival*'s popularity, its terms of reference, specifically the emphasis on exploration and map-making, have sparked the imagination of countless writers in this country – writers who both accept Atwood's thesis and/or playfully emphasize its limitations.

Whereas critics such as Davey point out the flaws in Atwood's model – flaws that stem from the fact that it views the whole of Canadian culture as a unified entity – other critics concentrate on the validity of the emphasis she places on metaphors of exploration in Canadian literature. Seemingly taking her cue from Atwood, Aritha van Herk offers a theory of why Canadians are driven to create maps. She, too, cites the fact that Canada is a relatively young country – young enough to still be engaged in the map-making process and to have 'almost perfect records of our own charting' ('Mapping,' 75). Currently, a growing number of critics and writers, including W.J. Keith, Germaine Warkentin, John Moss, Sherrill Grace, Rudy Wiebe, and Ian MacLaren, to name a few, are turning their attention to the importance of the legacy of exploration literature and its impact on the development of an English-Canadian literary tradition.[3] To underscore the link between the two, Keith points out that it was travellers and explorers such as Alexander Henry, Samuel Herne, Alexander Mackenzie, and David Thompson who showed the first signs of literary activity in this country (13) – paradoxically, because these people would never have categorized themselves as literary folk. While this model of literary development, which traces its roots back to the explorers, does not hold true for all writers (clearly few people actually have an immediate ancestral connection to the explorers who first sailed to this country and mapped its contours), nevertheless, this myth of origins constitutes a discourse that is available to contemporary writers. George Bowering invoked the tradition when he wrote his award-winning depiction of the voyage of George Vancouver, *Burning Water* (1980). In *Solomon Gursky Was Here* (1989), Mordecai Richler also refers to the myth when he playfully casts a Jewish explorer, Ephraim Gursky, in his version of the doomed Franklin expedition. More recently, in *A Discovery of Strangers* (1994), Rudy Wiebe draws on this same narrative of exploration to trace the initial contact between the members of the first Franklin expedition (1819–21) and the Natives who assisted them. Thus, regardless of their personal histories, authors can and do turn to this narrative and treat it as a fiction from which they can 'make metaphors for their own experience in the present' (*Survival*, 112).

As Keith points out, exploration narratives played a formative role in the development of Canadian literature, even though they were soon augmented by the literary contributions from settlers and travellers, who described their life in Canada so as to give potential immigrants a better sense of the country they would encounter. As Canada began to take shape in the second half of the nineteenth century there was a great demand for this type of narrative; during this period, travel literature became a dominant 'form of non-fiction' (Keith, 22) and a great deal of it was written by women. Susanna Moodie, her sister Catharine Parr Traill, Lady Dufferin, Elizabeth Simcoe, and Anna Jameson provided crucial information about the new land. Most of these women had left behind more or less cultured environments and when they arrived as travellers and settlers in Canada, where habitation was scattered and sparse, they found themselves displaced. As a result, they wrote, not only for the benefit of their fellow settlers, but also to orient themselves in an unfamiliar landscape.

Critics such as Helen Buss have suggested that, unlike their male counterparts who developed what has been called 'the garrison mentality' (Frye, *Bush*, 225), many of these women reacted to the strangeness of the Canadian landscape 'by merging their own identity, in some imaginative way, with the new land.' In her study, 'Women and the Garrison Mentality: Pioneer Women Autobiographers and Their Relation to the Land,' Buss concentrates on autobiographical accounts rather than traditional fiction and poetry to argue that women such as Susan Allison, Georgina Binnie-Clark, Martha Black, Mary O'Brien, and Elizabeth Simcoe achieved 'a realization of self in the wilderness through significant relationships and the act of writing to an intimate audience' (126, 130). While some women may not have responded to the landscape as men did, the need to determine one's place in the landscape affected men and women alike, and this preoccupation seems to have left its mark on Canada's literary tradition.

As I have suggested, writers as well as critics played a leading role in characterizing the concern regarding orientation as fundamental to Canadian literature. In his famous conclusion to the *Literary History of Canada*, Northrop Frye deems the struggle to orient oneself the primary and lasting concern of the Canadian sensibility: 'It seems to me that Canadian sensibility has been profoundly disturbed, not so much by our famous problem of identity, important as that is, as by a series of paradoxes in what confronts that identity. It is less perplexed by the question "Who am I?" than by some such riddle as "Where is here?"' (*Bush*, 220). Frye's comments and his method of thematic analysis were developed by Atwood and other thematic critics, such as D.G. Jones and John Moss. As noted earlier, Atwood went on to argue that the question 'Where is here?' was a national as well as literary concern for Canadians – a concern that was especially problematic because, in attempting to formulate an answer, Canadians had to struggle against a terminology that was 'foreign and completely inadequate to describe what ... [was] actually being seen' (*Survival*, 62). Again, it is important to recognize that neither Frye nor Atwood conjured concerns regarding linguistic alienation out of thin air. As David Staines argues in his book *Beyond the Provinces: Literary Canada at Century's End* (1995), the question 'Where is here?' has been 'a preoccupation of Canadian writers since the beginnings of our literary culture about a century ago' (7). Staines speculates that the question may hark back to 'the possible origin of the very word *Canada*, which may well come from the Portuguese word meaning "Nobody here"' (7). As early as 1858, Thomas D'Arcy McGee, Canada's most persuasive spokesman for Confederation, reflected on the problem facing Canadian writers forced to draw on borrowed traditions:

The books that are made elsewhere, even in England, are not always the best fitted for us; they do not always run on the same mental gauge, nor connect with our trains of thought; they do not take us up at the by-stages of cultivation at which we have arrived, and where we are emptied forth as on a barren, pathless habitationless heath. ... [I]t seems to me we do much need several other books calculated to our own meridian, and hitting home our own society, either where it is sluggish or priggish, or wholly defective in its present style of culture. (McGee, 262)

Viewed within this historical context, the problem of national representation, and, on a more personal level, self-representation, can be seen as something that started well before the current twentieth-century concern, and extends well beyond the interest of a few feminist writers. Dennis Lee explores this problem in his essay 'Cadence, Country, Silence' (1973), a work that relates public conflicts regarding national representation to his personal bout with writer's block, a frustrating and inexplicable period of silence. As he explains, 'the words I knew said Britain, and they said America but they did not say my home' (46). Similarly, Robert Kroetsch, a writer and critic, also believes that self-representation is a stumbling-block for every writer in this country. He recalls D'Arcy McGee and Lee when he suggests that the contemporary Canadian writer works 'with a language, within a literature, that appears to be authentically his own,' but is, in fact, a 'borrowing' because there is 'in the Canadian word a concealed other experience, sometimes British, sometimes American' ('Unhiding,' 43). In a recent edition of the *Globe and Mail,* Rick Salutin pointed to a similar confusion when he chastised the Canadian media for acting as if they were American because they consistently refer to 'President Clinton' and the 'Congress' without qualifiers, 'as if they're our president and our congress' (c1).

Despite the ongoing concern regarding orientation and national identity, some critics – notably David Staines – want to sweep the anxiety regarding orientation, articulated in the question 'Where is here?' under the carpet. According to Staines, Canadians have progressed beyond this infantile concern. As he explains:

Early twentieth-century attempts to probe the question led to mid-century denials of its relevance. Now, at century's end, the palpable absence of the question underscores a belated movement of Canada's literary identity from clinging to the seeming periphery to a confident claim that the centre, however indefinable, is none the less unmistakably both here and nowhere and everywhere.   (8)

He later repeats this view, insisting that the 'earlier obsession with the question "Where is here?" has faded into memory, a question no longer necessary, valid, or even appropriate' (27). On the whole, I do not agree that we can so easily dismiss questions pertaining to identity and orientation. Staines rightly argues that the question whether there is a *bona fide* Canadian literature no longer remains an issue. But surely the confusion generated by postmodern culture and the rifts caused by differences in gender, race, and class continually force us to redefine our identity and ask ourselves, yet again, 'Where is here?' In the light of the recent referendum concerning Quebec's desire for sovereignty, Staines's insistence on promoting a vision of Canada as a stable, happy family seems old-fashioned and unrealistic. As Lecker states, nowadays 'our understanding of the material conditions affecting cultural formations, our belief in the constructedness of literary communities, our valorization of postmodern self-questioning and fragmentation, and our immersion in a pluralist society all make it difficult for us to accept this dream' (95). Yet, while I agree with Lecker's analysis of the insufficiency of the dream of progress and the vision of 'homogeneous cultural unity' (95), I cannot accept his solution.

In the face of these very real concerns regarding orientation, Lecker champions a retreat into what amounts to a personal, romantic fantasy. Faced with this pluralist society, Lecker suggests that writers ignore the situation. As he says: 'whether or not there is or is not a coherent public out there is immaterial. If you believe it's out there, if you write to it, then it's there' (85). While I find the appeal to faith seductive, I have my doubts that murmuring the romantic credo 'If you build it, it will come' constitutes a practical solution to the contemporary social and cultural upheaval we are experiencing. With increasing cutbacks to writers and institutions that nurture and promote Canadian culture, I am probably not alone in wondering who will be left to dream this new community into being.

Ultimately, in contrast to these critics, I would argue that problems concerning orientation and identity continue to haunt us whether we like it or not. Reflecting on Canada's colonial situation in *Survival*, Atwood goes as far as saying that Canadians as a whole are lost. This does not mean that Canadians find themselves physically disoriented, because, for her, Canada refers to 'a state of mind ... the space you inhabit not just with your body but with your head. It's that kind of space in which we find ourselves lost' (18). If you are lost, you need a map. No one would disagree that the situation in this country has changed since the 1970s, when Atwood blithely lumped together everyone under the heading 'Canadian' and diagnosed the entire culture's malady in one fell swoop. Nevertheless, it would seem that, taken together, Canada's legacy of explorers and settlers, combined with the country's experience as a colony, has generated a host of discourses (including Atwood's) which have promoted and continue to promote a sensitivity to, if not a preoccupation with, problems of national as well as self-representation – problems often described as an inability to map oneself on the terrain.

Thus far, the historical context and critical discourses which stress problems regarding orientation apply to all Canadians and do not adequately explain why contemporary women writers are invoking figures of exploration and mapping in order to foreground problems specifically associated with representing female identity. Could there be particular factors that might account for female authors' interest in these discourses? While a reliance on the images of cartography and exploration is by no means solely a Canadian phenomenon, let alone an idiosyncratic feature limited to Canadian women's writing, studies of Canadian women's fiction have repeatedly drawn parallels between women's experience and Canada's colonial legacy. In her book, Howells points out the similarities between the 'search for visibility and identity so characteristic of women's fiction and the Canadian search for a distinctive cultural self-image' (Private, 2). She argues that women's experience of gender constructions and their problematic relationship to patriarchal traditions of authority 'have affinities with Canada's attitude to the cultural imperialism of the United States as well as its ambivalence towards its European inheritance' (2). Lorraine Weir expresses a similar view when she hypothesizes that 'women's texts are to the texts of patriarchy as Canada is and was to America and Britain' (68). Lorna Irvine puts it more emphatically: the female voice 'politically and culturally personifies Canada' (*Sub/version*, 11). Finally, in *The Dominion of Women*, Wayne Fraser dedicates an entire book to the exploration of the relationships between the interior colonization of women in a male-dominated society and Canada's status as a former colony. The connections between women's experience of the politics of gender and Canada's colonial inheritance are forged on the basis of women's sense of having been defined and controlled by patriarchal culture, just as the nation was defined and controlled through traditional, imperial practices of mapping. Similar practices of naming and claiming have been employed, either covertly or overtly, to construct and maintain both national and gendered identities; this may help to explain women writers' interest in images of exploration and cartography.

Historian of cartography Brian Harley points out that, for centuries, government maps have been 'ideological statements rather than fully objective, "value-free" scientific representations of geographic reality' (Harley qtd. in Monmonier, 122).[4] As such, a map constitutes 'the perfect symbol of the state' (Monmonier, 88), and nowhere is the map more a national symbol and 'an intellectual weapon than in disputes over territory' (90). Mark Monmonier clarifies the relationship between maps and European imperialism: 'Maps made it easy for European states to carve up Africa and other heathen lands, to lay claim to land and resources, and to ignore existing social and political structures. ... That maps drawn up by diplomats and generals became a political reality lends an unintended irony to the aphorism that the pen is mightier than the sword' (90). Simply put, in order to claim a country, one has only to map it. As Graham Huggan remarks, 'reality' as represented mimetically by the map 'not only conforms to a particular version of the world but to a version which is specifically designed to empower its makers' ('Decolonizing,' 127). According to G.N.G. Clarke, 'the map exists as a text of *possession*: a reconstruction of a culture's way with the world' (455). What emerges in this study is an awareness that the imperialist practices of map-making supported, and continue to support, the construction of gendered as well as colonized identities. Yet, as José Rabasa's reading of Mercator's seventeenth-century *Atlas* clarifies, maps always remain open to challenges because the supposed coherence of the colonial discourse is repeatedly contradicted by 'blind spots' in the map (Rabasa, 12). The existence of such 'blind spots' indicates that, although 'all maps seek to be both complete and consistent,' they are, nevertheless, 'always already divided' (Hart, 110). The internal divisions or contradictions within the imperialist discourses confirm Bakhtin's assertion that 'language, for the individual consciousness, lies on the borderline between oneself and the other. The word in language is half someone else's' ('Discourse,' 293). Because language, by its very nature, is not private, no one can completely control representation. It is this relative autonomy of the linguistic code that enables individuals (in this case, Canadian women writers inscribed within patriarchal and colonial discourses) to resist the ideological weight of colonization and imperialism through deconstructive readings of their repressive discourses – readings which, ideally, do not simply reverse the hierarchical order but challenge the philosophical assumptions on which the order is based.

In their efforts to deconstruct these discourses, all of the texts studied here rely on the images of cartography to thematize the way in which a set of traditional discourses has aligned women's bodies with nature and natural landscapes. This type of identification between human beings and the terrain is portrayed in the novels as a typical feature of colonialism. In her study of the pioneer period of American history, Annette Kolodny notes that the settlers, in their attempt to assert control over their environment, often employed metaphors of the land as woman. The works in this study demonstrate that the association between women and supposedly natural objects legitimated the practice of plotting the limits of the amorphous 'territory' of female being – female experience, sexuality, and desire. Alice, the narrator in Audrey Thomas's novel *Intertidal Life*, attests to the connection between the colonial endeavour to map or name territory and the mechanisms governing the production of gendered bodies, and she insists that what is at issue, in both cases, is who has control of language – who has the power to name. As she says, 'Women have let men define them, taken their names even, with marriage, just like a conquered or newly settled region, British Columbia, British Guiana, New Orleans, New Jersey, New France, New England, etcetera' (171). Alice tangibly underscores the connection between the mapping of geographical territory and the mapping of female bodies when she remarks that '[b]abies drop out of us from our most secret places, through channels the fathers have charted and laid claim to' (205). The ideological coincidence of women's experience under patriarchy and Canada's colonial experience may actually have enabled Canadian women writers to formulate their desire to exist as self-determining subjects because they were in a position to draw on the discourse of anti-colonialism (with its emphasis on 'place' and 'displacement') and apply it to describe the task of renaming or remapping female subjectivity (see Ashcroft et al., 174–7).

Both anti-colonialist and feminist writers have exploited the fact that inscriptions, whether cartographic or literary, are never entirely coherent, never entirely seamless. Thus, the imposition of colonial and patriarchal apparatuses never completely precludes the possibility of generating alternative readings which displace the privileged reading of the text. As Huggan asserts, a recognition of the contradictory coherence 'implied by the map's systematic inscription on a supposedly "uninscribed" earth reveals it [the map] ... as a palimpsest covering over alternative spatial configurations which, once brought to light, indicate both the plurality of possible perspectives on, and the inadequacy of any single model of, the world' ('Decolonizing' 128). Utilizing textual strategies such as temporal fragmentation, intertextuality, parody, and doubling, the fictions in this study both expose the 'blind spots' and generate alternative perspectives that were eclipsed by established discourses claiming to represent the Truth about female identity.

An examination of the way contemporary Canadian women writers concentrate on the mapping and recoding of female subjectivity must take into account not only Canada's historical relationship to exploration, the discourses based on this legacy of exploration and settlement, and the parallels between Canada's experience as a colony and women's experience under patriarchy, but also the intersection between feminism and what Fredric Jameson refers to as the new 'social and economic moment' known as postmodernism (Foreword, vii). While an exact definition of postmodernism remains elusive, it has been said to involve 'a radical break, both with dominant culture and aesthetic' (vii) – a break that is associated with a 'crisis in representation' (viii). In many ways, this so-called 'crisis' represents nothing more radical than a continuation of the epistemological upheavals generated by thinkers such as Nietzsche and Freud. As a result of these upheavals, certain established Truths were thrown open to question; one of the most important Truths to be affected is the belief in a universal, centred, and unified human subject. The waning of belief in this version of the subject, together with the more widespread erosion of 'the Truth' into plural truths, associated with the modern and postmodern upheavals, can be seen to dovetail with the feminist project to displace the concept of a unified male subject and to envision and construct a female subject.

For some feminists, however, the alliance between certain forms of feminist and postmodern projects breaks down because, while the latter recognizes the endless possibilities for discursive deconstruction, which seemingly undermines the potential for self-determination and the construction of an identity, the former stresses the importance of curtailing deconstruction and the deferral of meaning in favour of constructing a provisional and positional sense of female identity for the purposes of political agency. A number of feminist critics, in what has emerged as a common refrain, express their hostility toward and suspicion of the writings of poststructuralist and postmodern theorists who seem to silence women just when they are beginning to assert their rights and desires (Brodribb, xvii; Fox-Genovese; Hartsock, 163; Waugh, 6).

To speak of feminist and postmodern projects as if they were monolithic entities, however, does not do justice to the complexity of the diverse and often contradictory positions which tend to be erroneously conflated under both categories. Judith Butler, who manages to resist this impulse to categorize, asks a crucial question: what lies behind the motivation to 'colonize and domesticate' very different theories under 'the sign of the same, to group them synthetically and masterfully under a single rubric?' ('Contingent,' 5). Ultimately, she concludes that this 'gesture of conceptual mastery that groups together a set of positions under the postmodern, that makes the postmodern into an epoch or a synthetic whole ... enacts a certain self-congratulatory ruse of power' (5). She goes on to identify the practice of constructing totalizing definitions as a modernist gesture because it adopts as its implicit premise the modernist view that theories 'offer themselves in bundles or in organized totalities, and that historically a set of theories which are structurally similar emerge as the articulation of an historically specific condition of human reflection' (5). In keeping with Butler, I am aware of the pitfalls surrounding attempts to locate the postmodern, especially because, as she observes, critics typically invoke the term to dismiss a host of positions which threaten their epistemological foundations.

Postmodernism may pose a threat to feminism because, as Susan Hekman explains, the latter 'is both historically and theoretically a modernist movement with a legacy rooted in the emancipatory impulse of liberal-humanism and Marxism' (2). Yet not all feminists respond to this threat in the same way. A number of feminists, including Hekman and Jane Flax, argue that a postmodern perspective is necessary for feminist thought precisely *because* it challenges the background assumptions and contexts within which feminist debates are routinely conducted (Flax, 446). As Flax explains, postmodernism undermines 'the hope of innocent knowledge,' a hope which is linked to an outdated and dangerous Enlightenment dream. Recalling Butler's view, Flax asserts that the dismissal of postmodernist theory and the quest for the Real, on the part of certain feminists, conceal 'a desire to master the world once and for all by enclosing it within an absolute system' (Flax, 451). Whereas Butler, Hekman, and Flax urge feminists to come to terms with postmodern theorists, other critics, including Barbara Creed, Teresa Ebert, Nancy Hartsock, Patricia Waugh, and Somer Brodribb warn that such a coming to terms may prove harmful. Creed believes that attempts to amalgamate the two projects threaten to obscure the 'specificities of the positions of both feminism and postmodernism' ('From,' 66). Both Creed and Brodribb also condemn the tendency of postmodern theorists, such as Craig Owens, to absorb feminism into postmodernism, as if the former were merely – as Owens infelicitously suggests in his essay – 'an instance of postmodern thought' (see Creed, 66; Brodribb, xxv; Owens, 61–2).

Generally speaking, feminists' responses to postmodern theorists range from outright rejection of postmodernism as merely an 'addition to the masculinist repertoire of psychotic mind/body splitting' (Brodribb, xvi) to attempts to rescue postmodernism for feminism. For example, Teresa Ebert offers the type of masterful categorization that Butler emphatically rejects; and, in an ultimately futile effort to cleanse postmodernism of its supposedly relativistic implications, Eberts constructs a binary opposition between what she terms 'ludic postmodernism' and 'resistance postmodernism.' As one might expect, the division implicitly inscribes an opposition between good and evil. This difference supposedly allows Eberts to

dismiss her own creation, namely, 'ludic postmodernism,' because 'in deconstructing grand narratives (such as emancipation), identities (like gender, race, and class),
the referent, and experience as unfounded and divided by difference ... [ludic
postmodernism] ends up dismantling the notion of politics itself as a transforma-
tive social practice outside language' (887). Brodribb does not even contemplate
cleansing the term. She simply asserts that it is both possible and necessary for
feminists to reject postmodernism, and maintains that a complementary relationship between the two is out of the question (ix).

As we shall see, Canadian women writers have adopted varying positions on the
extent to which they align themselves with projects designated as postmodern and
the apparent fragmentation of the unified subject. For instance, Thomas's novel
portrays the horrors associated with the erosion of the unified subject and emphasizes that the instability associated with the breakdown of the 'molar' subject may
not be beneficial for women who have never had the chance to enjoy unified sub-
jecthood in the first place. The term 'molar' subject and its complement, the
'molecular' subject, are drawn from Gilles Deleuze and Félix Guattari's study *A
Thousand Plateaus*. These scientific terms, albeit a bit unusual in the realm of literary criticism, nevertheless prove useful in describing the shifts associated with the
breakdown of the unified subject. According to Deleuze and Guattari, 'molar' subjects constitute those entities which 'we know from the outside and recognize from
experience, through science, or by habit' (275). By contrast, 'molecular' groupings
signal that breakdown of forms in multiplicities, 'unfindable particles' (248).

Whereas Thomas emphasizes the horror associated with the loss of the molar
subject, writers like van Herk, who identify more strongly with postmodern theories, seem to revel in the molecularization of the subject. Although the novels differ
in their estimation of the benefits of molar versus molecular identity, they nevertheless display a common debt to postmodern, poststructuralist, and feminist theories – theories that have constructed vocabularies making it possible to escape
traditional binary systems of opposition in favour of non-hierarchical models of
'difference,' thereby opening up the possibility of conceiving of a subject other than
Man. Linda Hutcheon also points out that Canada's history, which promoted an unstable identity, may actually have primed Canadian writers for the 'paradoxes of the
postmodern' (*Canadian*, 4).

In an attempt to avoid the reductive manoeuvre involved in conflating a variety
of theories under the heading of 'postmodernism,' this study will analyse the fictions in light of specific writings by theorists such as Jameson, Foucault, and
Deleuze and Guattari – writings that posit crucial links between subjectivity and
cartography. For example, in his essay 'Postmodernism, or the Cultural Logic of
Late Capitalism,' Jameson identifies spatial issues as the fundamental organizing
concern for a hypothetical model of the contemporary political culture, and he

postulates the aesthetic of the new cultural form as 'an aesthetic of cognitive mapping' (89). Jameson describes the alienated city as a space in which 'people are unable to map (in their minds) either their own positions or the urban totality in which they find themselves.' By contrast, what he calls disalienation involves 'the practical reconquest of a sense of place, and the construction or reconstruction of an articulated ensemble which can be retained in memory and which the individual subject can map and remap along the moments of mobile, alternative trajectories' (89). His analysis of cognitive mapping recalls Atwood's assertion that a lost person (in her view, a Canadian) needs a map of the territory 'with his own position marked on it so he can see where he is in relation to everything else' (*Survival*, 18). As she says, 'For the members of a country or a culture, shared knowledge of their place, their here, is not a luxury but a necessity. Without that knowledge we will not survive' (19). In the case of the novels in this study, it is primarily a community of women who require new maps. However, these maps need not be restricted to representations of spatial elements. In his writings, Foucault describes the process of constructing a 'genealogy.' His understanding of a genealogy – a method for shaping historical narratives based on Nietzsche's writings – suggests a way of creating maps which facilitate orientation, not within the spatial dimension, but within the temporal sphere. The Foucauldian analysis of the genealogist's endeavour serves as an extremely valuable framework for understanding Daphne Marlatt's project in *Ana Historic*. The work of Deleuze and Guattari, which portrays a cartographic analysis of the lines of power and desire, takes Foucault's model one step further, by tracing possibilities for resistance to oppressive maps. Their work provides a model which sheds light on van Herk's portrayals of female, 'nomadic war machines.'

Thomas, Swan, and Urquhart do not overtly draw on postmodern or feminist perspectives. Therefore, I use theoretical materials to discuss features within the texts and not to intimate some intentional reliance on the part of the author. However, in the case of Daphne Marlatt and Aritha van Herk, I would argue that, whether there is a conscious intent or not on the part of the author, specific theoretical perspectives are delineated within the texts. This is not surprising, considering that Daphne Marlatt has admitted to being influenced by Québécoise writers such as Nicole Brossard, and French feminists, such as Hélène Cixous, Luce Irigaray, and Julia Kristeva.[5] Similarly, Aritha van Herk acknowledges the influence of postmodern writers and critics such as Robert Kroetsch. On the whole, this study utilizes theory primarily to highlight aspects of the texts, rather than to argue for some sort of authorial dependence on specific theoretical perspectives.

The analysis of contemporary Canadian women's fiction in the light of poststructuralist and postmodern theories signals this study's departure from earlier, ground-breaking analyses in the area of Canadian women's fiction. Although previous studies have noted women's interest in the area of exploration and mapping, they do not view this interest in terms of a response to postmodern society. As Coral Ann Howells writes in the introduction to her book *Private and Fictional Words*, many Canadian women's stories are concerned 'with exploration and survival, crossing boundaries, challenging limits and glimpsing new prospects' (5). Similarly, in her book *Sub/version* (1986), Lorna Irvine focuses on novels that foreground a female aesthetic in which 'female characters successfully complete both physical and spiritual journeys' (18). In *Territorial Disputes: Maps and Mapping Strategies in Contemporary Canadian and Australian Fiction*, Graham Huggan offers a detailed description of the affinities between the ideological implications of map-making and linguistic inscription, and he outlines the principles for a 'literary cartography.' While this is only an aspect of his overall goal, Huggan does discuss the feminist challenge to traditional maps and map-making strategies, and the ways in which contemporary women writers and critics view 'the ethnocentric tendencies of the map, its makers' choice to displace (or discard) what they cannot accommodate, as an analogue for the marginalization of women in patriarchal society' (11–12). According to Huggan, many contemporary Canadian women writers can be seen both as '*mapbreakers* engaged in the dismantling of a patriarchal system of representation, and as *mapmakers* involved in the plotting of new coordinates for the articulation of knowledge and experience' (13). Helen M. Buss's study *Mapping Ourselves* also forges a link between Canadian women's writing and cartography, but her research on women's autobiographical works does not trace images of maps and map-making within particular texts. In this case, the notion of mapping refers to a reading strategy which Buss advocates – a feminist practice which she believes will overcome the limitations of humanist and poststructuralist theories of female subjectivity.

In general, critics who analyse depictions of exploration and mapping have concentrated the issue of anticolonialism, and have focused on establishing the relationship between challenges to imperialism and Canadian women writers' interest in the figures of mapping and exploration. So far, few critics have traced the influence of postmodern theories on writings by Canadian women authors or examined the intersections between postmodern and feminist theories.[6] In fact, in her conclusion, Howells argues that there are not many English-Canadian women's fictions which 'could properly be called postmodernist' (Private, 185). She goes on to say that most English-Canadian women's fiction 'is written within the traditions of realism, though that framework is challenged with the shifts into fantasy and the counterpoint of the voices of tradition with the voices of female inheritors' (185). Although she draws upon feminist literary theory, Irvine, like Howells, also chooses not to examine the connections between Canadian women's fiction and postmodern theory. Irvine argues that it is not always prudent to reach outside of the literary domain and rely on theories that were not developed within a literary context (7–8). Huggan likewise confines his study to the investigation of the intersection between feminist and postcolonial theory. In the light of the fact that a number of critics have already addressed the intersection between Canadian women's writing and postcolonial concerns, this study, while pointing out this relationship, will put more emphasis on enhancing the reader's awareness of the links between postmodern theory and the texts under consideration.

At bottom, each of these studies noted above acknowledges that there is a radical difference between what men and women are interested in mapping and how they engage in this process. More specifically, many Canadian women writers are attempting to remap the female body in order to give women a sense of themselves as subjects rather than objects of desire. This insistence on the need to reinscribe women's experience of their bodies is taken up by feminist theorists such as Hélène Cixous. Drawing on the discourse of anti-colonialism, Cixous argues that the act of writing for women constitutes a reclamation of territory appropriated by men: 'By writing herself, woman will return to the body which has been more than confiscated from her, which has been turned into the uncanny stranger' (Cixous, 250).

In keeping with Cixous's comments, the novels in this study frequently seem to be intent on exploring women's sense of *Unheimlichkeit* or 'not-at-homeness,' the uncanny sensation, which, according to Freud, is evoked in response to something paradoxically both familiar and unfamiliar, like a secret, long-buried, that has come to light.[7] Many of the texts follow what Gail Scott calls 'the darker trails of being' in an attempt to probe the 'dark space' of the unthought ('Feminist,' 241). While both male and female writers are engaged in examining the unthought (it was a preoccupation of modernist literature and remains of concern to postmodern writers [Hoy, 21]), the nature of the unthought differs depending on one's perspective. As Scott explains, 'the dark space in which man sees women-the-object lurking isn't necessarily dark to her. ... What's "dark" (absence, gap) for him is something else for her. Lucidity, perhaps, inasmuch as she feels she exists as subject' (247). For a woman, what is dark or uncanny to her – the 'blind spots' on the map – may well be the nature of her own body and her own desires because they have so often been charted for her, but not by her. In their efforts to track 'the dark space,' the novels often combine the exploration genre, the picaresque, and / or the romance genre with Gothic and grotesque conventions. As Margot Northey explains, traditionally, the Gothic and grotesque genres have been used to provide alternatives to 'more familiar paths of realistic writers' (110). 'Gothic' has also been accorded a 'social connotation'; Gothic writing has 'sometimes been seen as a complex, revolutionary form of insight' (5). For this reason, these genres are especially appropriate modes for the 'revolutionary' inscription of female subjectivity on the part of contemporary Canadian women writers.

The study begins with an examination of Audrey Thomas's *Intertidal Life*, a text that employs the images of map-making and exploration specifically to draw attention to the ideological underpinnings of the narrative of romance. Thomas's novel foregrounds the fact that the 'quest' forms the fundamental structure of romance narratives. Through its examination of the structure of the quest, the novel emphasizes that romance operates in a fashion analogous to the imperialist paradigm, simultaneously inscribing both the male, hero-human, on the one hand, and the monstrous, female-obstacle, on the other. By exposing the mechanisms of the romance mode, the text reveals the way in which this literary structure creates the reality of the female-obstacle in the guise of describing it. The study opens with Thomas's text because its deconstruction of romance offers a clear picture of the complexity involved in challenging traditional discourses. It explicitly raises the question whether feminist challenges to the status quo are, at bottom, merely reversals of power rather than radical subversions of the patriarchal, imperialist worldview on which such claims to power are based. Wondering if it would have made any difference if the early explorers had been women, the narrator says, 'Probably not. It probably wouldn't have made any difference whatsoever. And yet' (15). The cautiousness with which the phrase 'And yet' is uttered clarifies that the work is far from a piece of feminist, utopian propaganda. Instead, *Intertidal Life* effects a tenuous probing of alternative visions, and it offers a particularly sobering message for women, namely, that the attempt to map out an alternative, female subjectivity often entails a radical and frightening upheaval; and furthermore, if the postmodern project of deconstruction is played out to its fullest extent, women may be liberated at the price of losing their ability to organize history, to make sense of a world in flux, and to create a coherent sense of self. In Thomas's novel, Gothic and grotesque elements associated with dismemberment and mutilation surface repeatedly, signalling the narrator's ambivalent reaction to the erosion of the unified subject. Despite the doubts and fears associated with the dissolution of this subject, the narrator acknowledges the necessity of refusing traditional representations of female identity generated within discourses such as romance, representations governed by a logic that privileges men at the expense of women. Within the work, the images of maps and map-making serve a double function. On the one hand, they emphasize the way in which women's bodies have been aligned with the landscape within colonial and patriarchal discourses, thereby supposedly legitimating their appropriation and exploitation; on the other hand, the images underscore the need for women to counter traditional, patriarchal narratives with their own accounts, which decentre the official representations of women and oppose the devaluation of women's experiences and their histories.

The next chapter focuses on Susan Swan's *The Biggest Modern Woman of the World*. Here the motif of exploration is linked to the travels of the protagonist, Anna Swan, a Victorian giantess. Swan's novel, like Thomas's, foregrounds the necessity of mapping women's marginalized history, based as it is on the life of a historical figure, an actual Canadian giantess, who travels to New York to work for P.T. Barnum. The narrative recalls earlier literary tales of (male) travellers who are gawked at by natives, and relies on the conventions of mock travel literature (of which *Gulliver's Travels* is perhaps one of the most famous examples). Swan's novel also draws on the lesser-known genre of the freak show pamphlet; these lengthy texts were distributed for a fee to audiences at freak show performances in the 1860s. By invoking the image of the traveller and the freakish circus performer, Swan's text calls into question woman's traditional role as exhibitionist, a spectacle which is 'simultaneously looked at and displayed' (Mulvey, 11). As in *Intertidal Life*, images of maps and map-making surface in Swan's novel in conjunction with a reinscription and subversion of the discursive positioning of woman as monstrous obstacle, the landscape which the hero must traverse and control.

Swan's narrative, which is set in the Victorian era, extends the parameters of this study beyond a consideration of literary discourses because, in addition to relying on literary intertexts, it invokes a host of nineteenth-century scientific and cultural discourses that charted women's physical and psychological nature and designated women as weaker vessels. At that time, 'experts' were busy categorizing even supposedly normal women as freaks because of their so-called perverse physiology. Swan's text simultaneously reinscribes and contests these various discourses through the use of parodic appropriation. In its challenge to the metaphoric association between women and landscape, the work corresponds to *Intertidal Life*; however, while both novels rely on the conventions of the Gothic and grotesque, Swan's treatment of women's erasure within patriarchal culture is far more comic than Thomas's because Swan utilizes what Margot Northey would call the 'sportive grotesque' (Northey, 87). In this section, Mikhail Bakhtin's discussion of the grotesque mode is invoked in order to illustrate how the novel's reliance on the 'sportive' or 'realistic' grotesque, as opposed to the 'romantic' grotesque (in Bakhtin's terms), serves to highlight the existence of alternative, unofficial perspectives on female identity – perspectives which, like the blind spots on Mercator's map, were partially obscured by the dominance of official nineteenth-century discourses. The novel specifically foregrounds the parallels between women's experience of patriarchy and Canada's colonial situation. At one point the narrator explains to her mother that 'to be from the Canadas is to feel as women feel – cut off from the base of power' (274). Very often parodic repetition of American and British nationalistic discourses serves to emphasize the bias and rapaciousness behind their portrayal of a Canada as a feminized, empty void, waiting to be appropriated and exploited. The text affords more than a critique of the official discourses, however, because it also establishes the legitimacy of devalued experiences, the knowledges of marginalized groups, and sets these up, in the context of a feminist, imaginative revision of history, as an alternative to the official discourses.

The third chapter analyses Daphne Marlatt's *Ana Historic*, a novel which, like the others, utilizes the imagery of maps and map-making to thematize women's alienation from language and naming, and, consequently, from history. Here the notion of mapping is translated from the spatial to the temporal dimension in order to discuss women's marginalized representation in official history. Marlatt's text goes to great lengths to foreground and denaturalize standard English to illustrate the way in which the language reflects the concerns of imperialism and inscribes 'reality' as constructed by the British Empire. Critics have suggested that, by providing 'some terms and not others with which to talk about the world' (Ashcroft et al., 44), standard or 'proper' English serves the imperialist process. Marlatt's text explores the way in which histories constructed from this language accorded women object-status. At one point, the narrator remarks that she learned that 'history is the real story the city fathers tell. ... a tale of their exploits hacked out against a silent backdrop of trees. ... (where are the city mothers?)' (28). The novel implies that women need to reconstruct, and, if necessary, fabricate temporal maps – ancestral trajectories – which reposition them as subjects of history. Drawing on Canadian pioneering history, the text directly challenges any imperialist version of history by making visible accounts of women's lives which were left outside the traditional frame. To this end, the narrative weaves together what I refer to as a 'genealogy for lost women,' which includes the story of the pioneer woman Anna Richards's experience in British Columbia at the turn of the century, an account of the narrator's life in the twentieth century, and a description of the life of the narrator's mother, who was mentally unstable. All three stories are linked by their mutual recognition of the legacy of patriarchal imperialism, which made it difficult, if not impossible, for women to exist as subjects in their own right. Each of the narratives focuses on the official portrait of female-gendered identity and the 'blind spots' of this discursive construct. In an effort to problematize the 'domesticated' version of female sexuality, the narratives portray the uncanniness of a repressed, female-centred desire, and reveal the brutality of the societal mechanisms that facilitated its repression. Like the previous texts, Marlatt's work explodes formal narrative structures, especially those of romance; however, of all the texts, Marlatt's gestures most visibly toward the darker realms of the female uncanny. Right from the start, the novel invokes the image of Mary Shelley's tale of *Frankenstein*; in this case, the monster comes to function as a trope for the feared and desired lesbian possibility. In its radical rewriting of history, *Ana Historic* reinforces the possibility that language can be salvaged because, to use Bakhtin's words, language 'lies on the borderline between oneself and the other'; thus, representation can never be saturated by any one inscription. By rigorously probing the 'dark space' of female desire, Marlatt's text succeeds in breaking the map and creates a feminist narrative out of the shattered fragments of Lacan's symbolic order.[8]

The next chapter treats the entire corpus of Aritha van Herk's writing because, of all the authors analysed, van Herk most consistently thematizes the construction of representations of female identity in terms of exploration and map-making. All of her texts portray women who don disguises and infiltrate masculine territory in order to challenge gender constructions that position women within the home or garrison and represent men as mobile adventurers. Once again, Gothic elements are used in conjunction with portrayals of female exploration, signalling women's interest in exposing the 'blind spots' on the map. For instance, *The Tent Peg* traces the adventures of a woman named J.L. who masquerades as a man in order to procure a job with a team of geologists trekking to the Yukon to stake out a mine. Gothic elements surface when J.L. takes her place among the team and is menaced by a fairly traditional Gothic villain – an ambitious geologist named Jerome, who believes that geology is 'a man's field' (27). Ultimately, the novel portrays a shift from territoriality to deterritorialization.

In *No Fixed Address*, van Herk continues to draw on the images of maps and map-making in order to offer a recoding of the picaresque tradition – a tradition that has always focused on the male rogue traveller. Here, the heroine is an underwear salesperson, Arachne Manteia, who drives a black Mercedes through the small towns of northern Alberta and Saskatchewan. Arachne is characterized as a sexually assertive, autonomous subject – a portrayal that subverts the traditional image of the masochistic, dependent, and passive woman. Drawing on the theories of Deleuze and Guattari, I argue that Arachne can be likened to a nomadic 'war machine,' in the light of her efforts to increase the availability of deterritorialized space. As the title indicates, van Herk's fiction offers a radical challenge to realistic narratives that definitively 'fix' or plot women in the literary terrain. Refusing a 'fixed address,' Arachne moves beyond the dualisms set up by traditional narratives to defy death itself.

In *Places Far from Ellesmere*, one of van Herk's most experimental works to date, the inscription of female subjectivity is once again revealed to be a fundamentally discursive project that collapses geography and fiction. For this reason, van Herk felt the need to create an entirely new genre and dubbed the text a 'geografic-tione.' Within this geografictione, the narrator muses on the nature of plots. She stages a rescue of the fictional heroine Anna Karenin from the death-dealing constraints of Tolstoy's nineteenth-century realism and goes on to imagine Anna's life on Ellesmere Island, so as to allow Anna to invent herself in 'an undocumented landscape, an undetermined fiction' (125). As I suggested earlier, in contrast to Thomas, who focuses on the dangers associated with the loss of identity, van Herk celebrates the erosion of the unified ego and women's shift toward imperceptibility.

The fifth chapter examines Jane Urquhart's *The Whirlpool*, a work which draws together many of the issues raised in the previous fictions – specifically, the links among imperialism, national identity, and the inscription of gender identity. Set in Niagara Falls in the summer of 1889, the novel explores the impact of imperialism on the lives of five characters (two men, two women, and a child). Urquhart's text highlights the effects of imperialism in several ways but perhaps most obviously by framing the events in Niagara Falls with an account of the last days of the poet Robert Browning. Both the prologue and epilogue, which feature the famous European poet walking through his beloved Venice, highlight the tension between the order of the Old World and the supposed chaos of the New – a chaos figured by the whirlpool – which the characters in Niagara Falls must negotiate.

In keeping with the other texts examined in this study, Urquhart's novel underscores the problems surrounding the translation of Old World modes of categorization onto the New World. Typically, the men in the novel impose the narrative of romance, with its binary opposition of the temple and labyrinth, as well as the aesthetic concept of the sublime onto the Canadian landscape. As in *Intertidal Life*, Urquhart's text explores the ramifications of coding the hero as male and the landscape as female. This chapter extends the discussion of romance and introduces a discussion of the sublime, with particular emphasis on the contributions of Burke and Kant. Both the traditional and contemporary accounts of the sublime, including those by Thomas Weiskel and Jean-François Lyotard, help to clarify the dangers involved in adhering to the concept, which is based on the sacrifice of the body and nature in favour of an illusory sense of power and transcendence.

In *The Whirlpool*, attempts at maintaining order through the imposition of both romance narratives and the sublime fail or, worse, prove fatal. Whereas the men cling to the Old World narratives, despite the cost, the text illustrates that there is a difference between the men's and the women's investment in these narratives. Given the opportunity, the women seize the opportunity to subvert traditional narratives covertly aligning them with the sublime chaos that the romantic hero seeks to master. Rather than unequivocally identify this act of subversion with women's flight and the shift toward imperceptibility – an identification that is readily apparent in Marlatt's and van Herk's texts – Urquhart's novel offers a more complicated, ambivalent response. In *The Whirlpool*, individuals do not necessarily have to escape into the uncharted wilderness in order to destabilize traditional narratives. Thanks to the subversive capacity of language, deterritorialization can occur even within the supposedly ordered 'temple' of the domestic sphere. *The Whirlpool* recalls other fictions in the study, by virtue of its interrogation of the effects of imperialism, its emphasis on the impact of the narrative of romance, and its presentation of subversive uses of language, but its complexity and expansive focus set it apart. I have chosen to conclude the study with this text partly because it offers an instructive contrast. For one, it takes the tragic fate of men who identify with Old World narratives as seriously as that of women.

Generally speaking, my decision to examine a variety of texts, rather than investigate the works of a single author, stems from a desire to emphasize the very different approaches that contemporary women writers are taking toward the construction of the female subject: I am not looking for a 'coherent, unifying vision.' Similarly, my use of a wide selection of theoretical approaches, rather than a single approach, is, as noted earlier, based on a reluctance to level differences among the texts by imposing an overriding theory. Instead, I have allowed the choice of theory to be governed by the specific concerns raised by each work. In practice, this means that theories discussed in one chapter may not be explicitly invoked in subsequent chapters. While this may appear to some as an erratic methodology, it allows for a case-by-case analysis of specific strategies of subversion – strategies that are not necessarily common to all of the texts. This method may well be postmodern, in that it does not foster the illusion that the texts share some underlying, essential, and unifying principle. The belief in some transcendent unity stems from a modernist faith in master-narratives – a faith which all of the texts are working to undermine.

In conclusion, I should also explain why the study focuses on five white authors. As I suggested earlier, these authors are all, on some level, writing their way out of a patriarchal and colonial tradition. This effort is related, yet remains distinct from, a project initiated by many contemporary indigenous writers including Lee Maracle, Beatrice Culleton, Jeanette Armstrong, Beth Brant, Joan Crate, Beth Cuthand, and J.B. Joe. Their works very often map out the tensions between what postcolonial critics refer to as the 'settler-invader society' and marginalized groups because of racism. Rather than conflate these two projects, I chose to focus on the way in which members of the settler-invader society have negotiated the 'maps' that they inherited. By the same token, I did not want to collapse concerns expressed in the works of white authors with those found in the texts of non-white authors, such as Dionne Brand, Claire Harris, Marlene Nourbese Philip, Himani Bannerji, Sky Lee, Joy Kogawa, and many others, who are investigating, among other issues, the connections and conflicts among race, ethnicity, language, and class. That being said, I believe that, with certain crucial modifications, the findings of this study can be of use to readers who examine the works of non-white writers.

2

Resisting Romance:
Audrey Thomas's *Intertidal Life*

Audrey Thomas's novel *Intertidal Life* (1984) invokes the traditional literary figure of the voyage to portray the dissolution of a woman's identity and her attempt to fashion a sense of self that subverts the boundaries established by inherited cultural and literary discourses. The protagonist sees herself, and women in general, as intertidal creatures, pulled by the tide and the moon, yet capable of survival. Each of the novel's three sections opens with an epigraph from *A Spanish Voyage to Vancouver*. This intertext establishes the primacy of the journey motif and the significance of mapping as a figure for the creation of a female 'subject in process.'[1] The epigraph to the first section offers particular insight into the relationship between quests and the construction of their fictional accounts:

Part of the following day was employed in arranging and setting in order our records of observations, charts and calculations, and the notes made on all matters which having been jotted down on board ship in the midst of toil and labour required to be systematically expanded in order that they might be in good order and not convey a confused idea of the information gained. ...   (1)

Taken from a book which the protagonist, Alice Hoyle, is reading during the summer of 1979, this quotation underscores the novel's major concern: namely, the link between quests and their linguistic inscription.[2]

  The excerpts from Vancouver's diary, which drift through the text, forge a connection between actual voyages undertaken by the early explorers for the purposes of colonization and the narrator's parallel 'anti-colonial' attempts to redefine her identity following the breakup of her marriage. Alice recognizes that the mechanisms of national colonization – the inscription of colonial power through the practice of imposing alien names on a country and its inhabitants – are related to the patriarchal apparatuses that effect her repression as a woman. The connection between colonization and her personal repression is clarified when she composes a list of men who gave their names to objects. At the top of her list are men such as Lord Cardigan, Mr Quisling, and the Earl of Sandwich; at the bottom is her husband, 'Mr. Hoyle' (146–7). Just as anti-colonial activity depends on the refusal of the 'conceptual and cultural apparatuses of the European imperium' (Slemon, 3), women's resistance to patriarchal repression likewise hinges on the rejection of the names imposed upon them. On some level, Alice understands that the construction of an alternate model for identity is inextricably connected to the production of discourses, and that women must claim the right to name and record their own quests if they hope to undercut traditional narratives which misrepresent, or worse, efface, their lived experience.

In her work, Thomas characteristically relies on the figure of the explorer or traveller, 'the person in flux who re-examines her life because she has become a stranger' (Wachtel, 'Guts,' 4). As Thomas herself notes, the motif of the journey serves both thematic and structural functions:

[A] journey implies a beginning and end and it's a way of creating a structure in the novel as well as in one's life. We often take journeys in points of our life when we feel as if our life has no structure. So we start at Point A and hope that by the time we arrive at Point B, we'll have found out something about ourselves that made us go on the journey in the first place. ('Audrey Thomas,' 60)

In the realist mode of the quest structure, the self is typically represented as an 'essence which might be "discovered" or as a unity which might be "willed" into existence' (Waugh, 23). Although Thomas relies on the quest plot, she breaks with this tradition, first, by casting a woman into the role of heroic explorer, and secondly, by underscoring that the plot's promise of a transcendent, unified identity cannot be fulfilled. As we shall see, the protagonist of *Intertidal Life* does not succeed in constructing a stable identity.

In accordance with the novel's emphasis on the importance of the fictional process as a potentially subversive activity for women, the narrator is a writer who is spending the summer with her daughter Flora in a cabin on one of Canada's Gulf Islands. In many ways, Alice's writing project parallels the explorer's task outlined in the first epigraph. She too desires to 'set her house in order' (272) and, in keeping with the maritime imagery, she wants to ensure that everything is 'shipshape' (280) before she undergoes a serious operation. In effect, the novel constitutes the sum of her attempts to understand and to elaborate on the events that unfolded over a period of ten years, beginning in the late summer of 1972. The story begins at a time when she first learned that her husband, Peter, was having an affair with their mutual friend, Anne-Marie. His affair precipitated the end of their fourteen-year marriage, estranged her from Peter, and shattered her identity as his wife. Almost by default, Alice finds herself launched on a quest to retrieve some provisional sense of ontological security outside the orbit of her husband.

The text portrays Alice attempting to sort through her life; like the explorers who puzzle over their records of observations, she peruses the scraps of narrative that she has collected over the years. As a result, the text includes inset elements such as dictionary definitions, lyrics from songs, African parables, and portions of the narrator's diary or 'commonplace book.' The presence of these elements establishes the text primarily as a novel about writing, belonging to the generic category of the *poioumenon* (Fowler, 123). At bottom, this genre is concerned with the 'formation of new selves, a process symbolized by the literary creative process portrayed. The great work is to bring integrated identity out of a chaos of possibilities' (Fowler, 125).

As Juliet Mitchell points out, historically, women have relied on literary forms to help them chart transformations in their subjectivity; literary forms arise 'as one of the ways in which changing subjects create themselves as subjects within a new social context' (Mitchell, 289). She suggests that early women novelists were trying to fashion new selves, to create a history from a state of flux: 'a flux in which they were feeling themselves in the process of becoming women within a new bourgeois society' (288–9). In a similar gesture, contemporary Canadian women writers, such as Audrey Thomas, are appropriating and transforming traditional literary forms to illustrate women's current attempts to redefine their identities within a postmodern culture. This culture is characterized by the breakdown of forms associated with bourgeois society, including marriage and the nuclear family. In interviews, Thomas acknowledges that the novel 'has a tradition of received morality behind it,' and she insists that, as a writer, she is working to deconstruct both the literary structure and the tradition it stands for (see interview with Twigg, 248).

Intertidal Life focuses directly on subverting the literary structure of romance, which explains the prevalence of the figure of the quest. As Northrop Frye suggests, the image of the journey forms the core of the narrative structure of romance – a mode whose complete form is 'the successful quest' (Frye, *Anatomy*, 187). According to Frye, romance 'brings us closer than any other aspect of literature to the sense of fiction, considered as a whole, as the epic of the creature, man's vision of his own life as a quest' (*Secular*, 15). Elsewhere, Frye notes that popular romance plays a role in consolidating what Thomas describes as 'a tradition of received morality,' and he specifically underscores the way in which this type of romance promotes the conservative idealism of the propertied middle class (see *Bush*, 236). *Intertidal Life* signals its association with the romance genre through repeated emphasis on the motif of the voyage, and through references to other textual representatives of this type. For example, the novel refers to well-known literary romances, such as Spenser's *The Faerie Queene*, and to anti-romances, such as Flaubert's *Madame*

Bovary. The book actually opens with Flora and Alice's discussion of contemporary Harlequin 'romances.' Alice tells Flora that they are 'crap,' and hopes that *Madame Bovary* will provide her with an antidote to the dangerous ideological message conveyed by the *Nurse Prue in Ceylon* (14).[3]

There is, of course, a vast difference in terms of both structure and content between Spenser's romance and the 'romances' churned out by Harlequin Enterprises, and I do not mean to collapse the historical differences. However, romances in their various manifestations are linked by a mutual reliance on a set of features common to the genre. For one thing, the central element of romance was, and still remains, the love story. The exciting adventures outlined in the traditional plot are normally a 'foreplay leading up to a sexual union' (Frye, *Secular*, 24). This element remains unchanged since Chrétien de Troyes first penned his romances between 1165 and 1181. Secondly, the combination of sexuality and violence has continued to remain a principal ingredient (*Secular*, 26). A critic of contemporary popular romances affirms that, in addition to emphasizing sexuality, cruelty and menace are 'equated with maleness and treated as a necessary part of the package' (*Snitow*, 134–5). Finally, romance, in all its various guises, is still tied to the 'wish fulfilment dream,' whose perennially childlike quality is marked by its extraordinarily persistent nostalgia, 'its search for some kind of imaginative golden age in time or space' (Frye, *Anatomy*, 186). Referring to romance's shift from romantic poetry to romantic fiction, Frye uses the term 'displacement' to discuss the technique of adjusting 'formulaic structures to roughly a credible context' (*Secular*, 36). He argues that 'the novel was a realistic displacement of romance, and had few structural features peculiar to itself' (38).

These links explain how a novel such as *Intertidal Life* can self-consciously manipulate and subvert time-honoured generic features of romance. Thomas remarks that her text has actually been described as a 'turned around' romance because it begins when 'all the happiness is over in the relationship between Peter and Alice' ('An Interview,' 29). Yet the novel is not so much an inverted romance as a romance told from an unusual point of view – a perspective that is more in keeping with contemporary romances, where the heroine's thoughts and evaluations make up the story line (Snitow, 135). What we have is not the hero's story, which, in this case, would be Peter's story because he is cast as the 'romantic hero' (181), although the outlines of his quest for enlightenment remain visible. Instead, we have Alice's story – a story told from the point of view of the woman whom the hero comes to perceive as an obstacle impeding his heroic quest and has left behind. It is as if Circe or Calypso, grief-stricken and outraged, had put pen to paper and written of her abandonment by Odysseus.[4]

In portraying history from the perspective of the 'castaway' or 'reject' (157), the novel follows the path of other feminist and postmodern texts which generally do not represent the exploits of typical historical figures: namely, the heroes. Instead, these texts give voice to the 'story and the storytelling of the non-combatants or even the losers' (Hutcheon, 'Politics,' 38). This shift in perspective in *Intertidal Life* prompts readers to question the ideology that informs the traditional romance mode and encourages them to re-evaluate the hierarchical structure of romance that traditionally privileges the hero. Thomas's novel points out the blind spots in Frye's ahistorical and non-gendered theory of romance by stressing that not all plots (or all facets of a plot) are available to women in every age. Teresa de Lauretis argues that romance narratives are overlaid with what can be described as an 'Oedipal logic' – a logic which works to inscribe two positions of sexual difference: the 'male-hero-human, on the side of the subject; and female-obstacle-boundary-space, on the other' (*Alice*, 121). This structural opposition ensures that powerful women are cast as monsters who must be 'slain or defeated so that the hero can go forward to fulfill his destiny – and his story' (110). In generating a fictionalized account of her experiences, Alice must immediately come to grips with this logic, which, as in Thomas's short stories, is presented as an 'unyielding, unitary, and patriarchal inheritance' (Davey, 'Alternate,' 14). Alice's biggest challenge lies in wrestling with the role she has been assigned within the traditional romance mode. While some part of her accepts her status as 'personified-obstacle,' the monster blocking the hero's spiritual ascent, she nevertheless refuses to co-operate whole-heartedly with a hierarchical plot that degrades her in order to secure an elevated position for its male hero. As we shall see in the following chapters, this patriarchal inheritance proves to be a formidable stumbling-block for women who want to be the subject, rather than the object, of discourse.

In *Intertidal Life*, the narrator tells her friends: 'Women have been shanghaied … and now we are waking up and rubbing our eyes and murmuring, "Where are we?" ' (170). Her comment echoes de Lauretis's assertion that women's evolution into gendered adults, according to the model Freud proposed, serves Oedipus:

[T]he itinerary of the female's journey, mapped from the very start on the territory of her own body … is guided by a compass pointing not to reproduction as the fulfillment of *her* biological destiny, but more exactly to the fulfillment of the promise made to 'the little man,' of his social contract, *his* biological and affective destiny – and to the fulfillment of his desire. This is what predetermines the positions she must occupy in her journey. (de Lauretis, *Alice*, 133)

In Thomas's text, Alice recognizes that women's bodies and lived experience have been colonized and mapped according to the dictates of masculine desire, and that women have yet to chart a course according to their own volition. She calls for a mutiny, hoping not necessarily to transcend, but certainly to arrest, the workings of the romance narrative.

In order to subvert the romance plot, however, the narrative of romance must first be invoked, and the text's reliance on romance conventions, even within a work whose ostensible aim is to discredit romance's ideological underpinnings, generates a paradoxical situation common to many postmodern texts – texts which challenge generic conventions even as they exploit them and depend on the reader's familiarity with them (see Hutcheon, 'Politics,' 32). Within the novel, although the fiction-writing narrator rejects many aspects of the genre, she nevertheless clings to certain romantic conventions. For one, she retains the well-established romantic belief in the elevated powers of the artist (Frye, *Anatomy*, 59); and, as noted above, she displays a basic faith in the quest model when she champions the right for women to go on quests, to exercise their imaginations, and to chart their own courses. To borrow Audre Lorde's metaphor, she seems to be using the master's tools – the quest motif – to destroy the master's house – the narrative of romance (Lorde, 99).

While the paradox generated within the text constitutes a recognizable feature of postmodernist texts, it is perhaps more accurate to interpret it as a symptom of the clash between postmodern and feminist attitudes toward the construction of identity. Whereas postmodern authors, for the most part, are saying goodbye to the myth of the bourgeois individual subject, and denying the possibility of self-representation, some contemporary feminist writers, as noted earlier, do not subscribe to this position, for the simple reason that, because they have been 'excluded from or marginalized by the dominant culture … , [women] may *never* have experienced a sense of full subjectivity in the first place' (Waugh, 2). In *Intertidal Life*, the portrayal of Alice's impulse toward constructing a sense of unified selfhood, 'a rational, coherent, effective identity' (Waugh, 6), reflects a modernist feminist inheritance informed by postcolonial discourses. On the other hand, the incomplete nature of this project, and the recognition that identity remains both a provisional and positional construct that is discursively produced, reflect a debt to feminist theories influenced by postmodernism.

As I noted earlier, despite the fact that each of the texts examined takes a different stance on whether a molar or a molecular identity is preferable, they nevertheless share a commitment to undermining traditional representations of female identity. In the case of *Intertidal Life*, it is important to appreciate that the appropriation of a literary structure, such as romance, for the purposes of revision, does not necessarily involve the replication of this structure and its ideological basis. Very often, the romantic elements that Thomas appropriates are adapted to reflect a feminist bias. For instance, while the narrator experiences the typical, romantic nostalgia for an earlier 'imaginative golden age,' she clearly opposes the regressive tendencies of the 'romantic' hippies who live on the island. Furthermore, her interest in writing does not lie in the romantic exploitation of 'a sort of tap-root into the world of …

childhood' in order to create a 'private dream-world' (Empson, 21). Rather than stress the individualistic and escapist function of art, Alice insists on art's social function; and unlike the typical Harlequin romance heroine who has no attachments, 'no visible parents, no ties' (Snitow, 137), the text depicts Alice enmeshed in a web of social relations and obligations. As far as she is concerned, it is not so much the journey itself as one's ability to remember and to relate one's observations to others that is at stake (201). Alice's goal involves leaving a map to serve as a guide, and, as van Herk points out, the impulse to create fictions for the benefit of others can be said to correspond to the desire to compose maps (*Rebound*, 3). At one point, the heroine of *No Fixed Address* explains that mapping is 'an act of faith, a way of saying, I have been here, someone will follow, so I must leave a guide' (118). In many ways, Alice seems committed to developing and operating within a specifically female community, which she calls a 'vast archipelago' (92) and a '[s]orority' (147). Yet the construction of a female-centred community never takes precedence over, or fuses with (as in the case of Marlatt's novel), Alice's role as a fiction writer. As we shall see, in *Ana Historic*, the notion of sorority and the development of a female frame of reference emerge as powerful tactics for the subversion of the masculine logic which governs the production of literary and cultural narratives; whereas Thomas's narrator strives to leave a guide for 'others,' Marlatt's protagonist struggles to create a map primarily as a guide for *women*.

In *Intertidal Life*, Thomas's primary concern lies in deconstructing the hierarchical romance structure that assigns men the role of the heroic explorer and women the role of the muse/monster/object. As Northrop Frye points out, romances are characterized by vertical divisions, featuring journeys of ascent and descent through what he classifies as the four levels of the mythological universe:

The highest level is heaven, the place of the presence of God. ... Level two is the earthly paradise or Garden of Eden, where man lived before the fall. ... Level three is the world of ordinary experience we now live in. Animals and plants seem to be well adjusted to this world, but man, though born in it, is not of it: his natural home is level two, where God intended him to live. Level four is the demonic world or hell, in Christianity not part of the order of nature but an autonomous growth, usually placed below ground. (Frye, *Secular*, 97–8)

Admittedly, Frye's analysis of the romance mode remains problematic because it tends to treat the mode, for the most part, as if it were a universal, apolitical and ahistorical form. Nevertheless, his careful anatomization of the genre's central features facilitates an analysis of works, such as *Intertidal Life*, which draw upon traditional romance motifs in an attempt to criticize the narrative's division of roles according to sex. In Thomas's novel, the mythological levels which Frye describes are clearly distinguishable, and while both Alice and Peter conduct quests, owing to their gender, their journeys take them in opposite directions. As Alice remarks, they are each in their 'little boat, giving the occasional wave or halloo' (165). As far as she can determine, Peter's quest sets him on the familiar path of the upward journey – the journey of 'a creature returning to its creator' (Frye, *Secular*, 157). By contrast, Alice's journey – the journey of the woman writer – takes the form of a quest through what Gail Scott describes as the 'dark space' ('Feminist,' 247) of memory in order to retrieve prizes, '[i]mages, single words. The occasional complete paragraph' (226). At one point when she is writing, Alice pictures herself 'sitting all day in a dark cave with a single candle. Trying to see, trying to see' (62). Statements such as this link her efforts as a writer with the shackled prisoners in Plato's cave. But, in this case, the struggle becomes a feminist quest for 're-vision' (see Rich's essay 'When'). Like her literary foremothers, Alice is trying to transform literary forms in an attempt to answer the question, 'What are men and women becoming?'

In addition to being a Platonic and contemporary problem, the motif of impaired vision is a familiar romance convention, often designating moral blindness. For instance, in the Harlequin romance that Flora reads, the hero is blind. Alice assures her daughter that he will regain his sight because Harlequin heroes are always physically flawless 'like Ken dolls' (13). Unlike these heroes whose vision and identity return in the end, Alice understands that the promise of clear-sightedness, wholeness, and order associated with romance is no longer attainable, or perhaps even thoroughly desirable; she must learn to live and work within the fog of a postlapsarian world. Shortly before she undergoes surgery, Alice clears out her house, laughing at all the amulets and talismans she has scattered about her room, 'a blind man's buffet' (275). It is significant that the novel begins with an image of the fog-enshrouded island and ends with Alice lost in a fog of anaesthesia. These images suggest that any ultimate restoration of vision, 'the making good of Oedipus' sight,' symbolizing the successful acquisition of a stable sense of self (de Lauretis, *Alice*, 125–6), has been suspended because the old story, *his*tory, has been undermined.

In many ways, the romance mode with its motifs of blindness and its hierarchical divisions into four 'levels,' according to Frye's model, serves as a perfect vehicle and target for Alice because its dramatic structure ironically reflects her actual experience as a woman in a patriarchal society following marital separation and divorce. In a self-conscious fashion, the text appropriates and transforms the structure of contemporary romance, which traces the journey of an isolated heroine who must overcome obstacles and misunderstandings before she accomplishes her journey of self-knowledge. Within the context of contemporary romance, self-knowledge and narrative resolution involve the recognition that the heroine does not fear the hero, but loves him; and that, despite evidence to the contrary, the hero has been in love with the heroine all along (Coward, 146). In Thomas's novel, this structure receives an ironic twist because Thomas's heroine must come to accept the fact that the hero does *not* love her, and, as the story progresses, the hero and heroine become more and more estranged. The hierarchical structure of the traditional mode is also adopted and modified in a similar fashion. Frye's model of the four worlds is reinscribed when Alice discovers that, while Peter moves upward along the vertical axis, she is carried downward to the third and forth level – levels which are related to the human unconscious (Frye, *Secular*, 56–7).

Typically, romance begins with a sharp descent in social status from 'riches to poverty' or the separation of a family (*Secular*, 104). Frye relates this change in status more generally to the 'motif of amnesia,' depicted as a break in memory or consciousness, which 'often involves actual forgetfulness of the previous state' (102). In *Intertidal Life*, this 'break in consciousness' is realistically effected through Peter's betrayal and subsequent decision to end the marriage. In essence, Peter, who reputedly has 'a very bad memory' (160), forgets that he was ever passionately in love with Alice (88). His 'amnesia' leads both to the marital separation and the breakup of the Hoyle family, and it initiates Alice's descent. As she explains to her friends, prior to Peter's departure she was Mrs Hoyle with an 'official lover and protector.' Everybody knew she was married: she 'had status' (172). Without Peter she loses social as well as financial clout: 'she had no real job, in society's terms, no credit cards, no credit' (235). Like a heroine in a Shakespearean romance, she finds herself impecunious and left to fend for herself in the unsettling lower realm of fertility, irrationality, violence, and death.

Far from embracing this change in status, Alice experiences profound ambivalence in response to her newly acquired freedom. In many ways, the text's depiction of her ambivalence signals women's 'simultaneous acceptance and refusal of the organisation of sexuality under patriarchal capitalism' (Mitchell, 289–90). For Alice, the united or 'happy family' she repeatedly invokes represents her version of paradise on earth (26, 47, 54, 276), and the blissful family outings she recalls emphasize the innocence and unity the family experienced prior to Peter's departure (7, 24–5). Alice's phrase, 'happy family,' is taken from the opening sentence of Tolstoy's novel *Anna Karenin*: 'All happy families are alike but an unhappy family is unhappy after its own fashion' (13). Later on, Alice elaborates on this statement, noting that happy women, in particular, 'have no histories' (92, 276). On a basic level, Alice's ambivalent attitude underscores the fact that change is often terrifying: it is a fearful task to move beyond the known world. Yet, as her reference to Tolstoy suggests, this step into the dark space must be taken if women are to achieve the right to become the subjects of their own histories. Interestingly enough, both Thomas and van Herk single out *Anna Karenin* in their work, although van Herk has no sympathy for Tolstoy or his 'happy family.'

Unlike van Herk's radical rejection of Tolstoy's conservative attitude toward the nuclear family, Thomas's narrative depicts Alice yearning for the security of the familial unit. Alice's ideal can be linked to what Frye terms the 'pastoral myth.' In his discussion of this ideal, Frye suggests that the 'nostalgia for a world of peace and protection ... is particularly strong in Canada' (*Bush*, 238–9). More pessimistic than optimistic, Alice describes the demise of the family as a disaster, which arrives 'like lightning hitting a tree. The family tree' (27). Envisioning the end of the marriage as an expulsion from paradise, Alice cites lines from *Paradise Lost*, which describe Adam and Eve leaving the garden, 'hand in hand with wand'ring steps and slow –' (92). In fashioning these two contrasting worlds, the paradise of marriage and the chaos of separation, the text once again draws on the traditional structure of romance, which typically presents a vision of polarized worlds; on the one hand there is the world we want and, on the other hand, the one we do not want (Frye, *Secular*, 58).

Cast out of the former, Alice initially feels abandoned. Although she is aware that the word 'abandon' also means 'to set free' (26, 171), it takes time before she can re-evaluate the end of her marriage and view it in any broader social context. When she finally does, she concludes that neither she nor Peter is to blame for bringing about the death of the relationship: '[t]heir ages probably did, and the age in which they lived' (225). Eventually Alice realizes that her marriage ended because the practice of ensuring that women are defined socially and economically by men has become a thing of the past: 'imperialism is over, for nations, for men' (171).[5]

As I noted in the introduction, Thomas's novel, like all of the works examined in this study, draws a parallel between the mechanics of colonialism and patriarchy on the basis of their mutual interest in 'map-making,' which involves imposing names on peoples and places. For example, the text clarifies that, by giving Alice his name, Peter followed in the footsteps of his forefathers, men who named and claimed in honour of their country. Despite the security provided by his name, it is a name that Alice had no part in creating. In interviews, Thomas stresses the importance of naming things for oneself, recalling how her grandfather urged her to name things: 'he wouldn't name anything for me. ... He would demand that I find an appropriate name for them' (interview with Coupey et al, 88).[6] In discussing her novel *Mrs. Blood* (1970), Thomas suggests that the protagonist, who calls herself Mrs Blood and Mrs Thing, is 'casting off that colonial name, presumably that her husband laid on her, or her father' (see 'Songs,' 23). Passages in *Intertidal Life* echo de Lauretis's assertion that women's bodies have been mapped according to masculine desire, especially Alice's remark, noted earlier: '[b]abies drop out of us from our most secret places, through channels the fathers have charted and laid claim to' (205). Alice insists that women must reject this type of colonialism: 'Do we really want somebody planting a flag on us and claiming us forever?' (171).

Alice's husband, Peter, a romantic hero who is British, stands as a representative of both British imperialism (31, 51) and male power, which, in the novel, are linked to the historical appropriation of the New World and to current explorations into space (16). Earlier, I noted that Peter appears at the end of Alice's list of household names, emphasizing his identification with the patriarchal power to name. In a flashback, Alice recalls the time shortly after they were married, when they lived with Peter's parents in Britain. Portrayed as repressive, hyper-critical individuals, his parents embody the very worst aspects of imperialism. The text underscores that Alice and Peter had to leave Britain before they could achieve any sort of autonomous existence.[7] Remembering the voyage from Britain that she and Peter took with their first child, Alice notes that as the ship pulled away, Peter's parents 'diminished to a manageable size' (277). The phrase 'manageable size' is followed by the words 'The Last of England.' This is the title of Ford Madox Brown's painting which depicts a couple and their child leaving England in search of the New World. In juxtaposing her departure with this representation of a historical departure, Alice underscores the connection between women's struggle for self-definition and the colonists' struggle to escape the 'order' imposed by British imperialism.[8]

The link between women's degraded status and the effects of imperialism is further reinforced with the introduction of the song Alice recalls about a woman in a dress made up of a map:

Her back was BRAZIL
Her breast was BUNKER HILL
And just a little bit
   Below
Was BORNEO   (70)

The song, which she used to sing at camp, like the comment regarding childbirth and the list of household names she composes, emphasizes that women have been treated like territory, anatomized and appropriated in the same way that the early explorers mapped and claimed the actual geographical terrain. Grief-stricken as she is by the end of her marriage, Alice still insists that it is time for women to go out on their own voyages of discovery and define the value of their own experiences, however difficult such an endeavour might be. The feminist map-making process she advocates involves not a reinscription of the colonial and patriarchal maps, but a remapping of women's bodies and their history from women's perspectives. Alice remains hopeful that this remapping will not lead to a simple reversal of power, but to a transformation of the nature of subjectivity itself. As the historian Gerda

Lerner argues, the insight that men are not the centre of the world, but rather that both men and women are, will 'transform consciousness as decisively as did Copernicus's discovery that the earth is not the centre of the universe' (Lerner, 13). Aware of the potential impact of this change, Alice echoes Lerner when she tells her women friends that what is happening between men and women is just as revolutionary as 'the discovery that the earth was round, not flat' (171).

As I noted in the introduction, in Thomas's realistic displacement of the romance genre, the perils women face in the real world remain evident. The novel makes no attempt to minimize the risks and doubts that female explorers must confront. The choice between questing and maintaining a relationship is always an issue. At one point, Alice wonders, 'Would our lovers wait faithfully for us until we returned?' (70). She understands that she and other women are forced to make a choice between maintaining their art and maintaining their relationship – a choice which she believes led to the destruction of her marriage: 'The stronger I got the more he [Peter] turned away from me' (174). Yet, when she signs the document legalizing her divorce, she crosses out the word 'housewife' and substitutes 'writer' for it (157), acknowledging the necessity of making the choice in favour of her art, even though it ended her marriage. On one level, the rejection of the label 'housewife' signals the narrative's complete refusal of the ideology conveyed by contemporary romances. As Joanna Russ points out, in these texts ' "Occupation: Housewife" is simultaneously avoided, glamorized, and vindicated' (675). In Harlequin romances, women's traditional roles, their supposed 'feminine mystique,' are consistently defended, and 'women are promised all sorts of psychological rewards for remaining loyal to it' (Russ qtd. in Snitow, 139). Alice's awareness of the heavy price women pay when they question the time-honoured 'conventional bargain between the sexes' (Snitow, 139) prompts her to acknowledge that many contemporary women might not 'want to go' on quests at all (70). Lerner specifically cites this 'price' as a factor which has traditionally kept women from fully participating in cultural spheres: 'No thinking man has ever been threatened in his self-definition and his love life as the price for his thinking. We should not underestimate the significance of that aspect of gender control as a force restraining women from full participation in the process of creating thought systems' (227). As we will see, in Urquhart's novel, evidence of a woman's thinking and the mere fact that she has a voice are enough to send a man into a rage. Nevertheless, in Thomas's novel, Alice decides that more pressing than these very real concerns is the need for 'new maps, new instruments to try and fix our new positions' (171).

In accordance with the first epigraph from *A Spanish Voyage to Vancouver*, the text reinforces the fact that one's position and the accounts of one's journey must be fixed with the aid of language. Taking the epigraph as a guide, it would seem that the creation of a useful, orderly text depends upon one's ability to read and decipher information and to shape a story out of notes written down 'in the midst of toil and labour.' In many ways, the first excerpt in *Intertidal Life* serves as a reflection of the development of the novel as a whole because, as critics have pointed out, the novel elaborates on images and themes found in several of Thomas's short stories, especially 'Real Mothers' and 'Natural History' from the collection *Real Mothers*, and 'Three Women and Two Men' from *Ladies and Escorts*.[9] The epigraph also corresponds to the narrator's method of organizing an account of her experiences, which proceeds according to the same process of expansion or elaboration described in the epigraph. Looking back to the information which she jotted down in her 'commonplace book,' the journal which she kept from 1972 to the present (1979), Alice expands her notes and creates a realistic story based on the events which led up to and followed the breakup of her marriage.

On another level, the epigraph, which implicitly deals with the construction of narratives based on personal experience, reflects Thomas's tendency as a writer to draw on autobiographical materials. Bowering argues that Audrey Thomas and Clark Blaise are two of the 'most obviously autobiographical fiction writers in Canada ...' (see 'Snow,' 64), and much of her fiction constitutes an elaboration on her own personal experiences. As she herself explains, her first real story, 'If One Green Bottle,' was 'real' because it had to be written: 'it seemed to be the only way I could organize the horror and utter futility of a six months long, drawn-out miscarriage in a hospital in Africa' ('My Craft,' 153). In interviews, she goes so far as to insist that she never writes about anyone other than herself: 'I really dont [sic] know anyone as well as I know myself. I find it really presumptuous to write about other people' ('Songs,' 14). On another occasion, she put it even more bluntly: 'I can only write about myself in the end' (interview with Coupey et al, 101). As a result of this stance, the narrators in her novels, no matter what names they are given, are always reflections of herself (see Wachtel, 'Guts,' 5). As Joan Coldwell says, Thomas's novels form 'a continuous semi-autobiographical narrative, a kind of *roman fleuve*, and it is clear that the narrating voice belongs to the same person at different phases of experience' (Coldwell, 'Memory,' 55).[10]

Thomas explains that her motives for writing are based on the need to organize 'pain and turn it into art' (see Wachtel, 'Guts,' 5). Thus the excerpt from *A Spanish Voyage to Vancouver* not only echoes the narrator's fictional process and the organization of the novel but also reflects Thomas's desire to organize the pain associated with women's experience in a patriarchal society. Given her belief that 'art is fossilized pain' ('Songs,' 22), it is not surprising that *Intertidal Life* treats distressing events that she herself experienced: Thomas was separated from her husband in 1972 and divorced in 1979, and the dates correspond to the time-frame outlined in *Intertidal Life* (see 'An Interview,' 7).

My point in drawing attention to the autobiographical tendencies in Thomas's fiction is not to suggest that there is a one-to-one correspondence between her life and her art. Instead, I am asserting that, by referring to her own experiences, she offers a challenge to the way we read, think about, and value fictions. In a postmodern and feminist gesture, *Intertidal Life* effectively blurs the borders between 'fact' and 'fiction.' The creation of this kind of indeterminacy, viewed in a wider context, underscores the fictional impulse at work in the construction of supposedly 'factual,' historical accounts. Like many postmodern texts, Thomas's novel points out the precariousness of making any clear-cut distinctions between the construction of history and the writing of fiction. Secondly, by casting personal experiences into the framework of romance, the text emphasizes that we cannot begin to think of our lives without recourse to fictional modes of organization. In *Intertidal Life*, Alice reminds Flora that our awareness of our lives is bound up with story-telling: 'All we know is what our parents and relatives choose to tell us' (277). Flora suggests that 'a lot of that is probably lies,' but Alice corrects her – 'I'd say "myths," not lies' (278) – in an attempt to help Flora recognize that fiction is not something 'out there,' a romance which we passively consume and push away when we are sated with falsehood. As Paul de Man asserts:

> [I]t is very difficult not to conceive the pattern of one's past and future existence as in accordance with temporal and spatial schemes that belong to fictional narratives and not to the world. This does not mean that fictional narratives are not part of the world and of reality; their impact upon the world may well be all too strong for comfort. What we call ideology is precisely the confusion of linguistic with natural reality, of reference with phenomenalism. (de Man, *Resistance*, 11)

Thomas's use of realistic, autobiographical information serves to highlight, in particular, our reliance on the romance mode. But she undermines the genre through the addition of details from her own experience – details that work against the romance convention of portraying 'stylized figures' rather than realistic human beings (Frye, *Anatomy*, 304). The reliance on actual experiences clashes with the official romance narratives, which typically feature perfect Ken-doll-type heroes, plucky heroines, and happily-ever-afters. The conflict generated between the official and unofficial narratives supports Howells's claim that women have 'to revise or even unwrite the old romantic fantasy narratives we have inherited' ('No Sense,' 111). Thomas's presentation of autobiographical elements also reflects a commitment to the feminist credo that the personal is political, and her work challenges the traditional belief that writers must portray history on an epic scale. In interviews, Thomas explicitly rejects the notion that women have to write about history with a capital 'H':

> [Y]ou can write your book any damn way you want to as long as it works and don't let

men tell you that it has to have the larger scene. I'm so fed up with hearing that. You know, you've got to write *War and Peace*, you've got to write this great diorama of history. ... You've got to set it in the context of the great social upheavals of your time. ('An Interview,' 45)

Thomas, like all of the writers treated in this study, is committed to presenting the story of a woman overlooked by history. As we shall see, she is in agreement with Swan, Marlatt, and van Herk, who likewise implicitly or explicitly reject the injunction that women, if they want to be taken seriously as authors, must produce epic fiction.

Thomas sees her project not as the replication of narratives akin to *War and Peace*, but as an attempt to give women 'a sense of their bodies' (see interview with Coupey et al, 107). In the novel, Alice (like her creator, Thomas) rejects the cultural and literary representations of women and the diminished value accorded to their experiences. In conjunction with Gerda Lerner, Thomas recognizes that women's experiences have come to bear 'the stigma of insignificance' because in Western society women are taught to devalue their experience: 'What wisdom can there be in menses? What source of knowledge in the milk-filled breast? What food for abstraction in the daily routine of feeding and cleaning? Patriarchal thought has relegated such gender-defined experiences to the realm of the "natural," the non-transcendent' (Lerner, 224). For Thomas and her fictional representative, Alice Hoyle, writing that portrays personal observations is not some frivolous pastime, but a necessary measure to keep one from remaining as the object of discourse, overwhelmed by alien terminology and confusing circumstances, and condemned to silence. Alice's first journal entry identifies her reasons for keeping the diary:

This was to be a commonplace book, where I would finally bring together all the words and definitions and phrases I have copied out for years on scraps of paper. But I need it now for something else, I need it to stay sane. ... I need to sprawl, to scrawl, to pull out from myself the great glistening sentences full of hate and fury and fling them, still wet and steaming onto these white pages. (30)

Her journal provides a receptacle for powerful emotions, and, in a culture that privileges cool, abstract thinking over feeling (Lerner, 224), the acknowledgment of these emotions alone constitutes an act of subversion.[11]

Within the novel, the two narrative levels (the first-person entries into the commonplace book and the third-person, expanded version) are framed by a third narrative level, in which an omniscient third-person narrator records events occurring in the present. Structurally, the novel shuttles back and forth among these levels, between past and present, covering the span of ten years. The juxtaposition of the three narrative levels forms a temporal collage; and, while all of the entries in the commonplace book are catalogued according to the month, it is not immediately clear what year is being invoked.[12] Elizabeth Komisar, discussing Thomas's earlier novel *Blown Figures*, which stages a woman's imagined journey to Africa to assuage the pain and guilt associated with the birth of a stillborn child, notes that Thomas tends to juxtapose 'one voyage against another ... crack[ing] the regular sequence of time' (interview with Komisar, 60–1). In *Intertidal Life*, a similar, though perhaps more subdued, oscillating time scheme alerts readers to the fact that they are witnessing a distressing voyage which takes place within the protagonist's mind. In an interview, Thomas confirmed that the quest reflected an internal, psychic voyage: 'I was trying to reproduce, or suggest, how people's memories work' (see review by Kareda, 50). Linked to the unconscious, this type of voyage captures what Thomas describes as '[p]sychological realism' ('Songs,' 14), and deconstructs traditional rules of temporal logic. As Freud suggests, unconscious mental processes are not arranged chronologically: 'time does not change them in any way and ... the idea of time cannot be applied to them' ('Beyond,' 28).[13]

In the end, Alice's record of the traumatic events associated with the dissolution of her marriage leaves the reader with only a sense of the cyclical nature of the seasons, an appropriately feminine temporal scheme. No orderly list of dates can be assembled, so that any attempt to construct a unified, causal history fulfilling the promise of progress is ultimately frustrated. While novels about writing, as well as romances, are 'almost always discontinuous' (Fowler, 124), Thomas's challenge to teleology reflects both a feminist and postmodern tendency described by Lyotard as 'an incredulity toward metanarratives' (xxiv); the novel's time scheme specifically subverts the narrative of historical and intellectual progress. Many of the novels in this study, particularly *Ana Historic* and *The Whirlpool*, interrogate historians' efforts to categorize the past – efforts that are typically associated with simplistic faith in progress. In *Intertidal Life*, the generation of a unified, progressive history must be replaced with a more provisional puzzling out of a set of thematically related events.

On the one hand, the temporal collage fashioned in *Intertidal Life*, which works against the vision of a circular or linear journey and the telling of a unified tale, can be related to the traditional structure of both the *poioumenon* and the romance. The latter has been described as a form that simultaneously 'projects the end it seeks and defers or wanders from a goal which would mean among other things the end of the quest itself' (Parker, 173). Seen in this light, the textual vacillations become a metaphor for fiction as a whole, which proceeds by way of expansion or dilation, and whose existence depends on the suspension of any final arrival or the procuring of some ultimate revelation. Alternatively, the vacillations can be linked to Alice's personal difficulty in accepting that one kind of story is over – the coherent story of her marriage to Peter – and that 'she must let it go' (225). At bottom, her reluctance to give up the 'happy family,' and the narrative associated with it, serves the fictional process by impeding closure. Her mind, which she describes as a 'midden' (227) or 'refuse heap' (*OED*), constantly dwells on the past and sifts through fragments of memory.

Alice's preoccupation with the past, taken together with her reduced social and economic status, leaves her in an 'alienated' state which, as we have seen, Jameson describes as 'a space in which people are unable to map (in their minds) either their own positions or the urban totality in which they find themselves' ('Postmodernism,' 89). On the surface, it would seem that there is a very real danger that, instead of becoming 'disalienated' and retrieving an account of her experiences, Alice will remain trapped in an endless process of reflection. Yet, Jameson's model, with its binary opposition between alienation and disalienation, may be too simplistic to capture the complexity of a text which self-consciously problematizes the possibility of ever achieving the kind of wholeness and order associated with disalienation. As Patricia Waugh notes, in its exploration of gender and identity, the work of contemporary feminist writers often 'does not "fit" into the dominant aesthetic categories of realism, modernism, or postmodernism' precisely because it balks at reconstituting the notion of a unified sense of self: 'Their work, implicitly or explicitly, recognizes the construction of woman as "other," but refuses the unitary concept of self which appears to be its self-evident opposite: the achieving, rational, autonomous, transcendent, successful "self"' (Waugh, 30). If disalienation is won at the cost of conforming to the symbolic system which divides the sexes, uses castration to symbolize this split, and positions the feminine 'over the point of disappearance, the loss' (Mitchell, 307), then jamming the system and settling for alienation may be a useful manoeuvre. In many ways, the strategies for subversion which I isolate in the following chapters proceed from this initial and risky tactic of arresting the system.

In accordance with this tactic, Thomas's text neither offers a representation of a transcendent 'self' nor completely dismisses, in a postmodern gesture, the possibility of achieving a coherent identity. Instead, the text focuses on the narrator's alienation and the difficulties associated with her attempts to map a subject position following the break-up of her marriage. *Intertidal Life* is not a success story, the hero's story. The epigraph to the second section, 'At every turn we encountered new obstacles,' (132), intimates that Alice increasingly encounters difficulties in her struggle to formulate a sense of self that offers an alternative to the prevailing narratives. Likewise, the song about the Lion Hunt that she sings with her children, which features a swamp that cannot be avoided, reinforces the sense that there is no getting around the patriarchal discourses which structure female subjectivity (151–2). Finally, the epigraph to the third and last section implies that Alice is unable to escape the 'currents' of the past: 'We put out our oars, endeavouring with them to counteract the current, but alas the efforts of the sailors were in vain' (245).[14]

Very often, the external landscape Alice inhabits mirrors her troubled mindscape. For instance, when she describes the boggy lake which she visits with Flora after her divorce, the lake takes on a 'swamp-like,' menacing aspect linked to the dangers of compulsive reflection, which precludes the construction of a unified sense of self:

The springy ground they sat on was a thin lid over the water that went back – how far? Nobody knew for sure. ... What if you went for a walk, pushed your way through the underbrush, explored a little farther? What if suddenly the ground gave way, would you have time to put out your arms or would you be sucked straight down, like water down a waste pipe? People out calling for you, getting anxious as it grows dark and you have not returned. And you, floating just beneath them if they only knew, dead in the yellow-brown water. (247)

The horror associated with the swamp may represent fears bound up with what Juliet Mitchell describes as 'the loss of oneself into one's own unconscious – into the gap' (307). As we will see, the horror associated with falling into a liquid abyss and the subsequent loss of identity are foregrounded in *The Whirlpool*, where the vortex below the Falls arouses ambivalent feelings of terror and delight in one of the male characters. In *Intertidal Life*, the image of the swamp can also be understood as a figure for Alice's internalization of societal discourses concerning women's diminished value; drowning represents a complete inability to escape from these discourses. Generally speaking, in Thomas's writings, water, especially the sea, serves as an ambivalent image. At times water symbolizes 'intertidal life' and the positive aspects of birth and female creativity. At other times, it takes on the type of demonic characteristics noted above and embodies a kind of pursuing fate. Frye remarks that, in the romance plot, the sea often functions as an image of the lower world, as well as representing the unconscious, 'which seems paradoxically to forget everything and yet potentially to remember everything' (*Secular*, 148). In Thomas's novels, the sea frequently corresponds to the unconscious. For example, the narrator of *Songs My Mother Taught Me* explains that, on occasion, her mother's past threatens to drown the children (*Songs*, 110). In a discussion of her earlier novel *Blown Figures*, Thomas refers to the narrator's struggle with a demonic past, which also takes the form of the sea that rises up and drowns her (see interview with Komisar, 60). In each case, patterns associated with the past threaten to impede efforts on the narrator's part to distance herself from an identity formulated in the past.

In *Intertidal Life* the threat of drowning is repeatedly invoked. Alice portrays her sadness as stretching before her 'like an endless sea' (24) and she describes herself 'struggling in the icy waters of Peter's rejection' (112). As Linda Hutcheon notes, the narrator makes repeated references to the figure of the drowning woman (*Canadian*, 119). The sea is most clearly associated with the past early on in the novel, when Alice and Flora go on an outing to Coon Bay. Walking out onto the rocks, Alice sees two people coming toward her in a canoe. One of them is Harold, a deaf man who had been living on the island during 1972, the year her marriage broke up. Confronted with this spectre from her history, Alice asks, 'Why should the past *rise up just now*, just now when she was trying to be, was succeeding in being, so calm' (18; my emphasis). Unlike the narrator in *Blown Figures*, who, according to Thomas, is 'drowned by the past' (she goes mad; see interview with Komisar, 61), Alice manages to take a stand, and she greets Harold, 'waving and smiling, as the deaf man and his companion came across the beach' (18).

In terms of the novel's structure, Harold's appearance triggers the first sustained flashback in the temporal progression and initiates what Peter Brooks describes as 'a *return* in the text, a doubling back' (100). As we shall see, this return is linked to Alice's inability to overcome a traumatic incident that took place in the past. After sighting Harold, Alice recalls her first impressions of the cabin as it was in 1972, remembering the plans and expectations that she had at the time. In keeping with the romance structure, where the 'normal means of transportation is by shipwreck' (Frye, *Secular*, 4), Alice likens the cabin to a less than seaworthy vessel: 'The original structure was suffering from rot and there wasn't a straight line in the place. It was a little like living on a ship' (19). Amid this initial flood of recall, one particular memory surfaces, a memory that is repeated throughout the text like the dominant note in a musical score. The significance of this memory is signalled both through repetition and by virtue of the fact that it is the first event entered in the commonplace book, appearing under the heading 'SEPTEMBER':

A month ago, up on the ridge he [Peter] asked me, Alice, what do you really want? I was so happy, so content, I answered 'Nothing.' I'd read my Shakespeare – what did I think would happen if I gave him an answer like that? But I was feeling so good! I had on my violet sweater and a long red paisley skirt. I had on a necklace of rose hips and cloves. That will become now, in my memories, one more of my 'crisis outfits.' I can always remember what I was wearing when a crisis occurred. ... Every time I wear that outfit I shall hear Peter's voice, feel the warm sun on the back of my neck, smell the scent of cloves. 'Alice, what do you really want?' (30)[15]

Unprepared for Peter's question, Alice answers off the cuff and claims that she wants nothing. Later, this response, like the tide, relentlessly comes back to haunt her because she understands that, on some level, her passive reply brought about the dissolution of their marriage. As she says:

If she had talked to him, then?
If she had caressed him? Put her hand between his legs?
If she had said I really love you I just don't know how to get through to you?   (35)

The fairy-tale repetition of the word 'if' implies a 'then,' an ideal image of the future in which the crisis and all the pain and isolation associated with her loss of identity have been magically averted, and she and Peter remain safe within the earthly paradise of marriage. In the passages cited above, Alice likens herself to Cordelia, who offered Lear the same truthful, yet foolhardy, response – a response that shattered the kingdom into warring factions and left the old king mad with shock and grief.

Even though Alice knows her answer was the wrong one, 'she is not sure what the right answer would have been' (38). All she is left with is an overwhelming sense of having been betrayed by the moment: 'The sun, the lichen-covered rocks, the pale green flesh of the arbutus trees, the hum of the bees – everything conspired to put her off her guard' (38). Her description of the Edenic surroundings suggests that, before she gave Peter the fatal reply, Alice enjoyed the existence that typically precedes the romance narrative. This is the state of existence in which there is nothing to write about because it occurs prior to 'once upon a time' and is subsequent to 'and they lived happily ever after' (Frye, *Secular*, 54); once again, we are reminded that 'happy women have no histories.' The text demonstrates how Alice tries to organize the pain associated with this event and with the adventures that followed in its wake by turning them into fiction within her commonplace book, and later on, in her third-person account. However, the recurrence of this particular episode throughout the text indicates that she has trouble laying the memory to rest.

This episode takes on heightened significance because her response to Peter's question led to his departure and the fragmentation of her identity. In its depiction of the trauma associated with this fragmentation, the text reinforces Deleuze and Guattari's opinion that one needs to keep 'small rations of subjectivity' in order to function (160). As I suggested in the introductory chapter, Thomas's novel demonstrates that the breakdown of identity must be undertaken carefully because, 'if you blow apart the strata [the organizing mechanisms] without taking precautions, then instead of drawing the plane [successfully exploring areas where identity remains fluid] you will be killed, plunged into a black hole, or even dragged toward catastrophe' (Deleuze and Guattari, 161).

In many ways, Thomas's text graphically illustrates the negative consequences associated with a sudden and drastic breakdown of identity. Throughout the novel, fragments of the fateful episode, as well as the repeated use of the word 'nothing,' recall the event (30, 35, 166, 222, 242); as a result, the episode takes on a kind of emblematic status. Whenever a related fragment surfaces, it creates a temporal wrinkle, a return to the past; it is the same, yet different, but never sufficiently transformed to allow Alice to leave the memory behind. As a result of her obsession with the past, the story which she hopes to write – the map that would serve as a guide for others – can barely be inscribed. In many ways, the repercussions associated with the blowing apart of the narrator's identity and the vacillations that result from this dynamic are best described by psychoanalysis.

In his work *Beyond the Pleasure Principle* Freud isolates a psychic dynamic which he terms 'repetition-compulsion,' which transcends the simple desire for wish-fulfilment. Forced to postulate why individuals suffering from war neuroses have dreams in which they return to the moment of the trauma (as opposed to dreams that are pleasurable), Freud suggests that there must be a psychic force that undergirds the pleasure principle. After linking the neurotic behaviour of those suffering from war neurosis to the play impulse of the child who throws away his toys, Freud canvasses several possible reasons for this type of behaviour, including a desire for mastery and / or revenge. In the end he concludes that individuals who have undergone a trauma, which is often forgotten and repressed, are forced to repeat the repressed material of the past as 'a contemporary experience' instead of '*remembering* it as something belonging to the past' (18). In referring to the dreams of his shock patients, Freud explains that the dreams which take them 'back with such regularity to the situation in which the trauma occurred ... are endeavouring to master the stimulus retrospectively, by developing the anxiety whose omission was the cause of the traumatic neurosis' (32). Simply put, individuals who are unprepared for a potentially traumatic event do not experience any of the apprehension that would normally prompt them to fashion a mental barrier to protect them from the oncoming excitation. The repetition-compulsion behaviour that follows the traumatic experience represents an unconscious effort on the part of the individual to restore the proper sequence between apprehension and event. Freud also notes that the repetition-compulsion observed in the case of neurotics can also be observed in the life of normal persons, where it gives the impression of a pursuing fate, a daemonic trait in their destiny (21). Freud's description of the demonic element associated with the repetition-compulsion dynamic sheds light on the recurring structural and thematic figures in Thomas's work, including the negative images of water noted above and the recurrence of the episode noted in the commonplace book.

In traditional romance narratives, the hero tumbles from one adventure to the next, remaining unscathed all the while. However, in Thomas's realistic displacement of the genre, which does not track the hero's escapades but the experience of the woman he has cast off, the sudden shift from Frye's mythological 'level two' to 'level three' (figured as an expulsion from her marriage) shatters the narrator's 'molar' identity. Like Freud's shock patients, her defence mechanisms were not mobilized when Peter posed his question. Inadequately furnished with a barrier against harm,

Alice can be likened to the hermit crabs that she and her daughters observe in the tidal pools – organisms that occupy 'snail shells or whelk shells into which they can retreat when alarmed.' However, the crab's safety is precarious because he chooses 'shells that are much too small.' He drags 'around his inadequate shelter, imagining he's safe' (268–9). Alice also unwisely mimics the behaviour of the limpet, a creature famous for its ability to cling to rocks even in 'wave-swept areas where few other forms of life can survive' (59). Long after Peter has left, she mistakenly believes that he'll come back and that she must 'hang on' (87). In this respect, Alice's obsession with Peter conforms to the conventions of contemporary romances, which are 'permeated by phallic worship' (Snitow, 134). However, in *Intertidal Life*, the heroine comes to identify this 'worship' as delusional; she realizes that she 'mythologized' her husband and that her attitude toward him exalted him 'in the eyes of others' (243). Alice's awareness of her complicity recalls Virginia Woolf's comment that women have served as 'looking-glasses possessing the magic and delicious power of reflecting the figure of man at twice its natural size' (*Room*, 35). For the most part, Alice lacks the capacity to reflect on her situation, and her traumatized and demonic imagination, like the tenacious limpet, is 'always returning to the same spot' (59); in this case, the spot is Peter, 'formerly Peter the Rock' (60).[16] As a result of the trauma associated with this 'crisis,' she is bound to recall this moment, to reproduce the past in the present, until she can somehow transform the meaning of her response – the signified – while remaining faithful to her original reply – the signifier, 'Nothing.'

In the meantime, her obsession with the past, '[t]his Peter nonsense, never petering out,' leaves her floating (and in danger of drowning) in her memories – 'currents hot and cold, lagoons and clashing rocks' (134). Unlike the typical hero of a romance plot who ultimately transcends the state of alienation, Alice remains unable to map a coherent identity. The alternating currents of her memory create the textual dynamic characterized by an oscillation between past and present, and constitute the medium of her seemingly endless voyage. However, the flashbacks are recorded with such intensity that they have the effect of freezing the narrative trajectory. On two occasions, the narrative explicitly invokes the image of freezing. Once, when Alice is reciting a lesson in lip-reading, she quotes the phrase 'We must freeze –' (26). This sentence, which is never completed, simultaneously signifies and enacts this type of suspension, which is a general feature of the narrative structure. Later on, Alice describes herself as a frozen pond with her heart like 'a little fish swimming vainly to and fro ... beneath the ice' (189–90). Here, she refers to the psychic 'freezing' associated with a trauma involving a miscarriage and/or abortion alluded to in the earlier novels *Mrs. Blood* and *Blown Figures*. In this case, the narrative trajectory is arrested for two reasons.

For one, this 'unspoken' trauma suspends the narrative because the reader must look outside the text to Thomas's other works for more information concerning the event. Taken together, Thomas's novels form a structure aptly described as a group of Chinese 'sliding panels,' which can be read separately or as a whole (see interview with Komisar, 59). As a result of this deferral to other texts within an unfinished corpus, the possibility of recovering meaning as plenitude or full presence remains suspended or frozen. Secondly, the narrative is interrupted because the vocabulary necessary to describe aspects of women's experience has not been developed. Thomas remarks in interviews that narratives written by men have rarely included discussions of the darker aspects of motherhood, the 'nasty things' that go on between the announcement of pregnancy and the appearance of a 'dear little baby' ('Songs,' 15). Gerda Lerner also suggests that this area of women's experience has traditionally not been considered worthy subject matter for literature; as such, it constitutes a 'blind spot' on the map. Critics discussing the presence of similar 'silences' within postcolonial writing have argued that one of the 'most persistent prejudices underlying the production of the texts of the metropolitan canon is that only certain categories of experience are capable of being rendered as "literature"' (Ashcroft et al, 88). In *Intertidal Life*, Alice explains that her husband did not understand her grief at the loss of the child, 'how fear and pain and all those vast quantities of blood, and the little dead thing in the basin had frozen her over' (189). Worse still, she could not describe what she had gone through, 'she had suffered a sea change of a most terrible sort and was dumb to tell about it' (189–90). Alice's trauma suspends the narrative because it marks the terrible gap in human communication and clarifies that women 'have been denied the full resources of language and have been forced into silence' (Showalter, 'Feminist,' 193).

In Thomas's text, this type of freezing or suspension, which subverts the romance narrative, becomes allied with repetition, which characteristically results in narratives which tend to be all middle:

Repetition ... appears to suspend temporal process, or rather, to subject it to an indeterminate shuttling or oscillation that binds different moments together as a middle that might turn forward or back. This inescapable middle is suggestive of the demonic: repetition and return are perverse and difficult, interrupting simple movement forward.   (Brooks, 100)

Brooks's claim, suggesting that simple movement forward (the Oedipal trajectory) is positive, while vacillation is negative, or worse, demonic, must be contextualized within a value system that privileges Oedipal logic. Theoretically, repetition itself constitutes a neutral strategy, one which has even received special attention from poststructuralist critics such as Derrida, who suggest that all writing can be understood as instances of citation or repetition predicated on the absence of a controlling presence or original author (see Derrida, 'Signature,' 326). However, in the case of the fiction Alice is creating, and with respect to the structure of the text as a whole, repetition is clearly aligned with a paralysing and destructive force that frustrates the narrator's ability to fashion a map for herself and others. As I suggested earlier, Alice becomes a reluctant quester because of her traumatic break with her husband; this shock generates a wrinkle in the text, analagous to the repetition-compulsion dynamic.

Deleuze and Guattari suggest that, in dismantling identity, 'there are times one courts death, in slipping away from signifiance [sic] and subjection one courts falsehood, illusion and hallucination and psychic death' (160). Once again, Thomas's appropriation of the romance structure serves as a perfect vehicle to express the protagonist's experience of hallucination and her brush with 'psychic death.' Very often, the demonic nature of Alice's obsessive preoccupation with the past is signalled through images associated with romance's 'lower world.' In the romance mode, the motif of freezing, here associated with the narrator's psyche, is a key feature linked to the lower mythological levels where human beings often freeze into 'some kind of invariable pattern' (Frye, *Secular*, 116–17). Even Peter, who tends to be preoccupied with his own search for enlightenment, can see that Alice is suffering, but he has little patience for her problems: 'Am I supposed to wait around while you go down inside and confront your demons? I have a life too!' (45). Alice herself is aware of the demonic qualities of her obsession. At one point, she reports fragments from an old Indian woman's conversation regarding the loss of one's soul, and she quotes a line from Emily Dickinson, 'One need not be a chamber to be haunted –' (125), tacitly acknowledging that she is the victim of a potentially harmful unconscious dynamic.

While Peter, embarked on his journey of ascent, views the end of his marriage as a chance for 'new life,' Alice feels 'as though there's been a death in the family' (63) and refers to the West as 'the land of the dead' (230). The lower mythological level is often associated with Egypt, the land of death (Frye, *Secular*, 114), symbolized by oracular figures such as ghosts (116). Throughout the novel, the narrator's imagination dwells on images of death and murder. When a radio announcer accidentally condenses the words 'murdered' and 'buried' into 'murried,' Alice suggests that it sounds more like 'married and murdered' to her (85), revealing her attitude toward Peter's decision to end the marriage and 'do away' with her. In many ways, Alice's distrust of Peter conforms to a well-known popular romance convention: very often, the heroine mistakenly believes that the hero intends to 'harm her' (see Radway, 131).[17]

In her commonplace book, Alice displays this same fascination with lower-world images. She compares the definitions of the word 'mummy,' the body of a 'human being or animal embalmed for burial,' with the word 'mother' (136). Later, she records the riddle: 'What does a Baby Ghost call his parents?' and the answer,

'Dead' and 'Mummy,' is written upside-down and backward (240). Through these repeated references to death and the association of her role as a mother with images of death, Alice emphasizes her preoccupation with death or 'absence' (Godard, *Audrey*, 25) – a preoccupation which, like the motif of drowning, is linked to her traumatic loss of identity – her brush with 'psychic death' – and to her more general sense of having been 'erased' by the dominant discourses.

The inversion of the riddle's solution intimates that Alice, like her namesake, the heroine of Lewis Carroll's *Alice's Adventures in Wonderland*, has crossed over into a looking-glass world and is trapped behind the mirror of the symbolic system, a frame which seals her off from others. (This image of the mirror recalls Alice's fear of being trapped in the bog.) In keeping with her identification with Carroll's heroine, who also embarks on an underground voyage, Alice echoes the conversation with the Cheshire Cat, when the little girl complains that she does not want to go among mad people. Suddenly made aware of the madness associated with an arbitrary system which degrades women, Alice repeats the Cheshire Cat's response, 'we're all mad, or we wouldn't be here' (123). She explicitly refers to herself as '[t]he cracked servant of the looking glass' (134).[18] Her use of the word 'cracked' underscores her own emotional conflict, but it also suggests that the spectre of Woman set up to serve men's desires has fragmented. Within the text, Alice's loss of social and economic status both foregrounds and shatters the mirror, as does Peter's decision to change from Peter the Rock into Peter Pan.

As with the narrative vacillations, the narrator's loss of identity and her awareness of being trapped within a fractured, looking-glass world find expression within the established terms of the romance mode. Within romance, the structural core of the 'motif of amnesia' lies in 'the individual loss or confusion or break in the continuity of identity.' This breakdown in identity has 'analogies to falling asleep and entering a dream world' (Frye, *Secular*, 104). As noted above, Alice's identity depended almost entirely upon her husband's ability to provide her with social and economic definition. When he becomes entranced with the 1960s counter-culture and joins the Lost Boys, Peter ceases to be a Real Boy (134–5). His 'break in consciousness' not only ends the marriage but also radically destabilizes Alice's hold on a reality mapped by imperialist, patriarchal discourses. Estranged from Peter and equally estranged from the traditional role of the housewife, Alice becomes fundamentally alienated from traditional societal structures and no longer sees a reason to distinguish 'real life' from 'unreal life' (40). She wonders where exactly she belongs: 'Was everybody just playing games? Was anything really real?' (123).

Thomas's parodic appropriation of romance conventions underscores women's experience in Western society, where their access to the 'real' and the related set of signifiers including the 'law,' 'money,' 'power,' 'knowledge,' 'plentitude,' 'authoritative-vision,' and so on is mediated by men who are more closely aligned with the privileged signifier or the 'phallus' (Silverman, 191). When Peter leaves Alice, she discovers that she has become invisible; as we shall see, this sense of erasure surfaces in all of the texts in this study. In *Intertidal Life*, the narrator experiences her loss of self-definition as terrifying, and it affects her most tangibly when she and Peter smoke up. In her drugged state, her awareness of the enormous, newly created symbolic rift between herself and Peter and her fears of disintegration are externalized. She hallucinates that she has become 'unreal' and believes that she can 'pass through people like a ghost' because she has become 'invisible' (49). The division between Alice's roles as domestic woman or 'Scorpio Housewife,' allied with the phallus, and the unallied artistic, autonomous woman whose mind is 'the heavyweight champion of the world' (226) effects an internal psychic split. When Alice tries to control the panic brought on by her hallucination, she experiences this terrifying inner division: 'She closed her eyes and began to scream and scream. No. Someone else was screaming for her' (50).[19]

Very often within the romance mode, loss of identity becomes aligned with an inability to determine one's name: the connection 'between naming, identity, and closure or ending remains a persistent romance phenomenon' (Parker, 5). Once again, the narrative conventions of romance highlight the parallels between the effects of colonialism and women's experience in patriarchal society. Alice wonders what she should be called now that she is no longer 'Alice Hoyle' (39). Although she knows that she is more complex than the generic or functional title 'mother' denotes, because, as a woman, she is operating within a language which does not adequately reflect her experience, she has trouble answering the question: 'And who was she really?' (14).

Commencing as it does with Alice's loss of identity, the novel follows the basic outlines of romance with one significant difference: in the novel there is no indication that the quest will conclude with the standard romance ending in which order and identity are restored or at least postulated in the not too distant future. In the text, the 'happy family' of Alice and Peter does not regroup and regain a seat in paradise. Ten years after her marriage has ended, Alice asks herself what she wants and decides that she would like to be a 'stone ... unmoving' (263). Her wish for stillness may be bound up with her unnamed illness, but whatever the cause, it indicates a desire for the peace associated with death – a release from her alienated position.[20] (Prior to wishing to be a stone, she imagines being buried peacefully in her garden [258]). As noted earlier, the work concludes with the ominous image of suspension: Alice lies on the operating table, asleep or frozen in a fog of anaesthesia. Thus, the sought-after conclusion to Alice's quest, which is bound up with the reader's quest for some coherent and meaningful conclusion to the narrative, seems to be infinitely deferred. The circular and/or linear structure of the traditional narrative, like the marriage (which was governed by the same symbolic order), has been shattered beyond repair.

In the text, the breakdown of the marriage – the traditional symbol of paradise on earth – and the impact of this breakdown on Alice's psyche are figured through repeated images of fragmentation. Journeying through the lower world where everything is reduced to an object, Alice views life as a perverse game and likens herself to a puzzle in disarray: 'Alice Hoyle: 1,000 Interlocking Pieces' (158). During the first year of their separation, Jehovah's Witnesses come to call, and when the woman asks if Alice has found 'some kind of peace' within her, Alice responds by punning, almost hysterically, on the word 'peace': 'Oh no peace, no peace. Everything's in pieces here' (66). Punning is, in fact, a trope which depends upon substitution and deferral of presence. Alice's predilection for this rhetorical figure emphasizes that, after the fall from paradise, language itself has ceased to reflect a stable meaning. As one critic suggests, the figure of the writer as castaway or exile becomes 'virtually inseparable from the differentiated, exiled nature of poetic language' (Parker, 224). It would seem that the romance narrative shatters because its constituent parts, the words themselves, can no longer be viewed as stable entities.[21] The note that Alice finds beside the telephone describes this situation perfectly: 'Everything is in a state of fux [sic]' (232).[22] Elsewhere, Thomas has described the separation between signs and referents using the image of 'halation,' a phenomenon observed in photography and stained glass. Halation refers to the spreading of light beyond its proper boundary. Thomas insists that 'words can do that too,' and that there is 'no "proper boundary" for words. Let them spill over from one language to another, let them leap out at us like kittens at play' ('Basmati,' 317).

In *Intertidal Life*, the fluidity of words, more often than not, represents a morbid symptom of the fallen world; Alice hears the 'end' in 'friend,' sees the 'rust' in 'trust' (30), and, crossing out the letter 'l' in the word 'lover,' she reveals the word 'over' (137). The most hopeful aspect of the mutability of words appears when Alice finally discovers another way to interpret her answer to Peter's question. As noted earlier, Alice's obsessive concern with her response stems from an awareness that by answering as she did, she was unwittingly conforming to the dictates of Oedipal logic, which characterize women as objects devoid of desire – objects which must be slain and discarded. However, because of the slipperiness of the links between signifier and signified, her original reply of 'Nothing' can be linked to the definition of 'nothing' used in the game of tennis, where 'nothing' can be substituted for the word 'love.' Burrowing through these contiguous verbal associations, Alice creates a path that enables her to change her story (and history) because she foregrounds the presence of her supposedly absent desire. The transformation of her answer illuminates the contours of female experience and female desire which are eclipsed on the imperialist and patriarchal map: '"Nothing," I said, "nothing." When what I meant was "love"' (166). In this way, fiction, like the transference situation between patient and analyst, constitutes a medium in which the past narratives can be represented symbolically (in her narrative, Alice casts events into the third person), making them accessible to intervention and reinterpretation.

Despite this hopeful aspect of the multivalence of language (which becomes a full-fledged strategy of subversion in other works, particularly *Ana Historic* and *The Whirlpool*), Thomas's narrator has a tendency to yearn for the security of a non-existent paradise. Her imagination broods on her diminished access to the 'real' and seizes on the negative aspect of mutability and dismemberment. In the bizarre newspaper headings she reads, Alice finds shocking and grotesque objective correlatives for the destruction of her marriage and security: a tidal wave off the coast of Japan, an assassination in one of the banana republics, a lady in Sweden who gave birth to seven infants that looked like rats: 'It's just one thing after another is it not?' (73). Her list concludes with the story of a man who 'caught a shark and inside was a human leg, complete with sock and shoe' (79), only one of the text's many images of dismemberment. Alice also reports that the unfortunate explorer Captain Cook was hacked to bits and 'presumably eaten' by natives (140). Even the natural world of the island she inhabits teems with mutilated victims: the shore crabs and starfish have legs missing – the savagery at work in the world is barely veiled. At one point, Flora asks her mother, 'Does everything just go around eating everything else?' Alice replies, 'Sometimes it seems that way' (270). Thomas's earlier novel *Blown Figures* offers a similarly disturbing vision of life as 'a roaring of tense colours and interlacing of opposites and of all contradictories, grotesques, inconsistencies' (157), and the novel concludes with a reference to cannibalism: the narrator, Isobel, who has gone completely mad, admits to having eaten the child in her womb (518). Similarly, in *Intertidal Life* the references to mutilation and cannibalism are horrific features of Alice's imagination.

Once again, these nightmare visions correspond to the conventions of the traditional romance mode. As Northrop Frye asserts, images of cannibalism relate to the 'cannibal feast' which is the darkest feature of the lower world: 'At the bottom of the night world we find the cannibal feast, the serving up of a child or lover as food. ... Such a theme is important not for its horrific frisson, but as the image which causes that frisson, the identifying of human and animal natures in a world where animals are food for man' (Frye, *Secular*, 118). However, in *Intertidal Life* the overwhelming evidence of mutilation specifically reflects the symbolic order's standard method of categorization, which positions women as subhuman and aligns them with the natural order and its inhabitants. The proliferation of images of mutilation mirrors Alice's sense of her own psychic fragmentation – her 'castration' – resulting from her severed association with Peter, who served as her link to the symbolic order. In popular imagery, castration is usually thought of in terms of dismemberment, as 'something cut off, missing, absent, a wound, a scar' (Mitchell, 307). The connection between the images of mutilation and Alice's sense of her own fragmentation becomes explicit when she recalls a sign she had seen in Victoria, 'War Amps,' and she wonders if there were 'love amps' as well, 'people who wandered around with parts of themselves, let's take the heart, for example, permanently missing. ... Wearing a badge which, echoed the words on the cenotaph. "Is it nothing to you?"' (242). Here again, the repetition of the word 'nothing' recalls Alice's fateful reply to Peter, which, as she recognizes, led him to believe that she was empty of meaning and therefore discardable: 'There was *nothing* new for him to find out about Alice, *nothing*. After fourteen years, he knew it all' (222; my emphasis).

According to Frye, within the lower world, human nature is not only fragmented but reduced to the non-human, a metamorphosis which is related to the image of freezing. The lower world is often populated by animals and human beings of the same structural type who are mute or inarticulate (Frye, *Secular*, 115). In *Intertidal Life*, after Peter's departure, Alice repeatedly associates herself with the animals that keep her company in her island cabin. She links herself in her role as a mother to the cat, Tabitha, and pads about the cabin 'mother-catlike' (119). She also thinks fondly of Flora as her 'last kitten,' occasionally wishing that she were more like a cat 'who never worries about the "father,"' and not so obsessed with the loss of her husband (31). Throughout the novel, Alice's sexuality – her 'pussy' (32) – and the animal attraction that exists between her and Peter (they stalk each other 'like two cats' and engage in 'fucking' rather than making love [42]) reflect Alice's awareness of her identification with the level of experience associated with the sensual, fecund animal world. On another level, her sexual awareness, her enjoyment of her body, and her desire offer a sharp contrast to the sexual 'inexperience' of most Harlequin heroines, whose desire is 'only ever triggered as a response, crushed out of her, as it were, as a series of low moans' (Coward, 147).

In terms of the structure of traditional romance literature, animals and animal companions are said to represent fertility spirits which are part of the death-and-rebirth pattern of the lower world (Frye, *Secular*, 115). Alice's cat, the mother of seven litters, clearly functions as this type of spirit. In the context of descent, however, animals represent chiefly Ovidian metamorphosis, 'the reducing of humanized beings to something subintelligent and subarticulate' (116). Metamorphosis of the Ovidian type, where something that has been human becomes an object in the world of nature, 'represents the falling silent of the world in its paradisal or humanly intelligible phase' (115). The narrator in Thomas's *Prospero on the Island* (1971) explicitly voices this fear, saying: 'Sometimes I'm afraid that we will stop talking and listening altogether. ... We will use hand signals like mutes, and no one will have anything to say to anyone else' (128). In *Blown Figures*, the central characters, Isobel and her husband Jason, are referred to as 'deaf-mutes' (48).

The deaf man, Harold, who appears on the beach and reminds Alice of the past, most clearly embodies the threat to meaningful communication in *Intertidal Life*. When Alice meets him for the first time, Harold reminds Alice of the 'the Frog Prince,' a title that signals his status as a human being reduced through some enchantment to something subhuman (57). Later, he is described as doglike, 'large, all over the place, sloppy' (103), and, in a sketch, said to resemble 'a satyr or Pan himself' (68). By virtue of his resemblance to animals and his deafness, Harold comes to represent the reduced or disabled state of human communication. He primarily serves as a foil for Alice, who, in her fateful conversation with Peter, kept silent and 'did not even try to speak what was in her heart' (35). When Peter tells Alice that he has been 'seeing' her close friend Stella, Alice imitates Harold's voice – a voice from 'deep inside a cave on the very bottom of the lake. "I can't hear you, I'm deaf"'' (240). Thomas, who is a careful wordsmith, has noted elsewhere that the word 'deaf' is related to the word 'absurd,' which comes from the Latin, *ab* from, *surdus*, deaf, inaudible, harsh, used metaphorically to mean deaf to reason, hence irrational ('Basmati,' 312). Thus, through this circuitous route, deafness becomes a sign, akin to fragmentation and mutilation, for the irrational and destructive forces at work in the lower or fallen world which accords women the marginal status of the 'other' in order to assure the subjectivity of the male.

As Frye notes, dogs are common lower-world symbols (*Secular*, 115). Viewed in this light, Alice's identification with the doglike Harold and the family dog, Byron, that was 'put down' after it bit a child can be seen as a romance convention. However, her identification with dogs more accurately reflects her status as a degraded female. Alice imagines that Peter and Anne-Marie probably regretted not being able to 'put her down like an old dog' (21); and later, when Peter has transferred his affections to Penny, Alice repeats this notion, saying, 'What a pity it is … that husbands can't put down obsolete wives the way one puts down a superannuated cat or dog' (166–7). At times, Alice finds herself behaving like Byron: after a visit from Peter, she howls 'like a forsaken dog' (43). Even her friend Selene, who strikes Alice as a paragon of virtue, admits that, at times, all she wants to do is follow her lover, Raven, around 'like a dog' (96). The impression gained from these references is that women, in their relationship with men, especially as wives, are positioned – and position themselves – as sub-male.[23]

The lower world of romance is traditionally the domain most closely associated with the cycles of nature, with fertility and with animals. As many writers have pointed out, women's identification with the order of Nature has a long pedigree. In an essay written in 1974, the anthropologist Sherry Ortner argued persuasively that women are consistently identified with this realm because in every known society women are viewed as being closer to nature than to culture.[24] While her study most accurately describes the ideology of Western culture, it offers powerful insights into the subordination of women, a practice that is upheld by religious, juridical, philosophical, scientific, and literary discourses. *Intertidal Life* clarifies that, within literary discourse, the romance mode is a powerful advocate of this type of subordination, comprising a 'major part of the western literary heritage ... with its roots in Greek mythology and the Bible, its pervasive presence in myth and fairy tale, its huge presence in medieval and Renaissance literature, especially in Shakespeare' (Davey, 'Alternate,' 14). In fashioning an account of the events which led up to and followed the breakup of the narrator's marriage, the text both acknowledges and challenges the narrative of romance, which constitutes the primary literary discourse perpetuating the hierarchical, Aristotelian perspective that devalues women.[25] In order to appreciate fully how she deconstructs the genre, her quest must be compared with Peter's.

Like Alice, Peter is also cast as an explorer. When the couple go for a walk along Spanish Banks, Alice forges a connection between herself and Peter and the early explorers Captain George Vancouver and Captain Dionysio Alcala Galiano (24). By profession, Peter is a visual artist, whose work reflects a preoccupation with masculine notions of ideal women. The nudes that he draws with 'loins of irresistible attraction, breasts like bloated wineskins ... lying on their backs and sides, with heads or faces hidden' are the stuff of male fantasy – passive, faceless women 'waiting to be penetrated' (31). His attraction to ideals persists in his liaison with Anne-Marie, who reminds Alice of an art-object, 'one of the nymphs on the Grecian urn' (26). According to Alice, Peter has no room in his binary scheme of whores and madonnas for mothers, and he leaves the marriage in search of romance. In this respect, Peter fits the description of one type of Harlequin hero: the man who is sexually active and has lots of girlfriends (Coward, 134). (Ironically, although he is sexually predatory, Peter suffers from 'performance-anxiety'; furthermore, his girlfriends were initially his wife's close friends.) Alice explains to her friend Stella that 'the minute I became a mother he was unable to love me any more. Romantically, I mean' (154). Although Peter's side of the story is filtered through Alice's consciousness, snippets of his conversations with her impart a sense of his motivation.

It would seem that Peter looked upon his married life with Alice as a period of stagnation, and he remains incredulous that his wife finds reason to grieve after he leaves her. As far as he is concerned, for fourteen years they lived as vegetables (45); his use of the word 'vegetable' reinforces his sense that his life with Alice took place on Frye's third level – the lower, vegetative, 'female' plane of existence. Alice imagines that Peter conceives of himself as an escaped prisoner, fleeing the repressive chains of marriage (80). The image of escaping from a prison-house is a figure many poets, including Wordsworth, use to represent an ascent from the lower world (Frye, *Secular*, 100). Throughout the text, Peter's movement along the upward trajectory toward paradise is constantly reinforced. As noted earlier, he looks on the end of their marriage as a 'new life' (63) and he emphasizes that his relationship with Anne-Marie goes *'beyond'* fucking, the base, sensual pleasure that Alice offers him (38; my emphasis). His claim that he and Anne-Marie have achieved 'something higher' (41) figures largely in Alice's imagination. She pictures them 'clasped in each other's arms, spirituality flowing between them' (42). Alice uses their supposed spirituality as a weapon against herself to confirm her own sense of her degraded, animal-like physicality. Ironically, Peter and Anne-Marie transcend the physical to such an extent that he is rendered impotent (38); this is only one clue among many that there is something wrong with Peter's quest for transcendence.

In the text, Peter's sense of himself as a superior being is graphically rendered. For instance, when Alice sleeps at their house in Vancouver, Peter sleeps *above* her in the loft. She considers telling him about her fears concerning the forthcoming operation and imagines climbing the ladder to reach him, but she predicts his cool response and remains below him, lying there as though they were 'in separate bunks on a ship' (13). Ladders are repeatedly used to depict the separation between Peter and Alice. When the Jehovah's Witnesses come to call on the Thanksgiving weekend, they interrupt Peter and Alice, who are picking apples in the orchard. After the couple leaves, Peter ascends the ladder, while Alice remains below him, crying (67). When Peter does manage to comfort Alice, his condescending gesture – he kisses the top of her head – only serves to emphasize his superior position (43). These images of Peter literally in a 'superior' position, which often feature ladders, correspond to the archetypal images of romance. Romance, as Frye asserts, takes us into 'the great Eros theme in which a lover is driven by his love to ascent to a higher world,' an ascent characterized by a number of images, including climbing or flying, ladders, mountains, towers, spiral staircases, the shooting of arrows, or coming out of the sea onto an island (Frye, *Secular*, 151). In accordance with his role as heroic quester, on a journey of spiritual ascent, Peter assumes traditional romantic postures and positions; and Alice, who is clearly familiar with romance imagery, portrays him accordingly.

Peter with his new soft voice (48) is also identified with the hippies from Coon Bay – the 'Peters with their Wendys' (94). The hippies assume moral superiority over anyone who expresses the so-called baser emotions: 'Anybody who got angry, jealous, suspicious, who even *raised their voice,* was somehow inferior' (95). Alice, watching the hippies embark as a group on a quest, determines that they are questers who are trying 'to go back to a paradise before the fall' (97), and images of ascent are repeatedly invoked in association with the counter-culture. Some of them, such as Raven, actually climb mountains (158), but most, including Peter, rely on drugs to get 'high' and to 'fly' (135). Their use of drugs as a short-cut to acquire the vision that comes from enlightenment reinforces the impression that the counter-culture's quest is merely a parody of the traditional romantic quest. This sense of parody is emphasized by Peter's association with Peter Pan, which also ironically harks back to a traditional feature of early romances, where the central character 'never develops or ages' (Frye, *Anatomy*, 186).

Alice harbours a great deal of scepticism regarding the behaviour of the counter-culture. Granted, she is resentful that Peter left her to join them, and this certainly colours her impressions, but she convincingly characterizes the representatives of the 'Me-Generation' as a narcissistic bunch of 'takers' (97), and compares them to Tennyson's lotus-eaters – questers who abandoned Odysseus's ship to sit 'on the hills like Gods together/careless of mankind' (67). At one point, Alice accuses Peter of being 'so far into … [his] romantic shitty dream' that he doesn't even listen (121). While Alice, who is most at home in her garden (258), is supposedly in danger of merging with the fecund, vegetative, subhuman world, the hippies are equally in danger of transcending their animal natures to the extent that they become entirely passive, shutting down their senses and losing touch with their humanity: 'They were takers. They did not care to change the world or make it better … they just wanted to be left alone. Their favourite position was sitting down' (97). In *The Whirlpool*, the pitfalls associated with the desire for transcendence are similarly portrayed, but, as we will see, Urquhart underscores the tragic, and even fatal, aspects of this desire to 'be left alone.' Perhaps because she is a mother, Thomas's narrator is outraged that the hippies have abdicated their parental responsibilities. She is appalled that Raven does not even know where his little girl lives (111), and she is anxious for the children of these lotus-eaters who want to behave like infants. As she says, 'Somebody's got to be the parent' (183).

At bottom, the text underscores that Peter and the hippies have adopted a misguided romantic attitude, and their tendency to march off into the unknown in a herd under the tender guidance of a guru – 'always male' (96) – suggests that, like the lotus-eaters, they are avoiding, rather than confronting, the true nature of a quest. According to Alice, 'one went on a true quest alone and, except for magical or divine intervention, one fought the terror of the dark wood alone' (141). It may seem paradoxical that a woman claims to possess a superior understanding of, as well as the right to criticize, the quest plot – a narrative model generated by men. Yet, as Virginia Woolf suggests, the sexes are often most astute when criticizing each other. As she says, 'there is a spot the size of a shilling at the back of the head which one can never see for oneself. It is one of the good offices that sex can discharge for sex – to describe that spot' (*Room*, 86). In offering her opinions regarding the shortcomings of the traditional quest model, Alice is discharging this type of service; she is also undermining and recoding the narrative structure of romance.

The real test afforded by a quest, according to Thomas and her protagonist, involves one's ability to analyse the journey and to compose an account out of the remembered fragments that will be worthy of passing on to others, which, as I suggested earlier, corresponds to the creation of a map. Yet in the journeys of the counter-culture, there is no 'real spirit of adventure'; worse still, 'there's no reflection either' (201). They have no interest in reading or creating stories (97). Alice prophetically claims, 'By their books shall ye know them' (103), confirming Frye's assertion that 'one becomes the ultimate hero of the great quest of man, not so much by virtue of what one does, as by virtue of what and how one reads' (*Secular,* 157). Alice tells her eldest daughter Hannah that Thoreau comes closest to her ideal image of the explorer because, although he had his faults, 'he did *observe*, he did think about things and try to organize those thoughts, to share them with others' (201). Ultimately, the goal of an explorer lies in the struggle to create stories (or histories) which make sense of the postlapsarian world. Given this requirement, one cannot succeed in a quest by dismissing the crucial role of narratives and the art of storytelling, and lapsing into forgetfulness. As we shall see in the chapters that follow, it is precisely this ability to generate an account of one's experience, to develop histories from a female-centred perspective, which surfaces as the most crucial tactic in any attempt to subvert traditional discourses.

In the case of *Intertidal Life*, the text's deconstruction of the romance genre also has ramifications on other traditional discourses. Associated as it is with a search for enlightenment – a search for truth – the romantic quest, which has its roots in the Bible, must also be seen in the context of the Christian quest, 'the journey of a creature returning to its creator' (Frye, *Secular,* 157). As it turns out, Thomas's re-coding of romance offers a challenge to Christian doctrine. Viewed in the biblical context, Peter's forgetfulness recalls the Christian story in which Christ's disciple 'forgets' his saviour and betrays him. Alice repeatedly aligns her husband with his namesake in the New Testament. Both are associated with fishing – the biblical Peter was a fisherman by trade – and Alice explicitly refers to her husband as 'Peter the Rock' (60), a reference to Christ's promise to his disciple: 'You are Peter, and on this rock I will build my church' (Matthew 16:18). According to the biblical story, when Peter followed Jesus to the court of the high priest's house, he denied his discipleship three times. When the cock crowed, he remembered that Jesus had foretold his denials and he wept. In Thomas's fiction Peter is called 'Traitor' (39) and he is also associated, somewhat playfully, with cocks. Under the heading for February in her commonplace book, the narrator records the etymology of the word 'cock,' and the entry is immediately followed by an account of a discussion between Alice and Stella about Peter, in which Alice remarks that Peter has a 'very bad memory' – an allusion to the forgetfulness of Christ's disciple (159–60).

While Peter's identification with his biblical namesake is somewhat ironic, the text's most radically subversive move involves casting Alice in the role of both Mary and Christ.[26] Presumably after the birth of her first child in Britain, Alice attended the ritual known as the Churching of Women, a rite which ensures that women who have recently delivered receive the sacrament. When she is offered a sip of the wine, said to be the blood of Christ, Alice wonders why the women did not 'put our hands between our legs, show him our blood' (53). This response to the rite directly challenges the Christian story, in which women and the experience of childbirth are treated as digressions unworthy of attention. Peter, who forgets his love for Alice and forgets when his children were born (51), perpetuates this dismissive attitude toward women and childbirth. In opposition to this cultural evaluation of the status of women's experience, Alice places women's capacity to reproduce on the uppermost rung, equal to, if not more valuable than, Christ's sacrifice. She recalls how the priest asked the congregation of women to think of the blood of Our Lord Jesus Christ which was shed for thee, and how her mind turned to Mary instead, who delivered her child like a beast, 'pushing and grunting and lowing' (52). Later on, thinking of her husband's transgression – his 'amnesia' concerning his children's birthdates – she repeats Christ's words at the holy supper: 'Take this in remembrance.' In this case, the words refer, not to the blood of Christ, but to the blood of women, shed in childbirth. By insisting on the significance of Mary's 'maculate delivery,' the text radically restructures the Christian story; it turns around the romance structure to include a recognition of women's experience, so that, to recall Gerda Lerner's words, there *is* wisdom in menses and in the 'milk-filled breast' (Lerner, 224). At one point, Alice rejects the hierarchical order espoused by the Bible, which eclipses women's participation in history, and creates her own feminist creed:

For the word is not made flesh, it's the other way around. The flesh made word, or rather, in the beginning, made cry, made howl. *Then*, later, the word, simple at first, all babies make it, race, color, creed do not come into it. Made word: Ma – Ma, Ma – Ma, the breast. And the breast, like the magic pitcher in a fairy tale, empties and fills up again.
    Take this
    Take this
    Take this
In remembrance of me.
    (and be thankful)   (53)

From this perspective, it is not man's ability to die but woman's capacity to engender life that constitutes the supreme sacrifice and the true miracle. In comparison to this miraculous and creative act, everything else, including the Christian sacrament, remains a pathetic echo. Writing, which Alice compares to pregnancy, comes closest to duplicating the fears and exaltation associated with the birthing process (107).

On the one hand, Thomas's subversion of the romance plot and the biblical narrative on which it is based serves to warn women of the dangers associated with a too rapid deconstruction of identity; on the other hand, it serves to recuperate the value of women's experience and offers hope for the future. In keeping with the text's aim to destabilize romance narratives, the conclusion to *Intertidal Life* offers an ironic comment on the standard outcome of Harlequin romances, which afford women 'uncomplicated access to a subjectivity which is unified and coherent' (Light, 142) and offer images of 'peace, security and ease' (143). Rather than transcend the symbolic system, Thomas and her narrator work within it, arresting the mechanism in order to challenge the traditional genre's hierarchical structure. The novel's suspension of any final outcome implies that, for women writers, the primary goal lies not in fashioning a definitive ending (providing a finished map) but in the resistance to the 'inherited codes and fictions' (Godard *Audrey*, 22). This does not entail abandoning traditional narratives altogether; instead, it demands careful analysis of the way in which women have been positioned within and erased from the linguistic terrain. Elsewhere Thomas has stressed that, for all their to-ing and fro-ing and travelling up Vancouver Island, the explorers sent from England and Spain to find the northwest passage ended up with the experience of the search itself: 'What they got was doing it. But that's it, what they got out of it was the search' ('An Interview,' 49). The same can be said for women; as Alice explains, the exercise of the 'enormous capacity we have for looking, reflecting, inquiring' (254) constitutes success, and, in the exercise of this capacity, women assume the role of 'officers and captains' (170).

Thomas's novel seems to suggest that the women who engage in feminist quests may not necessarily reap the benefits of their discoveries themselves; however, their efforts can effect changes for the next generation of women. In *Intertidal Life*, the narrator's daughter Flora most visibly profits from her mother's voyage. At the same time that Alice is undergoing her operation, Peter and Flora go out in the boat. Initially Peter rows the boat, but in an effort to comfort his daughter, who is worried about her mother, he hands over the oars, offering her the chance to steer: 'bracing their fishpoles beneath the seats, they carefully changed places' (282). Concluding with this image of exchange within a boat suspended on the water – an image which is juxtaposed with a description of Alice succumbing to anaesthesia and going 'under' (281) – the novel offers the possibility of establishing a more equitable distribution of power between women and men.

3

Citing the Body:

The Discursive Mapping of the Woman and the Subversive Domain of the Carnivalesque in Susan Swan's *The Biggest Modern Woman of the World*

Fold up the maps and put away the globe. If someone else had charted it, let them. Start another drawing with whales at the bottom and cormorants at the top, and in between identify, if you can, the places you have not found yet on those other maps, the connections obvious only to you. Round and flat, only a very little has been discovered.   (Winterson, 81)

In the previous chapter, I examined how Audrey Thomas's text draws on the figure of the quest to foreground and, ultimately, to subvert the narrative structure of the romance mode – a mode which, in its mapping of female identity, traditionally aligns the male with the heroic subject and the female with the monstrous obstacle. Susan Swan's novel *The Biggest Modern Woman of the World* also utilizes the quest motif and the figure of mapping, and plays on women's alignment with monsters or freaks. Here these strategies are used, not to call into question the ideology of the romance mode, but to problematize a wide variety of cultural discourses that arose specifically in the Victorian Age. As we will see, the novel draws on mock-travel narratives, such as Swift's *Gulliver's Travels*, but it also refers to the lesser-known generic conventions which structure the freak-show performer's spiel and the lengthy pamphlets which offered supposedly true accounts of his or her life. Swan's text utilizes all of these genres to highlight how modern notions of the Woman and the freak, and their interrelationships, were charted within the grid of the newly emergent discourses of modern science, industrial capitalism, and American nationalism.

One method of problematizing official discourses involves giving voice to the unofficial story; Swan's novel, even more explicitly than *Intertidal Life*, portrays events from the perspective of a woman overlooked by history, and draws on appropriately unofficial genres. *The Biggest Modern Woman of the World*'s protagonist is a historical figure, the real-life, seven-and-a-half-foot giantess Anna Swan, who was born in Nova Scotia on 7 August 1846. Anna Swan exhibited herself at Barnum's American Museum from 1862 until 1868. After leaving Barnum's employ, she travelled to Europe, and then settled in Seville, Ohio, with her giant husband, Martin van Buren Bates, devoting herself to 'church activities and [teaching] ... in the Baptist Sunday School' (Blakeley, 17). She died of consumption on 5 August 1888, just two days short of her forty-second birthday.

Nowadays few people know about her, partly because her fame has been eclipsed by that of the Cape Breton giant, Angus McAskill. Within the novel, Anna[1] complains that her famous counterpart was more widely known: 'In British North America, where I should be famous as the nation's first female entertainer, it is here an Angus, there an Angus, everywhere the McAskill from Cape Breton' (16). Although her erasure is treated with humour, the fact remains that her dual status as a woman and a freak ensured that she fell through the grid of history.[2]

In his book *Freaks*, Leslie Fiedler remarks that a *lusus naturae*, with the exception of a few dwarfs, rarely 'belongs to history' (58). One intention of Swan's book may have been to rescue Anna from her place in teratology (the study of monstrosities) and to restore her, as one critic said, to 'her rightful place in history' (review by Buitenhuis, 844). However, in fashioning an account of her history, the text works not so much to reinscribe Anna and restore her to 'her rightful place in history' as to complicate our ability to make clear-cut distinctions between historical fact and fiction. While the text, for the most part, portrays a historically accurate cast of human curiosities, including those who were employed by P.T. Barnum in the mid-nineteenth century, it plays fast and loose with the 'facts' concerning their lives. For instance, according to the novel, Zip, the black dwarf, William Henry Johnson (dubbed the 'What is it' by Dickens), is accidentally murdered by a blow from Angus McAskill, and subsequently stuffed and mounted by Barnum (84). In actual 'fact,' Zip lived to the ripe old age of eighty or more (Bogdan, 141). Conversely, the text's seemingly fantastic account of the fire at P.T. Barnum's American Museum in 1865, which portrays Anna being rescued from the burning building by a derrick, turns out to have been 'true' (Benton, 549–50).

The novel's playful exploration of the wavering boundary between fact and fiction characterizes it as a postmodern work. But this same feature has puzzled and angered individuals who believe that history ought to be dished out on one side of the plate and fiction on the other. To date, Susan Swan has received four letters from outraged elders of the giant Swan's family suggesting that the book be burned because, in their eyes, it is 'an inaccurate biography of their ancestor.' The author maintains that she 'mythologized the giant,' and she is exasperated that her heroine's family cannot 'recognize the difference between literature and biography' (Laderoute, 64). But the family's confusion points to an important connection between history and fiction because the inability to 'recognize the difference' between the two, on one level, clarifies the absence of difference. As Hayden White argues, historical discourses impose upon events 'the formal coherency that stories possess.'

Both historical and fictional narratives are plotted, 'put there by narrative techniques' and not '"found" in the events' (White, 24). If we grant that history and fiction are equally 'plotted,' that is to say, equally contrived, then Swan's novel can also be said to frustrate the possibility of ever achieving an accurate account of history, making a neat division between fact and fiction unattainable.

Yet, in her mythological portrayal of the giantess, the author teases us with the possibility of grasping the 'facts.' The novel conveys an accurate map of the contours of Anna Swan's life; by that I mean that the places that she lived and visited and the chronology of her life can be corroborated. Divided into four sections, the text portrays the heroine's travels in Canada, America, Europe, and Seville, Ohio. Born to a Scottish family living in the Mill Brook section of New Annan in Colchester County, Anna travelled to Halifax for her first exhibition in March 1851. At age fifteen, she moved from her hometown to Truro, Nova Scotia, to attend teacher's college. Unhappy with this experience, she subsequently signed a contract with P.T. Barnum to stand on exhibition at his American Museum. After working for Barnum, she joined a troupe of entertainers organized by Judge H.P. Ingalls bound for a tour of Europe. They sailed for Europe on 22 April 1871. In its depiction of Anna's journeys, complete with dates and chock-a-block with verifiable historical personages, the text gestures toward the concreteness of historical facts. However, within the seemingly solid bounds of these contours, a multiplicity of hidden, unofficial journeys can be traced.[3]

In *The Biggest Modern Woman of the World*, the motif of the journey serves, at bottom, to highlight the range of official and unofficial nineteenth-century discourses (some still in circulation today) that shaped prevailing notions about what it meant to be a Woman. Implicit in the use of the term 'Woman' is a notion of *sexual* difference – Woman versus Man. But this is difference which makes a difference not solely as a result of biology or even socialization, but because of 'signification and discursive effects' (de Lauretis, *Technologies*, 1). In using the term 'Woman,' I refer not to actual historical individuals (i.e., women), but to the product of various 'social technologies of gender' (de Lauretis, *Technologies*, 2) which assign individuals to a particular category that did not exist out there in 'nature' (4). As de Lauretis argues, we might say that gender, like sexuality as conceived by Foucault, is not a property of bodies or something originally existent in human beings, but 'the set of effects produced in bodies, behaviours, and social relations by a certain deployment deriving from a complex political technology' (Foucault, *History*, 127).[4] Gender technologies, mediated through a set of discourses, function in the same way that ideology does for the Marxist theorist Louis Althusser: they produce a set of differences and give meaning to these supposed differences.[5]

Swan's novel underscores the way in which a dominant set of nineteenth-century discourses wrote the female body into existence by scientifically classifying this body among other bodies. This hierarchical classification reinforced an understanding of the female body as inferior or abnormal compared to that of the male. While it is tempting to view these discourses as purely coercive instruments of patriarchal power, it is important to keep in mind that they did not serve solely as repressive mechanisms. Instead, they operated – and continue to operate – more generally as laws that create borders, distinguishing the speakable from the unspeakable, the legitimate from the illegitimate, so that, paradoxically, these discourses produce the objects that they come to deny. To the extent that these discourses serve to establish the boundaries of the gendered female body, 'instating and naturalizing certain taboos regarding the appropriate limits, postures, and modes of exchange' they can be said to have mapped the female body (Butler, *Gender*, 131).[6]

Within the novel, in a letter written to her lover Angus McAskill, Anna alludes to several of these budding discourses:

Angus there is a wind rustling my handbills whose name is PROGRESS. We are on a chasm. Enormous scientific changes are coming. We must prepare ourselves.

Have you read Whitman? I have.

Do you agree with Darwin? I do.

Will you advocate the rights of women?   (87–8)

Swan's metafictional appropriation of the past, with its parodic reproduction of its dominant discourses, prompts readers to reflect on the power these discourses have asserted within our own lifetime. This strategy of appropriation recalls Thomas's exploitation of romance conventions for the purposes of drawing attention to the genre's hierarchical structure.

Right from its opening pages, Swan's novel foregrounds not only the power of discourse and its capacity to shape what individuals come to perceive as the 'truth' but also the process of discursive appropriation itself. Initially, the narrator – the boisterous 'ghost' of Anna Swan – refers to the text as her 'never-before-revealed autobiography which contains testimonials and documents by friends and associates (from their perspective) of a Victorian woman who refused to be inconsequential' (2). By emphasizing that Anna's history is a patchwork creation composed of quotations culled from a variety of sources, the text underscores that identity is based on appropriation; it is 'linguistically and discursively constructed and displaced across the range of discourses in which the concrete individual participates' (Belsey, 61). Simply put, the text reveals that identity is a fiction – a necessary fiction, but a fiction nonetheless. From this awareness, it follows that the construction of the self-as-subject depends upon two factors: first, on the set of discourses in circulation at the time, and second, on one's ability to appropriate and manipulate these discourses in order to tell a story about oneself.

In offering this reading of Swan's novel, I hope to counter Frank Davey's view of the text as a failed *Künstlerroman*. According to Davey, the novel fails because the narrator does not 'achieve the transcending or distinguishing sense of identity' typical of this genre – a deficiency supposedly signalled 'early and throughout the novel by its multiple narrative viewpoints' (*Post-National*, 184). As Davey sees it, like the protagonists of the *Künstlerroman*, Anna 'relates her story in the first person, but, unlike them, not in a single, achieved discourse' (184) He goes on to argue that the 'insufficiency of her narrative as a ground for identity is emphasized by the numerous other perspectives the text offers. … This fragmented narrative signals a fragmented rather than achieved self' (184). Along these same lines, Smaro Kamboureli likewise suggests that Anna 'fails to becomes the subject of her own discourse' (106). 'This is most evident,' Kamboureli asserts, 'in the spiels written for her by her literary agent that she delivers during her lifetime' (106). Kamboureli proceeds to draw a parallel between Anna's inability to possess language and 'her failure to come to grips with her private self,' which is seemingly indicated by the fact that even 'when she is not on stage … but in the privacy of her bedroom writing in her journal, Anna lacks any sense of a cohesive self' (106). While one can certainly agree with Davey's and Kamboureli's suggestion that Anna fails to produce a traditional *Künstlerroman* and a traditional autobiography (just as Thomas fails to write a traditional romance), surely the point was never simply to reproduce these genres. Anna's narrative reads as a failure only if one adopts a traditional perspective that assumes an author wants to replicate familiar generic structures; the fact that both critics adopt this type of traditional perspective is evident in the language they invoke. Phrases such as 'single, achieved discourse,' 'achieved self,' and 'cohesive self' indicate that Davey and Kamboureli are implicitly relying on what has been identified as a masculine model of selfhood – a model which stresses independence and singularity rather than connection and hybridity (see Chodorow, 166–9; Gilligan, 24–63). Operating from within the context of this binary opposition of the achieved, authentic self versus the fragmentary, unauthentic self, both Davey and Kamboureli fail to recognize that Swan's text, by purposefully signalling the impossibility of 'inscribing a single achieved discourse,' may well be offering an altogether different model for mapping female identity. As Teresa Heffernan argues, in Swan's novel, the 'tradition of authority and objectivity are placed in a context which both allows for the inevitable connection between representations of the world and self interest and admits multiple and fluctuating perspectives that necessarily de-stabilize the notion of "fixed" identity' (31).

The first chapter, which opens with Anna's 'spiel' to the reader, not only reveals something about the fictive nature of identity but also covertly puts into practice the same type of discursive appropriation and manipulation that critics such as Davey and Kamboureli find troublesome. Anna solicits her readers the way any slick-talking barker would attract 'marks' or passers-by, by giving them a taste of the wonders that await them if they continue to read the novel:

Do you know how a giantess grows? Overnight? Like the sumac bush? Or slowly, like a cedar of Lebanon?

I, Hominida Pina Pituitosa Majora, a warm-blooded, viviparous, coniferous giantess, grew as an elephant grows, expanding in pounds as I rose in inches. My body weight doubled and then tripled by the time I was four.

I did not grow straight up like an Eastern White Pine, the largest conifer in North-East America, although I sprang from a Nova Scotian floor and learned to consort with livewood throughout the world without losing my needles. The LIVING LUMBER GIRL who walked and talked and juggled the Pre-Cambrian Shield (rocks to you, sir).   (1)

Far from being a product of her own genius, Anna's fantastic spiel draws on the well-established discourse of freak-show 'blowers,' whose lexicon consisted of a complex 'hodepodge of medical terminology and show-word hype' (Bogdan, 3). Even the lecture from Barnum's museum, which Anna quotes, turns out to have been written by her manager, Judge Apollo Ingalls; and he himself borrowed phrases from Barnum's handbills (4). Whereas Davey views the novel as a botched fairy-tale and an equally flawed *Künstlerroman* and Kamboureli refers to it as a failed autobiography, I would argue that the novel offers a successful representation of a host of unofficial genres. For one, the entire text bears a strong likeness to the detailed biographical pamphlets distributed, for a fee, to the audience at freak-show performances in the 1860s.

According to Robert Bogdan, with minor variations, a pattern had been established by 1860 and the pamphlets all corresponded to a particular format:

First, a short biography of the subjects was presented: where they were born, what their early life was like, how they were discovered, and what the condition of other family members was. This part concluded with a description of the exhibit's recent history – where they had been shown, who had seen them, and how patrons had reacted to them. Second, a description of physical condition was given, commonly written by or quoted from a medical doctor or a person affiliated with the natural sciences. Third, the pamphlets contained endorsements from people – elected officials, newspaper editors, royalty, and clergy – who had seen the exhibit and vouched for its authenticity, interest, and propriety for public viewing. ... In addition, most pamphlets contained drawings or photographs and, occasionally, songs or poems, either written by the freak or in celebration of the exhibit. ... Some pamphlets were forty and more pages long. ...   (19–20)

Viewed in the light of this type of pamphlet, the presence of multiple narrative perspectives in the work does not signal a flaw; instead, these contributions represent an integral facet of the genre.

With its emphasis on the production of stories and its generic resemblance to the freak-show pamphlet, Swan's text carries an important message for women (and other marginalized groups), namely, that one's ability to represent oneself as a subject rests on one's facility for appropriating and re-shaping a wide variety of genres and discourses. While it could be inferred that people are merely the sum of others' discourses about them – a position which precludes subjective agency – Swan's text emphasizes the individual's power to exert a measure of control over discourse through parodic appropriation. As I indicated in the introduction, this strategy goes beyond the mere repetition of official discourses because the ironic distance afforded by this type of parodic appropriation can transform imitation into 'a means of freedom' (Hutcheon, *Theory*, 35). Official discourses and traditional genres can be enlisted to serve radically different causes from the ones they were originally intended to serve.

In Swan's novel, textual production, linked to the production of the self, is conceived, not as the revelation of some unchanging 'essence,' but as a performance with the readers positioned as the audience.[7] In his study of the freak show, Robert Bogdan discusses the complexity of the relationship between the 'blower' and his audience:

The fabrications, the appearance of the freak, and the overall presentation were so outlandish that both the manager and most of the audience shared a sense of the ridiculous. The lecturer would acknowledge his participation in the farce with asides, humor, and commentary. In some cases he was quite subtle, presenting the exhibit to one segment of the audience, the more worldly, as a farce, but to the more naive, straight. (114)

Like the double-voiced discourse of the freak-show barker, Swan's text can also be grasped on several different levels: 'as straight story, as colourful social history, as pure entertainment, and even as a novel of ideas' (review by Wilson, 30). There is also something wonderfully tongue-in-cheek about the way in which the fictional Anna Swan takes on the role of her own 'blower.' She does not try to straighten out the misconceptions surrounding her identity (by, for instance, asserting that she is not a freak). Instead, she plays with the roles she has always been forced to occupy, and she sports with the audience's credulity.[8]

At the beginning of her narrative, Anna offers her audience three spiels. As Teresa Heffernan notes, in German *spielen* is to play, and *spiel* is a 'game' (26). In general, the emphasis on games and the process of discursive appropriation and manipulation practised throughout the text support Lyotard's conception of a postmodern 'game theory' of discursive practices, in which every individual can be seen to be 'located at a post through which various kinds of messages pass' (*Postmodern*, 15). His model is particularly valuable for marginalized and oppressed groups because it stresses human agency and the capacity of individuals to alter the messages relayed. No one, 'not even the least privileged among us, is ever entirely powerless over the messages that traverse and position him at the post of sender, addressee, or referent' (15).

According to this model, each language partner, when a 'move' pertaining to him or her is made, undergoes a '"displacement," an alteration of some kind that not only affects him[/her] in his[/her] capacity as addressee and referent, but also as sender' (16). (For example, the previous sentence, which invokes Lyotard's words, demonstrates this capacity to alter messages; whereas Lyotard's message refers solely and unself-consciously to men, as a 'sender' I altered the message to include women.) Furthermore, if, as I suggested earlier, identity is a fiction, then an individual's discursive move will have an impact on this fiction. For instance, by becoming her own 'blower,' and reframing the scientific terminology and show-world hype (incorporating it into her own story about herself), Anna effects a 'displacement,' which alters the meaning of these discourses. Ultimately, her discursive 'moves' work to displace the official version of history, a result which illustrates the revolutionary potential inherent in parodic appropriation. In the introduction, I suggested that all maps have hidden gaps of one kind or another; they are always internally inconsistent. In Swan's text, the giantess highlights the internal contradictions in nineteenth-century imperialist, patriarchal representations of Woman when she takes on the role of 'sender' in the language game.

Often a 'move' involves nothing more than allowing inconsistent discourses to rest side by side. The tension generated by this juxtaposition is sometimes enough to destabilize the official discourse.[9] To this end, the novel's multinational scope, enhanced by the heroine's extensive travels, furnishes an ample supply of inconsistent discourses. Swan's text, in keeping with Swift's mock-travel narrative, *Gulliver's Travels*, juxtaposes the multiplicity of cultural conventions among the different lands which Anna visits. This type of discursive comparison exposes the ways in which, in terms of their construction of the notion of Woman and of the freak, discourses can be 'both an instrument and an effect of power, but also a hindrance, a stumblingblock, a point of resistance and a starting point for an opposing strategy' (Foucault, *History*, 101). Swan's decision to focus on Anna's experience in the United States and England, in particular, facilitates the text's postcolonial project of rigorously scrutinizing the repercussions of American nationalism and British imperialism on English Canadians. As Davey points out, Anna and her pastoral Canadian family are displaced by 'the forces of emergent capitalism, which in both Europe and America are rationalizing and segmenting commodity production and alienating labour into purchasable quantity' (*Post-National*, 185).

The nineteenth-century discourses which the novel traces emerged in conjunction with the shift from mostly agrarian societies to industrial capitalism. With the decreased emphasis on household production, it became possible for women to consider new ways of life, and many considered entering the market and exchanging their labour 'for the means of survival' (Ehrenreich and English, 13). Within the novel, Anna initially follows this path, proclaiming that she wants more than 'a duty-bound life as Mrs. McAskill in the back waters of Cape Breton' (56).

By choosing to market her skills as a 'show biz personality' and to spiel before approving crowds at Barnum's, Anna believes she can escape rural life and traditional female roles. Gradually, however, it dawns on her that life as a female entertainer does not offer an escape because, as a Woman, she has always already been classified as a performer. In New York, Anna becomes fired up by all she has been reading, and she joyfully writes to Angus that she is in agreement that women ought to have rights. He dashes off the following scathing reply:

I have seen and done everything. And learned the truth. People are pigs and the worst are not among my sex. No other species is as eager to betray her husband, brother, father, than one of your kind. ... They disgust me, those snake charmers with their innocent airs – that faintly lisped 'hello,' that meek smile. ...

This is the suffering being to whom you would give the vote? This performer – better versed in theatre than you or me? Who makes a living by ruling the emotions of those deceived by her faint-hearted appearance?

All I can say is your letter was ridiculous. At least you are learning domestic craft [Anna's tutor was instructing her on the art of making shell boxes, seaweed albums, and wax flowers]. ... Perhaps your height is an excuse to avoid female duties.   (88–9)

Angus's misogyny stems from his frustration and fear that Anna will never consent to take up her role as his wife and return to Cape Breton. His reference to women's faintly lisped 'hello' recalls Hamlet's acerbic abuse of Ophelia: 'You jig, you amble, and you lisp' (Shakespeare, *Hamlet*, 3.1.146), which was likewise the product of the prince's anger and confusion. However, both speeches reflect the belief that women are all linked to Woman, and, on some level, all women are deceptive 'performers,' enigmatic and dangerous shape-shifters.[10]

Anna's female relations constantly remind her that she is a performer subject to the male gaze. In a letter to her daughter (penned by a man because she cannot write), Anna's mother supposedly states: '[A] ... lady's conduct is at the mercy of critics when she is in a public place ... and every passer-by will look at her if only for a glance to check for an unladylike action' (50).[11] Similarly, after Anna is pursued by a male gang in Truro, her aunt places the blame on her niece, reminding her that a lady 'sets the tone of a gentleman's behaviour' (54). Not only does this advice from the female chorus constitute a case of blaming the victim, it also demonstrates that women are pressured by other women to shoulder the burden that comes with their status as the object of the male gaze. As a result of this pressure, Anna learns to accept the 'traditional exhibitionist role' (Mulvey, 11), and she realizes that she has always had an audience. The only difference in becoming a *bona fide* performer lies in developing a 'professional attitude.' As she says, 'No performer should expend energy for groups that offer neither pay nor applause' (50). To her dismay, even when she becomes a professional, her roles still remain tied to her sex. For instance, in New York, although she longs 'to play serious drama,' Barnum continues to offer her limited dramatic roles in farce or melodrama – roles that he considers appropriate for her sex and status as a freak (93).

In the novel, it becomes increasingly clear that neither the freak nor the Woman may tread on the sacred and spacious ground of the 'serious' or the 'real.' When Anna pens her manual of 'Giant Etiquette,' Barnum urges her to 'save her serious thoughts for St. Paul's,' and he dismisses her attempt at being instructive. As he explains (not to her, but to her manager, Apollo Ingalls), 'Anna's appeal lies in her size. She is a wonder, the LARGEST OF HER SEX, not a philosopher.' Barnum subsequently points out that, although Anna must remain ladylike, her material must divert the audience because people 'want to laugh ...' (110). Anna senses that women, because they pose a threat to men, must represent themselves as a joke and never be seen to take themselves seriously; the majority of American men view women as 'a pretentious self-interest group out to thwart their manly pioneering spirit.' This distrust arouses a desire in men to see women humiliated, so that 'any female who is prepared to have a pie thrown in her face will be a success' (93). In *A Room of One's Own*, Virginia Woolf describes walking across the grounds of a famous university and being chased off the grass by an irate Beadle (7). In an analysis of this episode, Rachel Bowlby argues that the walk 'through "Oxbridge" approaches an allegory of the banning of women from the citadels of masculine authority, and it is all the more effective for its deployment of the imagery of territorial demarcations' (20). Just as the men guard the territory of male power in Woolf's narrative, in Swan's novel P.T. Barnum marks out the parameters of Anna's turf. As I indicated in the introduction, to claim a territory, one has to map it. Barnum's insistence on the bounds of propriety governing Anna's behaviour reinforces Huggan's assertion that the map conforms to a particular version of the world which is 'specifically designed to empower its makers' ('Decolonizing,' 127).

In Swan's novel, the contested terrain represents the realm of the serious, the normal, and the real. The norm, based on the average-sized white male, encompasses a wide domain, which, except for a token few, remains inaccessible to women and freaks. Positioned as outsiders *vis-à-vis* the norm, the freak and the Woman cannot, therefore, be taken seriously. In his study *Freaks*, Fiedler refers to the boredom experienced by freak-show performers who were 'doomed to play over and over the role to which their bodies [had] ... destined them' (148). His words apply equally to women. Swan's novel clarifies that the boredom experienced by the freak also plagued the woman, who was also doomed to 'inhabit a culture created by and for men' (Gilbert and Gubar, 120). When Anna finally leaves Barnum's employ, he begs her to stay and join his circus, promising her that she can play the roles of Glumdalclitch (the nine-year-old girl who befriends Gulliver when he arrives in Brobdingnag) and Lady Macbeth to her heart's delight; neither role allows her to play the hero. Faced with this offer, she admits to herself that the prospect of 'repeating the hackneyed old female roles filled me with horror' (157). On stage and off, Anna is hemmed in by these 'hackneyed old female roles.' Just as she tires of her theatrical roles, she grows weary of playing the role of 'wife,' and writes to her mother that, although she is sick of her wifely role, she remains 'unable to behave any other way with [her] … husband' (290). Even her affair with her manager Judge Apollo Ingalls, does not dispel her sense of being trapped within a 'farce' constructed by 'the perception of those who dwell within material reality' (the world governed by the norm). As she says, 'I was a prisoner in the thin dimension of ordinary life, looking for a way out' (306).

One way out of the heterosexist farce, according to several feminist theorists, involves playing the hackneyed female roles 'with a vengeance' (de Lauretis, *Alice*, 157) – that is, cold-bloodedly to make a spectacle out of oneself in order to make visible the fictive and therefore arbitrary basis of the construction of Woman. Within the novel, Anna adopts this strategy when she first goes to town. Initially, she is pinned by 'the angry loathing [she] … saw in the young men's eyes, and the understated little smiles of contempt on the faces of the young women' (22). The public's gaze causes her to experience the 'slow and dreadful tightening of limbs,' which she later associated with 'remorse over *making a spectacle*' of herself (23; my emphasis). After experiencing further humiliation at the hands of the crowd, she suddenly rejects the Canadian tradition of self-effacement. Instead, she rises, addresses the crowd, and proclaims, 'LADIES AND GENTLEMEN, FRIENDS AND PASSERS-BY: Forgive me. My body is showing' (24).

Luce Irigiray elaborates on the implications of this strategy of becoming a 'performer,' one who willingly 'resubmits' oneself to the gaze of the crowd in order to challenge the logic that determines the role one is forced to play:

To play with mimesis is thus, for a woman, to try to recover the place of her exploitation by discourse, without allowing herself simply to be reduced to it. It means to resubmit herself – inasmuch as she is on the side of 'perceptible,' of 'matter' [of body] – to 'ideas,' in particular to ideas about herself, that are elaborated in/by a masculine logic, but so as to make 'visible,' by an effect of playful repetition, what was supposed to remain invisible: the cover-up of a possible operation of the feminine in language. It also means 'to unveil' the fact that, if women are such good mimics, it is because they are not simply resorbed in this function. (76)

By asking to be excused because her 'body is showing,' Anna works within the existing discourse to reveal parodically the irrational element inherent in the discursive construction of women as Woman, who, if Man is aligned with Reason, must remain nothing but Body: that is the only thing she can be in men's eyes.

Barbara Ehrenreich and Deirdre English, discussing the representation of Woman in the nineteenth century, stress that the discourse of sexual romanticism effectively imprisoned women in this fashion. On the one hand, sexual romanticism, with its emphasis on separate spheres, put women on a pedestal. On the other hand, it demanded that woman be a *negation* of man's world, which left almost nothing for women actually to *be*: 'if men are busy, she is idle; if men are rough, she is gentle; if men are strong, she is frail; if men are rational, she is irrational; and so on' (109). Within the novel, Anna's gigantic stature can be taken as an allegory of women's predicament in nineteenth-century Western society. Positioned as 'the sex,' the 'Angel in the House' (Woolf, 'Professions,' 150) with an emphasis on *in the house*, women were forced to live within the cramped boundaries legislated by the dominant discourses. This was the limited space they were accorded on the map. As a giant Woman, Anna is subjected to a set of cultural interpretations that position her as a petrified symbol, a commodity, or the object of scientific scrutiny, and the impact of this interpretive framework on her life generates 'emblem fatigue,' a phrase coined by Angus McAskill (139).

In many ways, this fictional portrayal of Anna's experience in North America corresponds to historical accounts, which suggest that many men were uncomfortable with the new freedoms that were potentially available to women. According to Ehrenreich and English, at the same time that women were pondering new possibilities, men were discovering that women were themselves a question, and the question centred around the dilemma: 'What is woman's true nature? And what, in an industrial world which no longer honoured women's traditional skills, was she to *do*?' (4). From a masculine perspective, the Woman Question was a problem of control: 'Woman had become an issue, a social problem – something to be investigated, analyzed and solved' (4).

Within the novel, one of the most serious threats to Anna's ability to generate a positive sense of self comes from men, influenced by the scientific discourses of the day, who were bent on categorizing and measuring the female body. In their attempt to answer the Woman Question, scientists began seeking answers in the blood, bones, and tissue of their female objects. Physicians were the first of the new experts to pass judgment on 'the social consequences of female anatomy and to prescribe the "natural" life plan for women' (Ehrenreich and English, 4). Women's bodies with their 'rhythms and generative possibilities' appeared to these experts as 'a "frontier," another part of the natural world to be explored and mined' (19). As one historian asserts, 'It was no accident that medical misogyny, with its powerful definitions of moral and immoral female behaviour, reached a peak at precisely the moment when middle-class women were beginning to challenge the hegemony of the male professions' (Mort, 83).

In the previous chapter, I noted how Thomas's protagonist links the colonial project with efforts to map the female body. Swan's novel foregrounds how this type of mapping was supported by specific scientific discourses. In particular, a new science, gynaecology, arose in the nineteenth century to study women's *terra incognita*. It was the self-assigned task of this profession to map woman's natural physical and mental constitution. Practitioners of this science concluded that the female body was 'not only primitive, but deeply pathological' (Ehrenreich and English, 19). After scrutinizing women's biology, medical experts determined that women were at the mercy of their uteri, which were believed to be in competition with their brains.[12] Within the novel Anna suffers from profuse menstrual bleeding after she moves to Ohio, and her doctor worries that her womb is draining her mind of its 'mental faculties' (272).

Although the medical model of female nature presupposed woman's total submission to the 'sex function,' this did not make her a *sexual* being, and a firm distinction was drawn between reproductivity and sexuality (Ehrenreich and English, 121). This distinction generated a paradox of sorts. Although scientists believed that women's reproductive organs were locked in a death struggle with their brains, they were equally convinced that women were devoid of sexual desire. Acton's infamous comment conveys this sentiment perfectly: 'The majority of women ... are not very much troubled with sexual feeling of any kind' (112). Even the female physician Dr Mary Wood-Allen wrote that women embrace their husbands 'without a particle of sex desire' (194); and according to Mrs Eliza B. Duffey, in her *Relations of the Sexes* (1876), the more cultured the woman, the more the sensual is 'refined away from her nature' (219). Hygiene manuals warned against 'any spasmodic convulsion' on a woman's part during intercourse lest it interfere with conception (qtd. in Ehrenreich and English, 121).

In keeping with its parodic tone, Swan's novel does not simply reinscribe the official opinions on female sexuality. For some readers, the text's deconstruction of prevailing opinion regarding female sexuality may not seem far-reaching enough because lesbianism is never presented as an option, and eroticism remains 'constrained within a heterosexual framework' (review by Read, 29). In the next chapter, as we shall see, the women-centred relationships illustrated in Marlatt's *Ana Historic* prove to be powerfully subversive bonds that destabilize the patriarchal framework. However, Swan's avoidance of lesbianism as a tactic for subversion could be seen as a way of conforming to biographical constraints as well as acknowledging that, in the nineteenth century, women's sexuality could only be visibly expressed within the confines of what has been described as a 'compulsory heterosexuality' (see Rich, 'Compulsory'). Even though it works within a heterosexual framework, the text still manages to debunk dominant attitudes regarding female sexuality by giving voice to the unofficial discourses rendered invisible or taboo. As in Thomas's novel, in Swan's text women occasionally bond together in opposition to the supposed facts that have been proven by men. For instance, when the learned doctor suggests that Anna's womb is draining her mind, his wife, during a confidential visit, disagrees and suggests that it is simply the August heat that caused the giantess's monthlies to be so profuse. As it turns out, her opinion is shared by all the other women who come by to visit (272). Anna herself defies medical expertise when she tries to reassure her husband, Bates, that, even though he is impotent, he can make her 'dizzy with joy 100 times a night' by touching her 'sweet spot' (298). Her husband insists that he is an expert on women's physiology because he has been tutored on the subject by the learned Dr Beach. The doctor, however, was presumably ignorant of the clitoris or neglected to mention it to the giant, and so Bates responds by asking Anna not to 'make up tales' to save his pride (298). For a moment, Anna wonders if she is a 'freak' in her sexual response. Similarly, after Anna's manager, Ingalls, comfortably has sex with what he believes to be a sleeping giantess, he tells himself, 'It's a good thing she is a freak and does not have sexual desire' (220). (Given the nature of scientific theories at the time, it is not clear whether Ingalls refers to her as a freak because of her size or her sex.) But the text goes on to deflate Ingalls's version of events by presenting an account from Anna's perspective – the perspective of a woman with a healthy sexual appetite. Although he thought she was asleep, she was actually awake and enjoying the experience. Moreover, from her perspective, Victorian men are the 'mysterious species' because they expect women to be 'uninterested in the physical and are easily frightened if [women] ... express enthusiasm' (229–30).

Designating the white male as the norm, scientists promoted a hierarchical model that afforded an overlap between the discursive construction of notions of the freak and that of Woman. Just as Woman refers to that which is non-male, an essence that is supposedly inherent in all women, which has been seen as 'Nature, Mother, Mystery, Evil Incarnate, Object of (Masculine) Desire and Knowledge, Proper Womanhood, Femininity, et cetera' (de Lauretis, *Technologies*, 9–10), the freak also constitutes a discursive representation: '"Freak" is ... a set of practices, a way of thinking about and presenting people. It is the enactment of a tradition, the performance of a stylized presentation' (Bogdan, 3). At bottom, both categories, Woman and freak, are reserved for those who transgress socially determined boundaries based on the norm. Within the novel, when Anna makes love for the first time with Angus, she describes herself offering him up her 'secret world the way a barker lifts the tent flap on the mysteries of the sideshow' (57). This image reflects the extent of her own internalization of the categorical conflation between freakishness and female sexuality promoted by nineteenth-century scientific discourses.

Focusing as it does on the world of the freak show, Swan's novel underscores the mutually beneficial relationship that existed between freak-show managers and scientists, a relationship which enabled scientists to establish this hierarchical model. During the late nineteenth century, the physician Sir William Osler wrote that 'the spirit of science was brooding on the waters' (219).[13] As his biblical rhetoric clarifies, science was not a fully-fledged discipline, but the metaphor of 'brooding' suggests that science, like God's divine spirit, was *destined* to play a part in human history. Interestingly enough, the world of the freak show did a great deal to lend the scientists credibility and legitimacy, and helped the scientific profession gain ground. Until about the turn of the century, scientists were essentially amateurs. The discipline had not yet emerged in America as a full time occupation (see Daniels, 7 and Bates, 30). Fields such as endocrinology, genetics, and anthropology were in their infancy. Science had not yet developed its terms of classification, and many exhibits (such as the dwarf, William Henry Johnson) were referred to as the 'What is it?' – a title that reveals both the showman's promotional strategy and the undeveloped state of descriptive science at the time (Bogdan, 27). Both the showman and the scientist benefited by mutual co-operation. On the one hand, scientific interest in freaks legitimated the public's interest and boosted attendance. Scientists, for their part, who did not have the status they do today, 'gained visibility and authority by serving as "experts" in curiosity controversies' (Bogdan, 27). According to Bogdan, even the use of the word 'museum' in the title of many freak shows, including P.T. Barnum's, attests to the show world's close association with natural science (107).

Anna's museum lecture, offered at the beginning of the text, reflects this relationship and reveals the tenor of the connection established between the entertainment world and the world of science. According to the lecture, in Barnum's world of marvels, 'SCIENCE is the RINGLEADER, taming NATURE'(4). This claim exposes the violence inherent in the budding scientific discourse. The public is solicited to *watch* science 'taming' nature. In Angela Carter's novel *Nights at the Circus* (also about a giantess), the narrator reminds readers that 'to look is to coerce' (222). One imagines that there must be a multiplicity of 'looks' available in the world, some more coercive than others. (The look of the reader must be included in the set of all looks.) However, the gaze of science, as it emerged in the late nineteenth century, seems to have been the most coercive of all. Evelyn Fox Keller finds in the scientific discourse a recurrent thematics of conquest, domination, and aggression reflecting a desire to 'penetrate and subdue' the object of study (*Reflections*, 48). In a letter he wrote to his friend Weir Mitchell, Oliver Wendell Holmes, a doctor practising in the middle of the nineteenth century, reveals what has been read as the sadistic and voyeuristic impulse behind the scientist's desire to observe nature. As he says: 'I

liked to follow the workings of another mind through these minute, teasing investigations ... to see a relentless observer get hold of Nature and squeeze her until the
sweat broke out all over her and Sphincters loosened.'[14] Keller calls the association
of scientific thought with masculinity and of the scientific domain with femininity
the "'genderization" of science' (*Reflections*, 76). This type of representation becomes
all the more dangerous, according to de Lauretis, because, while the genderization
of science 'is admitted and encouraged in the realm of common knowledge it is
simultaneously denied entry or currency in the realm of formal knowledge' (de
Lauretis, *Technologies*, 42–3). The discourse of the sciences of man 'constructs the
object as female and the female as object' and that, argues de Lauretis, is 'its rhetoric
of violence, even when the discourse presents itself as humanistic, benevolent, or
well-intentioned' (45).

In some ways, women's experience as the objects of scientific scrutiny parallels
Canada's experience as a colony. Lorna Irvine's suggestion, noted earlier, that the
female voice 'politically and culturally personifies Canada' (*Sub/version*, 2) is reinforced by Northrop Frye's discussion of the way in which colonial powers subjected
Canada to a ruthless and objectifying gaze. According to Frye, after the Northwest
Passage failed to materialize, 'Canada became a colony in the mercantilist sense,
treated by others less like a society than as a place to *look for things*. French, English,
Americans plunged into it to carry off its supplies of furs, minerals, and pulp-
wood, aware only of their immediate objectives' (*Bush*, 221; my emphasis). Frye
goes on to remark that travellers visited Canada 'much as they would visit a zoo' (221).
Frye insists that Canada's experience as the object of imperialist scrutiny left its
mark, and that a 'feature of Canadian life that has been noted by writers from
Susanna Moodie onward is the paradox of vast empty spaces and lack of privacy,
with no defences against the prying or avaricious eye' (221).

Within Swan's novel, Anna, as a Canadian Woman, often finds herself the target
of seemingly benevolent individuals who wish to explore and chart her 'natural'
terra firma. Early on, in an episode in which the fourteen-year-old Anna trudges
to the spruce grove (the family uses the grove as a lavatory), the first aggressive
attempt is made to map her 'terrain.' While going about her business, Anna is spied
on by her neighbour, the dwarf Hubert Belacourt. The invasion of Anna's body
can be said to begin with this first act of voyeurism. Following this, like the ser-
pent in Milton's *Paradise Lost*, Hubert incites Anna's curiosity and preys upon her
ignorance. 'Do you know what a boundless universe lies inside you, Anna?' he
demands (32). When she shakes her head, he chides her for her ignorance: 'No?
Silly Anna! We mortals have an unknown terra firma within, with many roads and
rivers twisting up and down in fanciful routes.' He begs to be allowed to sketch
her 'spill channels, the short, wide head chute of the duodenum, the ropey coils of
the small intestine.' After he measures her large intestine at twenty-two inches, he

asks if she would let him measure 'the other highway uncurling in [her] ... great physique' (33). Choosing a mammoth icicle as his yardstick, he sets out to measure this 'highway,' which, presumably because it is a 'highway,' anybody has the right to traverse. When he maps her to the quick and ruptures her hymen, Anna's image of herself undergoes a transformation. She no longer perceives herself as a powerful being; instead, she positions herself as a 'female who, like every other female, could be penetrated in a way that no man could' (35). Her identity no longer rests on what she can do, but on what others – men – can do to her. Hubert's mapping of Anna's vagina recalls and graphically illustrates Alice Hoyle's point in *Intertidal Life* that the fathers have charted and laid claim to women's most secret places. Later on in the novel, when she is travelling to Europe, Anna's body is once again mapped out in the name of science. She undergoes a medical examination at the hands of the ship's doctor. Her travelling partner and fellow giant, Martin van Buren Bates, convinces the doctor (who is impressed with Bates's interest in the reproductive possibilities of the giantess) to let Bates spy through a peep-hole while the doctor conducts his examination. From the 'medico,' Bates obtains the statistics he desires, and he thanks the doctor for confirming his belief that 'the giantess is an unspoiled *natural resource*' (172; my emphasis). During this same voyage to Europe, Anna dreams that she is a ship and Bates the captain, declaiming to all her 'gross tonnage, displacement, and overall length' (185). Her dream is in fact a metaphoric account of her own objectification: Bates plans to marry her in order to exploit her generative capacity and to create a superior race of giants, enabling Americans to 'see over the heads of foreign nations' (174). As far as Bates is concerned, America's manifest destiny lies in climbing to the top of the evolutionary tree.

Bates's dreams of creating a superior race illustrate the way in which scientific discourses lent their support to nationalist discourses with their rhetoric of racism. The type of racist national mythology espoused by Bates gained acceptance with the popularization of the theory of organic evolution in Darwin's *Ascent of the Species* (1859), although its outlines were available as early as 1755, when Linnaeus developed the binomial system of nomenclature, according to genus and species (see Fiedler, 240). As Fiedler notes, the 'inclusion of humanity, wild and civilized, monstrous and normal, in the same taxonomic system may have served ... to demythologize "monsters," but it did so at the price of creating an invidious mythology of "race"' (240). Racist discourses, however, did not really flourish until Western imperialism had made possible a confrontation between white explorers and those defined as 'lesser breeds' (Fiedler, 241). When P.T. Barnum's American Museum was at its peak of popularity, Stanley and Livingston were lost in the 'dark continent,' and imperialist British were fighting those they were colonizing. This was a time of intense world exploration and Western expansion, and, in its account of this historical moment, Swan's novel traces the emergence and interlacing of the discourses of imperialism, racism, and sexism.

As John Haller and Robin Haller suggest, nineteenth-century medical society attempted to 'fix' the races and sexes in a natural order of ascendancy corresponding 'to the eighteenth-century's "Chain of Being," or for that matter, Aristotle's hierarchy of superior and subordinate forms' (48). Scientists further stipulated that attempts to get out of this place were 'unnatural and in fact diseased' (Ehrenreich and English, 117). By the 1860s, natural scientists could locate women's place on the evolutionary ladder: she was at the level of the Negro, who, according to one professor of natural history, Carl Vogt, shared the rung with the senile White and the child (Vogt, 192). The discourses of sexism and racism were mutually supportive; the doctors who advised a life of domesticity for American women gave arguments for women's inferiority which 'were almost identical with the century's rationalization for the inferiority of the blacks' (Haller and Haller, 38).

On the one hand, it has been argued that Darwin's *Descent of Man* (1871) marshalled evidence to show 'how the growth of moral faculties like self-control, love, and altruism were key elements in progressing towards a higher moral culture' (Mort, 111). But these same theories pointed to the 'precariousness of moral progress – how it could so easily slip back into animal chaos' (111). In the novel, Anna's manager, Apollo Ingalls, has a nightmare that betrays the anxiety generated by Darwin's model. In his dream, Ingalls looks into a mirror and sees a 'hairy ape face with deformed lips and a wide, squat nose. There is even hair on my forehead, and I have two rows of teeth in each jaw. I am so ugly I want to die, then I look down and see breasts poking through my suit vest. Dear God, I am a woman' (226). His nightmare exposes men's horror of becoming the Other, of slipping off their assigned rung and coming to rest alongside their ape-like ancestors. Furthermore, as his dream confirms, the rung of the animal, the non-human, and the freak is also the domain of the female. In the previous chapter, I noted how romance narratives align Woman with the non-human. Swan's text clarifies that even supposedly scientific discourses contributed to the construction and maintenance of this hierarchal framework.

Swan's mythological treatment of the fate of several of the characters reinforces the way in which the discourses of science, American nationalism, industrial capitalism, and racism worked together. For instance, the fictitious treatment of Zip, who is supposedly stuffed and exhibited by Barnum after his death, emphasizes that, within the context of the market economy gaining ground in America, human life is transformed into lifeless capital. But the episode concerning Zip reveals that it is even easier to reify a human life, if that life belongs to a black. Similarly, the novel suggests that Millie and Christine, the mulatto Siamese twins (who, like Zip, actually existed), are forced to travel from America to England in the hold of the ship, owing to their status as 'Bog-trotters.' When Anna argues on their behalf, Ingalls retorts, 'Niggers can't travel first class' (168). Lest readers assume that America is the only hotbed of racism, the text demonstrates that it is prevalent in the Canadas as well. Early on in the text, Anna's mother writes to her recalling her daughter's first exhibition, and Anna's naïve reaction to the treatment of the Micmacs. Ironically, her mother's comments convey a strong racist bias: 'They were an eyesore in vulgar colours and their great splay feet were clad in blanket moccasins. You studied their rag-tag group trudging in the carriage dust, and asked: "Poppa, how much do their families charge for people to look at them?"' (81). The emphasis on race in the novel reminds us that, in analysing the construction of identity, it is a mistake to concentrate solely on the impact of sexual difference because issues of race and class continually complicate the equation. In episodes such as this, Swan's novel highlights what I suggested in the introduction, namely, that the experience of a member of the settler-invader society should not be conflated with that of the indigenous peoples.

As Davey points out, at least six major oppositions mark the life of Anna Swan: 'pastoral versus industrial, large versus small, women versus men, "freakish" versus "normal," the United States versus Canada, and Confederate South versus Yankee' (*Post-National*, 182–3). In the light of the scenes noted above, I would add coloured versus white and native versus non-native. As Davey remarks, none of these oppositions 'can serve as a metaphor for another: their terms conflict; the affiliations they engender divide and redivide the individual' (183). As a result of this multi-levelled constitution, a subject is not 'unified but rather multiple, and not so much divided as contradicted' (de Lauretis, *Technologies*, 2).

By portraying events from the marginalized perspective of a Canadian, as well as female freak, the novel can effectively parody racist discourses and the discourse of American nationalism. Americans' habit of positioning themselves at the centre of the world, while remaining complacently ignorant of other cultures, is spoofed on several occasions by the Canadian giantess. For instance, when Anna and her mother first meet Barnum in the month of June, he asks the women in all seriousness if they are glad to 'be out of the ice and snow' (65). Anna quickly realizes that 'he hadn't stuck a big toe in the Canadas.' Barnum simply has his agents ship him curiosities 'as if they were fresh vegetables' (66). Later on, an Ohio physician also displays his ignorance of the Canadas, when he queries whether it is Nova Scotia or Quebec that is an American state. Anna gently informs him that Canada is a country of two nations which 'are not part of the American empire.' The Québécois strong man, Louis Cyr, who is travelling with Anna at the time, smiles at her as one who knows, and says, 'The Americans, Annie. They'll never understand' (265).

Swan herself has admitted that one reason she wrote the book 'was to tell Americans what it's like to grow up next to them' (interview, 'Susan Swan, Mythmaker,' 12). Anna, who seems to function occasionally as the author's mouthpiece, characterizes Americans as an 'energetic and warlike people who will sacrifice all to please their heathen god of financial gain' (140). The famous midget General Tom Thumb fits this description perfectly. In her encounter with the irascible midget, Anna specifically debunks the American Dream, which is based on the belief that anyone can be a success if they have enough 'gumption and get-up-and-go' (104).[15] Thumb boasts that 'every American is a Jason racing to get his golden fleece. Our great country is so free – that if you run hard and fast enough you may get the biggest fleece of all' (106–7). The word 'fleece' can also be taken in the sense of 'stripping of money or property' (OED), an interpretation which adds a sarcastic overtone to the naïve optimism of Thumb's speech. Although Thumb subverts his own legitimacy by his choice of rhetorical terms, Anna also takes it upon herself to deconstruct Thumb's speech by pointing out the blind spots in his argument. She remarks that his faith that anyone can become president is a 'Yankee superstition,' for the simple reason that the post is denied to members of her sex. Not only that, but the chance that any boy has of becoming president is so low that the contest 'may well be a lottery' (107). Finally, Anna warns that it may be a mistake for the Americans to think that their way 'is the only way' (107). Thumb responds to Anna's excentric insights by calling her 'an overgrown excuse for a female,' and he tells her to shut up. Generally speaking, Thumb's diminutive stature and his foul temper align him with the six-inch-tall Lilliputians in *Gulliver's Travels*, whose size likewise reflects their intellectual and moral baseness.

In contrast to the midget, the gigantic figure of Martin van Buren Bates recalls Spenser's Orgoglio, the symbol of fleshly pride, who, when faced with a courageous adversary, turns out to be nothing but an 'empty bladder' (*Faerie Queene*, 1.8.24). In the novel, the content of Bates's lectures illustrates the way in which Darwin's theories were appropriated to support the racist discourse of American nationalism. In his role as entertainer, the Kentucky giant lectures to sold-out crowds, declaiming his theories of 'The Survival of the Mediocre,' and he champions America's destiny to 'breed a superior species whose mental development will increase as the race grows in size' (118). When Anna ventures to ask his opinion of the Canadian, Bates responds that he is '[n]ot evolved enough to submit to my anthropometrics,' although there is 'every chance the Canadian will join us [the Americans] on the evolutionary tree!' (120). From her perspective, as a female Canadian, Anna sees that his tracts are flawed 'by his failure to recognize his subjective view behind his scientific idealism' (162–3).

Bates's dream of creating a race of American giants is parodied in the song entitled 'The Olympian Love Call,' which Anna and Ingalls (who is Australian) compose. Bates did not help much because he was too lazy to write the lyrics (178). Once again, the text emphasizes the importance of taking the opportunity to make a 'move' in the language game. With Bates out of the picture, the giantess and her manager are free to shape a unfavourable portrayal of Americans. In the 'warm-up verse,' Bates represents America during the machine age bloated with imperialist desires to exploit the vast Canadas: 'his eyes are like machines/whirring at the stars/his frost-free eyebrows are splashed/by river light'; and Anna takes on the role of the Canadas (178–9).

The second section, sung by Bates himself, is a blazon which recalls Frye's description of Canada's treatment at the hands of imperial powers. The song specifically parodies America's transformation of the Canadas into a veritable feast of discrete natural resources. In the poem (which, though long, deserves citing in full), the body of the woman becomes indistinguishable from Canada's geography:

THE KENTUCKY GIANT'S HYMENEAL

I will speak my will to Anna
that she will lie down
and tip south her giant womb
all by herself
she is the giantess next door
her name shall be
my all-American girl.

Take me in, New World Wahine
through your untapped vagina
to more mountain-rimmed gardens
where hot and cold airs
run together and averages
mean nothing.

Your eyes are like the future
gazing down on me.
Your head is the Far North
your neck – the long wolf's throat to the sea
the Near North is your shoulder
draped with trade staples and immigrants
who will learn to boast
of your bitter winds and thousands
of unproductive acres
your breasts are cod canneries
a continental refuge
for America's old head

your belly is a topped up
basin
fenced in by fir
and river valleys.

Come from your diversity, promised one.
Hurry down from the Canadian shield –
leave behind our inland tubs
from the Rocky Mountain trench
and from the Maritime shallows
from the zinc bars and spud flats.
You are my stolen limits
an eyeful of possibilities –
a half-strung boulder choker!
How infinite are your granite goods!
How vast you are my love, how vast –
your eyes behind your snowdrifts
are legends of mineral wealth
your hair like a flock of bison
streaming down Mount Rundle
your teeth like a caribou-herd
easily made domestic
by tundra and where trees end
by your fresh ice casts
off igloos and no floe
is the same size.
O beautiful mass!
Your lips are the north-west
passage waiting
for underglacial submarines
and your words are the wind
I can't see
if you yourself do not know
the ugly duckling you wear
around your neck
follow the frosty trail of frosty
arpents I will blast
from your rock necklace.

You are as remote as the white

whale on your Labrador coast
but there's no platitude
in your sweeping womb –
the grass triangle of pleasure.

The scent of your breath
is the fragrance of gas
and oil
your essence flowing
without restraint
into my appealing fist.

You will fall down
and invite me
your skin dripping sap
over my coffer knobs.

Let me in to our central concern,
the long sleeping space.

You are a sunflower
in Arcady

a white pine
among sumac bushes.

How propitious your roped slippers
your west riches spanning orchards.
I will kiss the demi-Eden
between your toes
and polish your gleaming nails –
the reflector of a dying mountain
where crystal waters rush off.

Beloved – I will rise up
in your empty heights
and plunge through your
regions of softwood
to the end of your Atlantic
depth once more

your grass bowl
will be exotic
with tropical life

our densities differ
but volume on volume
She is greater than me.
O Anna, *you* are the American Dream.
My will shall grow in your void.   (180–2)

Anna's response to this song, which positions her and, by extension, all of Canada as an absence waiting to be filled, is neatly summed up by the following verse, which she sings in reply: 'I'll be damned, Martin, / if I'll be crammed / on the seat of your / imperial fantasy' (183).

Despite her spirited rejection in the context of her performance, Anna never manages to escape Bates's clutches. After a while, she realizes that, within her marriage, she continues to play out the relationship between America and the Canadas, and she suggests, as noted in chapter 1, that 'to be from the Canadas is to feel as women feel – cut off from the base of power' (274). Both the poem and her reply attest to the fact that, in addition to the 'genderization of the sciences,' there may also have been a 'genderization of American imperialism.'[16]

In accordance with the song's prophecy, Anna's words become 'the wind / [Bates] ... can't see.' On the voyage to England, she finds herself passively agreeing to marry the giant.[17] Simultaneously, she loses her voice and she has to write her vows when she marries Bates in London. The loss of her voice represents the loss of her ability to control the discourses which shape her identity – a change which comes about when she agrees to submit to the institution of marriage, an ideological apparatus which silences her.[18] When she becomes mute, her husband and manager speak for her, and no one finds this unusual (186–7). This episode playfully illustrates Monique Wittig's assertion that the discourses of heterosexuality 'oppress us in that they prevent us from speaking unless we speak in their terms' ('Straight,' 105).

In the novel, Bates champions the discourses of modern science, American imperialism, racism, and heterosexism. Not surprisingly, on her wedding night, Anna compares Bates to a Cyclops whose monstrous gaze threatens to back her into a corner of herself. The 'blue light from his eye pouring into ... [her] interior' is reminiscent of the eye of the scientist, peering down through the tunnel of his microscope (208). As Evelyn Fox Keller suggests, the 'ferreting out of nature's secrets, understood as the illumination of a female interior ... may be seen as expressing one of the most unembarrassedly stereotypic impulses of the scientific project' ('Making,' 69). Despite the fear which he arouses in her, Anna refuses to suffer a complete 'eclipse of the spirit' (209).[19]

Although Anna eventually determines that the 'mudsills are stronger ... and will willingly suck the life out of any large being foolish enough to entertain them,' she still believes that she can find happiness elsewhere (157). She characterizes herself as an exile, an appropriate status for women and freaks, but she specifically states that she is also in exile from 'the ways of ... [her] childhood' (158). As she explains to Barnum, she has grown 'too sophisticated for the backwoods' (154). Her separation from her family constitutes a class rejection; she can no longer tolerate their crude furnishings. Once again, we are reminded that, in addition to being divided along the lines of sexual difference, individuals are also constituted along the lines of class.

Mistakenly, Anna believes she might be happier on the Continent, 'where centuries of culture have taught its inhabitants a civilized approach' (158), and so, like Gulliver, she sails off in search of a civilized domain. Yet, once she is in England, Anna discovers that the British treat her like a toy, and the text parodies England's colonial attitude toward Canada. At one point, a friend of the Prince of Wales sits in her lap and refers to her as his sofa, ordered 'from the colonies' (216).[20] Even the Queen, who considers herself a freak, uses Anna for her own amusement. When they are alone at the palace, the tiny Queen displays herself, parading before Anna like a sideshow performer. Victoria confides in the giantess, saying, 'If my people knew how I am riddled with imperfections, they would display me in one of Mr. Barnum's sideshows,' and she asks Anna, 'How can I manage the greatest empire ... when my intelligence is no bigger than my freakish size?' (195). The Queen represents herself as a freak because she has accepted the messages of the dominant discourses, and has constituted herself accordingly. Rather than use Anna's visit as an opportunity to question their mutual representation as freaks, Victoria chooses instead to position Anna as a Canadian and forces her subject to entertain her. Anna rightly surmises that, as a result of the Queen's decision, she 'ceased to exist for her as a person' (195). The Queen's behaviour further underscores the multiplicity of discourses in which subjectivity is constructed. Although both are considered freaks by virtue of their sex, the Queen can nevertheless draw on the power that is accorded to her as a British royal figure. In this way, she assuages the sting which comes from her recognition of the inferior, freakish status accorded to her as a Woman. Likewise, Anna's investment in the colonial discourse prevents her from refusing to play the role of Gulliver, and she allows the Queen to march through her legs like the Lilliputian king.

Althusser argues that individuals are constituted as subjects by virtue of the fact that they 'willingly' adopt the subject-positions 'necessary to their participation in the social formation' (see Belsey, 61). The process by which subjects are constituted rests on their capacity to 'recognize' themselves within ideological discourses (Althusser, 172–3). That is to say, individuals respond to the 'hailing' or the 'interpellation' of a discourse, much in the same way that you or I would spin around if another person shouted, 'Hey, you there!' (Althusser, 174). Eventually, Anna finds herself responding to the discourses which 'hail' her as a Woman. In the previous chapter, I suggested that the narrator's feelings of becoming 'invisible' were related to her awareness of the ways in which patriarchal culture effaces women and their experience. In Swan's novel, the giantess experiences, and on some level sanctions, this same type of devaluation. Her acquiescence is represented by her willingness to drink the tonic, Nelvana's Nordic Regulator, which Tom Thumb and his bride Lavinia Warren have concocted. This drink supposedly regulates people's height. Anna's manager, Ingalls, urges her to drink it on a regular basis, so that she will shrink. Although he knows that the tonic is a scam, Ingalls convinces Anna that she is shrinking. In many ways, this episode reveals the fictive quality inherent in all discourse. What matters is not that she really loses inches, but that she responds to the 'hailing' of a discourse that tells her that she is approaching the norm (just as it told her she was a freak, and continues to insist that she is a Woman). When she expresses uncertainty about ingesting the brew, Ingalls retorts, 'Don't you want to be one of the diminutive females our age idealizes, sweetheart?' (309). As de Lauretis notes, it is typically in order to satisfy another's desire that women make an 'investment' that leads them to take up a position in a certain discourse. This investment is 'something between an emotional commitment and a vested interest, in the relative power (satisfaction, reward, payoff) which that position promises (but does not necessarily fulfill)' (*Technologies*, 16). For a while, Anna drinks the potion to please Ingalls, but the irony of her predicament soon strikes her: 'I, who had defeated gravity for 32 years and who took pride in every inch of me, I had been as gullible as any thrill-seeking sideshow customer and allowed Apollo to convince me that I wanted to be shorter' (318). When Anna tells him that she does not want to shrink any more, Ingalls admits to the ruse, which involved adjusting the height of doors and fudging Anna's measurements, which he recorded in chalk. He explains that he staged the scam because he spent her circus salary. The mercenary motivation behind his plan to draw Anna and others toward the norm exposes the tremendous economic potential that lies behind positing categories of normality. When the crowd, listening to Anna proclaim the wonders of shrinking, goes wild and begins to 'scream confessions of dissatisfaction with their physiques' (318), it becomes apparent that all, including the Queen of England, when invited to compare themselves to the age's fictive ideal, can be made to feel ashamed of their 'imperfections.' Above all, people will pay good money to have their so-called imperfections corrected.

Given the overwhelming pressure to accept the dominant discourses' construction of female identity, one must finally ask what is it that allows Anna to avoid fashioning her identity according to the dictates of these discourses. What enables her to realize that her age's idea of a Woman is a symbol that bears little resemblance to lived experience? And why does she recognize that 'it is a grave mistake to mythologize biological facts to prove that one sex is better than the other' (230)? One answer may be that Anna can resist the pressure to conform to Victorian notions of what it means to be a Woman because she can tap into a specific unofficial discourse. She remains 'acceptable in [her] ... own eyes' because she has access to the Celtic folk traditions which oppose the set of modern discourses that align Woman with the freak and classify both as the primitive, pathological Other.

Anna's Scottish parents and her uncle Geordie – a man who felt 'the power of the little people and spoke in tongues' – are well versed in Celtic folk traditions (11). From her infancy, Anna listened to stories of fantastic beings. This made it possible for her to view herself as a *bean-grugach*, one of the magical women of 'large size and intelligence ... who are looked upon with respect' (258). Anna's father would gaze up at his daughter 'in awe' (25), in contrast to those who would look at her with contempt. He considered her to be 'a magic bairn whose voice made vegetables grow' (20). Throughout her childhood, the accessibility of this folk discourse allows Anna to experience her body and her size as 'her greatest delight.' As she says, 'in my early days I had no trouble accepting Poppa's and Uncle Geordie's vision of me as a special being with an important destiny. I wished for only one thing: that the race of dwarfs I sprang from would defy gravity and race up with me' (12).

The themes and images of the Celtic folk discourse correspond to Mikhail Bakhtin's description of 'grotesque realism.' This is an aesthetic perspective utilized by Rabelais, derived from the European folk carnival tradition, whose images of bodily life emphasize 'fertility, growth, and a brimming-over abundance. ... [I]t is a "banquet for all the world"' (Bakhtin, *Rabelais*, 19). At one point in the novel, Anna boasts that she is 'Rabelaisian in [her] ... giant core' (115). Many episodes depicted in the novel are suffused with the imagery of 'grotesque realism.'

In the section entitled 'The Great Event,' the narrator explains that her mother's stomach turned into 'a monster sphere during her pregnancy,' and that the delivery tore her mother's 'perineum from stem to gudgeon, turning inside out her anal sphincter' (9). In keeping with this introduction, the entire episode takes as its focus one of the primary sites of grotesque realism, namely, the lower region of the body – 'the fertilizing and generating stratum' (Bakhtin, *Rabelais*, 148). The violence associated with the birth also conforms to the bipartite vision of grotesque realism, the image of the 'double-body,' where 'the life of one body is born from the death of the preceding, older one' (Bakhtin, *Rabelais*, 318). Although Anna's mother does not actually die from delivering the eighteen-pound baby, she is virtually torn apart, and the depiction of her body 'turning inside out' represents a typical figure associated with 'all forms of popular-festive merriment and grotesque realism'

(Bakhtin, *Rabelais*, 370). Images of inside-out, vice versa, and upside-down are all graphic figures for the impulse of carnival humour to debunk the world of forms and ceremonies, to create a 'second world and a second life outside officialdom' (Bakhtin, *Rabelais*, 6).

In the account of the birth, the insistence on the material level of the body also demonstrates grotesque realism's insistence on turning people's attention to their link with life and with the cosmos. In keeping with this theme, the birth coincides with a bumper crop of vegetables. Nature's sympathetic response affirms the link between human life and the non-human, emphasizing that the grotesque body is 'not separated from the rest of the world' (Bakhtin, *Rabelais*, 26). Throughout the novel, Anna tends to view her body as part of the natural topography. In the poem which Anna composes at age eleven, she describes herself in terms that reinforce this seamless connection with nature:

THE INFANT GIANTESS

Anna, were you big when you were little?
Yes, I was large when I was small.

You should have seen my foot! All my toes
quarrelling for room, bent and curling, trying to wear
the landscape like a slipper.

The foot of a giant girl: it could squish house
and carriages between the roast-beef eater
and cried-all-the-way-home.

Cape Breton took shade under my ankle boss
farmers scaled my calves for thrills
swinging up on my leg hairs, fighting for the view
from my knee-cap.

Off the coast of Newfoundland,
fisher boats sighted my bones
expanding from their growing points,
white beanstalks hauling the flesh skyward
in a gush of arms,
hands, shoulders, face,
flowing from the earth up
with the determination of ants.   (13)

Phrases describing her 'trying to wear / the landscape like a slipper' and portraying her bones as 'white beanstalks hauling the flesh skyward' reaffirm the impression she has of herself as existing on a cosmic scale. Even her opening 'spiel' identifies her with the coniferous trees, and she calls herself the LIVING LUMBER GIRL (1). Bakhtin states that most legends connect natural phenomenan such as mountains, rivers, rocks, and islands with the bodies of giants, implying that human bodies in general are 'not separated from the world or from nature' (*Rabelais*, 328). This perspective offers an interesting counterpoint to the official discourses discussed earlier. In particular, Anna's poem reveals the inadequacy of Bates's 'imperial fantasy,' the blazon which, as noted above, represents the female body as a spiritually vacant, material entity waiting to be appropriated. Her positive construction of body as landscape challenges the imperialist version, and reinforces a recognition of the plurality of possible perspectives, and the inadequacy of any single model of female (or national) identity.

As I mentioned in the last chapter, in *Intertidal Life*, the narrator also aligns the female body with the colonial efforts to conquer and 'fix' geographical terrain (70, 171, 205). Yet a distinction must be made between Thomas's and Swan's perspectives. Although both novels draw on the grotesque tradition (by that I mean the basic association between bodies and landscape), Thomas's text tends to invest the association between the human and non-human realms with negative connotations. By contrast, Swan's text conveys the optimistic spirit of grotesque realism or what Margot Northey calls the 'sportive grotesque,' where jest or play is more dominant (79). In his study of the grotesque mode, Bakhtin clarifies the difference between the two main lines of the development of the grotesque genre, the Romantic and the realist tradition. In the Romantic tradition, the grotesque loses its regenerating and renewing capacity, and takes on a destructive, alienating character. The world of the Romantic grotesque is a 'terrifying world,' which promotes fear (*Rabelais*, 39) as well as abstract and spiritual mastery; in this world, bodily images seem vulgar (39). It is predominantly this mode which informs the treatment of the grotesque in Thomas's novel.

By contrast, Swan's novel is more closely aligned with the realist tradition, which forges a more playful and positive connection between human bodies and the natural world. Rather than look on her body with disgust, Anna yearns for everyone to rise up and attain her cosmic scale, as her 'growing song,' adapted from the Gaelic, illustrates:

I'm often asking the folk here, will you dance up, and can you rise higher; but then each one of you answers that I'm foolish to give my power to you.

I give my power to you, and I can't deny it. It's not a love of wealth, or ambition, but a love that grew in me when I was a child, and it will never wither until you leap higher. (29)

Although Anna's sense of herself as a magic, cosmic being is challenged when her hymen is pierced by the 'measure-mad' dwarf, and she grows 'ashamed' of her entire body, especially her 'over-grown vagina' (37), the folk tradition on which her earlier sense of herself as a magical being was grounded continues to function as a discursive reservoir for the construction of her identity and of the world. For instance, when she travels to New York and joins the other human curiosities at P.T. Barnum's American museum, she is invited to participate in a dessert-eating contest at the famous Delmonico's restaurant. Once again, the material body with its food and drink takes centre stage, and the body's connection to the universe is underscored. Anna, who virtually inhales nineteen puddings, claims that her stomach is 'the infinite bowl of the universe' (78). She loses the contest only because her corset becomes 'cripplingly tight.' As she says, she suddenly felt 'a vice clamp about [her] ... waist so viciously that [she] ... had to gasp for breath' (78).

This scene graphically represents the competing registers of official and unofficial discourses. The folk discourse of unbounded physicality meets the discourse of Victorian fashion head on. The seemingly innocuous device of the corset is, in fact, an ideological apparatus serving society's desire to subjugate women's bodies. I do not use the word subjugate lightly: the fashionable woman's corsets exerted, on the average, twenty-one pounds of pressure on a woman's internal organs, and extremes of up to eighty-eight pounds have been measured, leading Ehrenreich and English to suggest that the style of wearing tight-laced corsets, which was de rigueur throughout the last half of the century, 'has to be ranked somewhere close to the old Chinese practice of foot-binding for its crippling effects on the female body' (109). As one fashion magazine of the 1870s puts it, the corset is 'an ever-present monitor, indirectly bidding its wearer to express self-restraint; it is evidence of a well-disciplined mind and regulated values.'[21]

Despite the tangible 'pressure' of the various official discourses, Anna continues to use the folk discourse and her giant stature to deconstruct their rhetoric. For instance, after Tom Thumb declaims his version of the American Dream and calls Anna 'an overgrown excuse for a female,' Anna attempts to rescue him from an irate Commodore Nutt. She picks Thumb up, and, when he bites her, she treats him like the Yahoo that he is, dropping him first on the stove, and then into a bucket of water (108). Her response, although ostensibly arising out of a need to protect Thumb from his rival, nevertheless constitutes a carnivalesque mockery of all that the small-minded midget stands for.

Even more than her actions, Anna's thoughts reflect her alignment with the unofficial discourse of grotesque realism. While making love with Angus, she concocts fantasies that even the giant, suspicious of her imagination, cannot resist (116). Anna's tendency to view life from a carnivalesque perspective surfaces in her letter to Angus, when she writes about the series of fires that decimated Barnum's museums.

In her letter, she links these conflagrations to the 'old fire festivals of Europe' (141). She also reports that, after the second fire, she fled with a few others to the editorial room at the *New York Tribune* building, where she and the other women, with their weeping and urinating, nearly drowned the other occupants of the office (144–6). This episode is truly Rabelaisian, recalling the scene in Book One, in which Gargantua drenches in urine the curious Parisians who have gathered about him.[22] According to Bakhtin, the 'slinging of excrement and drenching in urine are traditional debasing gestures,' whose debasing meaning was generally 'known and understood' (*Rabelais*, 148). In addition to functioning as a traditional debasing gesture, the women's floods of urine and tears reflect the link between human beings and the cosmos, creating a link between bodily tides and the tides of the sea. In contrast to Anna's fantastic account of the fire and its aftermath, Jane Campbell's 'realistic' testimony is as flat and tasteless as a processed cheese slice: 'Well, I can tell you all she did was pee her pants in the newsroom at the *New York Trib*' (147). As one of those who dwells within material reality, Jane does not have access to the parodic 'Celtic tradition' (147) which is available to Anna and Angus.

Occasionally, Anna's sense of the grotesque leads her to hallucinate, as when, during a meeting, she sees her manager starting to grow, his bandy legs 'lengthening and curling in vine fashion.' By the time Anna's waking dream is complete, Ingalls has been transformed into a massive zucchini and Barnum's office is filled with giant writing (111).[23] Anna suggests that her vision was inspired by her sexual interest in Ingalls. In fact, her vision conveys very traditional images of the grotesque, as it was conceived in the sixteenth century. During this period, the word was used as an adjective to describe 'the monstrous fusion of human and nonhuman elements ... [which was] the most typical feature of the grotesque style' (Kayser, 24). Anna's waking dreams are strikingly similar to the 'dreams of the painters,' especially the grotesque figures that are discussed in Vetruvius's *De architectura*: 'bastard forms composed of flowers and human bodies [that] grow out of roots and tendrils' (qtd. in Kayser, 20).

As a result of Anna's early exposure to the folk tradition, she rarely loses sight of the cosmic element of the body. Eating, defecation, and love-making are suffused with Rabelaisian humour, and her vision of these human functions and of her own body reaffirms that there is another economy – a 'gift economy' – separate from the one based on dehumanized economic exchange.[24] Even when her life in New York proves ultimately disappointing, and she realizes for the first time that she will not attain everything that she desires, she still has access to the folk discourse. While ice-skating in Central Park, she repeats the words to her old growing song, 'saying it backwards,' willing New York to shrink 'with all the magic energy' she can summon (134). When the city shrinks to the size of a 'tourist trinket,' she picks up the 'miniature town' and pitches it as far as she can out into the Atlantic Ocean.

It is worthwhile comparing this episode to a similar scene depicted in Angela Carter's *Nights at the Circus*. In Carter's novel, the giant, winged 'Cockney Venus' named Fevvers effects this same type of transformation of scale. Pursued by a Grand Duke who wants to add her to his collection of objects, Fevvers escapes his clutches by jumping onto one of the Duke's toys, a miniature train, which has the words *The Trans-Siberian Express* painted on its side (191–2). After this episode the narrative continues, portraying Fevvers and the rest of the circus performers riding on this same train, which is no longer a miniature toy.

Both Swan's and Carter's texts violate the 'common-sense' boundary erected between the universe of the world of play (which contains toys and fictions) and the world of 'real life' (which tends to value only 'facts'). Swan's text, like Carter's, charts the life of a female freak destined not to be taken seriously who can, therefore, freely cross over into the dimension of the not-serious, or what Susan Stewart calls the domain of 'nonsense.'[25] On a figurative level, Anna's freakish size and her sex function as indicators of her 'excessive' relation to the norm. The domain of the excess includes all of the unofficial discourses, or, more to the point, what the official discourses make unrepresentable. As de Lauretis suggests, this type of excess functions as a potential trauma that 'can rupture or destabilize, if not contained, any representation' (*Technologies*, 3). With her extravagant size and Rabelaisian imagination, Anna challenges the world of 'petrified narrow seriousness' and insists on the power of unofficial discourses to alter the world. She can shrink New York and toss it out to sea, create floods, and cause people to grow. Whether or not she actually accomplishes these feats often remains a matter of subjective interpretation. For instance, when she has sex with Ingalls, she murmurs in wonder, 'Apollo ... I am making you grow' (296).

The connection between love-making and the domain of excess is not coincidental, and it raises an important consideration regarding the relationship between desire and unofficial discourses. In Margaret Atwood's novel *The Handmaid's Tale*, the captive heroine Offred explains to her commander that the builders of the new society did not take into account the unruly discourse of love, and it is this illicit discourse and the ties it establishes between individuals that eventually lead to the breakdown of the fascist state (231). Similarly, in Angela Carter's *Nights at the Circus*, a group of female prisoners fall in love with their female guards. Barred from contact, the lovers exchange letters written in blood, an act of inscription that underscores the link between the excessive, desiring body and the potentially revolutionary, unofficial discourse of desire.[26] Ultimately, the women break out of prison, marching off into the unknown with their lovers. In Jeanette Winterson's book *Sexing the Cherry*, an explorer discovers that his love for a woman actually transports him into another domain. From then on he leads two lives: 'the ideal outer life and the inner imaginary life' (102). The former is driven by society's demands, the latter, by desire. Both Lewis Hyde and Hélène Cixous align the domain of excess – the 'gift economy' – with the capacity to love without expecting anything in return (Hyde, 22), although Cixous specifically attributes this ability to women: 'She gives more, with no assurance that she'll get back even some unexpected profit from what she puts out. She gives that there may be life, thought, transformation. This is an "economy" that can no longer be put in economic terms' (264).

Unlike Carter's and Winterson's works, *The Biggest Modern Woman of the World* does not simply champion the utopian power of unofficial discourses. Instead, the text pits the potentially revolutionary force of the folk discourse and other nonsense discourses against the 'realistic' domain of the official discourses. At times, 'nonsense' rules, and the text's frame of reference shifts completely from the realistic dimension of everyday life into the nonsense realm. This occurs most often during Anna's childhood. For instance, when Anna is caught in a snow tunnel, her mother comes to the rescue with a broken sword, which she uses like a dasher in a butter churn. In the midst of this life and death situation, Anna's mother breaks into song: 'There's a click here, there's a clack here, there's a great/wet mass here. The carpenters will come, the constables will come,/the man with the yellow cap will come. The butter will/come in a rush' (15). Similarly, when Anna and her mother go on a visit to Angus to get serious advice about whether to sign a contract with Barnum, Angus recites a poem in Gaelic, which combines realistic elements ('soot-faced farmers' and 'fishers with crinkled palms') with descriptions that rival portrayals of Paul Bunyan's blue ox, Babe.[27] Angus can access the folk discourse because of his Gaelic roots. In the poem, he claims to have seen a wonder: 'an ox without hair, without flesh, dragging grass from the black earth' (40). Once again, the discourse of nonsense topples the boundaries of the everyday world. Later on, in one of his letters to Anna, he asks her to invoke a series of nonsensical charms he has devised:

Charm 1: Make a backwards turn in the service of rural route one
Make a backwards turn in the service of rural route two
Make a backwards turn in the service of rural route three and each backwards turn in the service of the backwoods and each back-wards rotation made on the backwoods for the sake of the back-woods and each backwards turn in the service of the rural routes that grow us. (91–2)

Susan Stewart stresses that the inclusion of these kinds of nonsense elements effects a 'transgression of common-sense interpretive procedures,' and not 'a simple rearrangement of the hierarchies of common-sense discourse' (37). This means that, although they are contained within the traditional, conservative form of the novel, they are not merely shifts 'of emphasis,' to borrow Coral Ann Howells's words. Quite the contrary: nonsense discourses remain potentially subversive. At the very least, they can make the official discourses seems less powerful (Hutcheon, *Theory*, 76). Unfortunately, the novel illustrates that few people can successfully operate in both domains, and there is a tendency for the dominant discourses to be more successful in 'hailing' individuals; sooner or later, they become its subjects.

Within the novel, Ingalls appears to be the one character who, like Anna, can operate in either domain. As Kamboureli remarks, allegorically, Ingalls 'eradicates the differences between freakish otherness and normal behaviour' (110). Right from the start, his penchant for gambling aligns him with the 'ludic' sphere (see Bakhtin, *Rabelais*, 236). Second, his frog-like mouth and his capacity to ingest great quantities also connect him to the material bodily principle at the heart of the realistic grotesque (Bakhtin, *Rabelais*, 317). Ingalls seems to be the one man who truly appreciates Anna and accepts her body. When Anna tells him that she loves him, he is amazed because he views himself as her inferior (249). After admitting that the tonic did not really make her shrink, he confesses to Anna that he never wanted her to become average-sized: 'I always liked you big. Your body has fed and loved me. A woman who can do that for a man is the best there is' (319). Ingalls sees Anna, not as a Woman, but as a woman. His ability to treat her as an equal may stem from the fact that, like Anna, he also comes from a colony, namely, Australia.

Despite his ability to operate in the economy of desire, Ingalls insists on keeping one foot firmly planted in the reified world of economic exchange. Within the novel, this world is epitomized by P.T. Barnum, the man who championed the values of the market economy where 'getting rather than giving is the mark of a substantial person, and the hero is "self-possessed," "self-made"' (Hyde, xii–xiv). In England, Barnum was looked upon as the vilest representative of the nation. *Punch* described him as a man who had 'honored the sacred name of Washington by exhibiting his nurse ... who had humbled the crowned heads of Europe by showing them slavering over a loathsome dwarf, and enriching him with a colossal fortune' ('Barnum,' 89). It must not be forgotten that Ingalls worked for Barnum. Within the novel, as his behaviour *vis-à-vis* the tonic scheme reveals, he, too, is willing to use Anna as a pawn to increase his cash flow. Not one to let 'romancing interfere with business' (169), he encourages her to marry Bates, whom he despises. When he finds out that Anna is pregnant with his child, he plans on living off what he would make 'exhibiting her and the kid' (228). Nor does he see the irony of his position, when he decides that it is better that his stillborn child not be exhibited but remain housed in the London Hospital. As he says, he would feel funny having his 'flesh and blood gawked at by nasty-minded strangers,' and he congratulates himself on being a 'softie after all' (244). His insight regarding the sensation aroused by being 'gawked at' never prompts him to think how Anna must feel. Ingalls merely concludes that she needs a tougher skin because a 'freak can't expect to have normal things happen to her' (243). Ultimately, Ingalls dies before making a choice between the official and unofficial domains, but the impression gained is that he cannot help but see Anna as a commodity. Nor does Anna develop a 'tougher skin,' and, if the conclusion has anything to say about the potential of the folk discourse to counteract the ever-growing phalanx of official discourses, the message is both nonsensical and discouraging.

In her study of nonsense strategies, Stewart suggests that ludic fiction 'refuses the uplifting note by which the world assumes a happy ending' (209). Swan's novel likewise ends 'not with a bang, but a whimper.' The final section of the novel records the birth of Anna's second child. One reviewer could not, for the life of him, understand why this detail was included in the text: 'The real Anna lost two children in childbirth, but there is no reason why the fictional Anna should' (review by Seamon, 152). What he fails to understand is that traditionally women have written history through their bodies. The fictional Anna attests to this, saying, 'I long to make a history the way women have made history since time began' (272). For this reason, it is fitting that the story of Anna Swan include this integral part of the historical process as experienced by women. Initially, when Anna finds out that she is pregnant, the news helps to assuage the feelings of loss associated with the loss of her lover, Ingalls. Her access to the unofficial discourse of the folk tradition and her Bakhtinian tendency to 'collapse the negative into the positive' (Hutcheon, *Theory*, 71) help her find solace in the pattern of death and rebirth: 'where death is, there also is birth, change, renewal' (Bakhtin, *Rabelais*, 409). She views the turn of events in the light of a mythic or cosmic scale: 'I had not lost Apollo. He was with me, after all. And if my body did its job, would not leave me again' (322). However, the episode concerning the birth of the child reveals that Anna's body is not allowed 'to do its job,' largely, as we shall see, because the prevailing official discourses exercise control over her body.

This birth takes place in the dead of winter in Seville, Ohio, and the scene offers a striking contrast to her own birth, the Great Event, depicted in the beginning of the novel, which occurred in the middle of a Canadian summer. The shift from summer to winter, from Canada to America, indicates that Anna has become estranged from her roots and from the unofficial folk discourse. When she bears her child, she is at the mercy of the American medical experts. The administration of chloroform, coupled with one doctor's ill-timed advice, brings about the collapse of Anna's abdominal muscles, which trap the child in the birth canal. The baby is born alive, but is too weak to survive, and the death of the child dashes Anna's hope that 'finally, someday ... [she] might have a connection with the odd world into which [she had] ... been thrust' (327). Viewed within the context of the folk discourse, the death of a child augurs ill for the future of humankind (and women in particular). The child's death intimates that, with their insistence on the denigration and control of women's bodies, the official discourses have effectively broken the natural cycle of regeneration and renewal. Just as in Thomas's novel, where the protagonist's abortion introduces a chilling gap within the text, in Swan's novel, the death of Anna's baby attests to the power of destructive forces that ultimately silence women. Anna's own death, which follows the child's by nine years, only confirms that the power of the folk discourse is waning; there is a shift in the novel from the realist grotesque to the Romantic, with its emphasis on alienation and terror.

The tension between these two perspectives is signalled in the first chapter, when Anna admits that her 'struggle with the two opposing views [about her body] has been the chief task of ... [her] life' (12). As I have argued, for the most part, she is able to align herself with the view that maintains that her body is 'not a curse but a blessing, a symbol of luck and hope for all us Swans' (11). Gradually, however, she succumbs to an outlook associated with the Romantic grotesque, which positions her body as a monstrosity and a vulgar curiosity. Her identification with this perspective strengthens with the birth of her first child. Initially, the giantess seems to be in fine form, spieling in her usual, joyous fashion; however, her boisterous announcement of the 'BIGGEST BABY GIRL IN THE WORLD!' ends abruptly. The giantess explains, 'I do not wish to go on with this bitter spieling. ... Alas! My darling girl was stillborn' (240). The death of her first child leaves her feeling 'female and flawed' (242), a sensation which she first experiences after she is violated by Hubert Belacourt. While Anna recovers from Hubert's prank, the death of her first child signals the waning of the regenerating power associated with realistic grotesque. For the first time, Anna's vigorous and imaginative spieling is cut down to 'cold humor, irony, sarcasm,' a transformation which marks the divide between the realistic and Romantic grotesque (Bakhtin, *Rabelais*, 38).

When she settles in Seville, Ohio, Anna increasingly identifies with the Romantic grotesque, a tradition that positions her body as a curse and a curiosity. Bakhtin suggests that 'the world of Romantic grotesque is to a certain extent a terrifying world, alien to man' (*Rabelais*, 38); and, in keeping with this theme of alienation, Anna finds herself shunned by the community and, as we shall see, alienated from her own body. At first, in an effort to be sociable, she arranges a tea-party for the ladies of the town. She longs for them to recognize and accept her as a member of 'the stoical sorority who endures in silence the pain and discomfort involved in populating our planet' (278). But the women insist on viewing her as a freak, and when she is called away from the party, they take the opportunity to mock her by going through her chest of clothes and trying articles on (280–1). After this insult, one misfortune follows another. Through a series of letters exchanged with her mother, Anna learns that her sister Maggie has contracted consumption (she later dies a horrible death), and that her youngest brother, David, has died before his second birthday. Eventually, Anna quarrels with her mother, and they do not write to each other for over a year. Everywhere, human communication and compassion are seen to have reached an impasse. When Anna takes up the correspondence again, it is only to admit to her mother that she realizes she may be 'wasting her life with Martin' (290). If these events were portrayed according to the tradition of the sportive grotesque, they would somehow be transformed into something 'gay and comic' (Bakhtin, *Rabelais*, 39). As it is, the letters retain the leaden seriousness associated with Romantic grotesque.

One hopeful event occurs when Apollo Ingalls arrives at Anna's farm, but his visit quickly turns into a trial because he coerces Anna to drink Nelvana's Nordic Regulator. As I mentioned earlier, whereas the realistic grotesque promotes 'fearlessness,' the Romantic grotesque is associated with 'fear of the world' (Bakhtin, *Rabelais*, 39). Accordingly, Anna's gradual shift in identification from the realist to the Romantic grotesque is expressed as a movement from fearlessness to fear. Initially, she is portrayed as utterly courageous. For instance, she refuses to be cowed by Bates on her wedding night (208–9). But, by the time she has settled with Bates in Seville and consented to Ingalls's plot to 'shrink her,' she is overcome with feelings of 'shock and terror' (311). Although she learns the truth, and discovers that she is not shrinking, the news does not restore any gaiety because she is immediately confronted by the fact of Ingalls's grisly death (he is run over by a circus wagon and cut into two pieces). As I suggested earlier, the sorrow of his death is mitigated somewhat by her discovery that she is pregnant with her second child, but the text clarifies that, by this time, Anna has lost touch with the cosmic, regenerative aspect of her own body. The perspective of the realist grotesque, which celebrates the body and bodily life, is eclipsed by images of fragmentation (including Ingalls's mutilated body), death, and alienation.

When she is pregnant with her second child and ready to deliver, Anna feels only an overwhelming sense of detachment from her body. Like Thomas's protagonist, Anna has succumbed to internal division, and a part of her remains trapped in the mirror: 'I felt out of touch with the huge, bloated Anna in the mirror but my alienation at least gave me freedom from responsibility. That morning when the first pains resounded through my gargantuan belly, it felt as if the labour was happening to somebody else' (323). Anna's feelings of detachment persist when she delivers her child; she describes herself as 'disembodied,' and the last words she utters before drifting off into the haze of chloroform constitute an apology to the physician for being 'so large' (325). Her apology contrasts sharply with her earlier refusal to cater to the crowd in Halifax when, she had the strength to mock the crowd by asking to be excused because her body was showing (24). Seen in this light, her final, drugged apology to the doctor confirms her acceptance of the Romantic grotesque's conception of the female body as 'a curse.' In the end, the text clarifies that Anna was ground down by a world governed by this perspective – a world that could only view her size as 'freakish.' Before she dies, she writes the following stern acknowledgment of this predicament in her diary: 'I have accepted my destiny. I was born to be measured and I do not fit in anywhere. Perhaps heaven will have more room' (332).

In my introductory chapter, I referred to Virginia Woolf's warning to women writers. Woolf advised women not to try to map themselves in the linguistic landscape of the modern era because 'nothing will grow there.' On one hand, Susan Swan's novel *The Biggest Modern Woman of the World* underscores the veracity of Woolf's prediction. The text's examination of the clash between the unofficial discourse of the folk tradition and the set of official discourses that emerged with the consolidation of modern culture helps to explain why the soil was so barren. But the novel, itself an 'authorized transgression' (Hutcheon, *Theory*, 101) that makes use of the unofficial genre of the freak-show pamphlet, still manages to deconstruct imperialist discourses by pointing out the blind spots on the map. Both deconstructive and reconstructive strategies are utilized in the text's efforts to chart an alternative, subversive representation of female identity that exceeds the bounds of the official discourses; and readers can choose to appropriate this unofficial discourse when they make their 'move' in the language game.

4

Daphne Marlatt's *Ana Historic*: A Genealogy for Lost Women

I do not think we can live as human subjects without in some sense taking on a history; for us, it is mainly the history of being men or women under bourgeois capitalism. In deconstructing that history, we can only construct other histories. What are we in the process of becoming? (Mitchell, 294)

As the analyses of the novels in the previous chapters suggest, various strategies have been adopted in an effort to challenge established representations of female identity generated within a variety of patriarchal cultural discourses. *Intertidal Life* subverts the traditional literary representation of Woman by suspending or arresting the mechanism of the romance mode. Alternatively, *The Biggest Modern Woman of the World* employs tactics of parodic appropriation, rather than suspension, to effect a rigorous deconstruction that destabilizes a set of nineteenth-century official discourses, including those of modern science, industrial capitalism, and American nationalism, which shaped notions of the Woman and the freak. Swan's novel also explores a technique that Luce Irigaray refers to as 'mimicry': performing the feminine with a vengeance in order to effect a displacement between the performer and the performance and emphasize that femininity is a role that because it can so flagrantly be put on, can also be discarded. Finally, Swan's novel raises the possibility that one can avoid positioning oneself as Woman, according to the dictates of official discourses, by tapping into specific unofficial discourses. This possibility is realized *by* the novel, but never fully attained within the novel, which portrays how the official discourses gaining ground at the end of the nineteenth century silenced the unofficial discourses. These are represented in the novel by the Celtic folk traditions, whose themes and images correspond to Mikhail Bakhtin's description of 'grotesque realism.'

Daphne Marlatt's novel *Ana Historic* explores yet another strategy for revising traditional representations of female identity – a strategy which I describe as mapping a 'female genealogy.' To appreciate the radical nature of Marlatt's project, it is necessary to expand the term 'mapping,' used to analyse the recurring figure that surfaces in the texts discussed thus far. Mapping is typically associated with the plotting of spatial co-ordinates; however, for individuals who have been virtually effaced from history, mapping the temporal dimension – recovering or, barring that, tracing a history – remains a crucial step in the construction of the self as subject of language. Marlatt's texts have consistently expressed an interest in the subject of mapping. As Lola Lemire Tostevin states: 'Mapping her way through a travel journal is a favourite form' (35). Similarly, Laurie Ricou argues that, with perhaps two exceptions, 'all Marlatt's writing is variations of the travel journal form.' She is continually 'wording herself in response to unfamiliar and once familiar places, moving though landscapes as through language' ('Phyllis,' 208–9).[1] While Ricou concentrates on spatial mapping, other critics have noted that Marlatt's attention has been divided between the mapping of spatial and ancestral trajectories.[2] In many ways, mapping this type of trajectory corresponds to what Fredric Jameson calls an 'aesthetic of cognitive mapping.'

In his analysis of postmodern culture, Jameson draws on Kevin Lynch's book *The Image of the City* to develop an aesthetic of cognitive mapping. As noted in the first chapter, he isolates Lynch's opposition between two concepts, 'alienation' and 'disalienation.' The former is characterized by people's inability 'to map (in their minds) either their own positions or the urban totality in which they find themselves' (Jameson, 'Postmodernism,' 89). Disalienation, by contrast, involves the 'practical reconquest of a sense of place, and the construction or reconstruction of an articulated ensemble which can be retained in memory and which the individual subject can map and remap along the moments of mobile, alternative trajectories' (89). Jameson locates an interesting convergence between the mechanics of cognitive mapping, as described by Lynch, and the model of ideology, as conceived by Althusser. According to Althusser, 'ideology represents the imaginary relationship of individuals to their real conditions of existence' (162). For Jameson, both the cognitive map and ideology 'enable a situational representation on the part of the individual subject to that vaster and properly unrepresentable totality, which is the ensemble of the city's structure as a whole' (90). Jameson transcodes the history of mapping and cartography into the problematic of the Althusserian definition of ideology to allow for the rethinking of cartographical issues in terms of 'social space' (91).

While I remain sceptical of Jameson's utopian vision of a united, Marxist challenge to the status quo, in which 'we [which we?] may again begin to grasp our positioning as individual and collective subjects and regain a capacity to act and struggle which is at present neutralized by our spatial as well as our social confusion' (92), I believe that an aesthetic of cognitive mapping can serve as an important tool for a feminist methodology. Adopting the techniques of Levi-Strauss's *bricoleur*, I have appropriated the model of cognitive mapping, with its emphasis on alienation and disalienation, to suggest that another 'we' (women without history, 'lost' women) specifically need to map histories or ancestral trajectories, if you like, in order to compose a life which offers an alternative to the one plotted by the Oedipal narrative, one which refuses both the heroic (masculine) subject and the structure of romance. Whereas in Thomas's *Intertidal Life*, Alice remains caught between alienation and disalienation, in *Ana Historic*, the narrator discovers or invents a type of temporal map, 'an articulated ensemble which can be retained in memory,' to use Jameson's words, in order to move from a position of alienation to one of disalienation.

My description of Marlatt's genealogical project may lead one to believe that I am suggesting that her work promotes a form of essentialism, but this is not my point at all; her project need not be read this way. As Foucault and Teresa de Lauretis clarify, it is possible to construct genealogies which do not seek to instantiate a fixed Truth or uncover a definitive origin. Nevertheless, some critics persist in labelling Marlatt's writing as essentialist. For one, Dennis Cooley argues that, in her work, the 'begetting self is presumed to be intact and prior to language' (71). In his analysis of *How Hug a Stone*, Frank Davey likewise isolates a preoccupation with origins that are prior to language, and cites Marlatt's phrase 'the old slow pulse beyond word' (*How*, 75, qtd. in 'Words,' 44). Finally, Lola Lemire Tostevin states that 'more and more her work relies on originary/original meaning' (35). Marlatt has been asked if it is possible to see her work as 'sliding towards the patriarchal essentialist trap' (see 'An Interview,' 104). She has responded by asserting that her project has been misunderstood (105).

In the case of *Ana Historic*, there is no reason to link the articulation of a female genealogy with an essentialist perspective. Teresa de Lauretis's essay 'The Essence of the Triangle or, Taking the Risk of Essentialism Seriously: Feminist Theory in Italy, the U.S., and Britain' clarifies the difference between a feminist genealogical project, on the one hand, and a search for an ahistoric essence, on the other. To drive a wedge between the two, de Lauretis uses the term 'nominal essence' in contrast to the term 'real essence,' and draws on Locke's analysis to suggest that 'nominal essence,' rather than reflecting an unchanging kernel of identity – a 'real essence' – refers instead to 'a totality of qualities, properties, and attributes.' She argues:

It is a totality of qualities, properties, and attributes that such feminists define, envisage, or enact for themselves ... and possibly also wish for other women. This is more a project ... than a description of existent reality; it is an admittedly feminist project of 're-vision' where the specifications *feminist* and *re*-vision already signal its historical location, even as the (re)vision projects itself outward geographically and temporally (universally) to *recover the past and to claim the future* [my emphasis]. This may be utopian, idealist, perhaps misguided or wishful thinking ... but it is not essentialist as the belief in a God-given or otherwise immutable nature of woman.   ('Essence,' 5)

It is in this spirit of a 'project,' rather than a description of 'existent reality,' that *Ana Historic* maps its genealogy for lost women or, as de Lauretis says, works to 'recover the past and claim the future.'

Turning to the novel, we see that the text begins to weave its ancestral trajectory by casting an eye on the past to give voice to the experiences of a real-life historical figure, Mrs Richards, a woman who actually appears in the Vancouver city records as the second schoolteacher at Hastings Mill School in 1873. Whereas historical materials regarding the giantess Anna Swan were meagre, the information available concerning Mrs Richards is virtually non-existent. The latter is only mentioned as having purchased a piano and, in Alan Morely's *Vancouver: From Milltown to Metropolis*, she is called 'a young and pretty widow' (see interview with Marlatt, 'On Ana,' 97).

Like Thomas's and Swan's novels, *Ana Historic* resembles other postmodern texts, in that it, too, portrays history from the perspective of the losers and / or non-combatants, rather than the winners and / or heroes. This is not to say the heroes' stories are not visible. On the contrary, the text does provide historical 'facts,' which predominantly concern work done in the public sphere, including the lumber industry, the laying of the Canadian Pacific Railway, and the establishment of the town's magazine, the *Tickler*. Yet these 'facts' do not occupy the foreground, as they do in traditional histories. Instead, they are relegated to the background, and the foreground is occupied by the recovery and invention of Mrs Richards's experience.[3]

Far from designating some sort of unified and definitive trajectory, the novel displaces traditional history, which the narrator describes as the story of 'dominance. mastery. the bold line of it' (25). The novel does not inscribe a single 'line,' but plays with the 'fact' that two different sources offer conflicting accounts of Mrs Richards's life, thereby offering what Jameson describes as 'mobile and alternative' trajectories. According to one source, Mrs Richards gave music lessons in her rooms in Gastown; another source reports that she lived in a small cottage behind the schoolhouse (interview, 'On Ana,' 97).

Very often, in its construction of a historical trajectory, the text must rely on invention rather than historical 'fact.' As a result, the novel raises what is, by now, a familiar problem regarding the wavering boundary between fact and fiction. However, as we will see, in Marlatt's text, the subversion of historical 'fact' by the products of invention is tied to a feminist project, in which the freedom to revise or 'invent' history is inextricably connected to women's ability to 'recover the past and to claim the future.' In interviews, Marlatt confirms that she 'invented' Mrs Richards: 'I invented a diary for her, I invented a past for her. ... I made her an immigrant from Britain, and I wanted to give her a different destiny from the one that history actually records' ('On *Ana*,' 97).

The text extends its genealogical network by adding another historical layer, juxtaposing Mrs Richards's life with the experience of the narrator, Annie. While doing archival work for her husband, Richard, a history professor, Annie stumbles across the account of Mrs Richards as well as her journal. Upon discovering these clues to Mrs Richards's existence, Annie decides to stop working for her husband and write a novel based on the historical fragments she has uncovered. Within the text, both of these historical levels are taken into account, and the resultant structure is a complex weave of historical re-creation, Mrs Richards's journal entries, Annie's speculation on the process of writing the novel, and details concerning Annie's life. The genealogy is further augmented when, in the course of writing about Mrs Richards (or Ana, as she is dubbed by the narrator), Annie gives voice to her mother's story. Like Mrs Richards, Annie's mother, Ina, was lost to history. She was a proper British lady schooled in colonial values. After emigrating from Malaysia to Vancouver with her husband and two children, Ina suffered from isolation and loneliness, finally succumbing to madness and death.

In interviews Marlatt suggests that Mrs Richards's story and Ina's story are related: 'They're analogies in some way ... They're not identical, so they're off-rhymes. ... But parts of the two stories echo each other' ('On *Ana*,' 101). The echoes do not stop there, however, because the story of Annie and Ina mirrors the relationship between Marlatt and her own mother. Marlatt admits that she wrote the novel as a way of coming to terms with her mother:

[W]e went through such a difficult time together during my adolescence when she had such a bad time with herself, and immigrating to Canada was the last psychic straw for her. We ricocheted away from each other, and she denied me and I denied her, and we never really got back to any kind of *rapprochement* before she died, so writing about her is my way of doing that, of getting to a place where I can feel some of that affection and empathy and understanding. It's a really different bond from the little girl's bond, because my understanding comes from empathizing with her experience as a mother, having had my own experience as a mother. And recognizing in myself the difficulties I had as an immigrant, and seeing how those were magnified for her. I can only realize what we had in common by also expressing where I felt she betrayed me as a mother, because she was in such deep psychological trouble herself that she couldn't go on mothering.   (Interview, 'Sounding,' 49)

Within the text, in an attempt to come to terms with Ina, Annie stages imaginary conversations between herself and her mother. When asked if those conversations were invented, Marlatt responded that she didn't know how to answer because 'sometimes they were in part remembered, and often enlarged' ('On *Ana*,' 97). The presence of these autobiographical elements within the novel reinforces the reader's awareness of the unstable border between historical fact and fiction. In interviews, Marlatt problematizes the distinction between the two. As she says, 'remembering is a fiction,' and so it is strange that we say 'remembering is real, and inventing is not – inventing is purely imaginary or fictional. What interests me is where those two cross' ('On *Ana*,' 96). Very often, the imaginary conversations between Ina and Annie self-consciously foreground the supposed difference between 'story' as 'lie' and 'history' as 'Truth.' At one point, Annie imagines Ina criticizing her for inventing aspects of Mrs Richards's life, charging her with 'simply making things up, out of a perverse desire to obscure the truth' (55). Annie responds by asking, 'whose truth, Ina? the truth is (your truth, my truth, if you would admit it)' (56). Annie's reply suggests that truth is not singular. Ultimately, the heated exchanges between Ina and Annie demonstrate how the culturally constructed distinction between invention and history reinforces a hegemonic perspective, which precludes the possibility of marginalized groups representing their 'truths' – truths which differ from the Truth of History.

Annie's awareness of the repressive impact of this singular notion of Truth fuels her desire to construct a female genealogy that confounds the distinction between invention and history-making. To this end, her novel blends historical elements seamlessly with imagined elements. On another level, Marlatt herself confuses the difference between fact and fiction by encouraging the conflation of the narrator's voice with her own. As she explains: 'Annie, the narrator, and I, at this point are both working against history because when I say I, I'm also saying I as narrator, who is Annie' (interview, 'On *Ana*,' 98). As a result of the novel's reliance on both invention and autobiography, it has been called 'an autobiographical novel of the imagination' ('On *Ana*,' 96). What remains to be seen is how this 'autobiographical novel of the imagination' constructs a female genealogy.

In a recent book published by the Milan Women's Bookstore Collective, the authors provide an account of a specific theory and practice of feminism which took place between 1966 and 1986, mainly in Milan. The book is entitled *Non credere di avere dei diritti: la generazione della libertà femminile nell'idea e nelle vicende di un gruppo di donne* (Teresa de Lauretis translates this as 'Don't Think You Have Any Rights: The Engendering of Female Freedom in the Thought and Vicissitudes of a Women's Group' ['Essence,' 14]).[4] These women suggest that the work done in the context of their group can be best understood as the creation of a 'female genealogy.' Arguing that freedom for women is not obtained through any adherence to the liberal concept of rights, they assert that such freedom is 'generated, and indeed engendered, by taking up a position in a symbolic community, a 'genealogy of women,' that is at once discovered, invented, and constructed through feminist practices of reference and address' (de Lauretis, 'Essence,' 14–15). The feminist practices specified include 'reading or rereading of women's writings; taking other women's words, thoughts, knowledges, and insights as frame of reference for one's analyses, understanding, and self-definition; and trusting them to provide a symbolic mediation between oneself and others, one's subjectivity and the world' (15). Their theory hinges on 'entrustment' – a concept that designates a particular relationship between two women, in which one woman gives her trust or 'entrusts herself symbolically to another woman, who thus becomes her guide, mentor, or point of reference' (22). As de Lauretis describes it:

[E]ach woman of each pair validates and valorizes the other within a frame of reference no longer patriarchal or male-designed, but made up of perceptions, knowledges, attitudes, values, and modes of relating historically expressed by women for women – the frame of reference ... [that] the book calls a female genealogy or a female symbolic. ('Essence,' 23)

Marlatt's novel, with its multi-generational female framework or, as Annie puts it, 'the cultural labyrinth of our inheritance, mother to daughter to mother' (24), also maps a female genealogy which, to use the words about the Milan group, is at once discovered, invented, and constructed through feminist practices of reference and address.[5]

In using the term 'genealogy,' in addition to referring to the work of the Milan group, I am also gesturing toward the analysis of genealogy which Foucault offers in his essay 'Nietzsche, Genealogy, History.' According to Foucault, the genealogist reverses the practice of historians, specifically, 'their pretension to examine things furthest from themselves' ('Nietzsche,' 156). Citing Nietzsche, Foucault emphasizes his distrust of supposedly 'objective' historians: 'those tired and indifferent beings who dress up in the part of wisdom and adopt an objective point of view' (158–9).[6] Following Foucault's injunction to write about what 'is closest' (156), the text draws on autobiographical materials relating to the author's life, her relationship with her mother, and the 'ahistoric' Mrs Richards, a woman who lived where Marlatt grew up.[7]

Foucault further stipulates that the genealogist must find the materials for a historical analysis in 'the most unpromising places, in what we tend to feel is without history' ('Nietzsche,' 139). He specifically links the task of genealogy to the exploration of what he refers to as disqualified or 'subjugated knowledges.' By this, he refers to the following:

[N]aive knowledges, located low down on the hierarchy, beneath the required level of cognition or scientificity. ... (such as that of the psychiatric patient, of the ill person, of the nurse, of the doctor – parallel and marginal as they are to the knowledge of medicine – that of the delinquent etc.), and which involve what I would call a popular knowledge ...

though it is far from being a general commonsense knowledge, but is on the contrary a particular, local, regional knowledge, a differential knowledge incapable of unanimity and
which owes its force only to the harshness with which it is opposed by everything surrounding it. ...   ('Two Lectures,' 82)

The knowledges the narrator conveys certainly fall under Foucault's classification
as 'subjugated knowledges'; in tracing her life and the lives of her foremothers, Annie
gives voice to the experiences of women not considered worthy enough to be inscribed in the 'book' of History (147).

Very often her materials concern 'what we tend to feel is without history.' For
example, as an adult, she describes the ontological shift she experienced with the
budding of her adolescent sexuality. Prior to this shift, her relationship to her body
emphasized autonomy: 'our bodies were ours as far as we knew and we knew what
we liked' (19). In adolescence, this relationship alters dramatically: 'now she was
walking her body as if it were different from her, her body with its new look. (o
the luck, to be looked at. o the lack, if you weren't. o the look. looking as if it all
depended on it)' (50). Annie's analysis of this 'ahistoric' event highlights the way
in which her self-definition was decentred by a system that privileges the male and
the male gaze: 'wanting to be the one looked at, approved by male eyes' (50). In
part, the shift in Annie's self-definition rests on a transference of approval, whereby
self-worth comes to be associated with an approving male gaze, rather than with
one's estimation of oneself. As in the previous novels studied here, Annie recognizes that she is positioned as an object, a spectacle for the male gaze. She remarks
that she acquired a body 'marked *woman's*. as if it were a brand name,' converting
all action 'into the passive: to be seen' (52). Annie's account of this 'event' corresponds to Elizabeth Grosz's description of the way in which power functions
directly on bodies by means of disciplinary practices, social supervision, and self-
regulation ('Inscriptions,' 64). According to Grosz, 'the subject is *named* by being
tagged or branded on its surface.' The messages coded onto the body 'bear the marks
of a particular social law and organisation' (65). Thus, Annie's sense of acquiring a
body 'marked *woman's*' can be located within the context of the operations of a
power-knowledge dynamic.

Raising the issue of power, as it does, Annie's inquiry into her attitudinal shift
foregrounds another aspect of the genealogical project. As Foucault asserts, the
task of the genealogist is to 'reestablish the various systems of subjection: not the
anticipatory power of meaning, but the hazardous play of dominations' ('Nietzsche,' 148). The ontological shift Annie recalls offers a record of a system of subjection. Annie recalls that this shift was experienced as a form of diminishment:
'from scavengers and traders we shrank into daughters' (80).[8] Alternatively, she
describes this change as a forced movement from one economy to another, where

the 'new economy we traded in was one based on the value of our bodies' (82). Her sense of moving from one economy to another recalls the distinction drawn in the previous chapter between the gift economy – the realm of excess – and the market economy. Within the latter, although women are supposedly at the mercy of their biology, their 'sex function,' paradoxically they are believed to have no desires of their own: they desire only to be desired (Ehrenreich and English, 121). Likewise, Annie's shift in self-definition is connected to the effacement of her desire. As an adult, she acknowledges this predicament, namely, the death of women's desire in the market economy: 'the small space desire gets backed into. boxed. off' (59). Ultimately, Marlatt's text, with its multi-generational framework, facilitates a historical analysis of the sexual conditioning and representation of women within Western culture's dominant discourses. During her examination of events 'without history,' the narrator traces the way in which women are alienated from their bodies, deprived of desire, and taught to feel ashamed of themselves.

Paradoxically, this sense of shame is an inheritance Annie claims to have received from her mother. In one of her many imaginary conversations with Ina, who has just died,[9] Annie complains, 'you taught me the uneasy hole in myself and how to cover it up. ... pride on the outside, and on the inside – shame' (60–1). Yet, as Marlatt suggests in interviews, only by expressing where she felt betrayed by her mother can she realize what they had in common (see interview, 'Sounding,' 49). In the end, Annie's recollection of her own sexual conditioning and her mother's betrayal enables her to see that, if she suffered from shame, the effacement of self-definition and desire, then her mother can be said to have died from trying to fulfil the requirements of a social code that positioned her as Woman.

It is at this point that the discourses of colonialism and patriarchy intersect. Musing over her mother's life, Annie concludes that her mother reached an impasse because she mistakenly transposed her English background with its phallocentric, imperialist ideology 'onto a Salish mountainside. and never questioned its terms. "lady." never questioned its values' (23–4). As a result of her unquestioned allegiance to the discourse of imperialism, Ina's energies were drained in a desperate attempt to conform to 'a rule, standard, or pattern,' which did not reflect her experience – her truth (18).[10] Recalling her mother's obsession with how-to-fix-yourself books, Annie plays with the word 'fix' to arrive at the word 'castrated,' and she concludes that this is what Ina was 'trying to live up to. the neuter' (35). Operating inside the representational system, without any critical perspective, Ina was caught 'between despair at being nothing ("just" a mother, "just" a wife [...]) and the endless effort to live a lie (the loveable girl in her Lovable Bra, the Chanel femme fatale ...) how measure up?' (57). Her sense of being 'nothing' reinforces Annie's opinion regarding Ina's castrated position – a position generated by the representational system which defines women as the zero:

While the sexes are represented according to a binary structure that reduces *n-sexes* to two, the binary structure itself reduces one term within the pair to a position definitionally dependent on the other, being defined as its negation, absence or lack. This is a *phallocentric* representational system in the sense in which women's corporeal specificity is defined and understood only in some relation to men's – as men's opposites, their doubles or their complements. This means that women's autonomously defined carnal and bodily existence is buried beneath both male-developed biological scientific paradigms, and a male-centred system of social inscription that marks female bodies as men's (castrated, inferior, weaker, less capable) counterparts.   (Grosz, 'Inscriptions,' 73)

In this description, one can hear echoes of Barbara Ehrenreich and Deirdre English's analysis of the nineteenth century's 'sexual romanticism,' which also catered to the demand that women be 'a *negation* of man's world' (109). In certain respects, the portrayal of Ina, a woman who has internalized the masculine paradigms, recalls Thomas's characterization of Alice, who, although far more articulate, also internalized patriarchal culture's construction of Woman as Man's castrated Other.

In Marlatt's novel, Ina's efforts to 'measure up' often target her body; similarly, many of Annie's descriptions of childhood memories also reflect a preoccupation with the attitudes and treatments directed at the body. This prolonged focus on the body is, once again, tied to Foucault's notion of genealogy, which, as an analysis of descent or *Herkunft*, specifically inquires into how the body functions as 'the inscribed surface of events.' According to Foucault, genealogy remains 'situated within the articulation of the body and history. Its task is to expose a body totally imprinted by history and the process of history's destruction of the body' ('Nietzsche,' 148).

In her effort to 'measure up,' Ina strove to inscribe society's version of the desirable body onto her flesh. As Grosz states: 'The body becomes a 'text' and is fictionalised and positioned within those myths that form a culture's social narratives and self-representations' ('Inscriptions,' 66). At one point, Annie recalls how Ina would fashion her appearance each time she dressed to go out for the evening. Seated at her dressing table, fixated on 'that hollow glance, that dark reflection' of herself, Ina 'lost' herself in the mirror, transforming herself into 'the brilliant reflection of no one [Annie] ... recognized. rosebud mouth, plucked brows, dark eyes intensified: the perfect implacable Garbo face' (57–8). Ina, like Alice Hoyle, finds herself trapped within a looking-glass world. In her book, *Les Guérillères*, Monique Wittig describes the psychic limbo experienced by women who, like Ina, are 'lost' in the mirror: 'They advance, there is no front, there is no rear. They move on, there is no future, there is no past. ... The silence is absolute. ... They are prisoners of the mirror' (30–1). They are purposeless and disoriented because they are positioned within a symbolic system that positions them *as*, as well as *in*, the mirror. Like Ina, they serve merely to reflect the image of men's desire, rather than their own.

Ina's identification with male desire is betrayed by her preoccupation with jewellery. Seated before the mirror, she adorns herself with gems. At one point, she tells Annie that 'emeralds are your stone, darling, they bring out the colour of your eyes' (57). This statement carries the implicit message that, by wearing the emeralds, Annie will enhance her capacity to attract the male gaze. Paradoxically, the gift *from her mother* (the emeralds) will augment, not her autonomy, but her value as an object for men, connoting 'to-be-looked-at-ness' (Mulvey, 11). Annie explains that it is a custom in the family to pass along these jewels from grandmother to mother to daughter, and that this transfer constitutes the only 'female line of inheritance.' Annie does not deal harshly with Ina, however, because she understands that, caught as she was within the phallocentric order, 'that was all [Ina] … had to give' (57).

In interviews, Marlatt refers to the ambivalent relationship between Ina and Annie: 'she wants to be nurturing, she wants her daughter to have everything she didn't have, but at the same time she's raising her daughter to accept the limitations of being a woman in a patriarchal society' (interview, 'Sounding,' 48). Ina's behaviour at the mirror, and her offer of emeralds to her daughter, emphasize that her behaviour is Janus-faced, partly nurturing and partly a form of coercion aimed at inducing Annie to accept her status as object.

By promising the jewels to Annie, Ina, like her mother before her, is, in fact, passing on 'the family jewels,' the Name of the Father, which is the traditional symbol and guarantee both of 'propriety' and 'property' (Felman, 37). Not surprisingly, Annie prefers her mother's costume jewellery, 'that fake stone your real breath would mist in an instant' (57). Whereas the emeralds stand for the Name of the Father and society's attempt to secure the male line by guaranteeing a steady stream of women who accept object-status, Annie's preference for fake jewels connotes a disregard for 'the original' (the phallus) and its privileged position. The presence of copies or 'fakes' introduces the possibility of subverting the system through substitution and replacement, essentially the principle of iteration, which 'unsettles completely the notion of unique referent, as Derrida has demonstrated' (Murray, 124). Although she is distressed and alienated by her position within the symbolic system, Ina does not believe in 'fakes.' For her, there is only the original, the single story, the one true plot; in her mind, there is no way to change the script. When Ina becomes psychologically unable to live up to the role of the 'neutered' wife and mother – when she 'cracks' like Alice in *Intertidal Life* – she is put into the care of psychiatrists.[11] As I suggested in the previous chapter, in conjunction with the scene depicting the death of the giantess's second child, science generally works in the service of the State, facilitating the control of women's bodies.

Elizabeth Grosz argues that efforts to incarnate society's image of the desirable body and efforts on the part of the psychiatric profession to inscribe socially desirable thoughts are located along a continuum. Within our culture, the inscription of bodies can occur both violently and by less openly aggressive means, namely, 'through cultural and personal values, norms and commitments,' the adornment of the body, its rituals of exercise and diet, as well as makeup. The more violent inscription of bodies occurs in 'prisons, juvenile homes, hospitals, [and] psychiatric institutions' ('Inscriptions,' 65). Grosz argues that psychiatric institutions inscribe bodies by 'traversing neural pathways by charges of electricity in shock therapy' (65). Whether the tactics involve covert or overt aggression, the body remains the primary target of the law. There are reasons why this is the case. According to Grosz:

[I]f the body is the strategic target of systems of codification, supervision and constraint, it is also because the body and its energies and capacities exert an uncontrollable, unpredictable threat to a regular, systematic mode of social organisation. As well as being the site of knowledge-power, the body is thus also a site of *resistance*, for it exerts a recalcitrance, and always entails the possibility of a counterstrategic reinscription, for it is capable of being self-marked, self-represented in alternative ways.   (64)

Ina's electric shock 'therapy' was supposed to erase the unreasonable thoughts that tormented her (144). Yet, as the official material cited in the text clarifies, these treatments did far more damage than simply erase a few painful memories: *'In the amnesia caused by all electric shocks, the level of the whole intellect is lowered'* (145). When Annie concludes that her mother 'died of reason,' she hears a peal of thunder, which makes her think of 'missiles going off' (17). The juxtaposition of Ina's death by reason and the deadly production of missiles forges a link between the two, intimating that the same logic or reason ('explanation, justification, normal mental state – that old standard' [17]) that led to her mother's 'therapy' also gave rise to North America's nuclear arsenal. The violence lying behind the supposedly rational 'therapy' is more fully exposed when Annie draws an analogy between her mother's treatment at the hands of medical experts and the management of timber: 'taking out the dead wood. pruning back the unproductive. it was all a matter of husbandry, "the careful management of resources." for everybody's good, of course' (146–7). Her comments locate Ina's 'therapy' within a society that envisions women as 'resources' to be controlled.[12] According to Annie, the doctors who treated Ina effaced her ability to represent herself in 'alternative ways' outside of her role of wife and mother: they took away her imagination, her 'will to create things differently' (149).

Through an examination of Ana's life, Ina's life, and her own life, Annie recognizes that she is implicated in this process – the production and maintenance of gendered female bodies. Within the cultural economy of 'the same,' which perceives only the Male and the not-Male (the neuter), women are inscribed as 'resources' of the male. In the face of this coercion, it seems that it would be almost impossible to express or inscribe a feminine identity which exceeds this binary opposition, an identity that is not merely a specular reflection of lack, but altogether different.

Given this predicament, women have had, to say the least, a problematic relation to history. In writing her novel, Marlatt hoped to address this issue: 'What I was interested in doing … was to do a woman's version of history, that being a difficult area for women because they don't inhabit history in the same way that men do. Their history is usually the unwritten history, it's the history that tends to get recorded more in oral histories. Women are not seen as world-makers' (interview, 'On *Ana*,' 98). In tackling the problem of women's invisibility, there is more at stake for Marlatt (and for Annie) than some sort of general project to balance out the attention given to male and female historical figures. Annie decides not to work for her husband, described as an 'Atwoodian map-maker and surveyor, symbol of the male eye of power' (Cooley, 76), because she is not, as the text puts it, interested in 'lot numbers and survey maps' (79). Although Richard encourages her to help him, Annie refuses to remain complicit with the system and merely modify official history: 'i'm no longer doing my part looking for missing pieces. at least not missing facts. not when there are missing persons in all this rubble' (134). As a result of her exposure to official history through her work with Richard, Annie understands that history serves Oedipus. Like romance narratives, history effaces women and transforms them into objects, the background for the heroic exploits of men. As I mentioned in chapter 1, in an imaginary conversation with Ina, Annie tells her mother that she has learned that 'history is the real story the city fathers tell of the only important events in the world. a tale of their exploits hacked out against a silent backdrop of trees. … so many claims to fame. so many ordinary men turned into heroes. (where are the city mothers?)' (28)

Paradoxically, although she is deeply suspicious of history, and she rejects 'history's voice' (48), Annie recognizes that she must engage in history-making because it is a vital element in the ongoing struggle to construct a female identity. As the epigraph to this chapter indicates, women must construct histories in order to determine who they are becoming. Juliet Mitchell, working within the context of psychoanalysis, insists that one must tell histories to survive: 'What can you do but disrupt a history and re-create it as another history?' (288). Histories must be generated in order to arrive at a story – and a life – that works. In Marlatt's novel, Annie's impulse to generate an alternative version of history is clearly tied to the process of individuation and the struggle to invent a life that can account for women's buried or repressed experience. In accordance with the postmodern tactic of contesting discourses which are simultaneously invoked, she does not attempt to do without history-making, although she rejects history as it has been fashioned: 'i wasn't dreaming of history, the already-made, but of making fresh tracks my own way' (98). Her project involves revising history, reading it against the grain, and working as a *map-breaker*. As she says, 'when you're so framed, caught in the act, the (f) stop of act, fact – what recourse? step inside the picture and open it up' (56). As I suggested earlier, the appropriation of an existing discourse is not necessarily a conservative 'move' that effectively replicates this discourse. As Derrida argues, change will not come about by dismissing a metaphysical construct: 'the passage beyond philosophy does not consists in turning the page of philosophy ... but in continuing to read philosophers *in a certain way*' ('Structure,' 259). Imagining a history for the ahistoric Mrs Richards – 'imagining things differently' – Annie invents a future for herself and continues the project of resistance which her mother was not allowed to finish. Yet, in order to construct a genealogy for 'lost women,' Annie must begin by finding out who was there. Only then can she answer the questions: 'Who do I really desire?' and 'Who is my real enemy?'

Not surprisingly, the novel opens by posing the haunting question: 'Who's There?' The phrase, spoken by the dreaming Annie, is followed by the words, 'knock knock' (9). With the addition of these words, the question is transformed into a riddle – a riddle that echoes the infamous riddle posed by Sigmund Freud. At the beginning of his lecture on femininity, Freud addresses this question to the audience:

Throughout history people have knocked their heads against the riddle of the nature of femininity. ... Nor will *you* have escaped worrying over this problem – those of you who are men; to those of you who are women this will not apply – you are yourselves the problem. (113)

Both Annie's and Freud's riddles pose the same question; however, Freud's formulation of 'the problem' neatly illustrates the effect of the phallocentric construction of femininity, which relegates femininity to object-status. As Shoshana Felman argues, Freud's question '"what is femininity?" in reality asks: "what is femininity – *for men?*"' (21). To the extent to that women are the supposed problem, they 'cannot *enunciate* the question; they cannot be the speaking *subjects* of the knowledge or the science which the question seeks' (21). Cast as objects, women are deprived of the opportunity to offer any subjective account of their own experience. As in the previous chapters, the silencing of women by patriarchal discourses emerges as a problem for women trying to exist as speaking and writing subjects.

In Marlatt's novel, the return of Freud's riddle – the return of the repressed – in Annie's dream alerts us to this problem: how can silenced women – women positioned as mute objects within the phallocentric order – speak? Juliet Mitchell answers this question by suggesting that women can only speak as hysterics. She describes hysteria as the woman's 'simultaneous acceptance and refusal of the organisation of sexuality under patriarchal capitalism' (289–90). She insists that a woman writer 'must speak the discourse of the hysteric, who both refuses and is totally trapped within femininity' (290).

Ana Historic acknowledges women's position as hysterics through its depiction of Ina, who literally becomes a hysteric within a symbolic order that diminishes her to the point where she is 'nothing.' The issue of hysteria surfaces again in conjunction with Annie's problematic relation to language. Annie inherits Ina's language – the language of British imperialism.[13] Yet, if she is to map an alternative trajectory, she must not repeat her mother's mistake and simply transpose an inherited language onto a new culture. However, in trying to erase her English 'difference' in an effort to become Canadian, Annie learns that her 'difference' is embedded in her speech: 'my English shoes and woolly vests. my very words' (23). She reaches an impasse because she cannot do without language. As she says, even the phrase 'my very words' constitutes a quotation from Ina. Similarly, when she describes writing her novel as 'just scribbling,' she is drawing on another quotation from her mother (81). Finally, Annie is led to ask: 'and what if our heads are full of other people's words? nothing *without* quotation marks' (81). Her question reinforces Derrida's assertion regarding the futility of any project to somehow transcend, rather than critique, an inherited language: 'We have no language … which has not already slipped into the form, the logic, and the implicit postulations of precisely what it seeks to contest' ('Structure,' 250). Rejecting the possibility of transcendence, Derrida argues that the 'quality and the fecundity of a discourse are perhaps measured by the critical rigor with which this relationship to the history of metaphysics and to inherited concepts is thought' (252). Using a familiar language, Annie operates, to a certain extent, with concepts which repress her experience of the world and assert a dominant perspective: 'words, that shifting territory. never one's own. full of deadfalls and hidden claims to a reality others have made' (32). Musing over words such as 'vagina,' whose etymological roots go back to the word 'sheath,' Annie discovers that words not only name and frame her experience of the world, but also contribute to her alienation from her own body: 'the words for our bodies betrayed us in the very language we learned at school' (62). Labelling by women's sexual organs 'sheaths,' means that their use-value is always already constituted in relation to a male economy, which privileges the 'sword' or phallus. Annie, like Ina, functions to some extent as a 'hysteric' because, despite her best intentions, her words reinforce the organization of sexuality within the symbolic order. Annie's concerns regarding language, which draw together the related issues of colonialism and patriarchal control, recall both Thomas's and Swan's exploration of these same forces and their negative impact on women's lives.

In the foreword to *Salvage*, Marlatt remarks that her entire collection represents an attempt 'to salvage the wreckage of language so freighted with phallocentric values it must be subverted and re-shaped, as Virginia Woolf said of the sentence, for a woman's use' (10). Given her belief that language can be 'salvaged,' she evidently does not subscribe to Juliet Mitchell's assertion that women are irrevocably bound to operate as hysterics within the symbolic order. By now, it is probably clear from the fragmented style of the quotations I have cited that, although Marlatt is working with and within the structures of a language that positions her as Woman, she is nevertheless *refusing* to co-operate with its Oedipal logic – the logic of subject-verb-object – which aligns women with objects. In the novel, many sentences begin without capitals (signalling both the narrator's thoughts, as distinct from the other textual elements, and her rejection of a system which is based on 'capital' and the reification of human beings). Very often, sentences consist of strings of nouns and noun phrases; pages are left blank or inscribed with only a few lines (43). The text also makes use of variable orthography, including handwriting (43), but more often, italics and bold-faced type, that designate the existence of alternative codes of communication contesting the privileged status accorded to standard English (see Ashcroft et al., 72).

This innovative treatment of the language highlights the fact that Marlatt holds out the possibility of operating *on the margins* of the dominant cultural discourse. In interviews, she refers to Shirley and Edwin Ardener's model of the relationship between dominant and muted social groups, which represents their interaction as two circles that overlap for the most part, but not entirely.[14] This model of partially overlapping circles has often been used to designate women's position within patriarchal culture, and it is a paradigm that affords the muted group a small crescent, described as a 'wild zone,' which is outside of dominant culture and language. According to this schema, then, women could be said to occupy a double position, located as they are both within and outside of dominant culture.[15] Working from the margins, it becomes possible to destabilize the ideological frame of the dominant culture's syntax and semantics: Marlatt shatters the shape of the sentence as well as the 'facts,' disrupting the frame which generates the type of subject positions for men and women so evident in Freud's riddle.[16]

As a genealogist, Annie must work against what has been characterized as a 'paternal genealogy' that silences women as subjects and authors of their own history. Sandra Gilbert and Susan Gubar have studied the omnipresence of this paternal genealogy, which is embedded in our culture. As they explain, 'the patriarchal notion that the writer "fathers" his text just as God fathered the world is and has been all-pervasive in Western literary civilization' (4). Within the terms of this genealogy, 'the poet, like God the Father, is a paternalistic ruler of the fictive world he has created' (5). They note the paradox at the heart of the metaphor of literary paternity, which creates a situation in which a male author both generates and imprisons his fictive creatures: 'he silences them by depriving them of autonomy (that is, of the power of independent speech) even as he gives them life' (14). For instance, Freud seemingly gives life to the feminine by inquiring after its nature, but he silences or, as Gilbert and Gubar put it, 'kills' women, by depriving them of the opportunity to speak in their own name.[17]

In her novella, *Territory & Co.*, Marlatt intimates that this paternal genealogy is an 'old story,' beginning perhaps with the story of Adam in the garden, naming all of the animals. Yet even after Adam and Eve left the garden, 'he kept track, he told the story, he passed it all on, father to son, desert camp to town. ... it's the name of the game. ... terri-stories' (*Salvage*, 72). The term 'terri-stories' forges an important connection between the paternal genealogy and the process of naming and claiming *territory*. Within *Ana Historic*, the various historical quotations that Annie cites from the archives illustrate that, within this discourse of 'terri-stories,' entities are categorized according to their use-value in relation to (white) men, and any sense of the entity having a life with its own purpose is left outside the frame. The following citation referring to the Douglas fir is a typical example:

Douglas fir and red cedar are the principal trees. Of these, the former – named after David Douglas, a well-known botanist – is the staple timber of commerce. Average trees grow 150 feet high, clear of limbs, with a diameter of 5 to 6 feet. The wood has great strength and is largely used for shipbuilding, bridge work, fencing, railway ties, and furniture. As a pulp-making tree the fir is valuable. Its bark makes good fuel. (13–14)

As one critic notes, the historical documents culled from the archives become denatured and break down into their components: 'the language of nominalization, categorization, hierarchization, domination, colonization, subordination, and control' (Banting, 125). Yet, these 'terri-stories' are not only applied to trees, but to women as well. Annie notes that the capitalized terms 'Proper' and 'Lady' – capitalized in both senses of the word – establish a link between 'Proper' and property, which underlies the sexual conditioning of females into 'wives or daughters-about-to-be-wives' (32). Thus, the paternal genealogy, which Gilbert and Gubar perceptively locate in the domain of literature, also gives rise to historical 'terri-stories.' After researching the archival material, Annie realizes that 'a sense of fraternal community runs through the records' (55).

In the face of the almost overwhelming repression and / or reification of the female within these historical 'terri-stories,' the question of 'Who's There' would seem doomed to remain unanswered. Yet, as Gilbert and Gubar insist, 'no human creature can be completely silenced by a text or by an image"; they argue that 'women themselves have the power to create themselves as characters, even perhaps the power to reach toward the woman trapped on the other side of the mirror/text and help her to climb out' (16). This is precisely what Annie does for Mrs Richards, her mother Ina, and, finally, for herself.

But women cannot reach the 'lost women' by appropriating the language and structures of the paternal genealogy or by merely filling in the gaps of history. Instead, they must 'reshape' phallocentric linguistic structures if they hope to get in touch with what is 'ana historic.' As a prefix, 'ana' means 'upwards' and 'forwards' as well as 'backwards' (*OED*). In the light of this definition, it is apparent that women like Annie, who are working 'from the margins,' are developing a practice of reading and recoding (in this case, history), which destabilizes and disrupts the official version.

Edward Said argues that the metaphor of paternal genealogy is built into the classical model of the novel through a series of genealogical connections: 'author-text, beginning-middle-end, text-meaning, reader-interpretation, and so on. Underneath all these is the imagery of succession, of paternity, or hierarchy' (162). In *Musing with Mother Tongue*, Marlatt registers the impact of this paternal genealogy, and locates it at the level of the sentence itself. She asks: 'How can the standard sentence structure of English with its linear authority, subject through verb to object, convey the wisdom of endlessly repeating and not exactly repeated cycles her body knows?' (47). Marlatt not only 'resists the sentence because she suspects its orders (as she suspects capitalist orders, its sentences, its capitals)' (Cooley, 68), she also resists the demand for continuity on the level of plot. In interviews, she has reflected on the nature of the plot: 'It's imperial in a way. It's the one line of development that is considered the most important, and it makes everything else secondary' (interview, 'On *Ana*,' 105). Furthermore, a plot, whether it is comic or tragic, demands a climax, demands a hero, and demands a specific conclusion; if it is a tragedy it ends in death; if it is a comedy, in marriage. As Marlatt states, historically, marriage and death 'have been the only two alternatives for women protagonists of novels' ('On *Ana*,' 105).

Within *Ana Historic*, novelistic conventions are consistently subverted. For one thing, the text, woven from a patchwork of official and unofficial discourses, breaks up the continuity of the plot. As noted above, it includes splices of archival material, excerpts from the *Tickler*, the official and unofficial writing which Annie composes about Mrs Richards, and the imaginary conversations between Annie and Ina. At one point, the reader encounters the following statement floating on the page: 'a book of interruptions is not a novel' (37). This comment self-reflexively foregrounds the impact of these interruptions on the traditional form of the novel. Secondly, Annie's unofficial writing subverts continuity on the level of the sentence. Retaining the shape of musings, her writings are typically presented as sentence fragments with no initial punctuation.

At first, Annie does not know what to make of the text she has created. Positioned within a patriarchal framework of reference and address, she imagines her husband's dismissive response to her work: 'this doesn't go anywhere, you're just circling around the same idea – and all these bits and pieces thrown in – that's not how to use quotations. ... but this is nothing' (81). In the feminist context of her relationship with Zoe, however, Annie learns that what has been described as nothing – the zero – is simply what remains unreadable within the phallocentric system of representation. Whereas, as Marlatt asserts, the 'cultural symbology for women centred on a hole, an absence, a zero, that background other against which the male subject takes form & definition' ('writing' 66), within a feminist frame of reference and address, the zero of phallocentric system becomes 'Zoe.'

Earlier, I noted that the Milan feminists suggested that the construction of a 'female genealogy' hinged on the concept of 'entrustment.' In *Ana Historic*, Annie's construction of a female genealogy is made possible because the text's frame of reference shifts from a patriarchal perspective to a woman-centred perspective (see Marlatt, 'Changing,' 129). This shift takes place gradually as Annie forms a relationship of 'entrustment' with Zoe. Before she even meets Zoe at the archives, Annie admits that she is 'looking for the company of another who was also reading' (45). In the absence of a like-minded reader, Annie imagined Richard reading and criticizing her novel. After they make contact, however, Zoe quickly becomes Annie's 'first' and 'ongoing reader' (132). Shifting her frame of reference from her official professorial and patriarchal spouse, Annie begins to address her questions to Zoe, trusting her to influence the novel's direction. It is Zoe who encourages Annie to abandon history's voice, 'the language of definition, of epoch and document, language explaining and justifying,' in favour of writing the 'words that flow out from within. ... the words of an interior history doesn't include ...' (90). It is Zoe who suggests to Annie that women 'read with a different eye' (107). As a result of Zoe's influence, Annie addresses her novel to women: 'she who is you / or me' (129). According to Marlatt, 'we don't really have a word for this relationship – guide, path-breaker rather than competitor, a witness for women's lives – and the reciprocity of this' ('Changing,' 129). To borrow the words about the Milan group, she chooses to write within a frame of reference 'no longer patriarchal or male-designed' (de Lauretis, 'Essence,' 23). In this way, Marlatt portrays an exchange which, to a great extent, operates outside of male discourses.

The etymology of the word 'zoe' is significant. According to Lewis Hyde, the Greeks distinguished two terms for life: *bios* and *zoe*. Bios is 'limited life, characterized life, life that dies. *Zoe* is the life that endures; it is the thread that runs through *bios*-life and is not broken when the particular perishes' (Hyde, 32). In interviews, Marlatt insists that her goal as a writer is to articulate what Hyde terms '*zoe*-life': to 'sound how everything is related and to reconstruct, in the face of these horrible separations and dichotomizations, the web, the network, the continual flux, the flowing, from one aspect to another aspect' (interview, 'Speaking,' 27).

This sense of flowing from aspect to aspect is also present in the interweaving of the lives of three women whose names, Annie, Ina, Ana, indicate the extent to which they overlap:

Ana / Ina
whose story is this?

(the difference of a single letter)
(the sharing of a not)   (67)

Annie self-consciously admits both to this blurring of identity (lack of a heroic subject) and to the lack of a heroic plot; like Thomas, Marlatt works to deconstruct the narrative of romance. Unlike her mother, who stayed married and tried to paint over the 'cracks in the whole setup' (26), Annie exposes the gaps in the plot, the way that the plot works to efface women. Refusing to 'pull [her]self together' (17) and present herself as a unified subject, Annie composes a novel without a hero: 'this is not a roman/ce, it doesn't deal with heroes' (67). As she says, 'far from leading my own life or my life leading anywhere (goodbye, hero), i feel myself in you [Ina], irritated at the edges where we overlap' (17). One critic commented on the 'problem' of the sliding point of view, the shifts between 'I' and 'you'; Marlatt responded by saying, 'Oh, that 'you' shifts around quite a lot, because sometimes it's 'you,' Mrs Richards, a lot of the time it's 'you,' Ina – and sometimes it's 'you' reflexive, anywoman's you' (see interview, 'On Ana,' 100).

The insistence between the unheroic 'overlap' between Annie, Ina, and Ana (not to mention Marlatt and Annie) not only reflects a desire to subvert traditional narrative conventions, but also indicates that the process of individuation for women may be radically different from that for men. As Marlatt states, the novel's framework takes in the whole generational system of individuation, which is how 'we come to personhood anyway': '[I]t takes a long time. ... [A]nyone who looks at any Freudian analysis of the family understands that it's much harder for women to individuate as daughters from their mothers than it is for sons. ... [S]ometimes it takes a whole lifetime' (interview, 'On Ana,' 101). Her statements draw on the work of Nancy Chodorow, whose studies suggest that men's and women's processes of individuation take radically different paths. Chodorow argues that the 'basic feminine sense of self is connected to the world, the basic masculine sense of self is separate' (169). This state of affairs arises because daughters tend to remain in a much longer pre-Oedipal symbiotic relationship with the mother than do sons. As a result of their prolonged identification with their mothers, women have less rigid ego boundaries. Girls come to experience themselves as 'less differentiated than boys, as more continuous with and related to the external object-world' (166–7). Whereas a boy has 'engaged, and been required to engage, in a more emphatic individuation and a more defensive firming of experienced ego boundaries,' girls see the world not as separations and hierarchies, but as a network (167).[18]

Marlatt's interest in investigating female individuation has led her to explore an area of experience which, as she notes, 'Freud didn't manage to talk about' (see interview, 'Sounding,' 48). The repressed territory in Freud's theory constitutes the pre-Oedipal stage, which Julia Kristeva designates as the 'semiotic' in contradistinction to the 'symbolic.' Whereas the symbolic order reflects the patriarchal order, ruled by the Law of the Father, the 'semiotic' is linked to the pre-Oedipal primary processes (Moi, 161). Once the subject has entered the symbolic order, the semiotic can only be perceived within symbolic language as 'contradictions, meaninglessness, disruption, silences and absences in the symbolic language' (162). It expresses itself, not as a new language, but as 'the heterogeneous, disruptive dimension of language, that which can never be caught up in the closure of traditional linguistic theory' (162). Thus, in *Ana Historic*, the effort to break up the continuity of both the sentence and the plot, as well as the flowing connections between characters, reflects an identification with the semiotic.

Although Marlatt acknowledges that we cannot consciously gain access to the semiotic, she argues that it is, nevertheless, 'there in our unconscious, it's there in all the repressed babble, the language that just ripples and flows – and it isn't concerned with making sense' (interview, 'Sounding,' 49). In the light of the relationship between the unconscious and dreams, it is understandable why Annie, woken from her dream by her own frightened articulation of the riddle, 'Who's There?' is able to recall the woman who was once there, namely, her mother, Ina. Moreover, Annie's memory of Ina is conveyed through a series of physical sensations: 'voice that carries through all rooms, imperative, imperious. don't be silly. soft breast under blue wool dressing gown, tea breath, warm touch' (10).[19] Memory, furnishing Annie with these discontinuous, rhythmic fragments, is clearly aligned with the pre-Oedipal pulsations of the semiotic. As Marlatt argues:

[M]emory seems to operate ... like a murmur in the flesh one suddenly hears years later. There is in memory a very deep subliminal connection with the mother because what we first of all remember is this huge body, which is our first landscape and which we first of all remember bodily. ... [Memory] is concerned with the feel; the 'feel' of words has something to do with the feel of that body, of the contours of early memory. (Interview, 'Sounding,' 49).

In an earlier interview, Marlatt was asked whether she felt that the 'best thing possible would be if the words would just stop, & we could get into something more full or more real or more the world than language.' She emphatically rejected this call to some essential ground, insisting that language is 'both a personal-making sense & an inheritance of all the other senses that have been made of 'reality,' 'history,' 'life and death' (interview, 'Given,' 59). Language is 'thought in action. You cant really think outside of words. You get senses of things, but you cant really think outside of words' ('Given,' 83). Marlatt's response suggests that she agrees that the mother/child dyad of the semiotic realm *must* give way to the triad, a shift which, as Toril Moi notes, necessarily involves loss:

When the child learns to say 'I am' and to distinguish this from 'you are' or 'he is', this is equivalent to admitting that it has taken its allotted place in the Symbolic Order and given up the claim to imaginary identity with all other possible positions. The speaking subject that says 'I am' is in fact saying 'I am he (she) who has lost something' – and the loss suffered is the loss of the imaginary identity with the mother and with the world.   (Moi, 99)

In *Salvage,* Marlatt describes the particular impact this shift has on the female child:

for the Word is His she will write as I distinct from mother-mine-o-lode, turning away in the script that writes her out of the reciprocal and into what she will become when narrative begins its triple beat about, about her/accusative.
this is all about framing.   (47; my emphasis)

Recalling the riddle posed at the beginning of the novel – 'Who's There? ... knock knock' – we can see that it too is 'all about framing.' By asking 'who's there,' the riddle simultaneously demands an answer to the questions 'Who do I desire?' and 'Who is my enemy?' and it also invites us to scrutinizes the 'frame' of the symbolic that we, as speakers, must negotiate: 'the unacknowledged door all of it got said through' (*Salvage*, 71). It is the configuration of this door – the way it precludes female self-definition, the female body, and female desire – which generates women's particularly debilitating experience of loss.[20]

Within the novel, after recalling the pre-Oedipal, rhythmic sensations of her mother's body, Annie concludes her reminiscences with the word 'gone' (10). Her mother's name, Ina, is literally broken open, just as the mother/child dyad is broken apart by the Law of the Father: 'I-na, I-no-longer' (11). However, as noted above, Ina's death is located on a continuum, which ranges from the covert effacement of the female to the more openly aggressive practice of electric shock therapy. Ina, who could 'outtalk, outname, outargue' her daughter any time, was erased systematically over time (20).[21] Following Ina's final disappearance – her death – it is up to Annie to represent her. As Gilbert and Gubar suggest, she must reach 'toward the woman trapped on the other side of the mirror/text and help her to climb out' (16). Annie echoes these words when, referring to Ina, she says, 'it's up to me to pull you through. this crumbling apart of words. ... you who is you or me. she. a part struck off from me. apart. separated' (11).[22]

Through Annie's efforts, a host of 'Lost Girls' are rendered visible on the other, historical side of the frame. It is not merely Mrs Richards and Ina who are lost, but Annie herself, as a result of her sexual conditioning, also becomes a 'she' (accorded third-person object-status rather than first-person status) who can only recall a time 'when i was she who did not feel separated or split' (11). If Annie's genealogical map is accurate in its depiction of the pain associated with the 'framing' of the symbolic order and its effacement of women, then one is led to ask why more women have not challenged its claim to Truth.

One reason may be that a revolt against the regime will be understood as madness. As many feminists have noted, in an effort to protect its vulnerable margins, the symbolic order casts anyone who refuses to submit to its sexual conditioning as a monster.[23] Once again, Marlatt's term 'terri-stories' proves extremely apt because it underscores that the paternal genealogy, whether it is articulated through literary or historical materials, serves to name and claim, as well as *terrify*. In this way, women are discouraged from enquiring too deeply into the nature of their self-definition, their bodies, and their desires. Even Annie experiences the frightening and uncanny sensation associated with a return of the repressed, when she poses the question 'Who's There?' and begins her journey into the 'dark spaces' of the unthought.

Right from the start, the reader is alerted that something fearful, something uncanny, is at work in the text. The words of the perverted riddle, 'Who's There? ... knock knock,' immediately introduce anxiety because they remind Annie of the time when she was a child left to babysit her younger sisters. Frightened of noises in the house, she would steal into the basement clutching a carving knife. First, she had to make her way down the staircase 'with its star scrawled on the yellow wall and COMRADE, an illicit word never heard upstairs' (9). Nobody seemed to see this word except her, 'like some signal blinking every time she had to go downstairs with the knife' (9). It is understandable that, in the 'cold-war Vancouver of the Fifties,' the word 'comrade' would have ominous overtones, conjuring up images from Major Hoople's talk 'about those sleazy reds who were always infiltrating from some foreign underworld and threatening to get under or was it into the bed' (9). Yet, when the word surfaces again, it is used to refer to the narrator's experience as a child, when, together with her 'sister-archers, her *camarades*,' they faced the task of defending their territory in the woods from others: 'what if the boys ... what if the men tried to bulldoze their woods? so what could we do?' (12). The word 'comrade' is defined as a 'mate or fellow in work or play or fighting, an equal with whom one is on familiar terms' (*OED*). This word may seem illicit to Annie because it offers the threat and promise of equality, which, for a woman who is supposed to be positioned as subordinate, is taboo. As the text unfolds, the reader understands that it is not communists, but *women*, who are infiltrating from some foreign world (writing from the margins), and threatening to get into the bed. At the end of the novel (which is not an ending in any traditional sense), this repressed possibility for equality is realized in the lesbian relationship, the 'cama-raderie,' between Zoe and Annie.

But even more uncanny than the word 'comrade' is the fear Annie experiences in the basement when she faces the intruder that she knows is hiding in the ward-robes: 'she stood in front of the darkest of the six-foot wardrobes, teak, too big to place upstairs, big enough to hide Frankenstein, stood feeling her fear, her desperate being up against it, that other breathing on the other side of the door she could almost hear' (10). Here, the door of the wardrobe functions as a metaphor for the frame of the symbolic. This becomes clear later on when the term 'wardrobe' is associated in Annie's imagination with 'whole wardrobes of names guarding the limitations' (152). Her treatment of the word 'wardrobe' emphasizes that the sym-bolic frame 'wards' or 'guards' against something, and that words themselves cover up the expression of alternative possibilities. In C.S. Lewis's marvellous tales enti-tled *The Chronicles of Narnia*, there is a wardrobe that leads to a magical world, the kingdom of Narnia. In *Ana Historic*, the wardrobe also operates as a door into an alternative order. This sense of possibility is reiterated in Marlatt's latest work, *Salvage*, where a poem begins, 'There is a door other than that which opens to the known world' (26). Of course, the image of the wardrobe and the anxiety associated with it also play on the fears surrounding 'coming out of the closet' as a lesbian.

When she enters into her relationship with Zoe, Annie discovers that the story about the monster lurking behind the door, the story of Frankenstein, is just a 'cover'-story. As she explains to Ina, the name Frankenstein is a *man's* name (Dr Frankenstein) *given to* the monster and now 'we call the monster by his name' (142). This anecdote concerning the naming of the monster operates as a parable for the position of women within the phallocentric representational system. Like Franken-stein's monster, women are defined by words such as 'vagina,' words that 'cover' their own experience. As Shoshana Felman puts it, women are the victims of a 'blind substitution of the masculine for the feminine,' which effaces femininity's poten-tially radical otherness (27). It is particularly significant that Annie's childhood anxiety surfaces in the familial home. The illicit word 'comrade' scrawled on the wall and the wardrobe big enough to conceal a monster are located in the base-ment. The location of these sinister elements leads one to suspect that the home is not safe or, more precisely, the familial triad of mommy, daddy, and me – the basis of the symbolic order – is threatened. As Marlatt acknowledges in *Salvage*, 'there's always some stranger knocking at the family door' (71). Within the novel, the anxiety produced by this threat to the family is related to a particular class of the frightening known as the 'uncanny.'

Challenging the assertion that the uncanny is generated by what is novel and unfamiliar, Freud argues that the uncanny (*unheimlich*) belongs to that class of the frightening which leads back to what is 'known of old and long familiar' ('Uncanny,' 220). To prove that something can be both familiar and unfamiliar, he traces the etymology of the German word *heimlich* (homely). The definition of this term reads: 'From the idea of "*homelike*", "belonging to the house", the further idea is developed of something withdrawn from the eyes of strangers, something concealed, secret' (225). In this way, *heimlich* comes to encompass its antithesis, *unheimlich* (uncanny). Freud also cites Schelling's account of the uncanny: the name for '*everything that ought to have remained ... secret and hidden but has come to light*' (224). Aligning the anxiety generated by the uncanny with his psychoanalytic theory of repression, Freud argues:

[I]f psycho-analytic theory is correct in maintaining that every affect belonging to an emotional impulse, whatever its kind, is transformed, if it is repressed, into anxiety, then among instances of frightening things there must be one class in which the frightening element can be shown to be something repressed which *recurs*. (241)

Freud goes on to suggest that the uncanny is in reality nothing new or alien, but 'something which is familiar and old-established in the mind and which has become alienated from it only through the process of repression' (241). This hypothesis allows him to establish a link between the uncanny and female genitalia:

It often happens that neurotic men declare that they feel there is something uncanny about the female genital organs. This *unheimlich* place, however, is the entrance to the former *Heim* [home] of all human beings, to the place where each one of us lived once upon a time and in the beginning. ... In this case too, then, the *unheimlich* is what was once *heimish*, familiar; the prefix '*un*' is the token of repression. (245)

Yet, if we accept Chodorow's assertion that men and women have different processes of individuation, then what is uncanny for men in Western society will not necessarily be uncanny for women. As Chodorow says, 'girls do not define themselves in terms of the denial of preoedipal relational modes to the same extent as do boys. Therefore, regression to these modes tends not to feel as much a basic threat to their ego' (167). Freud ought to have emphasized more strongly that the female genitals are uncanny, not for 'all human beings,' but primarily for *men* because they connote what the *masculine* subject must repress, if he is to take up his position in society – a position that is characterized by separation, rather than merging. Whereas men fear the removal of their power, signified by the phallus, and 'ward' against merging, which the sight of the female genitals arouses, women may well fear, not doubleness and merging, but the very mechanism that refused them power in the first place – the 'wardrobe'/wordrobe of the symbolic system, which positions the feminine so that it 'comes to stand over the point of disappearance, the loss' (Mitchell, 307).

Given Marlatt's aim to subvert the symbolic frame that guarantees masculine privilege, it is not surprising that, in *Ana Historic*, there is a concerted effort to move toward what Freud has characterized as 'uncanny.' In his study of this subject, Freud lists several prominent 'themes of uncanniness,' and each one is present in Marlatt's text. The first 'theme' relates to the 'doubling, dividing and interchanging of the self' (234). As noted above, Marlatt's sliding point of view deliberately dissolves any sense of a unified subject. The text seems to celebrate 'doubling,' and to suggest that the acknowledgment of a multiple and relational ego is an important part of women's recovery of their experience, which as Chodorow argues, involves remaining 'part of the dyadic primary mother-child relationship' (166).

A second theme of uncanniness, which Freud locates, involves the 'constant recurrence of the same thing – the repetition of the same features or character-traits or vicissitudes, of the same crimes, or even the same names through several consecutive generations' (234). In her role as genealogist, Annie discovers repeated character-traits in herself, in Ina, and in Ana. All three women (and even Annie's daughter, Ange) share related experiences, which are based on what Annie describes as 'the development of women's alienation from their bodies, suppressed hysteria' (133). This issue of hysteria can also be linked to another theme listed as uncanny. In his 1906 study of the uncanny, E. Jentsch suggests that manifestations of insanity were thought to be uncanny because they excited in the spectator 'the impression of automatic, mechanical processes at work behind the ordinary appearance of mental activity' (qtd. in Freud, 'Uncanny,' 226). In Marlatt's novel, the uncanniness Jentsche associates with madness or hysteria is subtly linked to instances of uncanniness, which, in accordance with Freud's suggestion, surface in conjunction with the repetition 'of the same crimes.'

Ina's madness, her hysteria, can be said to expose the 'mechanical processes at work behind the ordinary appearance of mental activity.' Here, as suggested earlier, the automatic, mechanical processes reflect the operations of power. While composing her novel, Annie traces a connection between Ana's fate at the hands of historians and Ina's fate at the hands of the psychiatric institution, and she forges a link between hysteria and history. She coins the term 'hystery' to characterize the relationship between these two violent mechanisms of the symbolic system, which promote the 'excision of women' (88). It is this mechanism, active in the scientific and historical discourses over generations, that generates the uncanny sense of the repetition 'of the same crimes.'

At the heart of the novel, the question 'Who's There?' is repeated in Annie's rhetorical address to Ina: 'who was it who cut your fingers, burned your skin, kept you insomniac and cursing all the neighbours' dogs? either that or gone in a morning-after fog of sleeping pills. knock, knock. who's there?' (88). In an earlier imaginary conversation, Ina demands to know whether Annie sees *her* as the monster hidden at the heart of the female 'cultural labyrinth.' After she contemplates her mother's suffering, Annie realizes that Ina is not the monster, although 'there is something monstrous here' (24). Eventually, Annie locates the monster, and answers the riddle in so far as she solves the question: 'Who is my enemy?'

The 'answer' that Annie eventually arrives at takes the form of an excerpt describing the brutal domination of women's bodies performed in the name of science:

Mechanical devices were invented for compressing ovaries or for packing them in ice. In Germany, Hegar (1830–1914) and Friederich (1825–82) were using even more radical methods, including ovarectomy and cauterization of the clitoris. The source of hysteria was still, as in Plato's time, sought in the matrix of the female body, upon which surgical attacks were unleashed. (89)

Thus, in Marlatt's text, the uncanny is ultimately *not* linked to the sight of the female genitalia, as Freud would have it, but to the brutal control of women's bodies. The monster Annie has always feared as real turns out to be the 'violence behind the kiss, the brutal hand beneath the surgical glove, the one who punishes you for seeing (through) him' (135). Furthermore, this brutality is uncanny (both familiar and unfamiliar) because, as the location of the wardrobe and the illicit word 'comrade' intimate, it occurs within the *familial* institution, where it is rendered invisible.

The family's role in subjugating women's bodies is revealed when Annie recalls the lyrics of the playful song, the 'hokey pokey':

you put your whole self in
you take your whole self out
you put your whole self in
and you shake it all about   (148)

The words to the song are juxtaposed with the recollection of Ina's electric shock therapy. In this context, the last line: 'and you shake it all about,' attains a sickening resonance. The hokey pokey is for the family, 'the magic circle we stepped inside of ... the family that holds together at the expense of one' (148). As Chodorow argues: 'What is ... often hidden, in generalizations about the family as an emotional refuge, is that in the family as it is currently constituted no one supports and reconstitutes women affectively and emotionally' (36). Through her genealogical analysis, Annie exposes the uncanny plot, the hidden mechanism at work within the family, which effaces women in order to clear a path for its male heroes.

The final theme of uncanniness that Freud isolates concerns 'all the unfulfilled but possible futures to which we still like to cling in phantasy, all the strivings of the ego which adverse external circumstances have crushed' (236). Whereas these 'possible futures' must remain repressed within the masculine paradigm, women are in a different position *vis-à-vis* the repressed. As Freud's association between the uncanny and female genitalia clarifies, women *are* the repressed; thus, they have nothing to gain from remaining complicit with the cover-stories, which, for them, are the kiss of death.[24] As we will see in the chapter on Urquhart's novel, women's slightly different position regarding the repressed also helps to explain why the female (and not the male) characters prove able to abandon traditional narrative structures. In *Ana Historic*, Annie decides to make what she describes as a 'monstrous leap of imagination' (135). Rather than reinscribe the historical version of Ana's life, which states only that she bought a piano and married Ben Springer, Annie rejects the 'diminishing glance' of history and refuses to close 'the lid [of the coffin?] ... firmly and finally' (48). As she contemplates Ana's pen poised above the words 'Today I have accepted,' Annie chooses not to allow Ana to marry Ben Springer and erase 'all the other selves she might be' (146). Unlike Ina, Annie profits from the gaps in the story, refusing to believe that one cannot change 'the writing on the wall' (142) or that fate – a woman's lot, 'too small for ... one mad Englishwoman' (79) – is irrevocable.

To appreciate the impact of Annie's decision, it is helpful to compare her choice with the decision made by the narrator of Alice Munro's short story 'Meneseteung.' Like Annie, Munro's narrator also shapes a story based on textual scraps from the past; just as Annie draws her material from the *Tickler*, Munro's narrator also fashions her character from hints provided by a similar small-town chronicle called the *Vidette*. Initially, Munro's narrator offers a factual summary of the life of the Victorian poet Amanda Roth. But the story soon shifts toward invention, as she goes on to create full-blown scenes depicting her heroine's life. Rather than portray Amanda encouraging her suitor and allowing her beloved countryside to be 'removed for her – filmed over ... by his talk and preoccupations,' the narrator describes Amanda choosing in favour of maintaining her own vision (61). She ultimately scripts a conclusion which portrays her heroine opting not to marry the local bachelor, Jarvis Poulter. The morning that she promises to go to church with Jarvis, Amanda abruptly changes her mind, retreats into her house, bolts the door, and sips her laudanum-spiked tea. In an opium-induced trance, she decides that so much is 'going on in this room ... there is no need to leave it' (69). Ironically, although the narrator rescues Amanda from marriage, she merely rejects one of the three options of the familiar script – a script that typically consigns female characters to marriage, madness, or death. Citing the *Vidette*, the narrator reports that Amanda succumbed to madness: as she grew older, her mind became *'somewhat clouded and her behaviour, in consequence, somewhat rash and unusual'* (71). In the end, the narrator confesses both to her inability to change the plot and to the fictiveness of her own rather tame invention. As she says, 'I may have got it wrong. I don't know if she ever took laudanum. Many ladies did. I don't know if she ever made grape jelly' (73). In comparison to her tentative adjustments to the story of Amanda's life (which are limited to filling in the gaps, but not substantially altering the pre-given plot), Annie's rewriting of the story of Ana's life appears scandalous.

In Marlatt's text, both Annie and Ana choose 'to fly in the face of common sense, social convention, ethics – the weight of history. to fly' (146). In taking flight, Annie invents for Ana a life which contains the possibility of becoming Birdie Stewart's 'secret friend' (108) and 'travelling companion' (146). Birdie Stewart, Vancouver's first madam, is mentioned in the archives. Her arrival coincides with that of Mrs Richards.[25]

Imagining Ana visiting Birdie in her sitting room, Annie envisions a scene in which Birdie's emerald green, bead-fringed lampshade functions as a metaphor for desire. Referring to the *fake* emerald beads, Birdie tells Ana, 'now this, you see, is the green that says yes, like certain eyes' (109). The reference to emeralds recalls Ina's earlier impoverished gesture – her promise to pass down the 'family jewels' to her daughter. In contrast to this female inheritance which would continue to position women as objects, Birdie's statement insists on the possibility of a female *subject* taking action; the eyes she imagines are not passive objects luring male desire, but eyes that say 'yes' to their own, very different desire. In the scene which Annie narrates, Ana catches sight of her own reflection in Birdie's eyes:

turning because of a spark, a gleam, your eyes are green (you had forgotten that) and you know them lit with the look of something you almost meet in Birdie's brown. you had not imagined – this

as history. unwritten. (109)

Ana's lesbian relationship with Birdie is uncanny – *for women* – in so far as it is both familiar and unfamiliar; as the reference to emeralds implies, it recalls the relationship with the mother which has been repressed. As Susan Griffen states: 'What is really feared is an open door into a consciousness which leads us back to the old, ancient, infant and mother knowledge of the body, in whose depths lies another form of culture not opposed to nature but instead expressing the full power of nature and of our nature' ('Way,' 645). The positive outcome of this desire, a lesbian relationship, challenges Freud's characterization of the final theme of uncanniness as 'all the unfulfilled but possible futures ... which adverse external circumstances have crushed' because the lesbian possibility has not been 'crushed.'

As noted above, Annie's question 'Who's there?' led her to consider her mother in the context of the question 'Who is my enemy?' When she poses the riddle for the last time, she answers the question: 'Who do I desire?' Throwing off the cover stories of Ina and Ana (who, because they overlap with Annie's identity, actually reflect parts of herself), Annie faces Zoe and the possibility of entering into a lesbian relationship which offers the prospect of reclaiming that part of herself that was struck off:

i want to knock: can you hear? i want to answer her who's there? not Ana or Ina, those transparent covers. Ana Richards Richard's Anna. fooling myself on the other side of history as if it were a line dividing the real from the unreal. Annie/Ana – arose by any other name, whole wardrobes of names guarding the limitations – we rise above them. Annie isn't Richard's or even Springer's. (152)

Ignoring the 'terri-stories,' dismissing the 'wardrobes of names,' the divisive frames of the symbolic, Annie renames herself 'Annie Torrent' in honour of the torrential desire women have always experienced but were never permitted to express (35). Her act of renaming disrupts the paternal genealogy with its implicit stipulation that women cannot speak and cannot write. Annie Torrent does speak, and, naming her desire, she tells Zoe, 'i want you. *and* me. together' (152). Thus, the monster, that other breathing behind the wardrobe, the thing that should have remained 'secret and hidden,' finally comes to light and it is terribly familiar, for what could be more familiar than oneself? As Annie says, 'it isn't even Frankenstein but a nameless part i know' (152). Elsewhere, Marlatt underscores the uncanniness of this type of relationship, noting that it is characterized by a feeling of 'familiarity and surprise' ('Changing,' 131). Annie's final act of self-naming confirms Elizabeth Grosz's assertion that the reason why the body is so rigorously controlled is because it possesses this capacity to be 'self-marked, self-represented' in alternative ways.

Some readers may be suspicious of the novel's tidy ending – an ending that could be said to promote a solipsistic view of human interaction because it seems to in-dulge in the narcissistic fantasy that other people are merely repressed facets of oneself. If taken seriously, this view could be used to defend the idea that one need not treat other people as individuals, whose differences must be addressed, because they are all, on some level, merely familiar reflections of one's own psyche. This perspective surfaces in Robertson Davies' novel *Fifth Business*, and it is worth comparing the attitudes regarding identity expressed in both Marlatt's and Davies' novels.

In *Fifth Business*, the hero, Dunstable Ramsay, embarks on a journey through life, only to discover that virtually everyone he meets constitutes an archetypal facet of his own personality. A believer in Jung's theory of archetypes, Ramsay discovers in his friends and enemies the eternal essence of his own 'shadow' and 'anima.' On a fundamental level, it does not matter who these people believe themselves to be because Ramsay remains convinced that the goal of his spiritual quest lies in discovering who they are within his personal psychodrama. When, as an adult, he becomes increasingly obsessed with a woman named Mrs Dempster, his spiritual mentor – a Jungian wise old man, if ever there was one – tells him to turn his mind 'to the real problem; who is she?' He goes on to clarify his notion of identity: 'Oh, I don't mean her police identification or what her name was before she was married. I mean, who is she in your personal world? What figure is she in your personal mythology?' (177). I would suggest that this view of identity represents a familiar retreat from the complexity of modern society: it functions as a defence – one used by a number of well-known modernist writers – against the fragmentation of the discourses which previously secured notions of Truth and meaning. Although the Truth can no longer be found 'out there' in the world, the method of classifying people according to archetypes ensures that wholeness and order can be located in a transcendent realm of unchanging aesthetic ideals: the mind becomes a warehouse of archetypes that houses, among other things, the Eternal Feminine. In *Fifth Business*, it becomes evident that, in the face of ever-shifting narratives (some of which threaten to represent the hero's insignificance), Truth cannot be definitively located, and Ramsay seeks solace in an aesthetic ideal that purports to guarantee spiritual truth. The text underscores the aesthetic nature of this ideal when Ramsay realizes that he confused Mrs Dempster with an image of the Holy Mother. Only after he discovers that it is the face of the Madonna who haunts his dreams in a cathedral in Salzburg does he abandon his obsession with Mrs Dempster. After he seizes on the aesthetic ideal, he no longer needs to control and possess the flesh-and-blood woman, and his yearning for the woman gives way to a longing for the artistic image. In the light of the fact that, as a disciple of Jung, Ramsay believes the image reflects his own anima, it makes sense that he would assert his ownership over Mrs Dempster and, later, over the image of the Madonna. In the case of Mrs Dempster, he insists that she would be his saint – and his alone (160). Similarly, when he gazes at the Madonna in the cathedral, he boasts, 'She was mine forever' (251).

Whereas Davies' novel portrays a world populated by unchanging archetypes – a view which springs from a fundamentally essentialist perspective – Marlatt portrays quite a different world. She does not so much look to some essential core as *invent* a new set of possibilities for human interaction. Along these same lines, I would suggest that, although her text foregrounds the interconnectedness among women, it does not base this connection on a fixed idea of the Eternal Feminine essence. Instead, as we have seen, her text explores a wide range of culturally and historically mediated discourses that engender women in a particular fashion and, in doing so, creates a subculture whose members are linked by 'a delicate network of influences operating in time' (Showalter, *Literature*, 12). As I suggested earlier in this chapter, rather than posit a 'real essence,' Marlatt gestures toward a 'nominal essence,' which, as de Lauretis asserts, does not reflect an unchanging kernel of identity – a 'real essence' ('Essence,' 5). In the light of the comparison with Davies' text, it becomes even more apparent that, whereas Davies relies on a fixed psychoanalytic model, Marlatt engages in a project of invention. To borrow de Lauretis's words: 'This may be utopian, idealist, perhaps misguided or wishful thinking ... but it is not essentialist as the belief in a God-given or otherwise immutable nature of woman' ('Essence,' 5).

This study began as an attempt to discover to what extent contemporary Canadian women writers were heeding Virginia Woolf's claim that, because of the shadow of the male 'I,' it is difficult for women to represent themselves in the literary terrain. More than any other writer examined thus far, Marlatt seems to be have taken Virginia Woolf's assertions to heart. Operating within the framework of a feminist practice of reference and address (under lesbian eyes), *Ana Historic* suggests that we can 'salvage' the linguistic terrain by mapping an alternative, ancestral trajectory, a genealogy for 'lost women,' which departs from the 'solid ground of fact' (111). Paradoxically, the territory which Annie charts for Ina – 'the bush[26] ... what you were afraid of, what i escaped to: anonymous territory' (18) – is not so much a place as a process which opens up the frame to make room for the possibility of representing female desire.

5

Abandoning the Map: From Cartography to Nomadology – the Fictions of Aritha van Herk

[T]he outsider will say, 'in fact, as a woman, I have no country. As a woman I want no country. As a woman my country is the whole world' (Woolf, *Three Guineas*, 125)

In the conclusion of the previous chapter, I noted that Annie informs her mother, Ina, that she has escaped to 'anonymous territory' (18), and that this 'territory,' which is, paradoxically, not so much a place as a process, allows for the representation of female desire beyond the frame delineated by traditional masculine discourses. In this chapter, I will focus on Aritha van Herk's treatment of a similar motif involving escape to unmapped territory. As it turns out, in conjunction with the images of mapping and exploration, the image of a journey into unknown territory constitutes a common thread linking the texts studied here. In *Intertidal Life*, following the breakup of her marriage, the narrator likens herself to a maritime voyager, and urges other women to emulate the explorers and mappers of the North Pacific in their attempts to move beyond traditional female roles and to 'fix our new positions' (171). Similarly, the protagonist in Swan's *The Biggest Modern Woman of the World* leaves Canada and embarks on a journey (reminiscent of the travels of the hero in *Gulliver's Travels*) to find out whether there is a place that can accommodate a giantess, a Victorian lady who 'refused to be inconsequential' (2). Finally, Marlatt's *Ana Historic* portrays Annie's quest to chart an ancestral trajectory, which affords an escape-route from patriarchal, historical narratives. In each case, the experience of travel, whether spatial or temporal, enables the characters to look at their home as a non-neutral space. In many ways, their rejection of 'home' and suspicion of the colonial and patriarchal discouses that structure their experience recall the fate of Swift's hero. After finally returning from his travels, Gulliver no longer retains his innocent view of imperial Britain. When he lands on his once-beloved isle, he retreats from his family into the stable – a retreat which symbolizes a rejection of Britain and its values.[1]

As I suggested in my introduction, the movement from chapter to chapter constitutes an account of increasingly subversive strategies for the dismantling of traditional representations of female identity; with van Herk's fictions, we encounter a gesture toward becoming imperceptible within the terms set by traditional, masculine discourses. This term, 'becoming-imperceptible,' is used in the work of Gilles Deleuze and Félix Guattari to draw a relation between 'the (anorganic) imperceptible, the (asignifying) indiscernible, and the (asubjective) impersonal' (279). In van Herk's writings, the notion of imperceptibility or invisibility specifically relates to women's refusal of traditional forms of representation – a refusal which, as noted earlier, is problematic for many feminists.

In this chapter, I will depart from the method of examining isolated texts because, in the case of Aritha van Herk, only a broader focus will allow for an investigation of her consistent reliance upon the figures of mapping and exploration, and the development of a complex, politically charged response to traditional representations of female identity in her writing. Works such as *Judith* (1978), *The Tent Peg* (1981), and *No Fixed Address* (1986) draw together many of the concerns raised in the fictions examined thus far. For example, texts such as *Judith* and *The Tent Peg*, like *Intertidal Life*, problematize women's status as monstrous or demonic obstacles within traditional narratives; second, like *The Biggest Modern Woman of the World*, all of van Herk's texts portray the cramped existence allotted to women within the dominant discourses; finally, in keeping with all of the works examined in previous chapters, van Herk's fictions explore tactics of subversion that enable women to escape their representation as Woman.

Although these texts continue to rely on the topos of the map, as I suggested earlier, this alone does not prove that they are replicating the ideologies of traditional narratives. In the case of van Herk's fiction, as we shall see, the texts engage in a feminist, subversive appropriation of the motifs of mapping and exploration to effect the deterritorialization of maps plotted by established, patriarchal discourses. While van Herk's texts stress the importance of mapping, they portray a procedure not predicated on the impulse toward mastery; they work to displace representations which claim to offer the eternal and universal Truth. In her fictions, the act of mapping is recoded, transforming it into a feminist process. In particular, *No Fixed Address* and *Places Far from Ellesmere* (1990) employ traditional figures of mapping and exploration to foreground a relationship between map-making and fiction-making that radically undermines both practices.

Of all the writers examined thus far, van Herk remains the most committed to a direct and literal focus on the figures of mapping and exploration. In her essay 'Mapping as Metaphor,' she confirms that the desire to map is a characteristically Canadian impulse. She argues that inhabitants of this country are driven to create maps because of the country's astounding size. As she says, Canada possesses the longest coastline of any nation in the world, and the 'sheer immensity of the country helps us to understand immediately the importance of measuring and charting, of imposing some kind of order on this overwhelming space. Mapping is necessary' (75). According to van Herk, two other factors also predispose Canadians to draw on images of mapping. First, as noted in the introductory chapter, Canada is young enough to have 'almost perfect records of our own charting'; and second, because we are a relatively new country, we are still engaged in the attempt to plot its outlines. Mapping remains 'both an on-going process and a metaphor for our particularity' (75).[2]

In this same essay, van Herk suggests that the impulse to map the physical landscape merges with the fiction writer's goal, in that both the cartographer and the fiction writer have the intention of making 'a place real in some representative way' ('Mapping,' 75). She emphasizes that cartographers never offer some objective and scientifically truthful portrait of the landscape. Instead, like fiction writers, they create imaginative representations:

As long as humans have tried to plot the landscape around them, they have repeatedly diagrammed not only the world they saw, but their own vision and interpretation of that world. What results is a map – not a tracing of shape but a means of shaping. The explorers and colonists did not passively record; they imposed their map on place regardless of whether or not the grid they chose was always appropriate. Clearly mapping, like language, is creation more than representation, and so it is not illogical to think of fiction writers as cartographers.   ('Mapping,' 77)

While she aligns writers with cartographers, van Herk – as a postcolonial, feminist author – nevertheless rejects the supposedly mimetic, inflexible grid that was imposed by the colonists and explorers.

In her writings, van Herk repeatedly underscores the necessity of generating fictional maps; yet she remains aware of the obstacles and dangers that confront the writer engaged in this process of creating maps. In a playful essay entitled 'Stranded Bestride in Canada,' she argues that western writers encounter problems fashioning fictional maps because they are ideologically divided. Their division stems from the fact that western Canadians like herself have had a rural background, but find themselves inhabiting a metropolis (11). The narrator of George Bowering's novel *Caprice* describes this same difficulty. He observes that by 'the 1890s the west started to shrink,' and, as the actual landscape became urbanized, the idea of the untamed west ended up becoming 'a style in eastern theatres' (109). Owing to the shift from rural to urban lifestyles, westerners with rural backgrounds find themselves disoriented because they cannot, in the manner that Jameson and Kevin Lynch have outlined, create cognitive maps to assist them in locating themselves in the urban landscape. Van Herk suggests that city-dwellers are doomed to confusion without fictions to facilitate orientation.[3] At one point, van Herk wonders how individuals could possibly orient themselves in a western city:

And how do you live here? Dream it, or dream something else? Feel yourself a fool because you cannot figure out which button to push when? Settle into calm acceptance, as oblique as the surfaces around you? Write a novel about it, write a novel about this city? That's it, write it into existence, then you can live here, you can recognize the place from your story. ('Stranded,' 11)[4]

Although van Herk views fiction as a possible antidote to urban alienation, she understands that the traditional fictions supplied by an earlier generation of writers cannot be relied upon by contemporary writers. For one thing, these fictions mapped a primarily rural environment, which is no longer home to western writers who inhabit the metropolis. Second, the method of perception utilized by the earlier generation of prairie writers cannot be appropriated because it was suited to their rural existence. Van Herk suggests that this rural mode of perception operates on the basis of the tangible, and that the inhabitants of rural areas perceived the world in relation to 'space and landscape and time, the inexorable time of sun and darkness' ('Stranded,' 11). How many city-dwellers continue to rely on the sun and the seasons to regulate their actions within their air-conditioned homes and glass-skinned office towers? She concludes that contemporary western writers are faced with the task of developing alternative fictions based on modes of perception that correspond to the urban environments they inhabit, where straight lines, square blocks, sheets of glass, and cubes of concrete have replaced the buffalo beans and the open sky.

In her opinion, western writers have not been successful in developing new modes of perception; nor have they been able to effect a neat division between their rural past and their metropolitan present. As van Herk explains, when she tried to write a novel about the city, she discovered that she had, in fact, described 'the place before the metropolis' ('Stranded,' 11). The resultant fiction took on the form of a palimpsest, bearing traces of the west's rural past. She sees this palimpsestic quality, which surfaces in her own work, as characteristic of western Canadian fiction in general: 'we carry our indigenous into the metropolitan, thus creating one of the unique literatures in the world' (13). Rather than view this division or hybridity as a drawback, which leaves Canadian writers stranded – 'we are nowhere and we are no one' – van Herk merrily points out that the edge is 'a fine place to write from' (13).

There are edges and then there are edges, however. As it turns out, women writers find themselves even more on the edge than their male counterparts because they are doubly displaced by traditional fictions. Van Herk does not shy away from discussing the impact that gender has on women's ability to assume the role of mapmaker:

I come from the west, kingdom of the male virgin. I live and write in the kingdom of the male virgin. To be a female and not-virgin, making stories in the kingdom of the male virgin, is dangerous. You think this kingdom is imaginary? Try being a writer there. Try being a woman there. ('Gentle,' 257)

Her message recalls Virginia Woolf's statement concerning the dangers facing women who try to map themselves onto the linguistic landscape. In *A Room of One's Own*, Woolf notes that works by male authors 'celebrate male virtues, enforce male values and describe the world of men' (97). Sixty-five years later, van Herk draws the same conclusion, but puts it more bluntly: 'The fact is, men write epic fiction: about life, about war, about what matters, including who they have screwed and whom they have killed. Sometimes, as an alternative, they write sensitive writerly novels about the male act of writing fiction' ('Double,' 276). If what matters to women differs from what matters to men, and if the former deserves to be articulated, then women writers are faced with the challenge of struggling against the belief that great literature, epic literature, is written by men.[5] Van Herk, like all of the writers examined thus far, insists on women's capacity and right to articulate their experience, their history, as opposed to epic History.

By far the greatest obstacle that women writers must negotiate when they try to get a word in edgewise is the legacy of masculine representations of the West and of Woman within western regional fiction. In *The Canadian West in Fiction*, Edward McCourt traces the development of literature in the western regions as it was depicted by its earliest chroniclers – fur traders, explorers, missionaries, mounties, and, later, travellers, journalists, and romantic novelists. As his study reveals, for the most part, the west has been seen and described from a masculine perspective. Van Herk points out that, in any list of western writers, Grove, Mitchell, Ross, Wiebe, and Kroetsch are inevitably cited; Margaret Laurence is the exception ('Women,' 15).

As far as van Herk is concerned, the western literary tradition is a thoroughly male terrain: 'the art that has defined it [the west] is masculine and it appears to have defined its art as a masculine one' ('Women,' 15). Within the traditional western fictions, women are 'fixed as mothers/saints/whores, muses all' (18). In *Caprice*, Bowering's narrator alters the terms, but offers a very similar view of women's position:

In the wild west, where men were men and life was hard, women were supposed to be one of two things – commodities or prizes. Bad women, such as those found in the dance halls and brothels, were the commodities. ... The beautiful or not necessarily all that beautiful daughters of ranch owners were the principal prizes, because they ... were likely to inherit land or stocks.

We are not here counting the wives of homesteaders, of course. They were neither commodities nor prizes. They were like anything that was likely to produce, used as devices to prepare the dream of a future.   (183)

Van Herk insists that the prairie is 'in bondage to an image' ('Women,' 17); the term 'bondage' may seem a trifle dramatic, but, when one reads the manifestos and fictions written by western male writers, the word seems appropriate enough. In his autobiography, entitled *In Search of Myself,* Frederick Philip Grove notes, in a self-evaluation made in 1912, that when he surveyed the work of the settlers on the prairies, they reaffirmed him in his belief that order 'must arise out of chaos; the wilderness must be tamed' (227). This impulse toward mastery continues to inform both the works and the criticism of male western writers. For example, Laurence Ricou, in his 1973 analysis of western fiction, isolates what he deems a prevalent image: the binary opposition between the vertical man and his horizontal world. Ricou cites an exemplary passage from Henry Kreisel's story 'The Broken Globe,' in which an old man surveys the land, to illustrate this characteristic opposition:

With a gesture of great dignity and power he lifted his arm and stood pointing into the distance, at the flat land and the low-hanging sky.
   'Look,' he said, very slowly and very quietly, 'she is flat, and she stands still.'   (Kreisel 58)

Not only is the feminized landscape portrayed as flat and still, but, as Grove's evaluation indicates, *she* is waiting to be conquered. The imagery which Grove employs and which Ricou isolates in many writers' works is, as van Herk emphasizes, undeniably masculine: 'a black line breaking up space. There is no entrance here, only imposition, juxtaposition, the hammer blow of an extrusive shape' ('Women,' 18).
   In his essay 'Passages by Land,' Rudy Wiebe offers one of the most clearly articulated examples of this impulse toward mastery over the supposedly feminine landscape:

[T]o touch this land with words requires an architectural structure; to break into the space of the reader's mind with the space of this western landscape and the people in it you must build a structure of fiction like an engineer builds a bridge or a sky-scraper over and into space. ... *You must lay great black steel lines of fiction, break up that space with huge design* and, like the fiction of the Russian steppes, build giant artifact. No song can do that; it must be giant fiction.   (259; my emphasis)

As I suggested earlier, in her own writing, van Herk champions the value of map-making, yet she wholeheartedly rejects the desire to 'fix' the prairie by imposing this type of grid, fashioned from a male perspective; and she likewise rejects the representations of women as Woman proffered by male western writers. By contrast, she remarks that the male west 'has to be earth-quaked a little, those black steel lines and the looming giant toppled. Not destroyed, oh no, but infiltrated' ('Women,' 24). In keeping with this philosophy, her increasingly experimental fictions explore alternative relationships between women and place – relationships based, not upon the capture and mastery of the landscape associated with the colonial enterprise, but upon the impulse toward deterritorialization. In the following analysis of her works, I suggest that this gesture toward deterritorialization resembles an ideologically subversive stance that Gilles Deleuze and Felix Guattari refer to as 'nomadology.'[6]

Van Herk's rejection of traditional representations of female identity is evident in her very first novel, *Judith*. Set in rural Alberta, this work traces the experiences of a young woman, Judith Pierce, who flees her life in the city and an unsatisfying relationship (a stereotypical affair with her boss) and takes up a rural existence as a pig farmer.[7] In the novel, Judith is initially portrayed as a wary and bitter young woman. Although she escapes the stagnant relationship with her lover/employer and returns to the rural neighbourhood where she was raised, she remains unable to generate a sense of her own identity beyond the roles that the men in her life have plotted for her (MacLaren, xix). In particular, she finds herself paralysed by the idealistic image she carries of her father. The bond between father and daughter runs deep; before he died, Judith's father was a pig farmer, and he taught his little 'Judy-girl' everything there was to know about farming. She helped her father run the farm until she was eighteen, and she was expected to take it over. However, when her parents wanted to hand over the operation, she rejected the idea, believing that it meant she would have to conform to the traditional gender roles associated with farm life: 'I just can't. Don't you see, it's here, this place, the life, all the women are house-wives and all the men are country louts. ... Every day is the same. I hate it, I hate it, I want to do things, can't you understand?' (92–3). Throughout the novel, Judith's struggle is linked to her desire to participate in farm-life, positioning herself not as a housewife but as a farmer. In this respect, the narrative recalls F.P. Grove's novel *Settlers of the Marsh*, which portrays a young woman named Ellen who also yearns to be a farmer. She, too, remains wary of men and rejects the hero's advances because, as she says, 'I had already made up my mind to become a farmer, though not a farmer's wife' (128). But, according to Grove's plot, Ellen renounces these desires and, like one transformed, asserts that she realizes that it is her 'destiny and [her] ... greatest need to have children' (264). In van Herk's novel, Judith successfully negotiates the transition and becomes a farmer, but, in doing so, she must take on her father's role and engage in certain rituals (such as the castration of the pigs) which he had taken great pains to shield her from when she worked with him. When she performs these duties, Judith realizes that they are basic, human tasks. She also understands that, in preventing her from participating in these tasks, her father was actually shielding her from the discovery that he, like his pigs, had testicles, and that he was merely mortal and not the god she had made him out to be: 'And so it was that she could love him, father/god perfect always, unfailing, showing her only birth and death and never the sordid in-between' (176). It is only when Judith finally sees through her over-idealized image of her father and ceases to identify herself as a little girl who will one day grow up and work for Daddy in an attempt 'to please him' (176) that she can generate her own identity. At the end of the novel, Judith experiences this 'sordid in-between' when she castrates her own pigs. Following this, she decides to redirect her mail from General Delivery, which 'is for folks just passin' through' (188), to a fixed address – she rents a box at the post office. According to Ian MacLaren, her decision to acquire a permanent address indicates that she has finally secured her own identity and located herself on the map (xix).

In her efforts to claim this identity, Judith must work through the masculine representations of Woman that have been imposed on her, including the role of the dutiful daughter and the mistress. The process of disengaging herself from the traditional female roles is facilitated by her isolation: by working alone on the farm, Judith escapes the male gaze. When she finds herself walking the way 'city women walk, as if stepping over cracked eggs,' she has to remind herself that no one is there to watch her, '[j]ust the pigs' (16). In addition to her isolation, the presence of the ten pregnant sows in her care also helps her to develop a sense of herself independent from the roles fashioned for her by men. In contrast to the masculine environment she must negotiate when she ventures into society, the fecund environment of the animals offers a locus of asylum: 'After the day in town, Judith entered the barn's loomy redolence eagerly. She was whole here, a part of their tumescent sanctuary of female warmth. It was that, their femaleness, the subtle scent that lifted from beneath their alert tails, surrounding her like a soothing conspiracy' (56).

In many ways, van Herk's presentation of rural life draws on the 1970s version of Romantic escapism. Yet, like Thomas's *Intertidal Life*, van Herk's fiction offers a feminist recoding of this tradition. On the one hand, the descriptions of Judith's pastoral life among the animals are clearly offered in contrast to her decadent experience in the city – an opposition that recalls Rousseau's slogan of 'Return to Nature,' which is, itself, based on the earlier classical distinction between the town and the country. In Grove's novel *Settlers of the Marsh*, the hero, Niels, dreams of escaping both society and women. As the narrator explains, he is consumed by a fantasy of escape:

A new dream rose: a longing to leave and go to the very margin of civilisation, there to clear a new place; and when it was cleared and people began to settle about it, to move on once more, again to the very edge of pioneerdom, and to start it all over anew ... That way his enormous strength would still have a meaning. Woman would have no place in his life. (139)

Whereas Grove idealizes this goal, van Herk makes it abundantly clear that the so-called 'Return to Nature' is never unproblematic or, in fact, actually an option for women: in the context of the masculine discourse of Romanticism, it appears non-sensical for a woman to desire to return to Nature because positioned as Woman, she *is* Nature. As Dorothy Jones suggests, the kingdom of nature, for women, 'is likely to be a place of exile, for to take possession of her own space a woman must all too often withdraw from a society which accords her little or no space at all' ('Kingdom,' 272). Judith's withdrawal from society, and her association with the pigs – characterized as a sordid and bloody affair – supports Jones's assertion, and clarifies that the text is not simply conveying an escapist fantasy.

Although Judith's relationship with her sows is a far cry from the lesbian relationship between Annie and Zoe depicted in *Ana Historic*, both alliances gesture toward a similar ideal, a realm which the Milan feminists describe as a frame of reference 'no longer patriarchal or male-designed.' Judith's friendship with her neighbour, Mina, further reinforces the existence of an alternative female frame of reference. Perhaps for this reason, when Mina first offers Judith her friendship, the event (which is witnessed by the pigs) takes on a quasi-mystical significance: 'the pigs saw Mina get to her feet, take Judith's hand in both her own and hold it there, the two of them caught together in the incantation of their joining' (102). In keeping with its emphasis on the significance of female friendship, the novel's final chapter concludes with an image of Judith and Mina, watching the comic antics of a boar trying to mount a sow. Both women reflect on the boar's 'limited usefulness' (186) in comparison with the sow's importance, and the chapter ends with an image of the two women dancing (187); Judith and Mina have moved beyond the patriarchal frame of reference, in which the boar would be positioned as the most important agent.[8]

There is, however, another way of interpreting the novel's presentation of Judith's transformation from secretary/mistress to 'Central Alberta Hog Farmer,' a transformation that underscores the more broad-based political repercussions of the subversion of traditional gender roles. The text's presentation of Judith's abrupt and surreptitious escape from the pink-collar ghetto (she tells no one that she is thinking of leaving and simply disappears) constitutes what Gilles Deleuze and Félix Guattari refer to as a 'line of flight.' Their notion of 'nomadology' highlights the political ramifications of this type of escape from traditional representations of identity.

In their book *A Thousand Plateaus*, Deleuze and Guattari outline a cartographic model of the lines of power and desire. In contrast to Foucault's view of the dynamics of power, Deleuze and Guattari's model offers the possibility for social and individual transformation; their model also shares many features of feminist strategies whose aim is to subvert phallocentric thought. Adapted, rather than adopted, the work of Deleuze and Guattari offers an innovative set of methods and procedures that can serve to displace the 'pervasiveness of the structure of binary logic that has dominated Western philosophy since the time of Plato' (Grosz, 'Thousand,' 7). The Deleuzian model is of particular interest to feminists because, in accordance with feminist theory, it displays an interest in viewing 'difference' outside the structure of binary pairs in which what is different 'can be understood only as a variation or negation of identity' (Grosz, 'Thousand,' 8). The subject, according to Deleuze and Guattari, is not an 'entity' or thing, or a 'relation between mind (interior) and body (exterior); instead, it must be understood as a series of flows, energies, movements … linked together in ways other than those which congeal it into an identity' (Grosz, 'Thousand,' 12). In this fashion, the Deleuzian model, like feminist models, destabilizes traditional modes of conceiving identity as unified and masculine.

Read in relation to the texts of Aritha van Herk, the work of Deleuze and Guattari, with its emphasis on the deterritorialization of identity, politicizes our understanding of the concept, referred to earlier, of 'anonymous territory,' which women flee to (or create) in an attempt to escape the rigid frame which defines the image of Woman. In their work, Deleuze and Guattari align attempts to subvert traditional representations of identity with revolutionary political struggles. Viewed in this light, the domain of fiction ceases to remain an aesthetically neutral realm which exerts virtually no influence on the lives of individuals. As far as Deleuze and Guattari are concerned, fictions are implicated in political struggles and can be used by minority groups to subvert the State apparatus. Thus, when van Herk argues that, if women hope to write fiction, they must reject their traditional identity as 'muse' and get out of 'this male structure' ('Women,' 18), she can be said to be aligning herself with what Deleuze and Guattari describe as a 'nomadic war machine.'

Van Herk shares with Deleuze and Guattari, as we shall see, an interest in using a cartographic model to discuss attempts to reformulate female subjectivity beyond the discursive positions sanctioned by the State. She specifically relies on cartographic models to describe women's attempts to reformulate representations of female identity in prairie fiction. Also, in her writing, van Herk suggests that women writers and characters must both escape; they must become invisible spies in an indifferent landscape. This notion of escape is in keeping with Deleuze and Guattari's concept of becoming imperceptible, and transforming oneself into a nomadic war machine. In her writings, van Herk portrays women as guerilla fighters, scouting out hostile territory; at one point, she boasts that women 'have an apron full of alternatives, all of them disguises, surprise weapons. We are beginning to dot this landscape but we can't be seen' ('Women,' 19). In a moment, I will look more closely at particular correspondences between van Herk's fictions and the theories of

Deleuze and Guattari; at this point, I will sketch some of the latter's major concepts.

In their study, Deleuze and Guattari begin by identifying the structure of binary logic with the State; they also characterize the State according to its essential function, namely, capture, which involves the stratification of space and the control of a variety of flows, including the flows of individual energies and movements, population, commerce, commodities, and money or capital (Deleuze and Guattari, 385). Working along molar lines, the State sets up its field of interiority and parcels out closed spaces to people, 'assigning each person a share and regulating the communication between shares' (380). On one level, then, the State's impulse to capture and control space is evident in a city's geographical grid; on another level, this impulse is evident in the images individuals use to organize and describe space. Rudy Wiebe's insistence that fiction writers must lay 'great black steel lines of fiction' across the landscape constitutes an example of the way in which this impulse toward capture informs literary descriptions of space.

According to Deleuze and Guattari, working in opposition to the State and its mode of binary thinking are a multiplicity of decentred, molecular entities, which are organized, not in the hierarchical or 'arborescent' manner of the State, but according to a 'rhizomatic' structure. They use the organic metaphor of a meandering root structure to describe assemblages based on multiple connections which 'bring together very diverse domains, levels, dimensions, functions, effects, aims and objects' (Grosz, 'Thousand,' 13). In many ways, this type of structure borrows from the feminist strategies of non-hierarchical organizational practices – what have been recently described as 'coalitional politics' (Butler, Gender, 14–16). According to Deleuze and Guattari, rhizomatic structures have the capacity to function as 'nomadic war machines.'

Understandably, many feminist have balked at the idea of appropriating the term 'war machine.' For one thing, what could be more male-identified than the military and war? Second, the term 'machine' makes feminists uncomfortable because the infrastructure associated with mechanical functioning and technocracies remains predicated on the exclusion of women (Grosz, 'Thousand,' 5–6). However, in working with the concepts of the State and the nomadic war machine it is important to remember that both of these terms refer to a constellation of characteristics, rather than to concrete, physical entities, which explains why they are used by Deleuze and Guattari to designate anything from organizations to modes of thinking. Used in this way, the terms are no longer reserved to describe male bastions. There is no denying that the use of the term 'war machine' to describe feminist projects remains problematic; however, it is necessary to re-evaluate arguments that assume that only supposedly 'feminine' terms and strategies are acceptable, while other, presumably 'masculine' strategies must be eschewed. If nothing else, Deleuze and Guattari's application of the term to describe the efforts of a variety of groups – including the feminists – destablizes any easy opposition between 'masculine' and 'feminine' techniques for subversion. In her essay 'A Manifesto for Cyborgs: Science, Technology, and Socialist Feminism in the 1980s,' Donna Haraway discusses many ideas which are in accordance with the theories of Deleuze and Guattari. Like Deleuze and Guattari, she utilizes a machine model (the cyborg) to discuss the breakdown of dichotomies between 'mind and body, animal and human, organism and machine, public and private, nature and culture, men and women, primitive and civilized' (205).

Deleuze and Guattari's writings constantly preclude the possibility of constructing simple dichotomies. For instance, they propose that the distinction between the State and the war machine ultimately can never be fixed because the border between the two is permeable; they argue that, throughout history, the State has constantly appropriated the revolutionary potential of the war machine. While their concept of the nomadic war machine is based on the characteristics of traditional nomadic tribes, the authors' goal lies in utilizing the idea of a war machine to describe the activities of isolated groups or packs 'which continue to affirm the rights of segmentary societies in opposition to the organs of State power' (360). They suggest that 'each time there is an operation against the State – insubordination, rioting, guerrilla warfare, or revolution as act – it can be said that a war machine has revived, that a new nomadic potential has appeared' (386).

In contrast to the State, which works to create stratified space, the nomadic war machine seeks to maximize deterritorialized or smooth space. For this reason, the shifting sands of the desert, whether sand or ice, are home to the nomad because, in the desert, there is no attempt made to enclose a landscape that is constantly changing. Even though the nomadic trajectory may follow trails or customary routes, 'it does not fulfill the function of the sedentary road,' which encloses space (380). Deleuze and Guattari emphasize that one's mode of perception changes in the desert because 'there is no line separating earth and sky; there is no intermediate distance, no perspective or contour; visibility is limited. ... It is a tactile space or rather "haptic," a sonorous much more than a visual space' (382). Whereas the line of power associated with the State is molar, the line corresponding to the nomadic war machine is the molecular path of escape or the 'line of flight': 'This is ... a line without segments which is more like the collapse of all segmentarity. It is the line along which structures ... break down or become transformed into something else. It is the line of absolute deterritorialization' (Patton, 65). It is this line of flight or transformation that subverts traditional binary oppositions – destabilizing, for instance, the distinction between the categories of man and woman, human and animal, as well as mind and body.

In their work, Deleuze and Guattari align the war machine and its line of flight with processes which they refer to as 'becomings.' These are processes which systematically break down binary oppositions constructed by State-thought. As Elizabeth Grosz notes, there is an order to these 'becomings':

There is, then, a kind of direction in the quantum leap required by becomings, an order in which becoming-woman is, for all subjects, a first trajectory or direction: becoming-woman desediments the masculinity of identity; becoming-animal, the anthropocentrism of philosophical thought, and becoming-imperceptible replaces, problematizes the notion of thing, entity. Indiscernibility, imperceptibility and impersonality remain the end-points of becoming. ... ('Thousand,' 23)

In my use of the theories of Deleuze and Guattari, I recognize, in conjunction with other feminist critics, that there are serious problems for feminists associated with their assertion that both men and women must engage in 'becoming-woman.'[9] Most obviously, Deleuze and Guattari's model of 'becoming' seems to appropriate women's experience once again, idealistically portraying it as a supposedly neuter, universal step which both men and women must strive to attain and then move beyond. However, even if their work replicates patriarchal structures to a certain extent, aspects of their theories can be usefully salvaged. As Elizabeth Grosz insists, it is important not to dismiss their work out of hand, but to determine whether it can serve as a 'powerful tool or weapon in feminist challenges to phallocentric thought,' even though their writings may be deemed patriarchal or phallocentric ('Thousand,' 6). Furthermore, any efforts to remain untainted by phallocentric thought, well-intentioned though they might be, remain highly problematic because, as Grosz underscores, 'no text – not even "feminist" texts – can in a sense be immune to this charge [of phallocentrism], insofar as the very categories, concepts and methodologies available today are those spawned by this history' ('Thousand,' 6).[10] In the debate between keeping feminism 'pure' and utilizing 'tainted' phallologocentric theories, I align myself with Grosz and other feminists who believe that we must employ all the theoretical tools at hand, just as we must shape them to our use; as Donna Haraway suggests, 'Cyborg writing is about the power to survive not on the basis of original innocence, but on the basis of seizing the tools to mark the world that marked them as other' (217).

Leaving this controversy aside, I want to look at the correspondences between the work of Deleuze and Guattari and van Herk's feminized, militaristic strategy for infiltrating the masculine terrain. Van Herk's insistence that women need to distance themselves from their traditional representations as Woman – 'mothers/saints/whores' – which surfaces in all of her writing, corresponds to Deleuze and Guattari's emphasis on 'becoming-minoritarian,' a transformation that separates individuals from their 'major identity,' and aims toward rendering individuals imperceptible

(Deleuze and Guattari, 291). Looking at *Judith*, we can see that the heroine's decision to become a pig farmer strikes a blow against the fixed boundary between gender roles. In a sense, by leaving her job as a secretary along with her subordinate
role as her employer's mistress and by taking up a 'male' occupation, Judith rejects
the binary opposition and male/female hierarchy of State-thought; she transforms the
fixed space of gender roles into deterritorialized space. According to Deleuze and
Guattari, this decision sets her on a path of 'becoming-minoritarian,' a process which
is related to another becoming, described as 'becoming-animal.' In their work,
Deleuze and Guattari suggest that the formation of an 'animal reality' – the fluid
dynamic associated with packs or bands – facilitates the subversion of the type of
relationships authorized by the State and the familial institution (242). They also
point out that the animals associated with the process of becoming-animal are typically those aligned with the 'demonic' (241).

The possibility of violence first arises when Judith ventures into the local beer
In the novel, Judith's relationship with her livestock recalls Deleuze and Guattari's
description of the process of 'becoming-animal.' Although Judith tries to domesticate her pigs – she is a farmer, after all – and her work is partially aligned with the
State's efforts to capture and stabilize 'flows,' the pigs still convey a sense of the
pack with its demonic undertones, and Judith finds herself becoming animal by
entering into their world. At one point, when she is feeding them in the evening,
she turns to find the animals watching her: 'a perfect succession of small eyes glow-
ing like lantern pinpoints in the dusty light. With a motionless and uncanny intelligence they watched her, holding her captive' (10). Later on, Judith's friend Jim
tells her that her pigs are 'spooky animals,' and she agrees, saying, 'They're super-
natural' (158). Not only are the pigs aligned with the demonic, but Jim insists on the
connection between Judith and her animals, saying, 'It's you. You're a witch. Somebody's gonna find out and burn you' (158). While these demonic attributes are in
keeping with van Herk's retelling of the Circe myth, viewed within the context of
'becoming-animal' the text's appropriation of the Circe myth can be understood as
a manoeuvre that involves more than a simple reiteration of a familiar tale. Instead,
the myth provides the outlines for a political stance that opposes the fixity associated with State-supported binary oppositions. By challenging the traditional representations of Woman, Judith aligns herself with the nomadic war machine, and
this link helps to explain why Judith's struggle for self-definition involves a measure of violence.

The possibility of violence first arises when Judith ventures into the local beer
parlour for a drink.[11] Inside the bar, she is taunted by a group of farmers, who are
affronted that a woman would dare choose to pursue an occupation reserved for
males.[12] Rather than accept men's jibes meekly, Judith stages a revolt, and starts a
bar-room brawl. She flings glass after glass of beer into the men's faces, 'her aim as
hard and flexed as her set, furious face' (143). In order to stop the fight, Jim has to drag

her bodily from the room. Unlike any of the works examined thus far, van Herk's text intimates that women must be prepared to become 'war machines' and resort to violence, whether physical or psychological, to secure their right to travel through territory arbitrarily reserved for males: in each of her texts, van Herk's heroines are clearly at war with State-thought.

It is useful to compare van Herk's violent heroine with the central character in Bowering's novel Caprice. Like Judith, the beautiful and dangerous *Caprice*, who rides a black stallion and carries a whip as a weapon, exceeds the traditional roles allotted to women as 'commodities or prizes' (183). However, whereas Caprice goes on a quest to avenge the death of her brother at the hands of an evil gunslinger, and directs her prodigious strength and capacity for violence to this end, Judith sets out to avenge the violence directed at her own body and women's bodies, in general. Van Herk's plot differs significantly from Bowering's: although violence remains a constant, her heroine's quest does not involve chasing a man to avenge another man's death.

Perhaps the most violent episode in *Judith* occurs when the protagonist takes it upon herself to castrate the male pigs, a job which, as noted earlier, was reserved for men. She does not flinch when it comes to slicing out the animals' testicles, emasculating each pig 'like the savage witch of pragmatism that she was' (175). The pigs' castration is described as Judith's 'atonement for the acts of barbarity she had committed on herself' to please her lover. She grows ashamed of the transformations she allowed him to orchestrate in her – 'his careful honing of her salient features into his special mold' (175). Her initial willingness to conform to this 'special mold' recalls Anna Swan's readiness to swallow Nelvana's Nordic Regulator, which likewise threatened to shrink the giantess 'into the zone of feminine perfection' (317); but unlike Anna, who merely weeps at the thought of this unwanted transformation, Judith takes 'swift and cruel' revenge (175–6). Judith's response is so brutal that it frightens her would-be lover, Jim, and causes him to rush off in horror. When he finally recovers from the shock of seeing a woman fearlessly castrate an animal, he returns and voices his anxiety: 'Listen, the way you went at those pigs this morning, how do I know what you'd do to me?' As a woman/war machine bent on subverting the system, Judith gives him the only answer possible: 'You don't' (183).

Van Herk's subsequent novel, *The Tent Peg* (1981), continues to develop this concern regarding the need to reterritorialize the terrain of female identity from a feminist perspective. Here, even more than in *Judith*, emphasis is placed on the notion of deterritorialization, and the need for women to take on the role of the nomadic warrior. The novel also continues to probe the necessity of testing the efficacy of violence as a means of securing the right to unimpeded access to male 'territory.' In this novel, a young woman named Ja-el disguises herself as a boy in order to join

an all-male geological team sent to the Yukon's Wernecke mountains to map potential mining sites. Pulling a hat low over her brow, she slips out of 'female' territory
and makes her escape by playing the part of a man. As Deleuze and Guattari point
out, to hide, 'to camouflage oneself, is a warrior function' (277). Once she reveals
her identity as a woman, however, she must defend her right to occupy male terrain. Each of the principal men in the camp – Mackenzie, Thompson, Franklin,
Hearne, Hudson, Cap, Ivan, Jerome, and Milton – is a product of the State, in
that each has been trained to expect women to operate within the pre-assigned category of Woman, and, in some cases, force them to do so.[13]

Interestingly enough, the protagonist hides behind both her hat and the gender-
neutral initials 'J.L.' Escaping her female designation and relying on the opacity and
inherent instability of language, she slips out of the restrictions which gender-spe-
cific names impose. Under the cover of a set of initials, she is able to fool the expedition leader, Mackenzie, into thinking she is a man and hiring her on as a cook. In
actual fact, her real name refers to the biblical story, in which a woman named Ja-el
led Sisera, the leader of an enemy tribe, into her tent as her guest, and then proceeded
to murder him after he fell asleep by hammering a tent peg through his skull (Judges,
4–5). Ja-el's courageous act initiated the first unified victory over Israel's enemy in
one hundred and seventy-five years; and Deborah, who was the judge of Israel at that
time, proclaimed it a moral deed (MacLaren, xxviii). Van Herk's novel self-consciously draws on this biblical story, which vividly depicts a woman behaving in a
fashion that violates Woman's supposedly nurturing and docile nature. Parallels are
drawn in *The Tent Peg* between the contemporary heroine, J.L., who ventures into
male territory, and her biblical foremother, who transgresses her assigned role as
hostess and murders her guest with the approval of Deborah, one of the finest judges
of the nation. Van Herk's novel abounds with references to the biblical story, and
J.L. even has a supportive friendship with a woman named Deborah, who is a singer.
Except for this contact, J.L. is emotionally and philosophically isolated in the
men's camp.

As in *Judith*, the protagonist in *The Tent Peg* maintains both an important friendship with another woman and a somewhat uncanny relationship with animals;
one could say that J.L., like Judith, engages in the process of 'becoming-animal.'
This process is initiated when J.L. forges a bond with an animal; as Deleuze and
Guattari suggest, becoming always 'concerns alliance' (238). When she and the pilot
are flying over the tundra, they disturb a female grizzly and her cubs (95). Later
on, this same grizzly makes an appearance outside of J.L.'s cooktent, and the event
is witnessed by the pilot and the radio-operator, who records what happens:

J.L.'s face is tilted up and the she-bear's face is tilted down and they're looking at each other
like they've met before. And then J.L. sweeps off her hat and bows at the same instant that

the bear seems to shrug, and drops to her feet. For a moment more they stand there as if in conversation, then they both turn. J.L. goes back into the cooktent and the bear lumbers away down the valley. From behind the corner of the tent two little cubs scurry to follow her. (108)

As in *Judith*, the men have a tendency to view the woman's bond with the animal as 'demonic.' In *The Tent Peg*, the pilot proclaims that J.L. is a 'witch,' primarily because she blurs categorical distinctions between the human and the non-human (109).

In the novel, J.L. specifically associates the blurring of gender boundaries with the existence of deterritorialized or unmapped space. Early on, after confessing to Mackenzie that she is a girl, she remarks, 'I want suddenly to touch him, to comfort him for all the *unmapped areas*, to tell him how truly sorry I am that I cannot stay a boy' (39; my emphasis). Her statement draws an implicit association between gender-identity and mapped versus unmapped landscape. In an interview with Dorothy Jones, van Herk reinforced this association by maintaining that she belongs to 'the region of woman' – a region defined by its characteristic 'sense of otherness' – which has not been represented by male western writers (see 'Interview,' 1). She emphasizes the difference between the two regions, saying:

[T]here's a very obvious difference between the region of women – that of the home and family, the traditional territory that women have, and now the regions they are reaching for outside, attempting to establish themselves in a different way – and the quintessentially male regions of fiction which have been the great theatres of the world. ('Interview,' 2–3)

As a writer, van Herk claims that she wants to stretch 'the borders of the region we inhabit as women' by inducing 'hair-line cracks, fissures, in all the things that men have defined as their territory, or the larger world' ('Interview,' 3).

In *The Tent Peg*, J.L. relies, for the most part, on the shattering impact of her behaviour and her words to introduce these 'fissures' into the men's consciousness; one by one, she pierces their phallocentric assumptions. Ian MacLaren argues that these 'pegs of understanding' can only be driven into the men's skulls because of the overall 'destabilization' of the camp, which J.L. induces (xxvii). Each of the men is forced to re-evaluate his assumptions regarding women and the roles women are traditionally required to play. For example, Mackenzie finally learns from J.L. why his wife left him after ten years of marriage. J.L. tells him, 'She left for herself. You were a good man but you couldn't give that to her, it had nothing to do with you' (202). When Mackenzie protests, saying he would not have 'prevented her from doing what she wanted,' J.L. remarks that the very idea that he could allow her or prevent her from leaving was what she found unbearable. Like the biblical figure of Sisera, Mackenzie feels the blow of the tent peg against his forehead: 'It is the sound of my own assumption that hammers in my temple' (202).[14]

In her efforts to destabilize the men's view of women as 'mothers/saints/ whores,' to use van Herk's words, J.L. is not afraid of using violence. As she says, 'It's time we laid our hands on the workman's mallet and put the tent pegs to the sleeping temples, if ever we are going to get any rest' (173). She calls for violence even though she knows that whenever women adopt the role of warriors and press for change, they are always denounced:

I know, we're supposed to change them with non-violence, we're supposed to show them by example, turn an oblique cheek until they wear themselves out. That's the slow way. I can think of a few methods to bring a quicker peace. All we need is the daring, the nerve. Of course, we'll be condemned for acting, we'll be forever traitors and bitches, have broken all the rules of hospitality, but we'll have gotten what we want. Peace. To hell with the historians and analysts. They always decide against us anyway.   (190–1)

J.L. clearly rejects the typically feminine strategy of non-violence; and, as I stated earlier, van Herk's portrayal of a feminine war machine makes it difficult to oppose masculine and feminine tactics for subversion in any clear-cut fashion.

In *The Tent Peg* violence is offered as a solution to violence, and both van Herk and her characters feel justified in offering this as a strategy to end women's subordination. In her writing, van Herk self-consciously addresses the fact that readers may be uncomfortable with this. As she says, 'You may feel that my spies, both writer and character, are violent, unredemptive. Only remember that they are spies, spies in an indifferent landscape up until now defined by other eyes' ('Women,' 24). Her philosophy is reminiscent of the one espoused in Monique Wittig's novel *Les Guérillères*, where a band of all-women nomadic warriors proclaim: '[L]et those who call for a new language first learn violence. ... [L]et those who want to change the world first seize all the rifles' (85). While J.L.'s wrath does not permanently transform her into the type of nomadic war machine described in Wittig's text, this same philosophy informs her actions; at one point, she, too, seizes a gun.

In the course of the summer, only one man, the assistant party chief, Jerome, remains unresponsive to J.L.'s campaign. Unable to alter his thinking, which is characterized by the binary oppositions typical of State-thought, Jerome maintains that geology is 'a man's field' (27), and that women 'just don't belong out there' (29). As Ian MacLaren points out: 'Faithful to his saintly namesake, the Church Father whose legendary sarcasm and invective van Herk retells superbly, Jerome remains so unregenerately misogynist that his hatred in fact spills over into a full embrace of misanthropy' (xxviii). Toward the end of the summer, Jerome takes it upon himself to punish J.L. for her supposed insubordination: '[G]et a woman in camp and she makes trouble, she does nothing but stir up shit. Well, I've had it, I, for one, think it's time she got put in her place, taken down a peg or two. The little bitch needs to be taught a lesson and I guess I'm the only one with balls enough to do it' (218). Sneaking into her tent at night like some Gothic villain, Jerome puts a gun to J.L's head and attempts to rape her. While he is fumbling at his zipper, J.L. knees him in the groin, grabs the gun, and fires a shot into the air. When Mackenzie appears on the scene, he finds J.L. pointing the Magnum directly between Jerome's legs with every indication that she intends to shoot. She is only dissuaded from castrating Jerome when Mackenzie quietly tells her, 'It won't help' (222). It is significant that the image of castration surfaces in both *Judith* and *The Tent Peg*. Without the secure possession of the phallus, the divide between male and female territory becomes blurred and flagrantly meaningless.[15]

Discounting Jerome, J.L. remains highly successful in her efforts to alter the men's attitudes about the nature of Woman. The fundamental reason for her success lies in the fact that the men have ventured into nomadic territory. They are at a disadvantage when they try to uphold State-thought because they are battling on her turf. Throughout the novel, the Yukon is portrayed as a 'magic place.' As Thompson explains, 'I know it, Mackenzie knows it. It's a place where reality is inverted, where you have to take strangeness for granted' (126). When she first learns from Mackenzie how to handle a gun, J.L. identifies her new-found power with the northern landscape:

It made me realize my own power, that I could turn a gun on them and pull the trigger, that up here there are no rules, no set responses, everything is new and undefined, we are beyond, outside of the rest of the world. There are no controls here.

It frightens me and yet I know now that I don't have to be afraid of them, no not afraid at all. Out here my anger is as real as theirs, can have as great an effect. (86)

The deterritorialized space of the tundra makes it possible for J.L. to escape the assigned female roles. Elsewhere in her writing, van Herk clearly identifies the ability to 'escape' with 'landscape': 'Landscape is technically a stretch of inland natural scenery as seen from a single point. A scape is a scene of land or sea or sky but the archaic meaning of scape is to escape, an escape, or means of escape. Landscape beckons escape' ('Women,' 16). In particular, for van Herk, the north functions as a desert, the home of the nomadic warrior. As I noted earlier, Deleuze and Guattari suggest that nomadic territory is 'tactile space' (382). In *The Tent Peg*, the Yukon is likewise identified as a tactile space, and J.L.'s association with it is confirmed when she sends the men home with scarlet sachets of moss which exude the 'faint lemony scent' of the tundra (224). As Ian MacLaren notes, her gift helps the men remember the space 'viscerally – by touch and by smell' (xxviii).

Ultimately, J.L.'s relation to the smooth space of the north is compromised when she assists in the staking of the gold mine. The men discover the seams at the end of the summer. In a race against time, they call on every last person to help drive the stakes into the earth, so that they can assert their ownership of the seams, dubbed by J.L. the 'Midas claims,' before competition arrives. For reasons which I will go on to discuss, J.L. willingly assists in the staking. According to Hearne, she pounds the posts into the ground 'with an intent seriousness that makes me think this staking has another importance to her, this is her farewell ritual to the Yukon, *an act of reference for her*' (210; my emphasis). Her rationale for helping the men, as Ian MacLaren suggests, lies in the fact that, by participating in the staking, J.L. claims 'a stake in the northern map of a hitherto unitary male discourse' (xxxi).

At this point, the novel foregrounds a dilemma that feminists must resolve – a dilemma that was also present in *Judith*. On the one hand, by claiming a stake in the northern map or, as in the case of Judith, by asserting a subversive identity in the prairies, women become visible members within an identifiable community. On the other hand, at the same time that they become visible and comprehensible within this community, they become aligned, to a certain extent, with the State and its mandate, which is based on capture, and when women capture and define a solid identity, they lose the creative potential offered by the line of flight associated with deterritorialized space. In the novel, this compromise is signalled when J.L.'s staking of the gold mine severs her connection with the she-bear. After the staking is complete and J.L. and the pilot are heading back to base-camp in the helicopter, J.L. catches sight of the she-bear for a moment. When the bear vanishes, J.L. is bitterly disappointed. Thompson understands and he puts a hand on her shoulder, but, as he says, 'she wants no comfort from me. She wants the bear' (209). Moments later, the bear makes one final appearance, rising 'monstrous, unforgiving, filling the frame of the sky between the mountain slopes, her silhouette like a huge, ragged omen against the light' (209). The animal serves to remind J.L. of the dangers associated with compromising her role as a nomadic warrior and joining in the State's efforts to capture and striate the landscape.

Van Herk's subsequent novel, *No Fixed Address* (1986), continues to investigate the relationships among mapped and unmapped territory and female identity. However, this work examines what happens when women do not ultimately align themselves with the State. As the title suggests, the novel does not conclude by positioning the protagonist within the 'fixed' bounds erected by the State. The term 'address' refers both to the type of physical location articulated in *Judith* and to the linguistic notion of address, which entails an understanding – or a lack of understanding – of the ideological 'location' of speakers in a given discursive situation. In this way, the title playfully signals the disturbance created in the linguistic terrain when women choose to become invisible within the terms designated by traditional representations of Woman.

No Fixed Address is composed of four sections, each bearing the same title, 'Notebook on a missing person.' The novel's picaresque heroine, Arachne Manteia, becomes this 'missing person' when she escapes into male territory as a travelling underwear salesperson. Throughout the novel, Arachne drives a 1959 Mercedes through a myriad of prairie towns, plying her trade.[16] Her profession and its relationship to the female body recall the emphasis placed on the treatment of the female body in the novels examined earlier. As one critic argues, underwear in *No Fixed Address* functions as 'a metaphor for the repression of women' (review by Leckie, 279). As I noted above, in Swan's novel, the control exerted over the female body is illustrated when the giantess experiences the agonizing constriction of her corset just when she is about to win the dessert-eating contest. More seriously, her second child dies because her body is placed at the mercy of the American medical institution when she goes into labour. In Marlatt's novel, this type of bodily domination is depicted in episodes concerning the narrator's gender training and her mother's experience as a psychiatric patient who was subjected to electroshock therapy in the 1950s. In *No Fixed Address*, although Arachne sells undergarments, which recall the time when it was '*taken for granted that woman's body should be prisoner, taped and measured and controlled*' (10), she herself never wears the stuff. Of all the characters examined thus far, she is the only one to have escaped this material aspect of patriarchal domination. Far from playing by society's rules, Arachne is an 'amoral, selfish, dishonest' woman (103). Unlike J.L., who briefly disguises herself as a man and then quickly discards the ruse, Arachne cheerfully maintains a variety of disguises (190). By far van Herk's boldest heroine, Arachne finds it easy to reject State-thought and become a nomadic warrior because she was never trained to be a Woman in the first place. Ironically, she must rely on her boyfriend, Thomas, to teach her how to don a feminine disguise in order to navigate in the '"real world,"' ... the respectable world, in which she is an imposter' (103).

Coral Ann Howells points out that *No Fixed Address* constitutes a brilliant parody of Canadian male exploration narratives and the European picaresque genre of which 'the American travelling salesman story is a variant' ('No Transcendental,' 113).[17] The text blurs fact with fiction because, in her travels to various towns, Arachne traces a route which can actually be followed on a map of the western provinces. In creating the character of Arachne, van Herk seems to have taken Robert Kroetsch's insightful characterization of the basic grammatical pair in the storyline of prairie fiction – the binary opposition of house/horse, female/male, stasis/motion (which he so comically exploits in *The Studhorse Man*) – and stood it on its head (see Kroetsch, 'Fear,' 100). Patterned on the character of the traditional male rogue, Arachne is a sexually casual, itinerant trickster, who, like the class of spiders she is named for, treats men like flies (see van Herk's interview, 'Kiss,' 86). As Arachne explains to her friend, Thena, men are 'just bodies, you could put a paper bag over their heads' (33). Unlike the prairie fictions in which the little woman waits at home, in *No Fixed Address* the situation is reversed, and Arachne's faithful lover, Thomas, a cartographer for the Geodetic Survey Company, chastely waits for her.[18] Furthermore, with the aid of the maps that Thomas and other map-makers like him draw, Arachne fulfils her insatiable longing to spider 'her own map over the intricate roads of the world' (223). Arachne's appropriation of Thomas's maps illustrates the extent to which van Herk has subverted the colonial practice of cartography. Here the cartographer, although male, is portrayed as loving and domesticated; and Arachne's enjoyment of the maps he produces indicates that maps, which are very often the products of colonial discourse, can be used for different purposes than the ones they were initially intended to serve. Arachne uses Thomas's maps to locate the boundaries of civilized society and to escape its borders.

Her wanderings can be aligned with van Herk's desire to expand 'the borders of the region we inhabit as women.' Not only does Arachne stray physically, but she also strays psychologically from the traditional image of Woman. For instance, Arachne is portrayed as a woman 'without a scrap of motherly feeling' (38). In accordance with the findings of Nancy Chodorow, Arachne maintains that motherhood 'is something socialized, something incubated in a girl child with dolls and sibling babies' (38). And that 'something' is the one thing she did not get from her mother, Lanie. One month after she was born, Arachne's mother left her alone and went off to work as a waitress, so that Arachne grew up 'without a mother hovering over her progress' (85). When Lanie wanted to go off to a bingo or a shoe sale, she would lock Arachne in the backyard as if she were a dog. At three years old, Arachne learned how to climb the fence and would spend her time wandering alone through the neighbourhood. As Arachne explains, her forays helped to shape her 'solitary and observant life' (42). Rather than receive a traditional education in the reproduction of mothering, Arachne is educated to become a nomadic war machine.

Her penchant for violence surfaces quite early. When she was a child, her dolls were 'clothespins divided into two armies who alternately attacked and decimated each other' (38–9). At fifteen years old, she founded and became the sole female member of a street gang, which she named the Black Widows (191). As Deleuze and Guattari point out, war machines are 'dark assemblages' which include war societies, secret societies, and crime societies (242). Gangs of street children also fall under the category of a war machine (358). In van Herk's novel, Arachne's gang is described as a 'clutch of swaggering city rats' (192). Deleuze and Guattari use this same image of a swarm of rats to describe the type of structure that subverts the molar organization of the State, arguing that 'the proliferation of rats, the pack, brings a becoming-molecular that undermines the great molar powers of family, career, and conjugality' (233). Thus, Arachne's early association with her gang primed her for an adult existence as a war machine.

   As an adult, Arachne continues to destablize State-thought in a variety of ways. Most obviously, her trade as a travelling salesperson allows her to indulge in a life-style antithetical to the type of fixed existence that women are encouraged by the State to adopt. Furthermore, as the narrator explains, 'Arachne travels to travel. Her only paradox is arriving somewhere, her only solution is to leave for somewhere else' (164). It is useful to compare the narrator's description of Arachne's 'lust for driving' (172) with Deleuze and Guattari's description of the nomad's attitude toward travel:

> The nomad has a territory; he follows customary paths; he goes from one point to another; he is not ignorant of points. ... But the question is what in nomad life is a principle and what is only a consequence. To begin with, although the points determine paths, they are strictly subordinated to the paths they determine, the reverse of what happens with the sedentary. The water point is reached only in order to be left behind; every point is a relay and exists only as a relay. A path is always between two points, but the in-between has taken on all the consistency and enjoys both an autonomy and a direction of its own. The life of the nomad is the intermezzo.   (380)

In van Herk's novel, Arachne, like the nomad described above, enjoys the process of travelling, the intermezzo, rather than the accomplishment of arrival. By contrast, as Ian MacLaren points out, in *No Fixed Address* the italicized voice of the narrator (who is desperately trying to plot Arachne's movements) represents the realist reader who is bent on establishing a map of Arachne's journey (xxxv). The narrator, neurotically obsessed with creating a realistic map of Arachne's movements, can be aligned with State-thought, whose vital concern is to 'vanquish nomadism' and to 'control migrations' (Deleuze and Guattari, 385). In the end, Arachne disappears altogether from the grid she has created. Like a spider, she creates her web only to abandon it, waiting for her prey to become helplessly tangled in the threads.[19]

   Whereas the plots of van Herk's two previous novels portrayed the heroines returning to the fold (Judith claims an address, and J.L. stakes a claim), *No Fixed Address* refuses to reduce Arachne's desire to travel to the confines of a realistic plot: the spider-like Arachne is never caught in her own web. Instead, she fearlessly crosses into unmapped territory. Moving beyond the conventional roles of daughter, wife, and mother, she remains sexually appetitive and adventurous – so much so, that she flouts social convention that relegates the elderly to an asexual limbo, and has a passionate affair with Joseph, a coppersmith who is almost ninety. One of the more intriguing boundaries that Arachne crosses is the division between life and death itself. Toward the end of the novel, Arachne dies. As the narrator explains, 'one of her lives [was] certainly over' (301). But the story does not end with her death because the text does not bow to the dictates of traditional plot structures, which, as noted earlier, always award marriage or death (or insanity) to the heroine. Instead, the inconclusive conclusion of *No Fixed Address* portrays Arachne, still very much alive, fleeing the law – a metaphor for the 'laws' of fiction, perhaps – driving north toward the Arctic. As the narrator explains, the Arctic '*is the ultimate frontier, a place where the civilized melt[s] away and the meaning of mutiny is unknown, where manners never existed and family backgrounds are erased. It is exactly the kind of place for Arachne*' (316).

With its emphasis on the north as anonymous territory, *No Fixed Address* continues to develop the link, first posited in *The Tent Peg*, between the unmapped northern landscape and the cognitive space where women can plot radical alternatives to traditional representations of female identity. More precisely, Arachne's transformations correspond to the Deleuzian model of 'becoming,' whose end-point, as Elizabeth Grosz indicates, involves becoming indiscernible, imperceptible, and impersonal ('Thousand,' 23). As Stephen Scobie remarks, in *No Fixed Address*, the most radical subversion of traditional representations consists in the refusal of representation itself. This occurs when Arachne becomes a 'missing person': 'She has certainly moved beyond the confines of an individual personality whether defined in the loose terms of the picaresque tradition or in the stricter terms of the fiction of realism. She has become a different person, a missing person' (review by Scobie, 40). Here the plotting of identity and the plotting of landscape fuse because, when Arachne drives to Long Beach in British Columbia, she drives over the edge, 'the brink, the selvage of the world' (291). As Scobie points out, the word 'selvage' is formed from the combination of the words 'self' and 'edge,' so that her journey literally takes her to the self's edge and beyond (39).

Van Herk discusses her fascination with the possibility of becoming imperceptible surfaces in the essay entitled 'Women Writers and the Prairie: Spies in an Indifferent Landscape,' where she encourages women to become spies who 'can't be seen' (19). This article concludes with an image of a woman who has emerged from her house on the prairie in the middle of a snow storm to collect her sheets from the clothesline. Instead of taking the white sheets back into the house, the woman uses them as a disguise. Hiding behind them, she has no outline, and she vanishes 'into the storm's curve': 'you should see her against the black square of the house door she will fumble open, you wait but it never opens and that blurred figure vanishes into the curve of the cool, sweet-smelling, clean-sheeted, indifferent prairie' (24). In *No Fixed Address*, van Herk offers a strikingly similar message, namely, that if women hope to escape the representation of Woman generated by traditional writers, they must be prepared to escape along a creative line of flight into anonymous territory. For Arachne, this territory corresponds to the unrepresented 'four-dimensional nothingness' of the north (317). In the end, the realist reader/narrator, desperate to capture Arachne, is left miserably following her trail of abandoned panties, those emblems of the repression of the female body, which are strewn along a road that never ends. Ironically, one reviewer, obviously sympathetic with the text's realist narrator, vents his frustration at the turn of events, which begins when Arachne abandons Thomas and the normalcy which he represents. According to the reviewer, after that, 'we're not sure what is real and what is not, so it hardly matters. Arachne is no longer a reverse role-model, but has become merely words on a page' (review by McGoogan, 34). Despite his frustration, McGoogan has hit on a key point. Unlike Judith and J.L., Arachne does not remain a reverse role-model. Instead, she moves beyond the frame of binary thinking, leaves the grid behind her altogether, and becomes unrecognizable as a real Woman (or Man, for that matter). Ironically, McGoogan does not recognize that the traditional image of Woman or Man and its mirror reflection were never more than simply 'words on a page' or their equivalent in the first place.

In van Herk's most recent novel, *Places Far from Ellesmere* (1990), not only is the traditional representation of Woman subverted, but the structure of realistic fiction continues to be destabilized as the narrator journeys from place to place and muses about the landscape, its history, its inhabitants, and, strangely enough, its graveyards. This text focuses most directly on the relationships between the mapping of place and the plotting of fiction, and the repercussions both types of plotting have had on fictional representations of female identity. At every instance, the narrator is, in fact, searching out possible sites for 'a future grave' (140). In her review of the text, Hilda Kirkwood describes van Herk as a 'contemporary mystic, quasi-religious, with a death-fixation' (29). However, van Herk does not have a 'death-fixation' so much as a desire to explore the nature of 'engravement,' which, as the pun indicates, concerns the process of engraving plots (*Places*, 23, 61). In the text, the word 'grave' pivots on this double meaning: a grave for people as well as a fixed *plot* for stories. As the narrator intimates, physical engravement, i.e., burial in the landscape, has affinities with the engravement or emplotting of fictions: 'to dare to stay after death, to implant yourself firmly and say, "Here I stay, let those who would look for a record come here"' (61). Writing, which is committed to paper, like a body committed to the earth, becomes both a record for others and an ambiguous icon: 'Enclosured, focussed, a possible fortress' (62). Although the narrator tests out the possibility of locating a plot in three different places, like Goldilocks in the fairy-tale, she is not permitted to make a final selection (140–1). Ultimately, she recognizes that she is destined 'to become ashes. Ashes alone' because it is not safe for women to choose a fixed plot (141).[20] Her insistence on remaining fragmentary and her awareness of the dangers associated with locating oneself in the literary landscape recall Woolf's assertion that it is dangerous for women to try to plot themselves in a masculine linguistic terrain. Perhaps this is the case because traditional plots only end in death, marriage, or insanity (a form of death) for the heroine or, as Teresa de Lauretis puts it, narrative serves Oedipus. In *Intertidal Life*, the protagonist conflates the words 'married' and 'murdered' to form 'murried' (85), reinforcing the presence of this trajectory. The narrator of *Places Far from Ellesmere* is likewise on her guard against this Oedipal trajectory, and she warns that women must resist the temptation to find a final 'home'/grave/plot because there 'are murderers at large' (141).

In *Places Far from Ellesmere*, the impulse to resist the temptation to rely on a traditional plot affects the structure of the work. As one reviewer writes:

What is this work? Certainly not a novel, not exactly an autobiography, although the speaker's name is 'van Herk' and its history apparently that of its author – up to a certain point. ... Perhaps it is what the American scholar Porter Abbott has called 'autography,' a self-writing that deliberately draws attention to its own fictionality while insisting on autobiographical significance.   (review by Beer, 36)

What remains clear, despite the confusion concerning genre, is that the self-conscious avoidance of plot, and the undermining of traditional forms of representation and gender roles, lead to the undermining of genre categories. It is a mistake, perhaps, to try to squeeze this genreless work into a rigid classification system that it is so clearly attempting to resist.

Van Herk herself has dubbed the work a 'geografictione,' in an attempt to describe the text's fusion of the processes of map-making and fiction-making. In accordance with its reliance upon cartography, each of the work's four sections maps a specific 'exploration site.' These sites include the author's hometown of Edberg; the city of Edmonton, where she attended university; Calgary, where she now resides; and, finally, Ellesmere Island, the Arctic desert where she journeyed with her partner, Robert Sharp, an exploration geologist. It is on this floating polar desert that the narrator enacts a rereading of Tolstoy's *Anna Karenin*, a reading that frees Anna from Tolstoy's murderous plot (82). In accordance with the Deleuzian model discussed above, the narrator journeys from one stratified site to another, where the individual is captured and enclosed, before she finally escapes to the smooth space of the desert.

As in *The Tent Peg* and *No Fixed Address*, in this 'geografictione,' the northern landscape offers a refuge for women from the overdetermined, masculine representations of Woman. When the narrator travels to Ellesmere, she brings Tolstoy's novel with her as 'a lesson, to solve a problem in how to think about love; to solve a problem in the (grave) differences between men's writing and women's writing' (82); once again, the word 'grave' can be understood to mean 'plot.' In addition, as Linda

Hutcheon suggests, the word conveys the sense of 'graveness' or seriousness typically associated with masculine, epic fiction. Rather than rewrite the masculine fictions of the prairie, as she begins to do in *No Fixed Address*, in *Places Far from Ellesmere* van Herk advocates abandoning them altogether: 'Go north. ... If there are westerns, why can there not be northerns? Northerns of the heart, harlequins in reverse. ... Anna has been punished too long. Take her with you to Ellesmere' (85). Like Thomas, van Herk is deeply suspicious of the romance mode that informs the Harlequin. However, whereas *Intertidal Life* employs the tactic of suspension to arrest the workings of the romance mode, van Herk endorses an aggressive rereading of the genre. From the above quotation, it is also evident that the narrator collapses the distinction between protagonist and reader by simultaneously addressing both the fictional character and the reader as 'you.' This mode of address is consistently employed throughout the text, and it precludes the construction of an individual, unified hero or heroine commonly associated with romance. As we recall, Marlatt employed a similar tactic. *Places Far from Ellesmere* goes to great lengths to stage the dissolution of romance by writing a Harlequin 'in reverse,' a sustained meditation on the dangers and desire for a traditional, permanent plot or 'home.'

In the first section, the narrator engages in a meditation on the nature of Edberg as home and as a possible site for engravement. However, the narrator quickly encounters difficulties in mapping the rural environment. The portrait of Edberg that emerges in this section indicates that the town is suffering the fate of other small rural outposts. In his study of western literature, Edward McCourt remarks on the tragic disappearance of the rural environment: 'the family farm, from time immemorial the foundation of an agrarian society, has all but ceased to exist' (122). The smaller towns, such as Edberg, are particularly threatened with extinction. Built originally on the railroad eight or ten miles apart, 'many no longer justify their existence. The new highways pass them by. ... But Main Street is more often than not lined on either side by empty rotting buildings and weed-grown lots' (122). Towns such as Edberg are dying primarily because people are leaving and moving to the city. McCourt concludes his study with the following provocative statement: 'Out of these changed social and economic conditions has evolved a theme of possibly tragic implications which so far none of our novelists has attempted to dramatize – the divorcing of an entire generation from its own past' (123). In *Places Far from Ellesmere*, van Herk dramatizes this very division. At one point, the narrator remarks on the farmers who sigh over their cups of coffee and speak of the town's children who have 'gone into the maw of larger and larger cities' (33). She even likens herself to a murderer because she understands that her defection from home has contributed to its demise (46). In its catalogue of the buildings that once existed and description of the 'remainders' – the barely visible remnants of these sites –

this first 'site exploration' offers an elegiac portrait of the disappearance of a small prairie town.

Despite the narrator's desire to offer an accurate map of the vanishing town, she recognizes that it cannot be contained:

> You cup your hands to hold it in, breathe deep. You want to command it into everlasting place like a horse or a dog, a patient animal. You look away: it moves, un/reads itself again, a sly alteration leaving you puzzled and groping for reassurement. You check with other originals, try to compare your grainy photograph with theirs. ... Impossible: their versions negate yours.   (37–8)

In passages such as this, the text foregrounds the fact that the Platonic distinction between original and copy cannot be sustained. The narrator remains unable to account for the site's multiplicity: 'Edberg goes on with its falling, one molecule at a time: and you too in your ache to archive it there to read/remember/blame. To unhinge, and to carve with words' (39).

Although she is unable to engrave or 'archive' it, she nevertheless understands that the town has informed her identity: 'Edberg has carved itself into the cleft above your mouth. Your nose has an Edberg slope to it. ... This is your self-geography, the way you were discovered/uncovered in Edberg's reading of your fiction' (36–7). In passages such as this, the narrator promotes a model of reading that dissolves the opposition between active, reading subject and passively read object; as she says, all people and places have 'acts of reading as their histories' (36). This statement counters the model of mastery located in Grove's text, as well as in Ricou's model of the vertical man/horizontal world opposition; it also challenges Wiebe's assertion that the fiction-writer's task consists in imposing 'great black steel lines of fiction' on the landscape (259).

Although she cannot capture the town in a fictional engravement, the narrator does provide some salient details regarding her hometown – details which emphasize its fortress-like nature. In her account of Edberg, she describes its 'six square blocks' and grid-like structure, stressing the emphasis placed on the control of flows (37). In her reading of Edberg's history and her early life in the town, she primarily remembers the set of prohibitions that were geared to restrict her movements. After reciting a long list of taboos, including going uptown at noon, playing ball, riding in a car with an adult over thirty, going to dances, smoking, drinking, and screwing, the narrator poses the following question: 'Who allows/forbids what?' (27). While her question remains unanswered, she concludes that what she was not allowed to express (all the flows that were dammed) to satisfy these prohibitions constitutes her unlived life, which remains '[m]issing: unread' (39).[21]

In contrast to the town's repressive character, the image of the platform at the train station, which stood 'on the lip of the world,' functions as a figure for desire and escape (16). It is on the platform that the narrator first imagines seeing Tolstoy's Anna Karenin 'in black velvet stepping down to take a breath of air on her way to one of the family estates' (16). Later on, she remarks that Anna 'will get off to pace the platform ... and to remember that illegitimacy lurks everywhere, she has only to read the story differently, her own story waiting to be un/read by the light of these places' (36). However, this image of Anna getting *off* the train highlights the crucial fact that a creative rereading of the story, what Deleuze would call a 'line of flight,' can only occur when one diverges from the linear narrative trajectories associated with State-thought, symbolized by the train-tracks.

In the 'geografictione,' the image of train-tracks corresponds to Rudy Wiebe's description of the writer's grid, those 'great black steel lines of fiction.' Within the section on Ellesmere Island, the narrator clarifies this association between the train-tracks and State-thought when she explains that Anna was railroaded into committing suicide by Tolstoy. She goes on to align Tolstoy with the mysterious peasant who appears in Anna's dreams and magically arrives on the scene when Anna commits suicide in the novel. Tolstoy and his alter ego, the little peasant '*working at the rails*' (Tolstoy qtd. in *Places*, 120), are held responsible for grinding Anna 'beneath the freight cars of the train' (119).[22] In essence, the train-tracks symbolize the rigid, prearranged structure of the Oedipal trajectory. The emphasis on the train-tracks also recalls Robert Kroetsch's parody of the quest-novel entitled *Gone Indian* (1973). In this text, the main character, Jeremy Sadness, a 'child of Manhattan,' believes his life to be 'shaped and governed by some deep American need to seek out the frontier' (5). Responding to this urge and fortified by his faith in the 'possibility of transformation,' Jeremy embarks on a journey to the untamed, carnivalesque Canadian northwest. In the end, together with his newly acquired lover, Jeremy vanishes into the blank indifferent geography of the Great Plains. Left behind in New York, his wife clings to a generous fantasy that features the 'romantic couple stepping down from their long and snow-scarred Pullman ... getting off the train at a whistle stop on the prairies. ... Making a clean break into the last forest' (153). In imagining a revised destiny for Tolstoy's Anna, van Herk may have been influenced by Kroetsch's protagonists, who likewise 'leap from the iron path' of fiction's familiar plot structure (157).

Like Jeremy Sadness, van Herk's narrator restlessly searches for an alternative to the traditional plot. In the second section of the 'geografictione,' she attempts to escape the prohibitions associated with Edberg by travelling to Edmonton, where she attends university. In this episode, the narrator highlights the problem of 'division' referred to earlier. As she explains, Edmonton is the urban environment that 'will divide you from the country, that will wean you from Edberg' (43). At this point, the narrator experiences the type of division that van Herk suggested is characteristic of many Canadian writers who grew up in a rural environment and moved to an urban setting. Although she travelled to Edmonton to get away from the prohibitions she experienced in Edberg, it turns out that Edmonton – this 'once-fort, Hudson's Bay Company stronghold' – like Edberg, is structured according to a grid (52). Associated as it is with the State and State-thought, Edmonton cannot possibly satisfy the narrator's desires for escape. The text offers a clue that this is the case when the narrator asks, 'what's to be expected of a fort(ress) set up to trade/skin Indians?' (43), and then likens herself to an Indian: 'you now the Indian coming with your skin, your fresh eyes up from the Battle River country' (44). As in the previous section on Edberg, the fortress is once again opposed to the smooth space of the desert.

Although the narrator's desires remain unfulfilled in Edmonton, she does manage to find some satisfaction in the books she reads (46). Literature takes the place of lovers as the repository for her desire, and she learns to savour fiction (47, 49). As we might expect, the 'space of literature' has been identified as a possible site of nomad-thought (Massumi, xiii). Despite her discovery of the pleasures of the text with its creative lines of flight, Edmonton itself remains a 'stagnation point' within the world at large. For the narrator, the city continues to be associated with the fortress it once was. Her memories of the city are of 'the darkness of winter and of buildings, of *enclosured* cold' (53; my emphasis). Far from offering a final resting point, Edmonton turns out to be merely the site of 'glacial long division, the self caught between origins and destinations: body and cemetery' (52). In this section, the image of Anna Karenin reappears once again, signalling the narrator's desire to escape what is clearly another of the State's fortresses: 'Russia is looming, luring, lurking, Anna's quick step on the platforms of desire reaches all the way to Edmonton' (48).

In the third section, the image of the fortress surfaces yet again. The narrator wryly comments on her new home, Calgary, saying, 'Found yourself a Jericho, have you?' (57). Jericho was, of course, the biblical walled city, which Joshua and the *nomadic* army of Israel destroyed. Each of Calgary's four quadrants is discussed in a separate section of the text. In keeping with van Herk's belief that contemporary western writers find themselves alienated in the metropolis, the narrator finds herself lost in the urban landscape. The shopping malls are described as labyrinthine 'bubbles of light and air that claim closure, insist on wholeness and order' where 'you wander, lost, cannot find the door you came in or any door at all' (72). Portrayed as a labyrinth, Calgary fulfils the primary goal of the State, which is to effect capture. At one point, the narrator likens herself to the minotaur trapped within a maze: 'Who can find you here, a clumsy bawling beast in the centre of a web of thread, a cat's cradle of encapturement?' (73).

Not only is Calgary a maze, it is also a fortress of sterility; the narrator explains that 'sex is too playful for Jericho' (73). Robert Kroetsch first described Calgary as a city of male virgins in an article that mocked the 'failure of sexuality' in the newly created city, and he concluded that Calgary is 'ultimately Christian in its sexual posture: women are the source only of man's fall' ('Kingdom,' 1). Van Herk takes up his assertion, but she emphasizes that Calgary is, in fact, only small part of a larger kingdom – a kingdom that encompasses the entire masculinized prairie and the fictions generated there. Both the cities and their fictions are described as chaste, idealistic, rational, and, above all, dangerous for women writers to inhabit ('Gentle,' 257).

In the midst of this discussion of the city's maze-like structure and its Christian idealism, the narrator introduces the concept of nomadology. She remarks that Calgary was begun by 'the oldest occupation, the nomadic herding of grazing animals,' and that the city's transient nature is the nomadic legacy of the ranchers (68, 69). At this point, when she poses the question, 'Where is home?' she recognizes that, from certain vantage points, home may not exist, and she realizes that there is 'no evidence of city' from certain points 'outside' the metropolis – points of view which belong to the 'nomad wandering the prairie' (71). Ultimately, the narrator decides that Calgary, a fortress built out of 'dragon's teeth that have grown themselves into monoliths' (71), is, in conjunction with Edberg and Edmonton, a place 'to run away from' (72). She winds up her tour of this exploration site with a plea in support of nomad-thought, and she urges individuals to escape Calgary's labyrinth of stone and return to deterritorialized space. In the end, she commands the city to shout, just as Joshua and his troops shouted in an effort to raze the walls of Jericho.

In the text's final section, entitled 'Ellesmere, woman as island,' the walls have shattered, the male west has been successfully 'earthquaked,' and the exploration site shifts to the deterritorialized, nomadic polar desert of an Arctic island. In this desert landscape, the female body ceases to be the site for the projection of masculine fantasies; the chimera of Woman gives way to a non-hierarchized body. As the narrator explains: 'You are only a body, here in this Arctic desert, this fecund island. Lungs, fingers, a stomach, legs and feet. This fragile world far tougher than you are, a floating polar desert for all characters to emulate' (77–8). In their work, Deleuze and Guattari invoke the concept of the 'Body Without Organs' to describe a body that is free from the restrictions imposed on it by State-thought. As Elizabeth Grosz suggests:

Their notion of the Body Without Organs (BWO) constitutes Deleuze and Guattari's attempt to both denaturalize the human body and to place it in direct relations with the flows or particles of other bodies or entities. ... Rather than, as psychoanalysis does, regarding the body as the developmental union or aggregate of partial objects, organs, drives, bits, each with their own significance ... which are, through oedipalization, brought into line with the body's organic unity, Deleuze and Guattari instead invoke Antonin Artaud's conception of the Body Without Organs (BWO). This is the body disinvested of all fantasies, images, projections, a body without a psychical interior, without internal cohesion or latent significance. Deleuze and Guattari speak of it as a surface of intensities before it is stratified, organized, hierarchized. ... [I]t is a limit or a tendency to which all bodies aspire. ('Thousand,' 14)

In accordance with this Deleuzian model of the Body Without Organs, the narrator portrays the interaction between body and environment on Ellesmere as one of free-flowing 'pleasure' and 'seduction.' The syntax used to describe the simple action of drawing water from a river reflects the extent to which the narrator's body is in direct relation with the flows or particles of other entities: 'buckets and water and stones and the muscles of shoulder and arm' (109). The conjunction of the human and non-human elements in this passage conforms to the rhizomatic structure of nomad-thought. As Brian Massumi explains:

Nomad thought replaces the closed equation of representation, x = x = not y (I = I = not you) with an open equation: ... + x + z + a +. ... Rather than analyzing the world into discrete components, reducing their manyness to the One of identity, and ordering them by rank, it sums up a set of disparate circumstances in a shattering blow.   (xiii)

With the aid of nomad-thought, the narrator is able to experience her body beyond the confines of its designation as 'the Sex.' Moreover, in conjunction with the destabilization of these binary oppositions, she is also able to deconstruct the static enclosure that characterizes the plot of Tolstoy's *Anna Karenin.*

The narrator explains that she could only take one book with her on her trip to Ellesmere. Although her friend, Rudy Wiebe suggested that she take *War and Peace,* she does not want to read masculine epic fiction. She chooses *Anna Karenin* because, as she says, she is looking for 'an image of a woman,' even one scripted by a man (81). According to van Herk, Anna Karenin is a 'lost' woman: 'Lost in Russian, lost in love, lost in the nineteenth century. The especial lostness of an invented character whose inventor revenged himself on her through the failings he invented for her' (77). This emphasis on 'lostness' recalls Marlatt's novel, *Ana Historic;* in fact, both works are concerned with women's status as individuals who have been lost or mis-represented within written history. In Marlatt's text, the resemblance among the women's names, Annie, Ana, and Ina, clarifies that all women have suffered this fate. Likewise, in van Herk's text, the narrator asserts that 'women are all Annas' (82) in that we have all been 'written by men' (85).

In an attempt to rescue Tolstoy's Anna, the narrator takes her to Ellesmere and unreads her (85). As I suggested earlier, the north is the home of the nomad – the deterritorialized space that lies outside the enclosed spaces of the State's fortresses. In *Places Far from Ellesmere,* the narrator underscores this, saying: 'these northerns belong to no nation, no configuration of [wo]man' (125). Even the puzzle-ice which covers the ocean provides a clue to the type of fluid unreadings made possible in this Arctic space. The narrator's / reader's unreading of *Anna Karenin* is likened to a thaw in the static mass of ice (93), and, at one point, the ice forms a picture of Anna herself (111–12). Ultimately, the image of the puzzle-ice transforming from molar masses to fluid molecular shards functions as a figure for the exploratory strategy of a feminist reading of Tolstoy's text: 'The words are stirred, mixed, like pieces of a jigsaw, broken up into their separate shapes and the whole picture lost' (113). As the narrator explains, 'reading is a new act here, not introverted and possessive but exploratory, the text a new body of self, the self a new reading of place' (113).

When she undertakes her unreading of Tolstoy's novel, the narrator discovers that Anna is punished as a result of her eroticism. Moreover, at the heart of Anna's desire for Vronsky and her love of books lies her fundamental desire to read her own life, an impulse that is not permissible in a society where female desire represents 'an unleashed demon that should be controlled and organized, scripted and domesticated' (107). In a close reading of the passage where Tolstoy arranges for Anna to commit suicide by throwing herself under the wheels of the train, van Herk highlights the fact that it is primarily Anna's ability to read that is negated by her death: '*And the candle by which she had been reading the book filled with trouble and deceit, sorrow and evil, flared up with a brighter light, illuminating for her everything that before had been enshrouded in darkness, flickered, grew dim and went out forever*' (Tolstoy, 802, qtd. in *Places*, 120–1). However, in the high Arctic of Ellesmere Island, the darkness into which Tolstoy casts Anna and the trains which he arranges to murder her are banished: 'The trains that shunt Anna back and forth between Moscow and Petersburg ... could not conceive of how to traverse Ellesmere. No amount of hammering could shape this floating woman / island into a metal bar. Within this endless light, she resists all earlier reading' (121). Ultimately, the 'site exploration' of Ellesmere Island offers a fierce condemnation of the imposition of the 'great black steel lines' of masculine fiction. Writing, in the service of the State, is revealed to be akin to rape. The narrator's use of the inclusive pronoun 'you' further emphasizes that all women have suffered from the rigid frame imposed by the representation of women as Woman: 'Anna murdered, *you murdered*, your body abandoned under its burden of blood and bone, the terrible violation of an iron writing' (142; my emphasis).

In *Places Far from Ellesmere*, Aritha van Herk grapples with the process of map-making, which, historically, has remained a profoundly colonizing activity. She utilizes the images of cartography and exploration to redraw the map, and she champions women's ability to reread and rewrite their way out of a fictional landscape plotted by male writers. Women, according to van Herk, can and must write their way out of a body deemed subnormal, submale, and pathological by scientific 'experts' – a body whose existence has been prearranged to culminate in death. As the narrator argues, escape from this prearranged plot is possible: 'You must live up to your fictions, all there is to it; you must help yourself achieve geografictiones of the soul, moments of erasure only available in fiction and on desert islands' (87).

With its emphasis on 'erasure,' *Places Far from Ellesmere* recalls the dilemma that surfaced in the previous novels – a dilemma that hinges on the dangers associated with erasure or the refusal of representation, on the one hand, and the construction of a 'fixed address' or a unified sense of identity, on the other. Van Herk's fictions delineate two prominent positions in what remains a current debate among feminists. On the one hand, many feminists argue for the necessity of asserting a recognizable and visible identity in language. For this reason, as I noted in previous chapters, they remain highly sceptical of post-structuralist and postmodern strategies that celebrate the dissolution of the unified ego. As Patricia Waugh explains, during the 1960s, when many male writers were waving goodbye to the idea of character in fiction, women writers for the first time in history were beginning to 'construct an identity out of the recognition that women need to discover, and must fight for, a sense of unified selfhood, a rational, coherent, effective identity' (6). On the other hand, writers such as van Herk realize that staking out an identity involves the risk of being co-opted by the State. To avoid constructing a totalizing structure to replace the representation of Woman, these feminists attempt to refuse representation altogether. Realistically, this dilemma can only be resolved within particular contexts. For instance, in the case of van Herk (a white woman working in an institution of higher education), there is perhaps more reason to break down a sense of 'unified selfhood, a rational, coherent, effective identity.' I suspect this would not be the preferred strategy if van Herk were a woman of colour. Instances such as this illustrate that it is crucial to emphasize the existence of feminisms, rather than feminism. An awareness of the variety of feminists and feminist strategies helps to explain why, at the same time that some feminists are fighting for visibility, others are championing invisibility; yet, these two strategies need not be mutually exclusive, as we shall see.

In her latest book of essays, *In Visible Ink: Crypto-frictions*, van Herk discusses a trip that she took to the Arctic, and, once again, she reinforces the pleasures associated with becoming invisible, a state which Deleuze and Guattari view as the endpoint in a series of 'becomings' associated with the rejection of the State and State-thought:

Yes, reader, I have cited space and measurement, time and quotidian gesture, all in vain. I cannot read these reaches. I have no language for *arctic*, impossible to convey the sensation. … Instead, it inscribes me, takes over my cullible imagination … invents me. … Effaces my referentiality, a transformation without continuity or chronology. I am re-invented by a great white page. Not *isolation* but complete invisibility, all causes and destinations blurred by causes other to causalities I believe I know. ... I am effaced, become an enunciative field, a page untouched by pen, no archive and no history. (8)

The notion of invisibility is problematized, however, because, at the same time that she engages in the process of becoming-invisible, she enters into an alternative language. In the journey referred to above, the narrator is led by an Inuit guide, Pijamini, who addresses her in his language, Inuktitut. As the narrator explains, 'He gives me *his* words, and thus names me, writes my invisible and unlanguaged self into his archaeology. I am written, finally, with that nomadic language' (10). This passage reveals that the dilemma noted above may not, in reality, be a dilemma at all; there is reason to believe that women must become invisible within the traditional systems of representation, at the same time as they become visible in terms of another, marginalized language, here represented by Pijamini's 'nomadic language.'

In *Gone Indian*, Kroetsch's hero idolizes 'Grey Owl,' the Englishman Archie Belany, who fled to Canada, claimed to be a Native, and went on to give lectures on behalf of 'his' people. Jeremy Sadness views him as a model frontiersman, and harbours a 'passion to become an aboriginal of some variety' 153). Although, as noted earlier, she likens herself to an Indian: 'you now the Indian coming with your skin, your fresh eyes' (44) – van Herk's narrator has not 'gone Indian' in the same way that Sadness does. Rather than attempt to 'become an aboriginal,' she experiences the joy of being *written into* an alternative archaeology – an experience which, although it flirts with the possibility of invisibility, does not involve dabbling in acts of impersonation.

In their work, Deleuze and Guattari suggest that women, in particular, must strive to oscillate between the two poles of invisibility and visibility in a strategic fashion: 'It is ... indispensable for women to conduct a molar politics, with a view to winning back their own organism, their own history, their own subjectivity. ... But it is dangerous to confine oneself to such a subject, which does not function without drying up a spring or stopping a flow' (276). In the case of Aritha van Herk's most recent text, it is difficult to determine whether the author achieves this balance. Some critics are unhappy with the balance that has been struck, arguing that, in the end, the text is a 'genreless book that makes a powerful argument for genre' (review by Thomas, 70). Ultimately, the ability to achieve this balance will determine the efficacy of any feminist strategy of subversion. As Deleuze and Guattari state:

You have to keep enough of the organism for it to reform each dawn; and you have to keep small supplies of signifiance [sic] and subjectification, if only to turn them against their own systems when the circumstances demand it, when things, persons, even situations, force you to; and you have to keep small rations of subjectivity in sufficient quantity to enable you to respond to the dominant reality.   (160)

In the light of van Herk's boldness and her successful destabilization of both traditional plots and representations of female identity, criticisms that dismiss her work out of hand seem far too harsh; worse, they reveal a misunderstanding of her project, which is not so much to change the map as it is to change the process of mapping altogether. What results is not 'a tracing of shape, but a means of tracing,' a 'geografictione' that instigates a shift from capture and cartography to deterritorialization and nomadology.

6

Emptying the Museum:
Jane Urquhart's *The Whirlpool*

I thought how unpleasant it is to be locked out; and I thought how it is worse perhaps to be locked in. ... (Woolf, *Room*, 24)

In the introductory chapter, I suggested that my interest in fictions by contemporary Canadian women writers was sparked by Woolf's claim that, in literature, the linguistic terrain is obscured by 'the dominance of the ... [male] "I"' (*Room*, 96). The epigraph to this chapter, also taken from *A Room of One's Own*, continues to explore the notion of terrain and boundaries as they relate to gender. The quotation concerns the reflections of the narrator, a woman visiting the fictitious university 'Oxbridge.' Lost in thought about the lecture she is preparing on 'women and fiction,' she suddenly finds herself being chased off the grass by an irate Beadle. This man, expressing 'horror and indignation,' confines her to the gravel path because only male Fellows and Scholars are allowed to walk on the 'turf' (7). Following this interruption, the narrator attempts to collect her scattered thoughts and wends her way to the library. When she opens the door, however, she is once again waved away by an elderly gentleman, who informs her that 'ladies are only admitted to the library if accompanied by a Fellow of the College or furnished with a letter of introduction' (9). What remains surprising is that the chapter does not close with a reminiscence of the curses the narrator placed on that venerable library. Instead, as the passage cited above indicates, the narrator possesses the intellectual curiosity and generosity of spirit to consider both sides of the equation. Astutely, she recognizes that a system that creates these divisions between insiders and outsiders is bound to be harmful to both parties.

I would suggest that a similar breadth of perspective, which takes into account the experiences of both men and women forced to negotiate an arbitrary divide, marks Jane Urquhart's novel *The Whirlpool* (1986). Woolf's image of the divide (the turf versus the gravel, and the door of the library) is particularly relevant here because it underscores the preoccupation with containment and its antithesis, chaos, that is also central to Urquhart's text. In many ways, Urquhart's novel recalls concerns raised in works discussed earlier: the way in which the narrative of romance enforces a divide between the male hero and the female obstacle. But here the image of a boundary is also linked, more generally, to the text's portrayal of the urge to conquer and organize the multiplicity of experience in the new world. This process of organization, which promises a form of transcendent vision, is, as we will see, associated both with the quest narrative and the discursive construction of the 'sublime' moment, which sometimes comprises a facet of the quest. In Urquhart's text the imagery of maps and map-making arises because, once again, an overlap exists between the mapping of physical divides and the plotting of narratives.

Set in Niagara Falls, Ontario, during the summer of 1889, *The Whirlpool* continues to explore women's problematic relationships with the maps that have been constructed for them – maps that position women as outsiders: muse, object, landscape, obstacle, or, in this case, whirlpool. As in the previous works, of concern is whether these maps contribute solely to the imprisonment and territorialization of bodies and desire or whether they can be made to serve the impulses of accommodation and even deterritorialization.

In Urquhart's text, perhaps as forcibly as in Marlatt's *Ana Historic*, these issues have an impact on the formal structure of the work. Framed by a seemingly unrelated narrative concerning the death of Robert Browning, the novel traces the intersecting lives of five characters. The chapters alternate to present the different perspectives of the historian, Major David McDougal; his wife, Fleda; the visiting poet from Ottawa, Patrick; and the local undertaker, Maud, and her young son. There is no single hero or heroine: this is no romance. In an attempt to remain sensitive to the structure of Urquhart's novel, this chapter will not simply trace the experience of the female protagonists (a tactic adopted in previous chapters). There are important links between the narrative of romance, specifically its archetypes of the temple and the labyrinth, and the text's related portrayal of the opposition between the home/museum and the whirlpool. The gendering of the romance narrative in Urquhart's novel is relevant here, as we shall see, specifically the way in which the whirlpool becomes aligned with Woman. I would suggest that the fears and desires associated with the whirlpool and related chaotic elements can be best understood in the light of the eighteenth-century aesthetic concept known as the 'sublime.' The novel's emphasis on the conflict between order and chaos highlights the extent to which this tension and the narrative mechanisms designed to deal with it (in particular, the quest motif and the sublime moment) constitute a legacy from the Old World. The chapter will conclude with an analysis of the strategies adopted by each of the principal characters in order to determine their varied responses to the divisive narratives inherited from the Old World.

Like many of the works examined previously, Urquhart's text interrogates the narrative of romance, which typically portrays an isolated hero engaging in a series of adventures. By contrast, the structure of *The Whirlpool*, with its shifting focus, ensures that whatever plot can be said to 'exist' owes its tenuous existence not to the unifying presence of the hero but to the reader's ability to fabricate meaning through a poetic process of association. I would argue, further, that the polyphonic structure, which invites readers to compare the experiences of the various characters, works in the service of deterritorialization because the multiple meanings that proliferate as a result of this type of associative structure frustrate any impulse toward containment. As we will see, this refusal of containment can be understood as yet another strategy of resistance – a strategy that is mirrored within the discrete sections themselves. Both formally and thematically, this tactic of subversion calls into question romance's quest for order.

Most critics agree that the goal of traditional romantic quests involves a transcendent vision or actualization of order: a return home, or a voyage to a place where the national unity and destiny will be affirmed (Abrams, 190–5). The Spenserian critic Angus Fletcher suggests that this place of unity is often symbolized as a temple. The structure of containment *par excellence*, the temple is 'strictly formalized, to frame the highest degree of order' (12). It is used to emphasize the concept of 'limit, edge, margin, boundary or closure' (18). While Urquhart's novel does not explicitly invoke templar structures, it nevertheless depicts nineteenth-century domestic versions of the temple, namely, the home.

Owing to the widening separation between the domestic and public spheres in the nineteenth century, the domestic space, set off from the workaday world, increasingly took on connotations of the templar structure. English author and critic John Ruskin explicitly links the domestic sphere to the temple in his writings on the ideal home:

This is the true nature of home – it is the place of Peace; the shelter, not only from all injury, but from all terror, doubt, and division. In so far as it is not this, it is not home; so far as the anxieties of the outer life penetrate into it, and the inconsistently-minded, unknown, unloved, or hostile society of the outer world is allowed by either husband or wife to cross the threshold, it ceases to be a home; it is then only a part of that outer world which you have roofed over, and lighted fire in. But so far as it is a sacred place, a vestal temple, a temple of the hearth watched over by Household Gods. ... so far it vindicates the name, and fulfils the praise, of Home.   (Ruskin, 136–7)

According to Ruskin, the temple is 'watched over by Household Gods'; as Fletcher states, the templar structure typically implies a 'ministry' of some kind (19). Women, idealized as the Angel in the House, were expected to fill the role of the temple's 'angelic ministers.'

Throughout Urquhart's text, the nature of 'home' remains a contested issue. When the novel opens, the historian's youthful wife, Fleda, has previously vacated one house and, more recently, left her lodgings at Kick's Hotel in the town of Niagara Falls in favour of dwelling in a tent set up on her husband's property, Whirlpool Heights. As the novel progresses, Fleda gradually moves closer to abandoning even this temporary structure. Eventually, she walks out into the woods and leaves her marriage, after thoroughly grasping the claustrophobic and stultifying implications of living in the home that is gradually being erected on the property.

In keeping with the anxiety surrounding the concept of 'home,' the visiting, reclusive poet, Patrick, has also recently abandoned his home and his marriage in Ottawa. When the reader encounters him, he has travelled to Niagara Falls and is staying at his uncle's farmhouse in an attempt to recuperate from a nervous breakdown. Early on, Patrick's and Fleda's paths cross when the poet goes for a walk on Whirlpool Heights. He glimpses Fleda and becomes instantly infatuated with her. Yet, rather than accept her offer to develop a closer relationship, Patrick continues to spurn anything faintly resembling the trappings of domesticity, until, finally, he embarks on his fatal, solitary quest to swim the whirlpool.

Patrick's quest links him and Fleda's husband, the historian David McDougal, with Maud, the local undertaker. Once again, in the sections of the novel which focus on Maud, the notion of 'home' assumes tremendous importance. In Maud's case, domestic relations are not interrupted because she has willingly left her spouse. Fate saw to it that Maud's husband and his family left her: they were killed off by an epidemic. Two years before the events documented in the novel take place, Maud found herself in possession of the family home and the family business, but the home that she inherits is far from welcoming. Instead, it is a museum-like structure filled with foreign objects donated by clients who bartered goods in lieu of paying their bills in cash. Moving through this space, Maud and her young son seem more like its prisoners than its owners.

Initially, both Maud and Fleda are constrained by their supposed role in the human 'ministry': angels in the domestic temple. Similarly, David and Patrick respond to their role as heroic questers, who must venture forth from this supposed 'place of Peace.' However, conflict arises when both sexes experience the limitations of their respective identities as angel and heroic quester. At one point or another, the over-determined nature of these traditional representations becomes intolerable. For the women, the templar home becomes a demonic parody of the sacred structure, which, as Fletcher notes, is 'always a prison' (36).[1]

In the novel, the identification between home and temple is complicated by the fact that the homes portrayed, stocked with the owners' possessions, bear greater resemblances to museums than temples. Moreover, the female occupants, who are fetishized and scrutinized, seem more like objects in a collection than angelic beings.

For this reason (and others, which will become apparent), I describe the process of deterritorialization deployed in the text as 'emptying the museum.' Before going on to investigate this subversive tactic, however, it is important to consider how the concept of the museum operates in conjunction with its antithesis, the whirlpool. In the novel, this opposition intersects with a set of cultural and literary variables. Earlier, I mentioned that the novel calls into question romance's quest for order, but it also interrogates the quests associated with nineteenth-century approaches to both history and science, as well as Victorian ideals of womanhood.

Virtually all of the characters (save Fleda, and Maud's child, who appears to be autistic) attempt to stabilize meaning through a rigid imposition of order and the maintenance of strict divisions between self and other. As Sylvia Söderlind notes in her study of Canadian and Québécois fiction, *Margin/Alias*, this practice owes a debt to the Enlightenment insistence 'on the sharp distinction between subject and object, observer and observed, reality and illusion' (26). In *The Whirlpool* this drive toward order typically culminates in the construction of a real or imagined museum. The historian dreams of the perfect museum; the undertaker constructs a personal museum from artifacts collected from bodies found in the river; and the poet collects wildflowers 'for his album,' but rapidly substitutes women for flowers. While the latter does not construct an actual museum, his habit of collecting and the separation he relentlessly imposes between observer and observed are, according to James Clifford, linked to the same ideology which gave rise to the museum in the West (2).

Critics of Urquhart's work have commented on her repeated use of the image of the museum and references to collecting. In interviews, she readily admits to her fascination with the drive toward order which, as she suggests, manifests itself in the act of collecting and is embodied in the museum. As Susan Stewart notes, collecting and museums go hand in hand: 'it is the museum ... which must serve as the central metaphor of the collection' (*On Longing*, 161). Urquhart's fascination with order and its concrete manifestations was sparked when she selected a museum as the setting for her third collection of poetry, *The Little Flowers of Madame de Montespan* – a collection that investigates the relationship between Louis XIV, the creator of Versailles, and his mistress. Discussing this project, she explains that she received ample education concerning control, power, and order after visiting Versailles:

I discovered through the landscape of the gardens there almost everything I wanted to know about power. The gardens of the Palace are gorgeous, but they have been controlled to such an extent by a single individual, Louis the XIV, that they are frightening. It's the difference between chaos and order, which is negative and which is positive. ... This fascinated and kind of appalled me and triggered two collections of poems. ... The idea of order versus chaos began to interest me to such an extent that I started to direct my travels in order to observe it more closely.   ('Interview,' 36).

In *The Little Flowers of Madame de Montespan*, Urquhart depicts Louis xiv, 'that great orderer of the landscape, stumbling through the forest at the edge of Niagara Falls in a nightmare' ('Interview,' 38). In *The Whirlpool*, this nightmare becomes a reality when all of the characters find themselves surrounded by the sublime geological chaos of the Falls. In an effort to master this chaos, many of the characters, following in the footsteps of Louis xiv, try to impose order by constructing museums, sometimes within their own homes.

The relationship posited in the novel between the house and the museum may strike contemporary readers as odd; yet the conflation of the two was commonplace in the late nineteenth century. For instance, in her book on collecting written for children in 1890, C. Montiesor urges her readers to create a museum within their own home:

[E]very house ought to possess a 'Museum,' even if it is only one shelf in a small cupboard; here, carefully dated and named, should be placed the pretty shells you gather on the seashore, the old fossils you find in the rocks, the skeleton leaves you pick up from under the hedges, the strange orchids you find on the downs. Learn what you can about each object before you put it in the museum, and docket it not only with its name, but also with the name of the place in which you found it, and the date.   (Montiesor, 192)

In the text, however, the images of the museum, the house, and the whirlpool do not simply reflect historically accurate cultural practices. As suggested earlier, these images, working along the same lines as the traditional romantic opposition between temple and labyrinth, recall a classic conflict between order and chaos.

Seen in this light, the various attempts on the part of the protagonists to create museums of one kind or another echo the primary function of the temple, namely, to stabilize meaning and eradicate chaos. By contrast, the labyrinth (figured here as the whirlpool located downriver from the Falls) signifies lost direction. In romance narrative, the labyrinth stands as the antithesis of home, closure, and the attainment of a goal or a truth; it symbolizes wandering, motion, process, and error. Once again, maps and map-making are inescapable; as Fletcher states, the form of the labyrinth is defined 'not so much as a material setting ... as a general condition of *unmapped* disorder' (29; my emphasis).

As the title indicates, in this case, the maze is a liquid one, but this is by no means unusual. In quest narratives, heroes wander over sea as well as land, and often the labyrinth is associated with sea voyages. According to Fletcher, the sinuous lines of the maze are frequently represented by the motion 'of waves and furious, redundant turbulence' (27). Urquhart's whirlpool, with its 'redundant' motion, constitutes a maze of this type. In fact, it is explicitly associated with the labyrinths found in traditional romance when the historian explains its origin to the poet.

As David states, the whirlpool below the Falls was formed because, at one point, before the 'ice age came along and filled it up with rocks and soil,' there had been a fork in the river. Even though the fork no longer exists, 'some of the water still wants to go that route. But, of course, it can't because there is nowhere to go so it turns back on itself' (103). He goes on to note that his wife, Fleda, interprets the whirlpool in terms of the quest structure of romance and views it as a metaphor for 'interrupted journeys. As if the river were Ulysses or something' (103). The poet agrees with this interpretation wholeheartedly: 'That's it, exactly, thought Patrick, amazed, delighted' (103). The novel not only sustains this identification between chaos and whirlpool but goes on to underscore the gendering of romance narratives and to demonstrate the links between the hero's response to the feminine abyss and the eighteenth-century aesthetic concept of the sublime.

The gendering of the romance narrative first becomes explicit when Patrick identifies the labyrinth as Woman. Early on in the novel, he finds himself intrigued with Fleda and the whirlpool, and actually confuses the two. While describing his plan to swim across the whirlpool to David, Patrick silently acknowledges the conflation: 'Suddenly, he was uncertain whether it was the water or the woman [Fleda] he was talking about' (102). The links between Woman and whirlpool and their opposition to order, figured by the image of the museum, are further underscored when Patrick subsequently wonders if he will 'be able to tour it [the whirlpool] like a museum or caress it as he would a woman' (102).

In accordance with the Oedipal aspects of the romance narrative, Patrick positions himself as subject/hero and treats the woman/whirlpool as background and/or obstacle: 'He stepped towards the river. The sound it made was like a woman's breath near his shoulder, incredibly gentle and quiet and calling. And then this fear of any action concerning the river, as if it were a woman' (221).[2]

In his study *Male Phantasies*, Klaus Theweleit discusses the prevalent association in literature between women and water:

A river without end, enormous and wide, flows through the world's literatures. Over and over again: the women-in-the-water; woman as water, as a stormy, cavorting, cooling ocean, a raging stream, a waterfall; as a limitless body of water that ships pass through, with tributaries, pools, surfs and deltas; woman as the enticing (or perilous) deep. ...   (283)

Theweleit argues that the representations by male writers of 'Woman-as-water' reflect pre-Oedipal desires for the dissolution of the Oedipal split between id and ego sustained upon entry into the symbolic order. He suggests, further, that the attraction / repulsion that often constellates around the figure of woman as water is indicative of the tensions experienced by a subject whose externally imposed identity is based on this split (204). Fletcher's analysis of romance inadvertently supports Theweleit's findings in that he too notes that contradictory feelings, ranging from terror to delight, are very often aroused by the labyrinth (32). Yet, as Jean-François Lyotard notes, between 'the seventeenth and eighteenth centuries in Europe this contradictory feeling – pleasure and pain, joy and anxiety, exaltation and depression – was christened or re-christened by the name of the *sublime* ('Sublime,' 198–9).

In his influential study published in 1757, Edmund Burke highlights both terror and delight when he characterizes the sublime as '[w]hatever is fitted in any sort to excite the ideas of pain, and danger ... whatever is in any sort terrible, or is conversant about terrible objects, or operates in a manner analogous to terror, is a source of the *sublime*; that is, it is productive of the strongest emotion which the mind is capable of feeling' (39).[3] Later on, he qualifies this statement, emphasizing that the sublime produces a feeling of 'delightful horror' (136).

Immanuel Kant's *Critique of Judgement* (1790) does not offer anything like Burke's empirical study of the emotions produced by the sublime, and is, instead, concerned with epistemology. Nevertheless, Kant also argues that during the sublime experience the mind feels agitated and experiences a rapid alternation of 'repulsion from, and attraction to, one and the same object' (115). While Kant disagrees with Burke's assertion that whatever is 'terrible' is sublime, and insists that sublimity is ultimately not contained 'in any thing of nature, but only in our mind' (123), he is in agreement with Burke that the sublime stimulates feelings of fear and astonishment mingled with delight. According to both authors, these emotions arise because sublime objects challenge the mind's capacity to organize experience. Either because of their seeming limitlessness (what Kant terms the 'mathematical sublime' [103–17]) or because of their awesome power (the 'dynamical sublime' [119–23]), these objects paralyse the imagination. As Burke explains, 'The mind is hurried out of itself, by a croud [sic] of great and confused images' (62).

For Kant, however, astonishment is only the first step of a complicated cognitive process which leads the mind to recognize *itself* as sublime and the source of the sublime in nature, and to substitute the humiliating awareness of our 'physical impotence' in the face of nature for the empowering awareness of 'an ability to judge ourselves independent of nature' (120–1). Initially, when the mental faculties cannot comprehend an object's magnitude or power and provide an instantaneous representation of it, the individual experiences pain (108). But this sensation is quickly replaced by one of pleasure after the mind 'sinks back into itself' and becomes aware of reason's demand for synthesis – a demand that would have remained invisible, ironically, were it not for the failure of the imagination (109). In Urquhart's text, the whirlpool can be taken as an image of the 'interrupted journey' or blockage experienced by the imagination – an image of the mind turning back on itself.[4] In the Kantian sublime, the individual transcends human frailty and mortality because the act of self-analysis acquaints the mind with reason's demand for totality – a demand that 'indicates a mental power that surpasses any standard of sense' (111). Fear mingles with pleasure when the mind becomes aware of 'its own sublimity, which lies in its vocation [its duty to obey reason] and *elevates it even above nature*' (121; my emphasis).

In Urquhart's novel, similar feelings of pleasure and pain, fear and desire, characterize Patrick's attitude toward Fleda and the whirlpool. However, it remains unclear whether he wants to transcend nature in the fashion outlined by Kant, or whether his ambition lies in healing the split between id and ego as described by Theweleit. Initially it seems as if Patrick wishes to efface boundaries.[5] While he meditates on his plan to swim across the vortex, he specifically expresses his desire for the dissolution of personal boundaries:

Submerge. To place oneself below and lose character, identity, inside another element. ... The world above. That's where he lived all the time now. Patrick had not swum for years. He remembered the liquid envelope, the feeling of total caress. Nothing but water and certain winds could touch him like that, all over. ... Patrick standing alone at the top of the bank, made a decision. He would swim again somehow. He looked out over the difficult whirlpool. He would swim there and take the world above with him, if necessary. This would be his battle and his strength. (80–1)

Although his claim supports the belief that he wishes to undo the work of the symbolic order and 'lose character, identity,' and return to a pre-Oedipal existence, his subsequent assertion that this would be his 'battle and strength' indicates that, quite the contrary, he will continue to position himself as heroic quester.

On the whole, Patrick's attitude toward the 'difficult whirlpool' recalls both Kant's description of the sublime encounter and the perspective of the quester of romance. As Fletcher suggests, while the labyrinth's 'lack of structure is threatening to the hero, he still persists in his quest, as if delighted by his good fortune in being awarded the heroic trial' (33). Tragically for Patrick, by maintaining the stance of the quester and by conforming to Kant's model of the sublime experience, which depend on mastery and the rigid separation between self and other, he forgoes the chance to experience the deterritorialization that he longs for. As the critic Nick Halmi argues, this type of sacrifice is integral to the sublime:

Because we are encouraged in writings on the sublime ... to believe in the opposition of the two constitutive elements, the mind and external reality, it is impossible to think of aggrandizing ... the one except by negating the other.

But such a strategy of opposition exists only as long as it preserves precisely what it is directed against, so that external nature is here assigned the hopeless role of the other that must be and cannot be suppressed for the integrity of the self to be confirmed. If the human mind were not challenged and threatened by the sensible world, there would presumably be no need to try to demonstrate its supremacy ...   (356)[6]

For the most part, Urquhart's portrayal of Patrick's position is in keeping with Halmi's description of the obsessive dance associated with the sublime. The poet's behaviour is also reminiscent of Woolf's description of the supposedly privileged male scholars who remain locked inside the library.

Having outlined the links between Urquhart's text and the narratives of romance, and discussed the ambivalent emotions associated with the feminine, sublime whirlpool, we must still investigate exactly what narrative mechanisms keep men like Patrick locked inside. In describing his desire to swim, Patrick forges a connection between his desire to lose 'character, identity' and the deconstruction of geographic order. He seems to conceive of himself as a prisoner of ordered, domesticated landscape. For him deterritorialization is figured as penetration into unmapped space:

Looking across the distance of the river to the foreign country [America] on the other side, Patrick considered how there was always a point where one set of circumstances ended and another began. Boundaries, borderlines, territories. This swim would be a journey into another country, a journey he would choose to make in full knowledge that he had no maps, that he hardly spoke the language.   (221)

This passage not only underscores Patrick's pre-Oedipal desire to escape the imposition of order and containment associated with national boundaries but also emphasizes something that we have learned from the previous novels, namely, that 'language' like maps, constitutes a powerful tool for instituting this order.

In *The Whirlpool*, concerns about order and chaos, while portrayed spatially (in terms of maps, map-making, and the architectural construction of houses), are revealed to be fundamentally discursive.[7] Moreover, the preoccupation with both order and chaos, according to the text, stems from Canada's colonial legacy. For example, throughout the novel, the historian's wife, Fleda, copies poems by Browning into her journal. On one level, this transmission embodies the material links between the transmission of literature and colonization. On another level, the poems themselves, which frequently portray images of houses, foreground the issue of accommodation and imprisonment.

In interviews, Urquhart admits that she set the novel in 1889 and introduced the character of Robert Browning precisely because she wanted to investigate the problems surrounding translation: the difficulties that arise from the imposition of Old World narratives onto the New World landscape. As she says:

> Part of the reasons that late nineteenth century Canadian poets were having problems, or at least in my opinion, was that they were trying to impose Wordsworth's daffodils in the total disorder of the Canadian landscape. ... In *Whirlpool Dream House*[8] a young man [Patrick] with an old world idea of what a poet should be is trying to live out that fantasy in nineteenth-century Canada. ('Interview,' 38)

Ultimately, the novel emphasizes that, as language users (readers and writers), individuals have a choice whether to support misguided attempts to translate European culture onto the New World or, by stressing the poetic and associative aspects of words, to support the efforts of deterritorialization.

Right from the start, the novel's frame story, concerning the last days of Robert Browning – the Old World poet who serves as a foil for Patrick – alerts the reader to this choice. It is the frame story, as well as Patrick's and Fleda's obsession with the Romantic poets, that highlights the fact that Canadians must negotiate Old World narratives, such as romance and the concept of the sublime. Seemingly unrelated to the principal text, which is set in Niagara Falls, Ontario, the prologue recounts Browning's final thoughts in December 1889, as he wanders about his beloved Venice and comes to the realization that his death is imminent. The novel opens and closes with this depiction of the poet at the end of his life. Taken together, these two brief sections offer a portrait, in miniature, of the concerns regarding order and chaos that affect the characters living in Canada during that same year.

The opening section portrays Browning as a stickler for order – a man who 'never once broke the well-established order that ruled the days of his life' (9–10) and never 'acted without a predetermined plan' (15). Only when he realizes that he is about to die does he finally probe his youthful obsession with the Romantic poet Percy Bysshe Shelley – an obsession which he repressed throughout his adult life. Confronted with the spectre of his own tidy death – he will be taken to the cemetery island of San Michele where he will join 'the island's clean-boned inhabitants sleeping in their white-washed houses' (17) – Browning admits that Shelley's chaotic death by drowning was infinitely more romantic and sublime than anything Browning could hope to achieve. He would gladly exchange all 'that cool white marble,' the contained, domesticated death in a 'white-washed house' which awaits him, for 'the shifting sands of Lerici' (237).

It is appropriate that the Victorian poet is haunted by Shelley's spectre because, for Browning, Shelley stood for everything that he repressed in his life and art. In essence, Shelley exercised the power of a fluid, rather than controlling, imagination: the 'formless form he [Browning] never possessed and was never possessed by' (236). Early on, Browning acknowledges wistfully that, while he idolized Shelley, he himself led an ordered, almost mechanical existence: 'He [Browning] had placed himself in the centre of some of the world's most exotic scenery and had then lived his life there with the regularity of a copy clerk' (11). Browning opted for the life of the collector or museum curator. But even though his life was a disappointment to him, he continued to position himself as a disinterested, objective voyeur, eavesdropping on imaginary noblemen and collecting lizards on his holiday. All the while, in his heart of hearts, he knew that Shelley's life was preferable.

In a subtle fashion, the frame story introduces the archetypes of the museum and the labyrinth. On one level, Browning's presence in Venice underscores this opposition in that a self-confessed lover of order locates himself in the most labyrinthine city of all. But the image of the labyrinth is also associated with Shelley and his sublime death by drowning; and it is in this context that we learn that there is a way to mediate between the two sides of this binary opposition. Ultimately, Browning's imagination enables him, however briefly, to escape the prison of his orderly existence. The deconstruction of the binary opposition takes the form of an image that encompasses Browning's control and Shelley's chaos. The seeds of this image are found in Browning's meditations on Palazzo Manzoni, a structure which paradoxically never attains a fixed shape. Palazzo Manzoni is the name of the house that Browning had wanted to buy, but never actually possessed. Because it was never attained, the house lives on in the poet's imagination, and constitutes one of the only facets of his life to escape his relentless control. As a house, it shares features of the temple / museum; yet, as an imaginative construct, it maintains a connection with the formless labyrinth. On his deathbed, Browning reconciles the antithesis between order and chaos in a dream where Shelley's drowned body glides through Palazzo Manzoni:

Now the drowned poet began to move into a kind of Atlantis consisting of Browning's dream architecture; the unobtainable and the unconstructed. In complete silence the young man swam through the rooms of the Palazzo Manzoni, slipping up and down the staircase, gliding down the halls, in and out of fireplaces. He appeared briefly in mirrors. He drifted past balconies to the tower Browning had thought of building at Asolo. ... *Suntreader.* Still beyond his grasp. (237)

This dream-vision mediates the opposition even as it continues to express Browning's troubled relationship with Shelley. Yet this vision and the prologue as a whole do more than introduce the preoccupations with chaos and order. By locating the opposition between these two archetypes within a European context and foregrounding two famous English writers, the frame structure emphasizes that these archetypes and the conflict between them have been inherited from the Old World.

Within the novel, the urge for control – embodied in the narrative of romance and the discursive construction of the sublime, and manifested in the act of collecting and in the construction of museums – is tied to the legacy of the imperial project and Canada's status as a former colony.[9] Each of the protagonists must come to grips with inherited European systems for organizing aesthetics, landscape, and gender. Reliant on European modes of categorization, including the narrative of the quest and the concept of the sublime, the characters are, for the most part, perplexed when confronted with Canada's distinctly non-European historical and geographical contours. In some cases, the dependence on Old World models is crippling. For example, Patrick, unable to deal 'effectively with the body or soul of the new country, had found himself, at thirty-three, eking out a subsistence salary as a clerk in the capital city' (69). Rather than investigate the possibility of constructing new paradigms or even, at the very least, acknowledge the disjunction, he looks to the Old World literature for escape from the Canadian landscape that he cannot fathom. As the narrator explains, night after night 'he disappeared into the old-world landscape with Wordsworth, Coleridge, or Browning' (69). But escape is impossible precisely because the Old World descriptions cannot account for the radically different features of the New.

In his contemporary account of the sublime, Lyotard focuses on Kant's description of the disruption of the harmony between the imagination and the demands of reason. Lyotard suggests that this can alternatively be understood as a disruption of the harmony that is derived from a system of categorization that guarantees 'a sharing of taste by an aristocratic public' – a system that assures 'the glory of a name' (202). Whereas critics such as Halmi read the sublime primarily an 'exercise' in 'self-reassurance' (356), Lyotard puts greater emphasis on Kant's repeated assertion that this reassurance is extremely limited and not practically applicable. Simply put, although the sublime experience enables individuals to become aware of the faculty of reason, they cannot know what reason asks.[10] In keeping with this uncertainty, Lyotard argues that, in the presence of the sublime, the artist 'ceases to be guided by a culture which made of him the sender and master of a message of glory: he becomes [instead] ... the involuntary addressee of an inspiration come to him from an "I know not what"' (202).

This is precisely the role that Patrick refuses. Even his uneducated wife recognizes the futility of his endeavour to continue bearing the message of Old World glory. Exasperated, she tells him, 'You're never going to find Wordsworth's daffodils here' (69). Patrick's insistence on using models from the Old World eventually jeopardizes his physical and mental health. He travels from Ottawa to his uncle's farm in Niagara Falls in order to recuperate from the effects of his alienation (at work and within the country as a whole), which have culminated in a physical and mental breakdown (69). His sickness and the attendant sense that words were being erased from his mind signal the danger of attempting to impose the linguistic order of the Old World onto the New. There can be no seamless translation, and the text repeatedly highlights the perils that result from engaging in this type of fantasy. As noted earlier, in Marlatt's novel, this same error of translation drove the protagonist's mother insane.

Like Patrick, twenty-nine-year-old Fleda voraciously consumes volumes of English Romantic poetry and repeatedly compares the landscapes described by the poets to her own surroundings. But rather than strive to render the process of translation invisible, Fleda recognizes the incongruity between the Old and New World. For example, at the beginning of the novel, while on her way to Whirlpool Heights, she peers out of the streetcar's window and carefully examines the geography beyond the city limits, and is immediately struck by the disjunction between the European landscapes she reads about and the actual landscape she inhabits:

The tough old rocks of the escarpment were in evidence everywhere, varying in size from the jagged edges along the road to the cliffs that dropped down to the river. ... The hill country of England, as Fleda imagined it, or gentle undulations of the Tuscan countryside, had *nothing to do with this*, nothing to do with this river side of the road. If she turned and looked through the windows on the opposite side of the car, however, she would see nothing but acres of rigidly planned, severely trimmed orchards. It was a geography of fierce opposites. Order on one side and, nearer the water, sublime geological chaos.   (31; my emphasis)

According to Sylvia Söderlind, this kind of recognition alone – the ability to allow the disjunction to remain visible – constitutes a deterritorializing strategy (19).

Whereas Fleda registers the disparity between Old and New Worlds, her husband, David, reacting to what he perceives as Canada's unhealthy Eurocentric focus, embarks on a heroic quest to sever Canada's ideological attachment to Europe and the United States. Unlike Patrick, who clings to European models, David apparently favours a strategy that celebrates and reinforces the divide. Ironically, his desire to free Canada from attachments to Europe and America leads him to embrace a form of nationalism that simply mirrors the models he claims to reject. In what follows, I will trace in greater detail the way in which David, Patrick, Maud, and Fleda respond to the narratives inherited from the Old World.

After delivering one of his tiresome public lectures on Canadian history, David greets Patrick and forcibly expresses his desire for an indigenous history:

Yes, we need real writers ... thinkers ... that think Canadian. Thinking Canadian is a very lonely business, my boy, and don't forget it. Do they think Canadian at the University of

Toronto? No, they don't. They think Britain ... the Empire and all that nonsense. Do they think Canadian in the churches? No, they don't. They think Scotland, Rome. Why not a church of Canada, I ask you? Surely we could at least have our own religion. I'll bet this group assembled here doesn't have more than one Canadian thought a day, and they pretend to be interested in Canadian history! (72–3)

In his capacity of military historian, David takes it upon himself to furnish Canada with a past of its own. Specializing in the siege of Fort Erie, he dedicates his life to proving that Canada won the War of 1812 against the Americans. His goal of providing Canada with an unambiguous past compliments his dream of creating a 'pure museum,' one where he could 'place the relics of the thin history of the country where he lived' (172). In her review of the novel, Aritha van Herk highlights this link between history and museum. As she says, David 'keeps the past that everyone else wishes to let go, collects it, writes it, in acts of military museumhood' (review, 'Summer,' 16).

David's attitude toward history and his dream of a 'pure museum' hark back to the Enlightenment strategies of containment which promote the belief that history and its artifacts can be organized in a logical, unambiguous fashion by a detached observer. As a critic of military history explains:

When you write history, especially military history, you break the relationship that exists between yourself and the event and the people involved – a relationship which demands an ethical response. Once history has been dealt with in this way, the event no longer occurs in the 'now': it has been set in perspectival, causal narrative. In this way, the historian situates himself 'outside.' He is no longer in the story. He is safe from history. (Jenkins)[11]

It is this longing for safety and order that prompts David to fabricate the 'Truth' of Canadian history. He wants more than anything else to enforce narrative closure by proving that Canada won the War of 1812 (73).[12] His version of history actually represents a flight from history, and, as such, it recalls Stewart's description of the escapist function of the museum: the collection 'does not displace attention to the past; rather, the past is at the service of the collection' (*On Longing*, 151). The museum 'replaces history with *classification*, with order beyond the realm of temporality' (151). For David, the museum represents precisely this type of flight from history, and it has a great deal in common with Ruskin's image of the home as a 'place of Peace':

There was peace here, and the major knew it. Emptied of drama and emotion these artifacts would not be making any further statements, any further journeys. They would remain here now, stunningly innocent and clear, years after their complicated performances involving death and pain. They had become three-dimensional documents locked away in rooms. (231)

David's fetishization of musuem objects confirms Andreas Huyssen's view that 'the point of exhibiting was quite frequently to forget the real, to lift the object out of its original everday functional context, thereby enhancing its alterity' (32–3). In the historian's eyes, the museum constitutes a temple, where objects are 'innocent and clear.'

In keeping with this templar structure and its link to romance narratives, David's desire to enforce a separation between the subject who writes history and the objects under observation also recalls the separation imposed between the heroic quester and the background/obstacle. Both the historian and the romantic hero share a common goal: their fundamental achievement is explicitly associated with a transcendent 'vision of native history' (Fletcher, 84). In keeping with romance tradition, David insists that he was commanded to engage in his quest for a 'vision of native history' by an authentically Canadian muse. As he explains to Patrick, the figure of Laura Secord appeared to him in a dream while he was in college, uttering the command: 'Remind them, remind them' (83). From that moment on, he took on the task of inventing Canadian history.

In the course of this endeavour, David not only shores up the Canadian identity but also defines his own. As Susan Stewart notes, very often collectors entertain the belief that they are the creators: 'the self generates a fantasy in which it becomes producer of those objects, a producer by arrangement and manipulation' (On Longing, 158). In Urquhart's text, this is exactly what happens to David. The narrator explains that often, 'when he was working on his battle histories he could actually feel the regimental energy flow from his pen, almost as if he, himself, were inventing the plan of attack' (49).[13] Patrick also notices the possessive nature of David's preoccupation with history: 'McDougal clearly felt the battle was all his, right down to the last death throes in the dawn hours' (82).

Ultimately, David's fantasies of ownership and his quest for an ordered vision of native history are revealed as deeply flawed. Ironically, his supposedly 'Canadian' historical narrative closely resembles the imperial narratives that he claims to reject: both rely on maps that efface the bodies, blood, and deaths that sustain them. Patrick, who is more sensitive to the presence of alternative narratives, realizes that, for both himself and David, death remains an abstraction: 'No mutilated bodies littering the landscape afterwards. Death would always appear in the form of a sentence for vast numbers of soldiers or as a paragraph for a particular hero' (125). The tendency to transform death into an abstraction is a classic technique for defending the self against the chaotic emotions associated with mortality. In his analysis of the sublime, Burke insists that when the 'danger or pain press too nearly, they are incapable of giving any delight, and are simply terrible; but at certain distances, and with certain modifications, they may be, and they are delightful' (40). Similarly, Kant repeatedly emphasizes that the sublime must be observed from a 'safe' distance (*Judgement*, 120, 121). One of the ways David distances death is by concealing it within a familiar narrative – the narrative of romance. The historian engages in this strategy when he speaks glowingly of a local stuntman who plans to shoot the rapids below the Falls. Initially, David celebrates the young man's project and views it in the light of the quest structure. Discussing the event with his wife, he boasts, 'Now you'll see ... Now you'll see what the river can do.' Fleda, already somewhat suspicious of this narrative, replies, 'Why do you always think you have to conquer something just because it's there. I already know what the river can do. No one has to prove it to me' (118). Despite her lack of enthusiasm, David continues to emphasize the supposedly heroic aspects of the event: 'Don't you think it's rather mythical ... the dangerous quest-like journey, braving the elements in the body of an animal' (118).

After watching the stuntman die a bloody death, however, David realizes precisely what his heroic version of history precludes: 'What he had never thought of, *what he had never placed on his maps* which drafted the details of endless marches, was the blood. It had simply escaped his imagination' (127; my emphasis). Yet even when confronted with this tangible challenge to his map-making and its abstract treatment of death, the historian proves unable to relinquish his attachment to the quest narrative; worse, he coerces his wife into playing a role in this narrative – a narrative which, as indicated earlier, intersects with the Victorian ideals of womanhood circulating in the late nineteenth century.

Early on in the novel, David brings home Patmore's book *Angel in the House* as a gift for his Fleda. The constraining nature of this overdetermined representation of Woman as angel / muse becomes even more pronounced when he asks Fleda who she would rather be, Laura Secord or Patmore's angel. Faced with this non-choice, Fleda lies, and says that she would rather be Patmore's wife. Later she admits to herself that she finds the stereotype repulsive: 'She wouldn't ever want to be Patmore's wife, Patmore's angel. Not now, not ever' (54).

David's desire to transform Fleda into his angelic muse figure illustrates the extent of his dependence on the quest narrative. His reliance on this narrative and Fleda's initial complicity are further emphasized when he grows bored with his analysis of the battles of 1812, and cajoles Fleda into dressing up as Laura Secord. This is a regular request and, while her compliance with his fetish temporarily satisfies his desire, it leaves her trapped within the all too familiar Oedipal narrative – a narrative that reduces its heroine to a lifeless object. As Fleda explains, 'She's the only woman in the whole story, so you simply romanticize her to death!' (51).

Positioned within this narrative, one of Woolf's 'insiders,' David cannot imagine that Fleda has an existence independent of his story. For this reason, when she abandons him at the end of the novel, his first thought is that she has simply wandered off to read Browning and forgotten about the time. Slightly miffed, he plans to 'give her the Laura Secord lecture' when she returns: 'What if *she* [Laura Secord] had decided to mope dreamily around reading poetry instead of delivering messages. What would have happened *then*' (228). Implicit in his response to the situation is the notion that women must be ready at all times to fulfil their role, not as subjects – the creators of meaning – but as objects, the bearers of (man-made) meaning. David's talk of messages recalls Lyotard's analysis of the sublime, which instigates a disruption, so that the individual 'ceases to be guided by a culture which made of him [or her] the sender and master of a message of glory' ('Sublime,' 202). For David everything constitutes a message – everything must be made to fit within a pre-given order. As night falls and Fleda still does not appear, his thoughts take another turn and he begins to suspect that Fleda has been captured by Americans (228). The irony is, of course, that David, who consistently views women as objects in his domestic museum, mere counters in the male game of power, never once considers that Fleda has left of her own free will.

Yet, after witnessing the death of the stuntman, he understands on some level the dangerous limitations of the quest narrative and his attraction to the sublime, specifically the way in which the sublime promotes alienation and abstraction from the particulars of everyday life. When Fleda vanishes, David finds himself recalling his aunt, a woman whose life progressively shrank to the confines of a single room. In the midst of this recollection, he comes to the realization that his desire for order is linked to the same fatal longing for stasis that attacked his aunt. Suddenly he realizes that his own life 'had been moving down a path which would eventually carry him through the door of his still unconstructed house. And while he had imagined walking through the door of the house, he had never considered stepping back outside' (230–1). His as yet unconstructed house at Whirlpool Heights will become a prison rather than a temple. Once again, we are reminded that being locked in may be a worse fate than being shut out. It is tempting to interpret the recurring images of the house in this novel as a figure for the individual trapped and isolated by his or her own improper use of reason.

The last time he appears in the novel, David is still stunned by the loss of his wife. But rather than try to find her, he heads 'directly to the museum to look at ammunition' (231). As the narrator explains, 'McDougal was comforted by the sight of these objects carefully arranged on fabric, safely catalogued and housed' (231). He chooses the deathly peace of the museum, which is akin to the solace offered by the whitewashed tombstones described in the frame story concerning Browning.

Initially, it seems that, of the two men, Patrick might succeed where David fails. Whereas the latter obstinately clings to a deathly order, Patrick is powerfully attracted to the antithesis of order, namely, the whirlpool. And unlike the historian, who insists on the incontestable nature of facts (and therefore on the possibility of ordering them), Patrick appreciates that facts are elusive. At one point, the poet listens to his uncle's version of the War of 1812 – a version that contradicts the historian's elitist, class-ridden representation (71). The existence of multiple versions of history leads Patrick to question attempts to organize the past: 'History, his story, whose story? Collections of facts that were really only documented rumours. When he thought hard about them, thought hard about facts, they evaporated under his scrutiny' (72). Using the fluid image of the cloud cycle and, by association, the whirlpool, Patrick affirms that history is unstable, liquid.

His awareness of the fictional nature of the past coupled with his interest in Fleda and the whirlpool would suggest that, while David may be doomed to live out his existence within the confines of a repressive order, Patrick at least has the potential to reject the type of Old World order embodied in the museum. Whereas Fleda's husband has no understanding of her desire to sell the house and live in a tent, Patrick's curiosity is piqued by her decision to exist beyond the confines of a domestic environment, in effect, to engage in deterritorialization: 'He wanted to know how she had managed her apparently fearless letting go – of domestic architecture, of closed spaces – how she had been able to turn away in order to embrace the open. He wanted to discuss the exact moment when the whirlpool had taken hold of her life' (107). Reminiscent of Anna Swan's manager, Judge Apollo Ingalls, Patrick straddles two different world views. On the one hand, he can converse with the order-obsessed David; on the other hand, he can also speak the poetic, deterritorialized language of Maud's autistic son.

As critics have noted, Maud's son constitutes 'the true poet of the novel' (review by van Herk, 17). As we will see, his ability to escape strategies of containment enables him to help others initiate the process of 'emptying the museum.' Patrick first becomes aware of the child when he is standing outside of the hotel where Fleda lived before she moved to the tent at Whirlpool Heights. The poet is determined to find out everything about Fleda that he can. The ultimate collector, he 'wanted her past ... her recent history, the seasons she had lived through before the tent, the architecture she had abandoned. ... He wanted an utter comprehension of the forces that had moved her into the forest' (107). In the midst of his quest for absolute knowledge, Patrick hears a small voice. Barely a whisper, it 'fluttered somewhere near the back part of his brain' (109). The voice belongs to Maud's son, and his message to Patrick stands in direct opposition to the poet's desire to know *everything* about Fleda: the message borne through the currents in the air is 'Nothing' (109).

In contrast to both David's and Patrick's efforts to make things mean something, to gather up random objects and events and imbue them with an abstract, static significance in order to stave off the 'nothing' of chaos, of death, the boy's linguistic practice emphasizes the wonderful instabilities inherent in language, the way in which language can become unhinged from its referent, signifier disconnected from signified. When Patrick asks the boy his name, the child replies, 'Parlour' (110). Faced with this transgressive conversational style, another person might turn away from the child in horror. But for Patrick, the 'child's uttered nonsense was a revelation, not unlike the intoxicating leaps he had known himself to take, only once or twice, in the manipulation of language. ... Suddenly, by virtue of its very randomness, the child's speech became profound' (112).

Patrick's attraction to the child's speech stems from his fleeting experience as a poet with the disruption of the syntagmatic flow of language.[14] Yet, in keeping with the narrative of romance and the eighteenth-century formulations of the sublime, Patrick never completely allows this randomness, this chaos, to 'press too nearly.' Whereas David constructs his distanced position by taking on the role of the objective, questing historian, Patrick assumes a similar position of safety by taking on the role of the questing scientist. Ultimately, for both men, the terror-causing threat is kept at bay, held back through similar processes of abstraction.

In Patrick's case, this abstraction is provided by the containing and controlling nature of the male gaze, which we have explored in earlier chapters. In accordance with nineteenth-century scientific practices, Patrick ventures into the forest to 'collect wildflowers for his album' (38). In the midst of his search, he catches sight of Fleda through his field-glasses, and in a seemingly effortless gesture, he substitutes the Woman for the flowers (39). Throughout the novel, Patrick conflates women and flowers. On one occasion, after Fleda cuts her hair and throws the strands to the wind, Patrick surreptitiously collects them (144), and the next time they meet, he explains that he is looking for a tiny rare orchid called 'Ladies' Tresses' (150). Toward the end of the novel, Patrick has a vision that once again aligns women with flowers (221). This repeated connection should come as no surprise, because, on some level, Woman was always already inscribed within the set of the 'natural.' Flower-like, women are aligned both with nature and the sublime, arousing fascination and dread. Although Patrick fantasizes about them, and admits that '[t]here was something in him that wanted to embrace them all,' he goes on to insist that 'there was something else, stronger, which turned towards denial' (221).

When he scrutinizes Fleda, Patrick is careful to sustain the necessary illusion of scientific detachment, the distinction between observer and observed, by framing her within the lens of his field-glasses:

Crouching behind a sumac bush, he once again, brought the glasses up to his eyes. Now he could see her more clearly, her downcast face, the sunlight on her dark yellow hair. In this setting, surrounded by the yellow-green foliage of late spring and seated in blue shadows, she looked to him like a woman in a painting, as though she had been dropped into the middle of the scene for decorative purposes, or to play a part in a legend. ... The lenses in Patrick's eyes and in his mind were wide open. (39)

From the discussions of male voyeurism in previous chapters, specifically the analysis of P.T. Barnum and his American Museum, Patrick's perspective is familiar. In this case, the frames surrounding Fleda multiply. The first frame, designated by the field-glasses, is scientific; the second, alluded to in the phrase 'she looked to him like a woman in a painting,' is aesthetic. We are also told that there are lenses 'in Patrick's eyes and in his mind.' All of these frames serve to reinforce the division between inside and outside, the gap between the mind and the chaotic sublime of nature. The multiple references to frames, mirrors, and lenses could also be understood to indicate that Fleda constitutes a mirror reflection of Patrick: she is his other. Whatever the case, the outcome of this process of framing and mirroring reduces Fleda to an object (akin to David's fetishized puppet), safely positioned to satisfy Patrick's scopophilic desire. In many ways, the image of the all-encompassing lenses opening in his eyes and mind is reminiscent of the description of Anna Swan's husband, Bates, who, on his wedding night, peers at his wife as if he is gazing at her through the lens of a giant microscope.

As the novel repeatedly illustrates, this distance between the scientist and the object of study is crucial. Without it, inside and outside become indistinguishable and the hero's identity is threatened: he is no longer transcendent, immune to pain and death. The precarious quality of this artificial divide is portrayed during Patrick's first 'encounter' with Fleda. Unaware of his presence, Fleda begins to stroll toward him. The diminishing distance between them causes Patrick to panic: 'His inclination was to bolt, run right out of the woods, back to the farm, onto a train. Vacate the province. Leave the country' (57). This response, treated humorously here, is triggered a second time when David invites Patrick to come to the tent at Whirlpool Heights for dinner. Anticipating the dinner with David and his wife, Patrick realizes that 'in his imagination, his fantasy, she [Fleda] was completely still. ... the idea of any activity taken as a decision her part did not connect with his vision of her' (97). As he approaches the tent, Patrick hears Fleda speak and he freezes: 'He didn't want her to have a voice, did not wish to face the actuality of her speech. ... One more step on his part and she would leave, forever, the territory of his dream and he would lose something – some power, some privacy, some control' (98). In the end, his desire for control, his need to occupy the sole position of subject, triumphs over his desire for contact, and he rushes away from the tent. Patrick's repeated desire to flee in order to maintain distance tangibly demonstrates the limitations of the experience of the sublime as described by Burke and Kant, and the romantic construction of the heroic quester, who, like Odysseus, only feels content when he away from home.

The necessity of maintaining this distance and diminishing Fleda's status to that of a silent object becomes blatantly absurd when Patrick finally comes face to face with her. Seeing no means of escape, he ignores her and pretends that she is 'not there at all' (124). In this ridiculous dance of insiders and outsiders, Fleda must be made to take on the role of 'no one' so that Patrick can maintain his identity as 'someone.' She must bear the burden of being 'nothing,' the haunting message Maud's son delivers to Patrick. Yet, not actually wanting 'nothing' because he needs the other to assure his own superiority, Patrick grows angry when he senses that Fleda's attention has shifted away from him to David: 'He wanted to capture her somehow, to put her where she belonged in *his* story, back inside the fieldglasses where he could control the image' (126). One of the most severe transgressions occurs when Fleda presumes to question him. This act reverses the roles between subject and object, observer and observed, transforming him into the object of inquiry; not surprisingly, he views her behaviour as an act of treachery (127–8). In romance narratives, the landscape or background is never conscious, it never 'acts'; nor does the cell under the microscope peer back at the scientist. Only the hero surveys and moves through the terrain in his quest for knowledge.

Whereas David strives for a vision of native history, Patrick believes that, by watching Fleda, he can attain a vision of the Garden of Eden. Put somewhat differently, he believes that his voyeurism provides him with a glimpse of a non-fragmented self – the self before the fall into language and self-consciousness. He fantasizes that he can experience Fleda in a 'pure and uncorrupted state' (128):

Patrick understood that, like a child at play, observed, but not conscious of observation, the woman would reveal sides of herself to him that she had revealed to no one else. He would experience her when she was whole, not fragmented into considerations of self and other. (107)

The irony is, of course, that she is tremendously conscious, and, as one who writes in her diary, she also is extremely self-reflexive, divided into considerations of 'self and other.' Furthermore, Fleda is aware of being spied on. She first realizes that Patrick has been watching her when, on impulse, she cuts her hair and leaves the strands to be blown by the wind. Returning to retrieve the scissors, she discovers Patrick 'collecting her discarded hair; stuffing first the pockets of his trousers and then his jacket' (144). Her initial reaction to being 'collected' is ambivalent. The knowledge that he had watched before, and often, both 'frightened and delighted her' (144). In her diary, she records the fact that she has begun 'to dress' for Patrick, just as she plays 'dress up' for her husband.

Fleda's references to feelings of fear and delight once again recall Burke's and Kant's analyses of the feelings which constellate around the sublime moment and its promise of transcendence.[15] Steeped in romantic literature, Fleda constructs her own 'story' about Patrick. She imagines that he will play the role of the demon lover who will carry her away from home and help her to discover who she really is. In her diary, she writes:

Perhaps I've always waited for the demon lover to leave the maelstrom and enter my house,
through some window while I slept on ... innocent and unaware.

One moment you are dreaming, the next terrifyingly awake, on board a ghost ship bound for
God knows where ... away from home. ... Would it not also be true that at this moment of dis-
aster you would know exactly who you were? Not necessarily who you had been, but who you
were right then?   (176)

For a long while, Fleda believes that Patrick will take on the responsibility for providing her with this type of transcendent self-knowledge and for freeing her from the
last vestiges of domesticity. In some ways, both Fleda and Patrick yearn for the
same thing: both desire an experience of wholeness. By playing the role of his muse,
she believes that her own world can be made whole – a wholeness reminiscent of
reason's demand for 'totality' outlined in Kant's conception of the sublime (*Judgement,*
111). As she explains, for 'the first time she felt the several parts of her world inter-
lock ... felt herself a part of the whirlpool, a part of the art of poetry' (145).

However, the text indicates that Fleda misjudges both her own tolerance for playing the static and inhuman role of the 'muse' and Patrick's ability to play the equally
reductive role of the sublime 'demon lover.' Even before he rejects her, Patrick's voyeuristic tendencies begin to grate on her nerves, and she wonders how much longer
she can play 'his vague illusive games' (168). Like the mythical hero Perseus, who
uses his shield as a mirror in order to slay Medusa, Patrick maintains his distance
and takes to looking solely at Fleda's reflection in a spoon, in her husband's eyes, in
the globe of a coal-oil lamp, and, finally, in Fleda's hand mirror (167). Even when
he faces her, he continues to look at her as though she were 'an eclipse, too dangerous to be perceived directly' (168).

Fleda's tolerance for Patrick's defensive gestures diminishes considerably when
they venture out on another occasion to gather kindling. She casually mentions to
him that she hoped that they might have been able 'to get close to each other. ... that
we might have been friends' (181). In response, he rushes toward her, clasps her
shoulders, thrusts his face into hers, and shouts:

I don't *want* to be this close to you. Not now, not ever. Look what happens ... when we're
this close we can't see each other at all ... not even each other's eyes. This close, you're a
blur ... and *I'm nothing ... completely nothing ... nothing but a voice.* You can't see me. My
voice is so close it could be inside your own head. I don't *want* to be this close, Fleda, I
want the distance.   (181; my emphasis)

Here again, Patrick expresses his greatest fear, that of becoming 'nothing ... completely nothing' – a fear which Kant suggests stems from the imagination's fear of
losing itself in the 'abyss' of the sublime (*Judgement,* 115). But Fleda challenges Patrick's

claim to 'want the distance' by betraying her knowledge of his voyeurism. This revelation utterly destroys his fantasy of transcendence:

He felt that his privacy, his self, had been completely invaded. He was like a walled village that had been sacked and burned, just when it was feeling most secure. ... How *dare* she? he thought as if she, not he, had been the voyeur. ... He was furious. It was as if this ordinary woman, this housewife, had turned his brain inside out so that she could examine it scientifically. His fantasy became a smear on a glass under a lens in a laboratory. ... Patrick did not look at her, would never look at her again. She was not supposed to be aware of the focus of the lens he had fixed on her.   (182)

After this episode, which destabilizes the illusion between inside and outside, and demolishes the fantasy of the 'wall,' Patrick recoils from Fleda and slips into David's territory, 'cunningly, as if he had been there all along' (195). Given the similarity of David's and Patrick's positions as heroic quester, it is tempting to suggest that he had, in fact, 'been there all along.'

At this point, Patrick determines to separate his lofty quest from the mundane housewife and the image of the soiled workaday world that she has come to represent: 'She became the smudge of the news on his fingers, the ink from his employment on his hands, the ugly red brick of his small house. Still, there was a swimmer in his mind and that swimmer would descend the bank without the woman, alone' (186). Patrick's decision to persist in his quest is ultimately a decision to retreat irrevocably from society – a retreat which culminates in what amounts to suicide. In her essay on the sublime, Frances Ferguson argues that the sublime promotes this type of withdrawal:

a kind of opting out of the pressures and the dangers of the social, because the sublime elevates one's individual relations with that mountain (or whatever natural object one perceives as sublime) above one's relationship to other human beings. Sublime experience cannot be taken away from you precisely because it is being set up as an alternative to the relationships among humans in society that make the question of referentiality have its force. Further, even though the sublime object is such because it is more powerful than the perceiving individual, any humiliation or abasement that may be involved in one's submission to a sublime object is preferable to humiliation by another person.   (73)

Patrick, a man who cannot stand crowds, who cannot control his panic and disgust in their midst, who must recite nursery rhymes to distract himself from the overwhelming sense of bodies pressing up against him, before fleeing from the smell of 'sausage on [the crowd's] collective breath,' is clearly unable to deal with 'pressures and dangers of the social' (122–3). Later, he suggests to Fleda that he wants to live 'weightless' (178). His flight from humanity represents a flight from the gaps in meaning, the instabilities, that mark communications among people. Like David, he finds comfort in the romantic notion of the solitary, pure quest: 'It was the landscape that he wanted and needed, uncomplicated setting, its ability to function and endure in a pure, solitary state' (192).

Patrick's ultimate refusal to engage in deterritorialization is clearly reinforced by his subsequent interpretation of his recurring dream; like Browning, Patrick also dreams of a house. In this dream, Patrick always finds himself walking through the rooms on the ground level of his uncle's farmhouse. All of the rooms correspond to reality, but when he reaches the end of the parlour, in the position normally occupied by a large window, he finds a door which opens onto a mirror image of the ground floor, except that the contents are 'entirely scrambled':

In this space, the dining room with its cold, blue walls and perfectly regular flooring, was filled with wheels and teeth and blades and smelled of damp, rotting burlap. The harsh, golden light of the kitchen, on the other hand, would expose undulating sinks and counters, soft tables and doughboards resembling the overstuffed furniture of the parlour. The parlour had become as smooth and untouched as ice; its surfaces reflecting not its own contents at all but those of rooms Patrick had never even imagined until that moment.

He would awaken, always, with blood pounding in his head and an intense fear that all the objects in the room where he slept would suddenly be unfamiliar and out of context. (191)

Recalling this dream immediately after his confrontation with Fleda, Patrick asserts that 'for the first time [he] understood its meaning, its message':

Keep the sequence of fear, of quest, of desire in logical order – compartmentalized and exact. ... Do not confuse fear with desire, desire with quest, quest with fear. Otherwise the world scrambles, becomes unidentifiable, loses its recognizable context.

A simple shift of objects, events, emotions, from their rightful place brings chaos. And the world you live in enters nightmare.

He had dislocated and mixed categories, had confused the woman with the whirlpool, had believed, in some crazy way, that she *was* the landscape. ...

There would be no more confusion. He was through with the woman. From now on, whenever he visited Whirlpool Heights, and he knew he would visit often, it would be the landscape he was courting. (191–2)

At first, Patrick's acknowledgment that his initial conflation of the woman with the whirlpool was misguided would seem to be a positive step. As Klaus Theweleit argues, the sexualization of males (and females) involves the manipulation and control of desire. The young boy's 'desire is – indeed is *required to be* – directed solely toward women. All of the growing boy's ideas, hopes, dreams, and plans must be focused and fixated on the conquest of that one object, woman' (375). Arguing that this disciplined desire, which takes the initial form of an incestuous desire for the mother, is reductive and forecloses choice because it is 'installed in the subject from without, by society' (377), Theweleit asserts that, in fact, desire 'cries out for something else: 'It isn't my mother I wanted. It was never her – or even simply a woman. I wanted to know the world, produce it, people it with my creations. I wanted to explore every possible connection, visit every site on earth and leave again' (376). It is this recognition that Patrick seems to attain when he chastises himself for believing that it was the woman he wanted, rather than the world.

However, while he rejects the conflation, his desire still remains fixated on an ideal notion of 'pure, solitary landscape,' which indicates that he remains committed to maintaining his defensive position; he still wants to keep the elements in his life 'compartmentalized and exact.' Rather than explore the possibility that his recurring dream offers him a glimpse of what is he longing for, and what he has repressed, namely, deterritorialization, he interprets it as a warning to maintain an even stricter order. Henceforth, he will police the division between self and other with even greater vigilance.

When he meets Maud's child in the street for the last time, this renewed commitment to order and boundaries is apparent. In the course of their hilarious, poetic exchange, it becomes obvious that the boy does not understand the meaning of pronouns. More precisely, he does not know the difference between 'I' and 'you,' and so Patrick takes it upon himself to teach him this difference. Although the boy successfully makes the distinction, an aura of disappointment hovers over this achievement. Patrick muses to himself: 'Self and other. That's the way it always was. To merge was impossible except for short periods of time. Impossible and undesirable' (188). His remarks seem sensible, the product of a rational mind, but the narrator clarifies that he has failed because, despite any assertions to the contrary, he longed for closeness but he was never able to break down the boundary that separated him from others. His whole life 'had been a departure from certain dramas which should have been his destiny. A dance in which the partners turn away' (220). Yet this dance was 'choreographed,' in part, by the Old World narrative of romance and the sublime; as Weiskel asserts, the price of this enhanced sense of self is alienation (58–9). As we will see when we turn to Maud's experience, she makes the opposite choice in this same dance. She turns toward her partner.

In the end, Patrick fulfils his desire to heal the split between ego and id, but only in the most perverse fashion: he ventures into the whirlpool and drowns. As noted, his death is in keeping with the alienation that results from conforming to the demands of the sublime. As Weiskel states, by privileging the mind over nature (including our natural bodies), one of the 'things the sublime enables us to discount is our life' (95). Retrieving Patrick's corpse from the river, the River Man notes that the body assumes the posture of a newborn: 'the body was being drawn forward from its centre, the rope looking like a thick umbilical cord, the limbs trailing loosely, slightly behind the torso' (226). The connections among purity, wholeness, and death are further emphasized when Patrick is laid out in the funeral parlour. Surveying the body, Maud suggests that, aside from the film across his eyes, the 'rest of him was undamaged, perfect. He was like a dead child' (232). The allusions to infancy would suggest that Patrick has returned 'home.' He has returned to the abyss, the womb-like space associated with death and the time preceding birth. And yet, rather than 'escape' the order associated with the Old World, he becomes its victim. His death, the result of a desire for mastery and control on the part of a virtually unknown poet, parodies the accidental death of the renowned poet, Shelley, by drowning.

Ultimately, both David and Patrick remain trapped inside the museum. The text, however, in keeping with the frame story, does not simply leave the binary opposition intact. Several characters, specifically Maud, her son, and Fleda, discover ways to destabilize this construct. By now, it probably comes as no surprise that women are more effective in their attempts to destabilize traditional narratives. As noted in previous chapters, women's position regarding the romance narrative is complicated by the fact that they are identified with nature as 'obstacle': it is their bodies and desires which are effaced in order to guarantee the unified sense of self enjoyed by men. As a result, there is more at stake in their efforts to subvert traditional narratives. Furthermore, as noted in the chapter on Marlatt, women's individuation may not leave them with the same fears associated with the breakdown of interpersonal boundaries. To recall the words of Nancy Chodorow, 'the basic feminine sense of self is connected to the world, the basic masculine sense of self is separate' (169). It is this alternative path toward 'closeness' and deterritorialization that I will now go on to trace.

Immediately following the introductory segment concerning Browning, the narrative focuses on the life of Maud Grady, the undertaker's widow. Two years before the action in the novel takes place, an influenza epidemic took the life of her husband and his parents. In the blink of an eye, Maud found herself in possession of the family home and business. Dutifully following the cultural codes, she transformed herself from a proper wife to an equally proper widow: she became the 'perfect symbol of animate deep mourning,' encasing herself in folds of crape for two full years (22). Her willingness to wear this costume recalls Fleda's decision to don outfits for her husband and for Patrick. In Maud's case, however, the costume is more clearly tied to notions of imprisonment and punishment. The emphasis on clothing here recalls the analysis of the repressive function of women's clothing in van Herk's *No Fixed Address*.

In *The Whirlpool*, the narrator dwells on the fact that the fabric of Maud's costume comes from Halstead, England, and is woven by employees at Courtault Limited: 'The workers – mute, humble, and underpaid – spent twelve hours a day, in hideous conditions, at their steam-powered looms pounding black silk threads into acres of unpleasant cloth' (21). This digression into the history of the cloth only makes sense when viewed in the light of the text's more general concern regarding the origin of the repressive order that regulates life in the New World. The Old World order that determines Maud's choice of costume also governs both David's and Patrick's choices. The history of Maud's mourning garb clarifies the harmful aspects of the unself-conscious translation of values and practices from the old world to the New World. In particular, the exploitation that characterizes relations between factory owner and employee at the Courtault establishment is reinscribed on the bodies of women who find it necessary to wear the fabric in Canada.

From the description of the noxious material, it would seem that the cloth is designed solely to punish women for having the audacity to survive their husbands: 'It encased the female body ... in a suit of crumpled armour. ... it scraped at the neck and dug at the armpits. It clung to the limbs and rasped at the shoulder blades. It lacerated the spine if that series of bones ever dared to relax. And it smelled, always, of grave mud and sorrow' (21–2). As if to impress its mark even deeper, this material bleeds onto Maud's skin, imprinting itself indelibly on her flesh (22). In her dreams, Maud imagines escaping the onerous task of wearing this costume. Instead of wearing the crape herself, she offers a cape made of the stuff to her dead husband. But 'he would reject it, outright. ... [and] after this refusal, Maud would once again drape the heavy material on her own shoulders realizing, as she did so, where it rightfully belonged' (23).

The notion of costumes surfaces again when one of Maud's employees returns from a funeral and describes having witnessed the marriage of a young girl on her deathbed. Apparently, the girl was too sick to dress herself, so they simply laid the wedding dress on top of the covers. But afterward, because she was dead and could not resist, her mother made her wear the dress in the casket. Maud, already beginning to identify her own oppression, carries this story around with her 'for the rest of the day, thinking about costumes':

Lord, she thought, they are always dressing you up as something and then you are not yourself anymore. This young girl, the frozen, immobilized bride, coerced into it and then dead and unable to ever grow beyond it. No one now would even remember her name. Anecdotally, she would always be the bride, the one who was married and buried in the same breath.[16]

Just as Maud in her costume ... would still be 'the widow,' were she to stop now. Bride, wife, widow. She would not stop now. (149)

Like the young girl, Maud is trapped within her garments of widowhood, but her refusal to be reduced to this static identity is indicated in her final assertions that she 'would not stop now.'

But Maud is not simply trapped within her costume; the novel highlights the fact that she has been a prisoner of a deathly order throughout her married life. The text emphasizes that Maud's former husband, Charles, who had an obsession with spiders, kept her imprisoned in his domestic web and virtually embalmed her. In the novel, the connection between Charles and spiders is first made explicit when the narrator asserts that Charles's passion for the undertaking business was only exceeded by his passion for spiders. His fondness for these creatures seems appropriate in the light of the fact that Charles and his friend, Sam, were the first licensed embalmers in Canada (26). But Charles's passion takes on a crazed aspect. In conjunction with the other collectors in the novel, he studied spiders 'obsessively, collecting members of the species, recording their activities in a growing series of notebooks' (23).

As noted above, the text's emphasis on spiders and weaving (the references to the crape produced by the factory workers as well as the weaving of spider webs) recalls van Herk's tale of Arachne. However, unlike *No Fixed Address*, *The Whirlpool* subverts the traditional associations among women, spiders, and weaving. In this case, spiders are associated with men and industrialization, their mutual impulse to contain and control. By emphasizing that the crape comes from factories within England, the novel discredits the notion that women design and choose their own confining costumes. On a more figurative level, the links between Charles and spiders can be taken as a clue that women are not the weavers or plot-makers, but are, instead, caught within the narrative webs.

Within her own home, Maud literally moved among a myriad of spider webs. While her husband was alive, their house constituted his museum; he refused to let Maud clear any webs from the premises. Once, in an attempt to persuade him to let her clear away some of the old, empty webs, Maud suggested that perhaps the spiders might need help in clearing them away. Her comments merely enraged him: 'Spiders *never* need help. ... They *always* know exactly what they are doing' (90). For Charles, spiders represent perfection, a dream of order – akin to the historian's vision of the pure museum – which his wife had no right to disturb.

In fact, there was little in the house that Maud was allowed to disturb. Charles and his parents expected Maud to live in a state of suspended animation:

[W]hen she was newly married, the periods of enforced quiet had disturbed Maud – times when she had sat dutifully over some senseless piece of embroidery while downstairs mourners had recited measurements for coffins. It had been as if, in her own life, emotion had been held in suspense, so that the rest of the world could live and love and, more importantly, die. So the rest of them could respond. ... (43)

Her experience of 'enforced quiet' in her home recalls Patrick's wish that Fleda would remain completely still. But Maud's position, and the 'enforced quiet,' specifically invokes the earlier discussion of the association between home and temple in the nineteenth century. It is within a temple, after all, where one expects to find this type of quiet. Fletcher describes the temple as being at a remove from the ordinary world we live in: the 'still point of the turning world' (22). In Maud's case, the home is specifically allied to the museum because of the pervasiveness of Charles's spider collection, and because it is filled with objects that formerly belonged to other people. After the epidemic takes its toll, Maud looks around her and realizes that the furniture and decoration scattered about the house have all been brought there by clients 'who had been unable to pay their accounts at some time or another over the period of the last sixty years' (43).

Not surprisingly, it is within this larger museum that Maud constructs her own personal museum; in keeping with her newly acquired role as the town's undertaker, she collects relics from the dead. After her husband's death, Maud assumes the responsibility for looking after the members of the community who die as well as the tourists who drown themselves 'sometimes accidentally, more often not,' in the Niagara River, while attempting to cross the Falls or navigate the whirlpool's upper and lower rapids. The bulk of her work begins when tourist season arrives in the spring. The River Man, mentioned earlier in conjunction with Patrick's death, assists her in collecting the bodies or 'floaters,' as they are termed by the initiated. But these unnamed and unclaimed bodies or, in some cases, fragments of bodies that arrive at her door trouble her greatly. She feels an urgent need to impose order onto the chaos wrought by the whirlpool, the force that erases the identity of each body. Her method of imposing order involves writing down all available information concerning each corpse (articles of clothing and personal artifacts) into a book, entitled 'Description of Bodies Found in the Niagara River, Whirlpool, etc., 1887 – '. Ironically, when she first opens the book in the spring, she finds that 'the book itself was unidentified' because the gum label which had adorned the leather cover had disappeared over the winter (48). The threat of chaos never ceases.

Maud's initial commitment to preserving order – her desire to restore the name – links her to the male questers in the novel. In her struggle to maintain order, she becomes both historian and curator of her own museum. On a concrete level, Maud's private museum consists of a cupboard filled with numbered canvas sacks, each one filled with the possessions of an unknown and unnamed body. As the narrator explains, the cupboard 'was Maud's own personal reliquary. She wanted to enclose and protect the fragmented evidence of these smothered lives, to hold memories of their memories. This was her museum' (96). From her collection of objects, including coins, tie-pins, charms, medals, watches, rings, and eyeglasses, Maud builds 'a frail network of history around each death. ... This was how she maintained order, how she gathered together some sense out of the chaos of the deaths around her' (165).

Understandably, Maud feels sympathy for those whose lives, like her own, have been 'smothered.' But her decision to take on the role of historian/curator only makes sense in the light of the fact that she has been thoroughly trained in this role. As noted earlier, her life in the home of her in-laws taught her to suspend her own desires. As a result of her experience in the domestic museum, her own subjectivity has been virtually effaced; other people's lives seem more real than hers. Recalling an anecdote told to her by her husband, Maud confesses that her husband's memories had become more real than her own: 'the stories that he had recounted about events that took place when she was not present ... [became], for the moment, stronger than her own personal past, until, at times, she thought of herself as the keeper of his memories rather than the keeper of his memory' (93). Thus, when she begins to gather the fragments of other people's lives, to become a vessel holding the 'memories of their memories,' she merely extends her former role as the 'keeper' of her husband's memories.

Treated as if she herself were dead by her husband and his family, Maud responds by reifying other human beings, dead or alive. When the novel opens, she is portrayed as a woman who has minimal contact with the outside world. Her only attachments are perverse, involving 'relationships' with the bodies of dead children, her little 'angels,' as she calls them (137). As Aritha van Herk argues, Maud is 'an angel in the house of death' (review by 'Summer,' 15). Her position reveals the dangers of the nineteenth-century ideal of the Angel in the House expressed by Patmore – an ideal which, as Ehrenreich and English assert, left 'almost nothing for women to actually *be*' (109): if the man is to be 'something,' the woman must be 'nothing.' However, Maud does not remain a static angel, and the force that sets itself in opposition to this nineteenth-century discourse and ultimately frees her is embodied by her son.

In contrast to Maud's death-in-life existence, this strange child, who remains unnamed throughout the novel, is 'vehemently alive' (27). Seemingly autistic, he is silent until Maud forces him to speak. But even after he is compelled to talk, he continues to resist the symbolic order. As illustrated in his encounters with Patrick, mentioned earlier, the boy's poetic use of language consistently severs the links that normally bind signifier to signified. Both his silence and, later, his parodic speech effectively preclude his inscription into the order that initially claims his mother.

Maud's violent attempt to force the boy to speak offers a tangible representation of the role language plays in wresting order from chaos, and illustrates the nature of the symbolic order. The episode begins when Maud takes her child into the garden and tries to impress on him his adamic role as namer of the world. 'Garden,' she says to him slowly, pointing to the expanse. To her consternation, he gives no indication that he is even the slightest bit aware that she is speaking to him (64). Frustrated, Maud is forced to recognize that this 'absurd naming of objects had become one of the rituals of the day' (65). Inside the house, she can calmly utter an inventory of the objects, but when she is no longer within the confines of these four walls, where the number of objects to name is supposedly finite, 'the enormity of the task confounded her' (65–6). Her difficulty recalls Kant's discussion of the mathematical sublime. Unlike the 'dynamical' sublime, where the imagination is paralysed by the awesome power of nature, in the case of the mathematical sublime, the imagination is faced with the impossible task of synthesizing a seemingly infinite number of data – in Maud's case, the names of objects.[17] The futility of her task, coupled with her child's unresponsiveness, drives her into a rage. In her anger, she pins the boy between her legs, jerks his head upright, and peels back his eyelids, so that he is forced to stare directly at the sun. Then she screams the word 'SUN!' again and again into his ear.

The choice of this object, the sun, is significant. Located at the centre of our universe, the sun has traditionally functioned as an image of ultimate order. In his writings, Copernicus articulates the sun's function as ruler:

In the middle of all sits Sun enthroned. In this most beautiful temple could we place this luminary in any better position from which he can illuminate the whole at once? He is rightly called the Lamp, the Mind, the ruler of the Universe; Hermes Trismegistus names him the visible God, Sophocles' Electra calls him the All-Seeing. So the Sun sits as upon a royal throne ruling his children the planets which circle round him. ... Meanwhile the earth conceives by the Sun, and becomes pregnant with an annual rebirth.   (Copernicus qtd. in Bernal, 408)

Not only does the sun function as an image of ultimate order, but it is also viewed as male. As Susan Griffen asserts, the sun symbolizes 'God the Father' (*Woman*, 8). Taken together, these associations would suggest that Maud's gesture constitutes an attempt to subject the boy to the symbolic order. This scene is reminiscent of the biblical fall into consciousness, which likewise took place in the Garden and involves the notion of 'vision' – 'the eyes of both were opened' (Genesis 3:7).

According to Lacan, the child's first use of language constitutes a fall into alienation and reification because, when an individual represents himself, he does so as if he were an object among objects. In the confrontation between Maud and her son, the sense of alienation or split introduced by language is signalled by the boy's first word, 'sun,' spelled phonetically as 'sawn':

From his lips came an almost unidentifiable sound, more like the moan or low growl of a terrified cornered animal than anything human.

'S-a-a-a-w-n,' he groaned, followed by a long, slow, sob. 'Sa-a-a-w-n!.' ... Maud placed
her hands on his shaking shoulders and turned him gently away from the blinding fire.
That was his first word.
Those were his first tears. (67)

The unusual spelling of the word 'sun' as 'sawn' connotes the severing of the mother-
child dyad, concomitant with the child's entry into the symbolic order. The sense
of the split is further reinforced by the word 'tears,' which, by virtue of its dual
pronunciation contains this notion of a fissure.

Despite this attempt to conscript the boy into the symbolic order, he does not
relinquish his role as a force of subversion. The very presence of the puns noted
above emphasizes that linguistic instabilities can never be banished altogether. The
child continues to work, not in the Name of the Father, but in the unnamed efforts
of deterritorialization and poetry. His commitment to deterritorialization first becomes explicit when he studies a school of fish in a pond in his mother's garden. As
the narrator explains, the boy 'wanted to move the fish around, to remove them from
their various prisons. ... Why should they not have the rest of the garden, the rest
of the world?' (75). The boy sees what his mother, at this time, cannot, namely, that
containers do not constitute homes, but prisons.

In this same scene, the boy articulates his contempt for those people who are bent
on 'keeping' things. He watches his mother digging up a cannon ball in her garden
(her garden occupies the site of the Battle of Lundy's Lane). As she prepares to take
it back to the barn, where she hoards the other artifacts she has unearthed, her son
stares at her, with 'something approaching contempt altering the features of his small
face,' and he begins to repeat the word 'keeping' (78). The child utters this word on
only one other occasion, during his conversation with Patrick. At the time, Patrick
is in the midst of experimenting with the child. As the narrator explains, he wants
'to lay his own obsessions out in front of him [the boy] like clothes on a bed, just
to experience the word this boy might attach to them.' When Patrick says, 'Swimming,' the boy replies, 'Keeping' and, later, 'collar' (112). I would suggest that, in
accordance with his role as a force of deterritorialization, the child names both his
mother's and Patrick's obsessions for what they are, efforts to contain and control.

Ultimately, the child engages in a range of bizarre linguistic practices, including, among other things, mimicry, recitation, and parody, all of which constitute
forms of quotation. As such, his playful utterances demonstrate the impossibility
of 'keeping' or enforcing stability or ownership of language. This idea behind this
verbal refusal of origin and ownership, which is foregrounded in the decontextual-
ization of the quotation, is echoed in the boy's physical reorganization of his mother's
house. As Aritha van Herk points out, the 'child de-houses' both language and the
museumed objects of the novel (review, 'Summer,' 17).

By far the most significant intervention, the boy's complete transformation of his mother's home recalls Patrick's recurring dream concerning his uncle's farmhouse, where all the objects are 'scrambled.' The child effects this same type of scrambling, as the narrator explains: 'Objects had been grouped together, classified somehow, though it was difficult for Maud to determine the criteria for these new configurations. Her domestic geography had been tampered with, her home had become a puzzle' (204). Rather than feel anger, or the type of horror that Patrick experiences at the loss of order in this 'domestic geography,' Maud experiences only curiosity. Unlike Patrick and virtually all of the men in the novel, she is not dependent on the effacement of the Other to maintain a sense of identity. By contrast, she understands that this alternative system of classification may be an expression of the other, which she has been searching for all along: 'These strange little assemblings might be the key to the child's mind; a garden she'd been denied access to for years. In her heart, she felt like letting him continue. Rearrange it, she would say, it might be better' (206).

But the child not only rearranges her house, he also invades and disassembles Maud's museum, emptying the canvas sacks and removing the labels from the shelves, so that all hope of resurrecting the 'incredible classification process' is lost. As a result of this obvious introduction of chaos, Maud is finally forced to stop obeying what Kant describes as the 'law of reason' – the law which insists on 'the idea of a whole' that the imagination can never adequately represent (*Judgement*, 109). In Maud's case, this 'whole' is associated with the belief that she can restore an absent identity in its totality through a relentless process of collection. Until her son interrupts this process,[18] she behaves as if, by patiently collecting fragments from the nameless dead, she will ultimately discover the name and put an end to chaos. However, her son's gesture of 'emptying the museum' forcibly demonstrates that these fragments were never parts of some greater, unified whole, and that reason's image of wholeness remains an illusion in the world of experience. Kant repeatedly insists that reason's demand known as the 'moral law' must be understood simply as a regulative principle; it constitutes a 'supersensible substrate (which underlies both nature and our ability to think)' (*Judgement*, 112).[19] When the boy interrupts Maud's impossible quest, he pierces to the heart of this illusion of totality. As the narrator explains, the child 'had caused all the objects that surrounded her, all the relics she had catalogued, to lose their dreadful power. He had shown her what they really were: buttons, brooches, tie-clips, garters ... merely objects' (215). To an extent, Maud's experience conforms to the description of the resolution of the Kantian sublime. As Weiskel explains, in the case of 'an excess on the plane of the signifieds, the syntagmatic flow must be halted, or at least slowed, and the chain broken up if the discourse is to become meaningful again' (28). However, Maud's resolution does not conform to Weiskel's description of the latter stages, whereby the 'absence of a signified itself assumes the status of a signifier, disposing us to feel that behind this newly significant absence lurks a newly discovered presence, the latent referent, as it were, mediated by the new sign.' According to Weiskel, 'indeterminacy signifies' (28). By contrast, for Maud, indeterminacy ceases to signify; her release represents a complete rejection of the sublime. She no longer engages in the process of sublimation, which previously led her to view objects in terms of abstract values 'assessed and assigned by the mind' (Weiskel, 39). Her son has released her from alienated position entrenched by the sublime.

The boy's act of deterritorialization illustrates a fundamental aspect concerning objects as well as language. The objects Maud has collected do not bear any essential relationship to the person to whom they once belonged; in this respect, they correspond to words and language itself, a code that functions on the basis of the arbitrariness of the relationship between signifier and signified, and on the basis of the fact that words, like 'buttons, brooches, tie-clips, [and] garters' can, practically speaking, be used by anyone. Viewed in this light, what seem to be arbitrariness, breakdowns in the system, and intrusions of disorder are, in fact, enabling violations. Language does not cease to be meaningful because words can refer to two different things (i.e. 'tears') or because someone else can quote my words in my absence. Quite the contrary, it functions because the code *is* adaptable and remains independent of individuals.

Ultimately, the child enables Maud to appreciate the dangers of the misuse of reason, and he forces her to reconsider her position as a curator and collector. As the narrator explains, 'Maud perceived that he [the child] was the possessor of all the light and that it was she, not he, that had been the dark wall. She had never, since her husband's death, allowed the child access to the other, brighter side of that masonry, she had never allowed him to try to pull it down' (215). Unlike Patrick, who can never deconstruct the 'walled village,' the arbitrary divide between self and Other, order and chaos, Maud seems grateful for the opportunity to remove this obstacle because she wants to understand her son and achieve 'closeness.' In the final section featuring Maud, we see this formerly isolated woman pulling her son 'closer to her own warm body' (233).

As I noted earlier, Fleda expresses similar desires for 'closeness,' but her fate takes a different turn because, unlike Maud, she does not have the benefit of the child's subversive energies; instead, she turns to Patrick for this closeness. In tracing Fleda's path toward deterritorialization, it becomes apparent that her recognition of the constraining nature of the Old World order occurs prior to Maud's discovery. Before her husband was posted in Niagara, he and Fleda had lived in a house, which, as she says, 'became a kind of fortress.' She occupied this structure, reminiscent of Patrick's 'walled village,' sequestered with her 'companions,' the English Romantic poets, until she knew 'the geography of Venice, of Florence, of the English Lake District, better than the streets of Fort Erie, the hotels of Niagara Falls' (141).

Fleda, like the other characters, initially privileges European aesthetic values. Early on in her diary, she records her vision of appropriately 'picturesque' views and suggests that the Canadian landscape is attempting to mimic the European landscape, which pleases her:

I feel sometimes that my own special group of cedars is trying desperately to become cosmopolitan, to resemble their Italian cousin, the cyprus, and it makes me glad since I believe it to be unlikely that I should ever be fortunate enough to travel to that enchanted land. (35)

At this point, she still has some faith in the narratives that position her as the angel in the house, and she looks forward with anticipation to the construction of her new home on Whirlpool Heights. Yet, on some level, she understands the relationship between domesticity and keeping, the house and the prison, and considers herself an '*ex-prisoner*' of her former lodgings in town (36). Although she claims that she is excited about the construction of her house, her behaviour tells a different story. For instance, while she lives in her tent on Whirlpool Heights, she builds campfires using the log cabin method. As the narrator explains, she constructs a 'tiny house, a doll's house' so as to experience the pleasure of burning it 'to the ground' (32). This gesture indicates that Fleda will never find peace in the domestic museum.

Later on in the novel, Fleda recalls moving from her house, and the description bears a strong resemblance to the child's dismantling of Maud's museum. What she remembers most is 'emptying the cupboards':

Such debris! Such endless rooms filled with kept things! Such hoarding behind such firmly closed doors. Everything out of sight for years. Shoes, belts, corsets, stockings, gloves, buckles, feathers, shawls, hats, hat-boxes.

Plates, cups, saucers, vases, urns, relish dishes, mustard pots, salt and pepper shakers, candle snuffers, silver trays, pickle tongs, cruets, spooners, goblets, sealer jars.

And behind the doors of the upright cupboard in the parlour: papers, papers, old letters, newspaper clippings, recipes, photographs of deceased uncles, and of distant cousins, a survey of the property.

What is marriage, then, if not an accumulation of objects? (105)

Fleda, like Maud's son, rejects the 'museum mentality' and the obsession with collecting. When she moves to Whirlpool Heights and lives in a tent, she begins to experiment with chaos and gradually becomes aware of the dangers associated with enclosures (105).

For Fleda, as for her beloved Browning, home remains 'a dream, a piece of imaginary architecture whose walls and windows existed in the mind and therefore could be rearranged at will' (141). Initially, the house at Whirlpool Heights is akin to Browning's imaginary Palazzo Manzoni. But when the first stakes are driven into the ground, Fleda realizes that if her dream were 'laboured into permanence, [it] would produce a similar fortress and the feeling of caged torpor she was now beginning to associate with her last dwelling' (142). At this point, Fleda confronts the same dilemma as J.L., the heroine of van Herk's *The Tent Peg*. In both texts, the act of staking offers the possibility of acquiring a 'solid' identity; however, this solidity is also associated with a curtailing of the creative potential associated with deterritorialized space.

Whereas the women in the town of Niagara champion the type of feminine identity associated with the emerging house (the angelic wife and mother) and are scandalized by Fleda's transgressive behaviour, asserting that she 'should be having babies and minding house' (71), Fleda knows that this 'solid,' scripted identity holds no appeal for her. Recalling the carpet-sweeper that she once owned, called 'Mother's Helper,' Fleda admits that she found the name mildly ironic, 'since she had never been, and somehow knew she would never be, a mother' (140). Unlike J.L., who participates in the staking, Fleda chooses the deterritorialized existence over an ordered domesticity. It strikes her that, while she still performs chores around her campsite on Whirlpool Heights, 'there was nothing here like the insistent pressure of a house that wanted putting in order. There was hardly any call to order at all' (140).

Gradually, Fleda comes to value her own landscape over the tidy landscape of Europe. She begins to imagine poems 'filled with the smell of cedars carried on the breath of a northern wind. Scotch pines, white pines. Roots in the ground, needles in the sky' (119). Her willingness to accept the actual landscape, rather than yearn for the European ideal, underscores the fact that she has begun to distance herself from European notions of order, specifically the order associated with the domestic prison. As the narrator explains, when she 'closed the door for the last time. ... [s]he took her books with her into the real landscape of her own country' (141).

As the novel progresses, Fleda recognizes her unique situation in the New World and appreciates the fact that she has acquired a sense of freedom that the European poets could never even imagine: 'She had broken out of the world of corners and into the organic in a way that even her beloved poets in their cottages and villas hadn't the power to do. ... Released from boundaries, from rectangles, basements, attics, floors and doors' (142). The text highlights that Fleda's departure from domestic space constitutes an abandonment of all facets of pre-established order and of a predetermined female identity:

Departure from everything she had assumed she would be; from the keeping of various houses, from the sameness of days lived out inside the blueprint of artificially heated rooms, from pre-planned, rigidly timed events – when this happened in the morning and that happened in the afternoon, just because it always had and always would. (143)

Although Fleda relinquishes the repressive order associated with domesticity, she does not believe that she will remain alone in this; like Maud, she, too, yearns for 'closeness.'

Fleda knows that Patrick is fascinated by the fact that she has, to borrow his words, 'integrated herself with the terrain around her' (74), and she anticipates that he will join her. But as she reads her beloved Old World poets, Fleda begins to understand Patrick's position and his hesitation: *'Reading Browning. Learning Patrick'* (151). More specifically, in Browning's 'Andrea del Sarto' she recognizes both the compelling invitation to *'come out from behind your walls into the scenery. Let the view change around you ... forever'* and the refusal to embrace this change: *'the weak-eyed bat no sun should tempt / Out of the grange whose four walls make his world'* (151).

Despite the fact that Fleda is aware of Patrick's fear, she is stunned and hurt when he abandons her. Like Alice, the protagonist in Thomas's novel *Intertidal Life*, Fleda experiences pain of abandonment, the fate reserved for obstacles that impede the hero's quest. The withdrawal of Patrick's attention leaves Fleda 'flat and empty,' but more important, 'the life she had lived before became impossible to re-enter' (194). She cannot continue playing dress-up for her husband and planning views from the windows of her imaginary house – a house that is gradually being 'laboured into permanence.' To make matters worse, although Patrick spurns her, he continues to visit Whirlpool Heights. During one of his visits, he reminds Fleda that her freedom is being curtailed: 'Next year I'll come back and you will have built it, a house, right here, where once there was nothing at all' (195). His message also indicates that the forest which she loves remains invisible, *nothing*, to him. Increasingly, the prospective house takes on connotations of a prison:

> Corners were being introduced into her geography, accompanied by enthusiastic comments from the men. The building was a woman. 'She looks good, don't you think? Shouldn't she have a back door too? She'll be big enough for two good-sized carriages.' Pushing their hats back, they stood looking upwards at timber, at straight lines and corners, at the artificiality of geometric order. (195–6)

More and more, Fleda finds herself at odds with masculine notions of order and transcendence, which transform the particulars of everyday life into 'an abstract medium of exchange' (Weiskel, 58).

Toward the end of the novel, Patrick and David celebrate this order when they discuss the War of 1812 and the glories of dying for one's country, although David silently acknowledges that 'he didn't care at all what they were fighting for as long as he could write about it afterwards' (209).[20] At one point, Patrick asks David why General Brock sacrificed himself. Carried away by the glamour of sublime self-sacrifice, David replies, 'the whole thing was so wonderful. A young country like

ours needs dead heroes. Someone to mourn. Someone to make a monument for'
(209). When Patrick interjects that Brock was English, David dismisses his objec-
tion, explaining that he was English 'only when he was alive. After that he became
entirely Canadian. ... Canada claimed him and nothing will ever change that' (209).

During this absurd conversation, Fleda parodies the heroic ideal of the self-as-
fortress by singing patriotic hymns from the *Canadian Hymnal*:

> *Leave no unguarded place*
> *No weakness of the soul*
> *Take every virtue, every grace*
> *And fortify the whole*   (208)

Ultimately, the anger that she feels in the face of Patrick's 'vain masculine will' drains
away and she stops 'responding to either one of them' (212). At this point, she understands that, committed as they are to the narrative of romance and the sublime,
they will continue to position her as 'nothing' and ignore her and her desires. Following this realization, she begins to make her own plans for escape: 'an idea was form-
ing, taking vague shape. Departure. She could no longer live the closeted life of the
recent past.' (218).

Toward the conclusion, Fleda notes in her diary: '*The men keep wanting to build
things; to order lumber, hire workmen, draft plans, take measurements. They keep wanting to deliver* concrete *messages and plan battles*' (219; my emphasis). Her refusal to
bear this oppressive Old World message is clarified when she writes:

> *I think about Laura Secord living for sixty more years in the same house, dreaming of one
> long walk she took in the wilderness, telling the story, over and over to herself, to anyone else who
> would listen.*
> *Nobody understood. It wasn't the message that was important. It was the walk. The journey.
> Setting forth.*   (219)

This insistence on the importance of the journey as opposed to the goal recalls Audrey
Thomas's insistence on the fact that what the explorers sent from England and Spain
ultimately gained was the experience of the search itself. When Fleda leaves David,
she follows 'Laura Secord's route but she carried with her no deep messages' (234). The
emphasis in these passages on delivering 'messages' once again recalls Lyotard's
reading of the sublime, which, as noted earlier, instigates a disruption, so that the
individual 'ceases to be guided by a culture which made of him / [her] the sender
and master of a message of glory' (202). Viewed in this context, Fleda does not
remain the bearer of a message of glory but becomes 'the involuntary addressee of
an inspiration come to ... [her] from an "I know not what"' (Lyotard, 202). Like

Arachne in van Herk's novel *No Fixed Address*, Fleda literally walks off the man-made map. She leaves her husband's property – ceases, in fact, to be his property, and escapes into the uncharted territory beyond the frame of the story.

If Urquhart's novel had ended solely with David's retreat into the museum, Patrick's death, and Fleda's journey into the woods, one might be tempted to presume that the only way to negotiate the 'divide,' the order associated with the narrative of romance and the writings on the sublime, lies in this type of flight into the untamed landscape. However, the fact that Maud remains with her son in the parallel section suggests that Fleda's rejection of domesticity and motherhood and her flight into the wilderness are not integral to deterritorialization. There are many ways to effect a shift from closure to open space. Although David and Patrick do not succeed in this endeavour, the child, Maud, and Fleda successfully employ different strategies to 'empty the museum,' ensuring that, to borrow Woolf's image of the woman standing before the library door, no one need remain bound by the arbitrary, yet powerfully entrenched, divisions between insiders and outsiders.

7

Epilogue: Strategies for Re-vision

There must be another name, somewhere, if only one had the eyes to read it. (van Herk, *Places*, 97)

As I suggested in the introduction, in many respects what emerges from an analysis of the fictions in this study is a range of tactics of subversion used to challenge traditional, patriarchal discourses, which have charted the terrain of female identity. The common feature linking all of the texts is the consistent deployment of imagery associated with travel or exploration, maps, and map-making. These images are used to call into question the privileged position of a wide variety of literary and non-literary discourses that have informed constructions of female identity. Although the novels focus on widely divergent discourses, specific to such disciplines as literature, science, religion, and history, they nevertheless expose similarities in the way in which these established discourses inform a world-view that hinges on a belief in two basic positions: the male hero-human, on the one hand, and the female monster-obstacle, on the other. Each of the novels emphasizes that, in their construction of this binary opposition, specifically in the transformation of women into Woman, these discourses displace and devalue women's perceptions of their experience.

In many ways, the construction of the Man/Woman dichotomy corresponds to the colonial tactic of manufacturing the 'Other,' the looking-glass reflection of the equally fictitious entity designated as the 'self.' As critics have noted, in order to maintain authority over the Other, imperialist discourse strives to 'delineate the Other as radically different from the self, yet at the same time it must maintain sufficient identity with the Other to valorize control over it. The Other can, of course, only be constructed out of the archive of "the self," yet the self must also articulate the Other as inescapably different' (Ashcroft et al., 103). Gayatri Spivak elaborates on the strategy of 'Othering' and suggests that this process is based on the assumption of authority, 'voice,' and control of the 'word' – essentially, the 'seizure and control of the means of interpretation and communication' (qtd. in Ashcroft et al., 97). Yet, as we saw from the analysis of the texts in the previous chapters, this colonial process has strong affinities with patriarchal mechanisms; the tactic of 'Othering' has clearly played a part in generating the hierarchical relations between men and women – relations that are legitimated by the various discourses outlined above.

All of the texts in this study demonstrate that, at the very least, the basic strategy of appropriation (which includes the appropriation of the role of 'author') must be adopted in the hopes of transforming the discourses that have alienated and silenced women, while according men privileged access to communication and interpretation. Using various tactics of subversion, the novels signal an awareness of women's marginalization, their displacement from the privileged centre; to a certain extent, all of the writers examined in this study are 'violent' and 'unredemptive' spies working in a 'landscape up until now defined by other eyes' (van Herk, 'Women,' 24).

However, the very existence of these texts suggests that meanings can shift and that discourses, like maps, can be used in ways that are radically different from the ones they were originally intended to serve. As I have repeatedly pointed out, the novels clarify that the goal of a disruptive involvement with discourse does not lie in simply reversing the hierarchy, but in bringing about a complete transformation that will change the conditions of reading. This transformation, likened in Thomas's text to a Copernican revolution, will be achieved through a rigorous deconstruction of the framework that accords meaning and value. In Urquhart's text a similar desire for this type of transformation is expressed. When Maud discovers her son's deconstruction of their home, she responds, 'Rearrange it ... It might be better' (206). The ultimate target of this type of scrutiny is the medium of language itself: the medium in which conceptions of 'truth,' 'order,' and 'reality' are established.

As I noted earlier, within the texts, the images of exploration and cartography serve a double function. On the one hand, they highlight the way in which female identity has been fixed by traditional discourses; on the other hand, these same images emphasize the fact that the texts are engaged in attempts to remap established representations of female identity through a detailed analysis of the 'blind spots' on the map. In Thomas's text, the 'map' selected for analysis is none other than the literary genre of romance. In its parodic appropriation of this genre, *Intertidal Life* concentrates on the principal element of romance, that is, the quest motif. In the novel, the structure of the quest is linked to the imperialist and patriarchal conquest of the 'territory' of female experience. As in all of the novels analysed, in Thomas's work, parallels are drawn between women's experience of the politics of gender and Canada's colonial legacy. In this case, the text adopts and adapts the rhetoric of colonialism to suit a feminist agenda, with the implication that women must attempt to name their experiences and recolonize their identities by taking on the role of officers and captains and undertaking quests themselves.

If we take the narrator's quest as an example, we see that these alternative voyages do not resemble the traditional, ascending quest structure – the journey of a 'creature returning to its creator' (Frye, *Secular*, 157). Instead, Thomas's female quester finds herself exploring the 'dark space' of a world in flux. From her unusual perspective – the perspective of the castaway – the narrator finds herself in a position to offer a critique of the framework of romance. Gradually, what emerges from her critique is an awareness that this literary structure freezes participants into hierarchical relations in which the woman is locked into position by the assumed moral superiority of the dominant hero. Within the grid of romance, women are represented as Woman, the specular reflection of Man, and thereby characterized as devoid of desire – as 'nothing.'

In her radical refusal of the structures of both traditional and popular romances, Thomas's narrator never stages a return to the pastoral ideal of the 'happy family.' Instead of achieving some form of coherent identity, she hovers between alienation and disalienation. While this strategy assumes negative connotations because it emphasizes the very real dangers of psychic fragmentation, and does not offer tangible alternatives to an identity that positions women as man's degraded Other, it still manages to avoid the simple inversion of the power structure. To its credit, Thomas's text succeeds in arresting or freezing the mechanisms of the romance narrative altogether. In many ways, it is crucial that the narrator never finishes sorting out her journal and that her account of events lacks the cohesion typically associated with systems that guarantee unified maps of experience and subjectivity; the novel's relentless portrayal of a world in 'flux' provides a useful characterization of a postmodern world in which meanings are unstable, and identities, if they are assembled at all, remain both strategic and provisional fictions.

Generally speaking, in its critical exploration of romance, Thomas's text adopts several recognizable feminist, postcolonial, and postmodern strategies which, as we have seen, are also deployed in other novels in this study. For one, in all of the texts, events are narrated not from the hero's perspective, but from the perspective of society's outcasts. Second, intertexts (which include canonical and non-canonical inset elements) are used to highlight the gap between the official story (as related by the canonical materials) and the unofficial story. This gap serves to illuminate the 'blind spots' on the official map and expose the contradictions and the instabilities inherent in the binary model of self/Other. At times, the texts simply leave the gap to stand as a marker signalling the indeterminacy and inadequacy of any one system of communication. At other times, subjugated knowledges are revealed within the gap – knowledges that were previously eclipsed by the bipolar model. The texts' presentation of these knowledges throws the legitimacy of the traditional discourses into question because the novels open up the possibility of representing differences without subjecting them to the controlling mechanisms of hierarchical structures. Very often, these subjugated knowledges consist of autobiographical materials that blur the categories of 'fact' and 'fiction,' and they undermine the implicit assumption that only certain categories of experience are capable of being rendered as 'literature' (see Ashcroft et al., 88). In most cases, the presence of autobiographical and/or biographical materials concerning women's history intimates that women need not support the devaluation of their personal experience by conforming to traditional practices and portraying history on an epic scale. Instead of writing history with a capital 'H,' all of the writers in this study inscribe local and personal histories.

In Susan Swan's novel, we can see that many of these same strategies are at work. Her portrait of the Victorian giantess draws on the generic conventions of the mock-travel narrative and the freak-show pamphlet to call into question the discursive positioning of women as landscape and woman as monstrous obstacle, even more emphatically than *Intertidal Life*. Here the patriarchal and imperialist logic that guarantees this type of division is exposed within a set of nineteenth-century discourses, including modern science, industrial capitalism, and American nationalism, which charted the category of Woman and aligned it with the equally fictitious category of the freak. Although Swan's target is not the literary narrative of romance, like Thomas she reinscribes and resists a world-view that constructs 'reality' by establishing the male as normal and the female as subnormal.

Within the novel, images of travel, maps, and map-making are used to emphasize the way in which nineteenth-century scientists attempted to solve the 'Woman Question' by charting the terrain of women's bodies. Yet, these images are also recuperated for the purposes of subversion: whereas the men engage in quests to map and measure for science and profit, elements of the quest motif also surface in conjunction with Anna's search for a place that will accommodate a 'Victorian woman who refused to be inconsequential' (2). At bottom, in both Thomas's and Swan's novels the problem of women's representation as Woman within the symbolic order is at issue. While Swan does not rely on autobiographical material, her novel does draw on biographical information concerning a real-life giantess, and, like Thomas's text, reflects a concern with the process of history-making.

In Daphne Marlatt's *Ana Historic*, which takes, as its point of departure, archival information – albeit meagre – concerning Mrs Richards, the concern regarding history-making occupies centre stage. Given the changes and additions Swan and Marlatt introduce into the scant biographical details concerning their subjects, one might question whether these authors betray, rather than rescue, their subjects by reinventing their lives. Chastised for writing what relatives of the giantess viewed as 'an inaccurate biography,' Swan insists that she never set out to write non-fiction. Instead, she wanted to offer a mythology of a female giant, presumably to counter the numerous stories about male giants such as Angus McAskill, Paul Bunyan, Gulliver, Goliath, the Cyclops, Gargantua, and Pantagruel (see Heffernan, 25). Marlatt has also been challenged on similar grounds. In an interview with George Bowering, she admitted to her desire to give her protagonist 'a different destiny from the one that history actually records,' whereupon Bowering asked, 'You're not allowed to do that, are you?' Marlatt replied, 'As a novelist I'm allowed to do anything' ('On *Ana,*' 97, 98). Both Swan's and Marlatt's responses underscore their refusal to be condemned for appropriating factual details to fabricate their fictions. As Marlatt's reply indicates, she holds her ground because a myriad of authors, ranging from Chaucer to Michael Ondaatje, have invoked historical information in their fictions. Both Swan and Marlatt know that this remains a standard practice of writers – satirists, historical writers, and biographers, in particular. It is strange that Bowering, of all people, questioned Marlatt for inventing a life for Mrs Richards, in the light of the fact that he won a Governor General's Award for reinventing the life of George Vancouver and shaping this man into a nasty, gout-afflicted homosexual in his novel *Burning Water.*

Like male authors, then, women demand the right to imagine history differently. In *Ana Historic*, Marlatt employs many of the same subversive strategies outlined above, but the text differs from Thomas's and Swan's in that it shifts the boundaries of the notion of cartography. In Marlatt's novel, the notions of mapmaking and exploration are allied with the temporal rather than spatial dimension. Despite this shift, the text persists in analysing the consequences of the metaphoric connection between women and landscape, and, in keeping with the other novels, *Ana Historic* identifies this metaphoric association as a legacy of both patriarchy and imperialism. In interviews, Marlatt suggests that 'the patriarchal oppression of women and colonialism are two different faces of the same coin' (interview, 'Sounding,' 54). This comment seems somewhat misleading – unless it refers to the operation of colonialism and patriarchy during a specific historical 'moment' – because patriarchal oppression, as Gerda Lerner argues, pre-dates colonialism and very often survives the dismantling of colonial structures.

Of all the texts studied, *Ana Historic* puts the greatest emphasis on exposing and destabilizing the mechanisms responsible for the brutal erasure of women's bodies and women's desires. In its blending of autobiographical, historical, and fictional passages, and in its use of intertexts and fragmentation – right down to the microfragmentation at the level of the sentences – *Ana Historic* stages a veritable assault on the structures of the symbolic order. In conjunction with its rigorous deconstruction of the mechanisms of the symbolic order (as Lacan has described them) and the institutions supported by this order, Marlatt's novel, like all of the texts in this study, works with a dual agenda that involves both decoding and recoding the maps that have established the terrain of female identity. Thus, at the same time that the map of official history is being deconstructed, the novel is simultaneously reconstructing (retrieving and inventing) a history of the 'dark space.' What emerges is a map of an ancestral trajectory or, more precisely, a genealogy for 'lost' women fashioned from the fragments of the shattered symbolic frame.

What is perhaps most unsettling about the stories is that, in their deconstruction of various discourses, they reveal the pervasiveness of mechanisms that effect the repression of women. In particular, in each of the texts, marriage and the nuclear family are revealed to be dangerous, 'uncanny' institutions that marginalize women and force them to operate as hysterics. In its exploration of an alternative to these paths (which lead only to marriage, madness, or death), *Ana Historic* simultaneously exposes the violence at the heart of the symbolic system and locates a strategy for resistance. While Thomas's and Swan's texts traced only the faintest outlines of a 'sorority,' in Marlatt's novel, the creation of this type of alliance constitutes a fundamental strategy for contesting the symbolic order. Here, the creation of a female frame of reference, established in terms of the friendship between Annie and Zoe, has the capacity to undermine the frame of the symbolic and open up the possibility of representing female desire.

No strategy is undertaken without risk. In the case of *Ana Historic*, the risk centres on the construction of a female symbolic, which, if too closely identified with a specific identity, namely, lesbianism, could lead to the reinscription of yet another binary opposition – one that valorizes some sort of unified (and potentially totalizing) homosexuality. This outcome would hardly effect any improvement upon the standard naturalized compulsory heterosexuality that currently holds sway. As Judith Butler insists in her discussion of Monique Wittig's writings, perhaps the most potentially subversive positions are not either straight or gay (*Gender*, 121–2). Marlatt, who uses terms such as 'salvage,' is clearly in favour of adopting stances that include a recognition of such features as hybridity. She is particularly insistent that the poetic convention of seeing woman as landscape cannot be discarded, but must be transformed. In interviews, she has been asked to explain how this poetic convention – the 'territorialization of the female body,' which Annette Kolodny has referred to as 'the lay of the land' – is treated in her writing. Her response emphasizes her awareness of the need to illuminate the contradictions and inconsistencies that exist within established structures, rather than to reject these structures altogether. As she says:

Obviously one doesn't want to be stuck with the whole image bank that male writers have given to the female. And yet, it's very dangerous for us to totally deny it because we would then deny an important part of ourselves. Betsy [Warland] and I have talked about this a lot, and we're trying to reclaim it in a way that is meaningful for us. For instance, if I talk about our sexuality as a hidden ground, then I have to make a distinction between ground that is laid out, gridded, cleared for use, dry land versus unmapped, uncharted, untamed land that is wet and swampy and usually discarded. So there is a difference within the landscape metaphor. ('Speaking,' 27)

In general, Marlatt seems wary of portraying alliances based on notions of correctness, purity, and authenticity; associations based on these features remain suspect no matter which group (dominated or dominating) invokes them.

Aritha van Herk's fictions avoid the risk noted above because they do not depend upon the construction of a female frame of reference as a tactic for subversion. Instead, the practice of forging alliances is augmented to include bonds that transgress traditional dichotomies such as man/woman and human/animal. In van Herk's fictions, we find some of the most overt expressions of resistance to masculine narratives and their representations of women as Woman: 'mothers/saints/whores, muses all' ('Women,' 18). Like all of the fictions analysed in this study, van Herk's novels continue to trace the connections between the feminization of the landscape and the appropriation and exploitation of women. In many ways, the text's treatment of the colonial and patriarchal imposition of names, and its emphasis on the way in which this practice secures the paternal genealogy, recalls Thomas's treatment of this same phenomenon. The following statement, taken from van Herk's latest text, could easily be mistaken for a comment made by the protagonist in *Intertidal Life*: 'These names, every mapped configuration male/lineated ... names on everything, on every physical abutment ... one's father's name, the names of other men, the names of absent and abstracted/ideal women' (*Places*, 88). In conjunction with the other texts, van Herk's writing foregrounds the power of the male gaze, the power of the name, and draws parallels between the stratification of the Canadian landscape portrayed as female and the stratification of the roles and behaviours assigned to men and women on the basis of sex. In her texts, images of maps and mapmaking are primarily invoked to signal a challenge to the boundaries erected between the supposedly masculine and feminine 'regions.'

Like the other writers in this study, van Herk rejects the belief that women must inscribe epic history. Much of her writing eschews the universal and transcendent in favour of the local and immediate. In *No Fixed Address*, the narrator celebrates the marginal; she seduces a cast-off old man and visits minor towns such as 'Redland,' whose existence is so ephemeral that it is not found on the map and can never be relocated after the initial chance encounter (34–6). In *Places Far from Ellesmere*, the narrator celebrates the shifting, unstable geography of the Arctic desert, deterritorialized space which, in this subversive text, takes precedence over the metropolitan 'fortresses' of Edmonton and Calgary, cities that bear the marks of stratification in their 'square blocks' and 'straight lines' ('Stranded,' 10).

To a certain extent, the depictions of the conquest of the landscape within her texts (especially in *Places Far from Ellesmere*) recall Northrop Frye's analysis of the grid which was imposed on the country as a whole:

> Civilization in Canada, as elsewhere, has advanced geometrically across the country, throwing down the long parallel lines of the railways, dividing up the farm lands into chessboards of square-mile sections and concession-line roads. There is little adaptation to nature: in both architecture and arrangement, Canadian cities and villages express rather an arrogant abstraction, the conquest of nature by an intelligence that does not love it. (*Bush*, 224)

Whereas Frye suggests that individuals continue to look upon the mapping impulse and the grid with suspicion, van Herk intimates that the maps can be wrested from the hands of the cartographers and adapted to suit the needs of feminist explorers. Even if the grid proves too inhibiting, feminist 'spies' can always resort to the strategy of 'earth-quak[ing] ... those black steel lines' ('Women,' 24). By 'black steel lines,' van Herk refers to the grid which, as Frye notes, was imposed on the landscape by both explorers – settlers and western writers – but, unlike Frye, van Herk emphasizes that the 'grid' was imposed on women as well.

Van Herk's texts imply that one way to escape the paternal genealogy, which governs both literary and historical discourses, lies in moving off the beaten track, the grid of the black steel lines, and venturing into unmapped territory. Her texts repeatedly identify the Arctic as the deterritorialized space in which traditional practices of representation can be resisted. As noted earlier, van Herk's characters adopt the practices of what Deleuze and Guattari term 'nomadic war machines.' In many ways, it is not surprising that a regional western writer should adopt the strategy of 'nomadology.' As Frye asserts, Canada is both immensely vast and sparsely inhabited compared to other countries, and as a result of these two factors, transportation and communication have always been crucial: in Canada, the rhythm 'of nomadic movement over great distances persists' to the present (*Bush*, 223).

In many ways, the glorification of the Arctic expressed in *The Tent Peg, No Fixed Address*, and *Places Far from Ellesmere*, corresponds to Frye's analysis of what he terms the 'second phase of Canadian social development.' According to Frye, at this stage, the conflict of man and nature expands into 'a triangular conflict of nature, society, and individual. Here, the individual tends to ally himself with nature against society' (*Bush*, 245). As an example of this tendency, Frye cites John Robin's *Incomplete Anglers*: 'I can approach a solitary tree with pleasure, a cluster of trees with joy, and a forest with rapture; I must approach a solitary man with caution, a group of men with trepidation, and a nation of men with terror' (qtd. in *Bush*, 245). In van Herk's writing, the exaltation of the deterritorialized domain of the Arctic recalls this 'triangular conflict'; however, in her fictions, 'man' does not refer to the supposedly universal category but to *bona-fide* males.

In van Herk's later texts, the characterization of the Arctic as an 'agent,' rather than passive background, which 'reads and writes' the narrator (*In Visible*, 5), leaving her 'invisibled by awe,' echoes the tradition of the romantic sublime and the Wordsworthian sense of nature as teacher, which, as Frye notes, is visible in Canadian literature 'as early as Mrs Traill' (*Bush*, 245). This tradition receives an ironic twist because the narrator's claim to have been rendered 'invisible' is profusely and richly described 'in visible ink.' In pointing out the resonances of earlier traditions within van Herk's fictions, I am simply indicating that, as a feminist discourse of liberation, her texts, like the other works in this study, have taken up and reshaped discourses from established, masculine traditions.

At some point, one must ask whether van Herk's fictions, which typically represent the Arctic as 'the ultimate frontier,' promote a playful rejection of genres such as the western and the northern, which typically invoke the image of the Arctic as 'no man's land,' or whether her fictions, on some level, reproduce the imperialist projections that gave rise to the western and account for its pervasive description of an empty, feminine landscape waiting to be conquered. This question surfaces with decided urgency because, historically, descriptions of the north as a no man's land have had tangible political repercussions. In *The Tent Peg*, J.L. transforms herself into an angry gunslinger who revels in her freedom from the constraints associated with civilized society – a transformation that highlights the story's reliance on the traditional western (see Slotkin, 403–4). When Arachne ventures north, she, too, behaves like any other westerner, searching for a frontier that can be colonized. As the narrator states: 'She is steeling herself to enter the blank, the dislocated world of the North. ... After this there is no turning back. ... Perhaps she will be able to find a place to settle in, colonize' (302). Whereas van Herk's earlier fictions tend to replicate the rhetoric glorifying machismo and the conquest of a virgin territory, in her most recent collection of essays, she seems to realize that the desires of a western feminist for escape – desires that are predicated on the representation of the Arctic as a blank space – must be negotiated within a broader context that includes the perspective of the Inuit, who read this space, not as a blank, but as home.[1]

At bottom, none of the authors in this study assumes that she is operating in a textual vacuum or that a *total* escape from representation constitutes anything more than an energizing, imaginative fantasy. In Urquhart's text, for example, the ability and willingness to reshape inherited discourses, to 'empty the museum,' are crucial attributes that are linked to the physical and mental health of individuals who find themselves in the New World. Each of the principal characters is compelled to engage in some form of translation when it becomes obvious that traditional European discourses, specifically, the narrative of romance and the aesthetic concept of the sublime, cannot simply be imposed on the Canadian landscape. Of the five characters, only three – Maud, her son, and Fleda – succeed in reshaping the narratives inherited from Europe; the men cannot or will not give up their attachments to these narratives. As Patrick sees it, loosening his grip on established narratives, which position him as the scientist-hero, would mean renouncing power and control or, worse, becoming 'nothing.' While his choice seems regressive, he is at least cognizant of the fact that he has the ability to choose. By contrast, the historian appears unaware of the existence of other narrative options. He dutifully bears the Old World message, its belief in progress and its 'museum-mentality,' what Frye describes above as 'an arrogant abstraction, the conquest of nature by an intelligence that does not love it.' Like Patrick, he, too, becomes a victim of the Old World order.

On the whole, it is the text's awareness that inherited stories can and must be changed that links it to the other novels in this study – a link that is strengthened by the presence of other related features, including a desire to deconstruct the narrative of romance, a healthy suspicion of History with a capital 'H,' an awareness of the power of the male gaze, and, finally, a penchant for interrogating the uncanny and oppressive nature of domesticity. But *The Whirlpool* differs from the other novels in that it takes equal pains to emphasize that men, as well as women, suffer from the rigid imposition of imperialist and patriarchal narratives. Identification with these narratives, which are based on binary oppositions and the orderly division between male and female, human and non-human, entails a profound sacrifice of one sort or another, regardless of one's sex. This tragic sacrifice can only be averted if individuals make a leap of faith – a leap into what appears to be chaos – in order to transform the fictions they live by.

In general, the necessity of taking this step and engaging in a process of appropriation and manipulation of established narratives highlights once again that representations are not fashioned in isolation. This means that altering notions regarding female identity involves not some transcendent search for a 'new self' free from ideology, what Atwood has called a 'new land cleaned of geographies' ('Reincarnation,' 60), but a contestatory practice that takes place within the terms of the existing 'geographies.' In Urquhart's text, when Fleda leaves, she follows Laura Secord's route, but does not carry the same 'deep messages' (234). As Sally Robinson argues, 'while it may be true that masculine and feminine positions oppositionally conceived are the only two positions *offered* by hegemonic discursive systems, it does not necessarily follow that others cannot be *constructed*, or even wrenched from within those very systems' (18).

Looking at the texts in this study, we see that van Herk and Thomas occupy opposite positions in terms of their attitude toward the breakdown of a unified identity. However, the tension between these two positions emphasizes that there is no single strategy and no single goal that all feminists can adopt in their attempts to revise traditional representations of female identity. Furthermore, as R. Radhakrishnan insists, the positions from which one speaks necessitate different practices, depending on the relative power afforded by those positions. Thus, whereas 'the dominant position requires acts of self-deconstruction, the subordinant position entails collective self-construction' (277). Once again, we are reminded that, in discussing 'identity,' we must keep in mind that we need to think of 'identities,' which are both temporary and strategic (Riley, 136). It is imperative, however, that, in a bid to construct these strategic and temporary identities, women do not allow themselves to be marginalized yet again. It is all too easy for women writers to unwittingly render themselves invisible by grouping under the banner of postmodernism and/or postcolonialism. As I have demonstrated, women writers have a great deal in common with groups who are attempting to throw off traditional or colonial apparatuses; they even use rhetorical tactics that are common to both postmodern and postcolonial fictions. Nevertheless, while the means may be similar, the ends are quite different. In the struggle to regain their voice and chart out their experience and desires, women writers are not simply working for the liberation of an oppressed and colonized people. (Ironically, within supposedly postcolonial countries, patriarchal oppression often remains as rampant as ever.) Likewise, in constructing their fictions, Canadian women writers are not toying with the latest continental or American rhetorical trends, namely, poststructuralism and postmodernism. If the achievement of self-representation within these texts can be said to involve 'moves' in a postmodern language game, then it should be clear from the analysis of the novels within this study that it is a game being played in earnest, where the stakes are people's minds and bodies.

To conclude, what began as a quest to discover if and how Canadian women writers were responding to Virginia Woolf's statement that it is dangerous for women to map themselves onto the linguistic terrain has generated a multiplicity of responses. From a survey of the fictions examined here, it seems that Canadian women writers feel that there is no choice other than to map themselves in this precarious terrain. Language and literary forms cannot be abandoned altogether because, as mentioned earlier, they constitute a medium 'in which changing subjects create themselves as subjects within a new social context' (Mitchell, 289). Perhaps Thomas best describes this wary and ambivalent relationship to language when she says, 'language was my enemy for a long time, so, what do you do with your enemy? You wrestle it to the ground' ('An Interview,' 39). In their attempts to fashion identities within a postmodern culture – identities that subvert the hierarchial dualisms of bourgeois identities – women writers must draw on the maps that are available, but this does not mean that the masculine framework cannot be 'earth-quaked' a little before the work of salvaging begins.

Notes

1: Introduction

1 In her essay 'Professions for Women,' in *The Death of the Moth*, Virginia Woolf uses the term Angel in the House to describe the image of the perfect woman – a phantom which would leap to mind whenever Woolf put pen to paper and exclaim, 'Never let anybody guess that you have a mind of your own,' effectively preventing her from writing (150).

2 For a detailed description of the debate surrounding *Survival*, see McCombs, ed., 7–8.

3 A number of these critics, myself included, gathered to discuss the intersections between exploration literature and Canadian fiction at the 'Arctic Narrative Symposium' held at the University of Ottawa, 21–3 April 1995. John Moss is currently preparing a collection of the talks presented for publication by the University of Ottawa Press.

4 For an excellent analysis of the way in which maps function as ideological tools in the service of the state, see the introductory chapter of Graham Huggan's study *Territorial Disputes: Maps and Mapping Strategies in Contemporary Canadian and Australian Fiction*, 3–34.

5 Marlatt discusses her debt to a variety of theorists in 'Sounding a Difference,' her interview with Janice Williamson, 47–8.

6 There are, of course, notable exceptions, including Barbara Godard, Lorraine Weir, and, of course, Linda Hutcheon. In particular, the chapter '"Shape Shifters": Canadian Women Writers and the Tradition' in Hutcheon's book *The Canadian Postmodern*, 107–37, offers an analysis of a selection of texts which utilize postmodern strategies.

7 See his essay 'The "Uncanny,"' in *The Collected Works of Sigmund Freud*, 17:218–52.

8 In my use of this term, I draw on Chris Weedon's definition of the 'symbolic order' as 'the social and cultural order in which we live our lives as conscious, gendered subjects,' which is structured by 'language and the laws and social institutions which language guarantees' (52). For Lacan, meaning and the symbolic order as a whole are 'fixed in relation to a primary, transcendental signifier which Lacan calls the *phallus*, the signifier

of sexual difference, which guarantees the patriarchal structure of the symbolic order'
(Weeden, 53). See Lacan, 67, 198–9.

2: Audrey Thomas's *Intertidal Life*

1 The term 'subject in process' is one that Juliet Mitchell (288–9) uses in her book to
describe the endeavours of women writers of the seventeenth century, women who were
trying in their writing to describe the process of becoming women within a new bourgeois society.

2 In her essay 'Sailing the Oceans of the World' (285), Lorna Irvine suggests that the
motif of exploration functions as a metaphor for the process of female creativity.

3 In her essay 'A Fine Romance, My Dear, This Is,' Thomas emphasizes the dangerous
ideology that informs Harlequins, asserting that 'millions of women are buying the violence and abuse, the humiliation, along with the happy ending' (11).

4 In Thomas's short story 'Natural History,' in *Real Mothers*, the narrator worries that if
she stays on her island forever she 'will end up like an old witch in a witch's cottage'
(32), a fate paralleling that of both Circe and Calypso. Critics Robert Diotte and
Wendy Keitner both relate Thomas's narrators to the female characters in *The Odyssey*.

5 In conversation with her daughter Flora, Alice recalls how she and her girlfriends would
literally 'brand' the initials of their boyfriends onto their skin, by tanning with adhesive
tape on their backs (10–11).

6 In Thomas's novel *Songs My Mother Taught Me*, a similar episode occurs. The narrator's
grandfather asks the narrator, 'Why take a name that someone else has given ...?' Realizing that people as well as things are named, the narrator asks, 'Is my real name not
Isobel?' Her grandfather replies, 'It might be. Wait and see' (98).

7 In *Blown Figures*, the narrator admits that she accepted her mother-in-law's order as
'more valuable than [her] ... own chaos' (160). Alice's relations with her in-laws provide
a microcosmic example of the ideological tensions that existed between the colonies
and the British empire.

8 Several critics have analysed Thomas's fiction in the context of postcolonial fiction,
including Susan Ash, Chris Prentice, Arnold E. Davidson, and Chantal Zabus.

9 For a discussion of Thomas's use of earlier short stories in developing the novel, see
Brigitte G. Bossanne, 'Audrey Thomas and Lewis Carroll: Two Sides of the Looking
Glass,' as well as Joan Coldwell, 'Natural History and *Intertidal Life*.' Linda Hutcheon
focuses more broadly on Thomas's elaborate use of intertextuality in her book *The
Canadian Postmodern: A Study of Contemporary English-Canadian Fiction*, 111–19.

10 In her book *Audrey Thomas and Her Works* Barbara Godard links Thomas's tendency to
write a *roman-fleuve* with Hugh Hood's work and suggests that Thomas's impulse
toward autobiography can be linked to the influence of the Tish group, who were guided
by phenomenology (6–7).

11 During an interview with Pierre Coupey et al. Thomas discusses the North American insistence on the repression of emotion (88).

12 I, for one, am at a loss to explain why the dog, Byron, said to have been put down (8), is suddenly lying at Alice's feet the morning of the operation (279).

13 Thomas self-consciously deconstructs the temporal logic in many of her novels because, as she says in her interview with George Bowering, 'I'm not interested in time. I don't believe in time. I don't know what time is' ('Songs,' 14).

14 Note that the length of the sections decreases proportionally, so that the second section is roughly half as long as the first, and the third section is half as long as the second. This structure gives me the impression that the text is winding down, much like a drowning woman running out of air.

15 Alice's attention to her clothing may be a parodic allusion to Harlequin romances, in which tremendous space is filled up with descriptions of the heroine's attire (see Snitow, 135).

16 In my treatment of the intertidal creatures as ambivalent symbols, I refer to their status in the novel as well to George Bowering's discussion of the relationship between memory, pain, and intertidal organisms in *Mrs. Blood*: 'Mrs. Blood says that she is encrusted with pain, or with memories ... Mrs. Thing is covered with pain, & Mrs Blood is covered with memories' ('Songs,' 22). In *Mrs. Blood*, the narrator says she is 'covered with memories like barnacles' (148).

17 In her essay 'Somebody's Trying to Kill Me and I Think It's My Husband: The Modern Gothic,' Joanna Russ confirms that this fear is also a familiar convention of Gothic fiction.

18 Thomas has admitted to her fascination with Lewis Carroll's work and with mirrors. See Eleanor Wachtel, 'The Guts,' 4, and Wachtel, 'An Interview,' 39. Thomas also uses the words of the Cheshire Cat as an epigraph to *Mrs. Blood* and in the conclusion to *Songs My Mother Taught Me*. In the first chapter of their book *The Madwoman in the Attic*, Sandra Gilbert and Susan Gubar provide an excellent analysis of women's use of the image of the mirror to describe the sense of being trapped by patriarchal discourse.

19 Wendy Keitner and Phyllis Gottlieb examine the pronounced rift in *Mrs. Blood*, where the narrator divides herself into Mrs Blood and Mrs Thing. They argue that this division suggests the fragmented nature of women, 'divided not only from other women, but also from herself, by language, tradition, religion and law, in order to *be* for someone else' (368).

20 Occasionally, Alice puns on the word 'peace' and plays on its homonymic relationship to 'piece' and 'pieces' (66). At one point, her Peace roses, which grow in her garden, are linked to fragmentation, when she imagines having her ashes (pieces) buried beneath them (258). These plays on 'peace' support the sense that Alice desires to escape the pain and confusion associated with the fragmentation of her molar identity.

21 Godard, in *Audrey Thomas and Her Works*, suggests that Thomas's studies in Old Norse and Old English 'gave her an interest in philology and also a sense of the instability of the word as sign' (6).

22 This comment recalls Juliet Mitchell's assertion that women turn to literary forms to create a history from a state of 'flux' (288–9).

23 Thomas's novel *Latakia* repeatedly emphasizes the association between women and dogs, and features a 'Dog-Lady' or 'Dog-Girl' (17, 35–6). The narrator cynically thinks of her lover's wife as 'a faithful dog-wife' (86).

24 Sherry Ortner, 'Is Female to Male as Nature Is to Culture?' For a critique of Ortner's arguments refer to the chapter 'Gender and Status,' in Henrietta L. Moore, 12–41. Dorothy Jones also addresses the link between women and nature in a literary context in her article '"A Kingdom and a Place of Exile": Women Writers and the World of Nature.'

25 For an excellent analysis of Aristotle's attitude toward women, see Lerner, 205–9.

26 In *Mrs. Blood*, the narrator similarly casts herself as Mary and as Christ. For an exploration of the victim/host relationship in Thomas's novel, see Anne Archer's essay.

3: Susan Swan's *The Biggest Modern Woman of the World*

1 I will refer to Anna Swan as Anna in order to reduce the confusion between her and the author, Susan Swan. Although they share the same name, their kinship remains unverified. The author explains that she knew about the giantess as a child because they have the same surname and because her branch of the family is tall (see Read, 28).

2 Linda Hutcheon suggests that, as a female Canadian forced to relate to American males, the 'historically real giantess manages to become a paradoxically ex-centric Everywoman figure' (*Canadian*, 120).

3 Teresa Heffernan points out that, as a feminist, Swan 'must write Anna into history,' and to do this she employs the conventions 'that have governed the traditional recording of history – the narrative is continuous, it locates an origin, it is concerned with connections … and it involves a chronology of facts borrowed from the real Anna Swan's life' (25). But Heffernan goes on to suggest that, even as the author invokes a chronological narrative, 'the possibility of a continuous, coherent, autonomous agent or a consistent, objective historical account recedes as the author acknowledges the artifice and the inevitable biases inherent in generating narratives' (27).

4 Judith Butler uses Foucault's insights into sexuality to argue that gender is a 'fantasy instituted and inscribed on the surface of bodies.' Gender is 'produced as the truth effects of a discourse of primary and stable identity' (*Gender*, 136).

5 For a discussion of the function of the Ideological State Apparatuses, see Althusser's essay 'Ideology and Ideological State Apparatuses.'

6 In speaking of the 'body,' I am referring to what Butler describes as 'a set of boundaries, individual and social, politically signified and maintained' and not 'a ready surface awaiting signification' (*Gender*, 33). Butler partly derives her conception of the body from Mary Douglas, who argues that the body is a social construct, in which the 'powers and dangers credited to social structure' are reproduced in small on the human body (115).

7 Butler reinforces this notion of self as performance, arguing that gendered identity is 'performatively constituted by the very "expressions" that are said to be its results' (*Gender*, 25).

8 Anna's strategy, which operates here by subverting discourse from within, implies that subversion, if it is possible, will take place within the terms of the law.

9 As Michel Foucault suggests, 'there can exist different and even contradictory discourses' operating within the same 'field of force relations' (*History*, 102, 101). Mary Douglas also affirms that any 'structure of ideas is vulnerable at its margins' (121). With this in mind, we can appreciate why cultural margins constitute especially vulnerable sites, and why the juxtaposition of inconsistent discourses generates tension.

10 The English philosopher Herbert Spencer adapted Darwin's theory of evolution to suggest that modern woman gleaned from her ancestors, through inheritance and selection, the capacity to conceal her feelings from the male: 'Women who betrayed the state of antagonism produced in them by ill-treatment were less likely to survive and leave offspring than those who concealed their antagonism' (Spencer, 342–3).

11 I stress Anna's mother's inability to write because, as the novel underscores, this puts her at a disadvantage as a player in Lyotard's language game. Without an ability to read and write, other 'players' (here Herbert Belacourt) can put words into her mouth, thereby using her turn or 'move' for their own advantage.

12 The scholar A.L. Smith wrote that 'overexertion in mental activity would cause females to suffer from "ovarian neuralgia," resulting in the inability of the body to supply both the brain and generative organs with sufficient blood' (qtd. in Haller, 59).

13 Osler's speech is quoted in Ehrenreich and English, 69. Ironically, she refers to Osler as 'America's only titled physician,' although he was born and educated in Canada (Pratt, 3–8). Osler travelled to America in 1884 to take charge of Johns Hopkins hospital. He left the hospital to take up the post of Regius Professor of Medicine at Oxford in 1903, and, in 1911, he was made a baronet at the coronation of King George V.

14 Oliver Wendell Holmes's letter appears in Anna Robeson Burr's *Weir Mitchell: His Life and Letters*, 82–3. Ehrenreich and English cite it in their book to support their argument regarding science's 'sexual sadism' (76).

15 In response to Barnum's claim that 'the individual is what makes America great,' Anna remarks that the 'individual is a business gimmick' (156), emphasizing, once again, that identity is a fiction.

16 For a discussion of the way in which the American landscape was associated with the female body, see Annette Kolodny's book *The Lay of the Land*. Northrop Frye also notes that the Canadian landscape was conceived of as an 'unseizable virginity' (*Bush*, 220). In her reading of the novel, Linda Hutcheon sees the inability to separate national differences and politics from sexual differences and politics as a 'postmodern conjunction' (*Canadian*, 120).

17 Her reason for marrying Bates is offered in the terse and enigmatic assertion that she is

a 'creature of show business, after all' (187). Perhaps this equation between marriage and show business implies that, if women want to play a part in human history, they must accept an available role, which, at a certain stage, is that of the 'wife' (or 'spinster').

18 The fact that Anna 'is reduced to uttering only gurgling sounds and chuckles while she resides in Great Britain,' as Smaro Kamboureli suggests, also 'allegorizes the colonial status of her already dwarfed Canadian identity' (109).

19 Linda Hutcheon notes that Bakhtin describes fear as the emotion that contributes most to the power and seriousness of official culture (*Theory*, 73).

20 This episode bears some resemblance to the treatment of Lavinia Magri and her sister Minnie by members of the royal family and their friends, when the sisters appeared at Windsor Castle in 1865. According to Magri's report, the Duchess of Argyle took Minnie on her lap (79).

21 This passage is taken from Cecil W. Cunnington and Phyllis Cunnington, *Handbook of English Costume in the Nineteenth Century*, 499, qtd. in Haller, 148–9.

22 For a discussion of this episode in Rabelais's work, see Bakhtin, *Rabelais*, 147.

23 Her gigantic writing, which covers the walls and furniture, offers a discursive resistance to Barnum's speech: her script is superimposed upon a monologue in which he proposes that Anna should help him stage a dramatization of his life by playing the part of his wife.

24 The phrase 'gift economy' is borrowed from Lewis Hyde's book *The Gift: Imagination and the Erotic Life of Property*. In using the term 'separate economy,' I do not mean to suggest that this economy is positioned 'outside' culture. As I pointed out earlier, the Celtic discourse is a discourse of folk *culture*; thus, it still exists within the bounds of culture. Further, the capacity of this 'unofficial' discourse to disrupt dominant cultural discourses suggests that the latter are not unified and impermeable.

25 Susan Stewart, *Nonsense: Aspects of Intertextuality in Folklore and Literature*. Daphne Read also suggests that the novel is, at one level, 'about play' (review, 28).

26 The use of blood as a medium for inscription is apt in that blood – especially menstrual blood – is a bodily fluid that traverses boundaries between inner and outer, thereby challenging the notion of the body as self-contained and unified. As noted earlier, Mary Douglas suggests that social systems are vulnerable at their margins. Bodies, as specific instances of social systems, are likewise vulnerable at their 'margins.' Furthermore, the 'matter issuing from them is marginal stuff of the most obvious kind' (121).

27 This combination of fantastic elements with realistic journalistic detail conforms to the model of grotesque realism as described by Bakhtin (*Rabelais*, 436).

4: Daphne Marlatt's *Ana Historic*

1 Ricou suggests that *leaf / leafs* and *Frames of a Story* are not travel journals. Yet, as Marlatt argues in interviews, *Frames* was 'about being lost' (see 'Given,' 41). When she was writ-

ing the work, she had the sense of 'charting a territory that was unknown ... & having to map it out in order to discover where I was' (63).

2 For example, critics such as Barbara Godard and Frank Davey note that many of Marlatt's text focus on a search for a lost or absent mother (Godard, 'Body I,' 491–4; Davey, 'Words,' 40–6).

3 In an interview with Brenda Carr, Marlatt suggested that this figure/ground reversal, 'trying to shift that ground which is usually background for the figure so it becomes foreground. The shift in values that's involved is also what feminism is about' (103).

4 Marlatt refers to de Lauretis's essay and the work of the Milan group in an interview with Brenda Carr (105).

5 Marlatt's emphasis on the thread of female ancestral connections recalls Thomas's description of the bond among Alice and her daughters, which is described as a 'sorority.'

6 Foucault refers to Nietzsche's *Genealogy* (158; ch. 3, sc. 26), where he states, 'I do not like these weary and played-out people who wrap themselves in wisdom and look "objective."'

7 In an interview with George Bowering, Marlatt describes her home in Vancouver, and it is remarkably similar to Annie's home in *Ana Historic* (see 'Given,' 32–3).

8 In the previous chapters, the Lacanian symbolic order's impact on women was also associated with shrinking or becoming invisible. In *Intertidal Life*, Alice fears that she is becoming invisible (49); in Swan's novel, the giantess is fooled into thinking that she is shrinking (307–19).

9 In an interview with George Bowering, Marlatt emphasizes that Ina 'just died, so she is present, but not in the flesh' ('On Ana,' 100).

10 In an interview with Janice Williamson, Marlatt stated: 'The patriarchal oppression of women and colonialism are two different faces of the same coin' (see 'Sounding,' 54).

11 In recording Ina's experience of her treatment, Annie is once again fulfilling her role as Foucauldian genealogist, recording the subjugated knowledge of the psychiatric patient.

12 In the previous chapter, I suggested that the giantess's corset, which leaves her gasping for breath, represents just such a material instance of control. In this case, the medical technology labelled 'electric shock therapy' constitutes the material embodiment of an ideology bent on disciplining individuals who threaten the symbolic order.

13 Marlatt explains that she wrote *Ana Historic* because she had to come to terms with the oldest layer of her language: 'the language I inherited from my mother which was generated within certain national class and period mores' (interview, 'Sounding,' 56).

14 Marlatt refers to this model in an interview with Brenda Carr (105). It is cited in Elaine Showalter's famous essay, 'Feminist Criticism in the Wilderness,' 199–200. For an indepth treatment of the model, see Edwin Ardener's essay 'The "Problem" Revisited,' 19–27.

15 In the introduction to *in the feminine*, Marlatt writes that women are living 'within such

constant doubleness, we live both within and outside of the culture that contains us …, we speak both within and outside of the language that speaks of us …, we are both citizens and aliens of a country that fails to guarantee our rights' (12)

16 Marlatt has often forged an association between the frame of a photograph and the way in which 'facts' are framed. In *Ana Historic*, Annie defines the word 'fact': '(f)act. the f stop of act. a still photo in the ongoing cinerama' (31). Marlatt's essay 'Distance and Identity: A Postscript to *Steveston*' contrasts this type of framing with the open-ended quality of her writing. She notes that Susan Sontag calls photographs 'maps of the real' because a photograph is 'never less than the registering of an emanation (light waves reflected by objects) – a material vestige of its subject' (Sontag qtd. in 'Distance,' 43). As far as Marlatt is concerned, a poem is not 'located in time as a photograph is. … [I]t exists in continuing time, because, in the time it takes to read it, we re-enact the forward-streaming of its sentence or sentences' (43). In an interview with George Bowering, Marlatt emphasized that '[t]he single frame is the trap, because experience is constantly moving forward' ('Given,' 50).

17 For a critique of this model of literary paternity, see Showalter's essay 'Feminist Criticism in the Wilderness,' 187–9, as well as Nina Auerbach's review of *Madwoman*, in *Victorian Studies*.

18 The image of the net is central in Marlatt's work; she has even entitled a collection of her writings *Net Work: Selected Writing* (1980). In interviews she has discussed her sense of the web as a figure for 'relationship, & how tremendously interwoven all of our lives are with all of these other lives around us. … What we move in also in terms of history. We move in an accretion of time, which we dont recognize' ('Given,' 81). For a feminist analysis of the importance of web-like relationships in women's lives, see Carol Gilligan's chapter 'Images of Relationship' (24–64).

19 In a conversation with George Bowering, Marlatt stated that 'I've always been fascinated by whatever that other was – what is beyond the self, outside the self; & and the fact that we're really restricted in all our perceptions to what's here' ('Given,' 45). In her opinion, there is no need to try to understand 'the other' through reason. As she says, 'rationalism is only one of the ways we receive the world, & it's one that I particularly distrust' (58). Instead, '[y]ou have to experience it. … [Y]ou have to somehow let it in. … [T]urn off all the lights. … [Y]ou can be just as clear in the dark. What you do is feel your way, you dont see your way' (45).

20 Annie understands at one point that the frame is a trap, and that her mother 'needed someone to knock holes in the walls instead of showing … [her], calmly, how the doors worked' (136).

21 The stories she wrote 'lost their humour in description, faded away in proper sentences' (20). She rendered herself 'invisible in the mirror' (58). Finally, she disappeared in madness, which, according to Marlatt, 'is like death' (interview, 'On Ana,' 105).

22 This act of representation is not the evocation of some essential presence because, as

Marlatt stresses, language 'does not stand in place of anything else, it does not replace the bodies around us' (*Touch*, 45).

23 Barbara Creed suggests that monstrous figures represent what Julia Kristeva calls the 'abject': that which does not respect '"borders, positions, rules" ... that which "disturbs identity, system, order"' (Kristeva qtd. in Creed, 'Horror,' 45). In Gilbert and Gubar's *Madwoman in the Attic*, the authors describe how women's 'intransigent female autonomy' is consistently represented in the traditional novel as the 'monster-woman, threatening to replace her angelic sister' (28).

24 Marlatt has stated that Annie 'has to unwrap a lot of cover stories, and the principal one is her own cover story, the story of her own sexual conditioning, and this comes up very strongly in her dialogues with her mother' (interview, 'On *Ana*,' 98).

25 The name 'Birdie,' as well as the emphasis on flying, echoes Hélène Cixous's assertion that '[f]lying is a woman's gesture – flying in language and making it fly.' Cixous points out that the word for flying in French *voler* has a double meaning because it could also mean 'to steal.' As she says, '[i]t's no accident: women take after birds and robbers just as robbers take after women and birds. They ... take pleasure in jumbling the order of space, in disorienting it, in changing around the furniture, dislocating things and values, breaking them all up, emptying structures, and turning propriety upside down' (258).

26 In the book *Double Negative*, which Marlatt co-wrote with Betsy Warland, there are frequent references to the word 'bush' – references that clarify that this term refers, not only to vegetation, but to the vagina. My sense is that Marlatt is evoking this same *double-entendre* in *Ana Historic*, which would leave open the possibility that Ina was a closeted lesbian.

5: The Fictions of Aritha van Herk

1 In her talk 'Darwin as Gulliver,' Gillian Beer suggested that travel from island to island enables explorers to view their home as an exotic space on a par with the other countries they have visited. By adopting this perspective, travellers are in a position to view the laws and customs of their own country critically. Beer's insights into nineteenth-century travellers such as Darwin help to explain the emphasis on, and importance of, travel within works by Canadian women writers.

2 Van Herk's suggestion that Canadians are particularly inclined to draw on the figures of mapping and exploration confirms my earlier assertion that the country's legacy of explorers and settlers, combined with its experience as a colony, may have promoted a preoccupation with questions of orientation and mapping. See the first chapter of this study, 7–11.

3 Her concerns recall Northrop Frye's assertion that the Canadian sensibility is preoccupied with the question 'Where is here?' (Frye, *Bush*, 220), as noted in ch. 1.

4 As noted in the introduction, the faith in literature's capacity to function as a map,

expressed in this passage, echoes Margaret Atwood's belief that Canadians can rely on a literary map to orient themselves in what remains an unknown territory (Atwood, *Survival*, 19).

5　In her latest novel, *Places Far from Ellesmere*, the narrator recalls Rudy Wiebe's jibe that women will never be great writers because they do not set themselves great subjects. Instead of writing about war and peace, women supposedly 'write only out of their visceras.' The narrator sees through this illusory belief, however, and wryly notes that the visceras of men are 'larger and more dangerous, hidden as they are in an inflated sense of themselves centring the subject of greatness' (80–1).

6　For a detailed discussion of this concept, refer to their chapter, '1227: Treatise on Nomadology: – The War Machine,' in their book, *A Thousand Plateaus: Capitalism and Schizophrenia*, 351–423.

7　In interviews, van Herk suggests that, in writing this novel, she was motivated by a desire to retell the story of Circe. Her interest in the Circean myth recalls Audrey Thomas's allusions to Circe in *Intertidal Life*. Both novels emphasize the importance of hearing the other side of the story – the story told from the perspective of the marginalized woman left behind by the hero. As van Herk says, 'I am so sick of never hearing the Circe side of the story' (qtd. in MacLaren, xvi). Margaret Atwood also renders Circe's point of view in her 'Circe / Mud Poems' (*Selected*, 163–85).

8　In a fascinating essay entitled 'Restoring the Temples: The Fiction of Aritha van Herk,' Dorothy Jones compares the female friendships in van Herk's novels to the mythical bond between Persephone and Demeter. She also notes that, during the festival honouring Demeter, pigs played a significant role: in the ancient world, pigs 'were images both of female sexuality and of the mother goddess'; thus, in her eyes, the pig barn 'resembes a temple of female divinity' (418).

9　For a discussion of the reservations that feminists have articulated in response to the work of Deleuze and Guattari, see Elizabeth Grosz's study, 'A Thousand Tiny Sexes: Feminism and Rhizomatics,' 2–5. Grosz delivered this paper at a Deleuze conference at Trent University in Peterborough, Ontario, on 16 May 1992, and I believe that she intends to include it as a chapter in a forthcoming book.

10　I was disturbed by a talk at the Canadian Women's Studies Association, 30 May to 1 June 1992 because it focused on the supposed evils of poststructuralist theory. In a session, entitled 'Postmodernisms: Feminist Critical Responses,' Somer Brodribb spoke of the dangers associated with 'touching the phallus,' and the tendency of phallocentric, poststructuralist theory to undermine and obfuscate the clarity of truly feminist strategies.

11　In an essay, van Herk reminds readers that, by law, women were not allowed to enter bars in the prairies ('Women,' 18).

12　This episode parallels Judith's recollection of the time when she and her father went to visit the feed mill. There the employees would tease Judith by addressing her father, saying, 'Hey, Jim, she oughta be a boy. Whatdya say, Judy, wouldn't it be better if you were a boy?' (125).

13 As critics have noted, the names of Hudson, Hearne, Mackenzie, Franklin, Thompson, and Cap Kane eponymously keep the 'male map firmly before van Herk's reader' (MacLaren, xli). Barbara Godard also remarks on van Herk's choice of names in her review of *The Tent Peg* in *Fiddlehead*, 92.

14 As Dorothy Jones points out in her essay 'Restoring the Temples,' the strength of female friendship, the appearance of the bear with her two cubs, and the departure of Mackenzie's wife, Janice, with her two children are thematically related (423–4).

15 The text consistently treats the possession of the phallus quite playfully. For example, in an early episode, all the members of the camp erect their tents only to have them blown down by the gusts from the helicopter. Significantly, it is J.L.'s tent alone that remains erect: 'For a moment everything is still, and then, hat on her head ... J.L. steps through the flap of that still-standing Jutland – her cooktent – and starts to laugh. She laughs loud and wide at the lumpy heaps of tents' (43).

16 In interviews, van Herk has suggested that the three novels, *Judith*, *The Tent Peg*, and *No Fixed Address*, form a trilogy because they portray 'three tough and unusual women who are making their way in the world' (interview with Jerve, 70).

17 Susanne Becker notes that the picaresque is related to a set of genres including the romance and the feminine Gothic. For a discussion of the way in which the novel transforms some conventions of the feminine Gothic by ironic displacement, see her essay 'Ironic Transformations: The Feminine Gothic in Aritha Van Herk's *No Fixed Address*.'

18 Bowering's heroine Caprice also subverts this binary opposition so aptly summed up by Kroetsch as the horse/house dichotomy. As the narrator explains, Caprice's lover complains that he feels uncomfortable with the reversal: 'It did not seem right, he had told her, that I am bound here, that I have to stay in this one place while you are riding all over the country, whenever you feel like up and moving' (174). Yet, for all her 'up and moving,' Caprice is resolutely chaste – a domestic trait which separates her from van Herk's voracious heroine, Arachne.

19 My thanks to M. Harry at Saint Mary's University, Halifax, for pointing out the behaviour of spiders, which Arachne emulates.

20 This comment also recalls Alice Hoyle's image of being cremated and having her ashes buried under her Peace roses (*Intertidal*, 258).

21 The notion of a restricted flow surfaces here as well as in Marlatt's text, where the narrator wonders what a woman does with her own 'unexpressed preferences, her own desires,' and concludes that they are probably 'dammed up, a torrent to let loose' (35). Ultimately, Marlatt's narrator breaks free from the prohibitions restricting the flow of her desires, and renames herself 'Annie Torrent' (152).

22 Van Herk refers to the Penguin translation of Tolstoy's classic, *Anna Karenin*, 802.

6: Jane Urquhart's *The Whirlpool*

1 In her book *Romanticism and Gender* Anne Mellor discusses the way in which the home, 'the theoretical haven of virtue and safety,' becomes the site of sublime terror, because of the exercise of patriarchal authority (93).

2 There is nothing understated about this association; at times, it seems as if the characters are merely wooden examples of traditional narrative patterns. This didactic quality diminishes, however, when the characters begin to question the narratives that they embody. For instance, although Patrick initially conflates Fleda with the whirlpool, he gradually comes to reject this identification, and his relation to traditional narratives becomes increasingly complex.

3 There is, of course, a long history concerning the sublime that predates Burke. However, what is at issue in this study is not the sublime as a rhetorical device for persuading through emotions, as described by the Greek critic Longinus. Instead my interest lies in non-rhetorical theories of the sublime which stress its subjectivism; and, as Samuel Monk notes in chapter 5 of his study of the sublime, Burke's *Enquiry* constitutes a key contribution to this approach. Monk also argues in his introduction that the eighteenth-century aesthetic of the sublime has as its 'unconscious goal' Kant's *Critique of Judgement*; it is for this reason that I concentrate, for the most part, on Burke's and Kant's treatments of the topic.

4 For a thorough treatment of this concept of 'blockage,' see Neil Hertz's essay 'The Notion of Blockage in the Literature of the Sublime.'

5 In his study of the sublime, Thomas Weiskel suggests that these two seemingly antithetical positions are contained in the response to the sublime. As he explains, 'It would appear that the negative sublime [his term for the Kantian sublime] as a whole is the expression of two separate sets of defenses intimately linked. To put it sequentially: the excessive object excites a wish to be inundated, which yields an anxiety of incorporation: this anxiety is met by a reaction formation against the wish which precipitates a recapitulation of the Oedipus complex; this in turn yields a feeling of guilt (superego anxiety) and is resolved through identification (introjection)' (105). Essentially, Weiskel's theory accounts for both the pre-Oedipal urge for the dissolution of boundaries, described by Theweleit, and the split or alienation of mind and nature (the key to Kant's formulation of the sublime), which occurs when the mind identifies with reason.

6 Weiskel also describes, how this conflict between mind and nature assumed 'the form of tragedy' (46), when Kant's version of the sublime was taken to extreme forms of alienation by Schiller and Schopenhauer. As Weiskel so eloquently puts it: 'The sublime begins as an excessive interest in nature and ends with an excessive disdain of nature' (76).

7 The use of spatial images to refer to discursive practices recalls Wittgenstein's famous image: 'Our language can be seen as an ancient city: a maze of little streets and squares,

of old and new houses with additions from various periods; and this surrounded by a multitude of new boroughs with straight regular streets and uniform houses' (Wittgenstein, 8).

8 This was the working title of the novel.

9 According to Weiskel, we 'hear in the background of the Romantic sublime the grand confidence of a heady imperialism ... a kind of spiritual capitalism, enjoining a pursuit of the infinitude of the private self' (6).

10 Kant discusses the transcendent nature of the Ideas of Reason in *The Critique of Pure Reason*, in a passage entitled 'The Regulative Employment of the Ideas of Pure Reason,' which is contained in an Appendix to the Dialectic (B 670–96).

11 Weiskel discusses this same process of abstraction and argues that it is a 'specific instance of the general economic law of sublimation, whether of labor (capitalism), of sexuality (narcissism), or of perception (abstraction).' As he says, sublimation 'is the transubstantiation of what Marx called "individualities" and Blake called "minute particulars" into an abstract medium of exchange. But the price of this freedom for will or ego – and of this enhanced sense of self – is alienation from particular forms of primary experience. ... The formal properties of the perceived particular are cancelled and replaced by their "significance," values assessed and assigned by the mind' (58–9).

12 An interesting comparison can be made between David and Atwood's female military historian, Tony, in her novel *The Robber Bride*. Whereas David's research has a clear-cut goal and an implicit bias (his aim is to prove Canada won), Tony 'doesn't take sides: all battles are battles, all contain bravery, all involve death.' And unlike David, she isn't even sure 'what she's really collecting, or in memory of what' (19). Finally, whereas David firmly believes that he can assemble a coherent story, Tony, with a postmodern awareness of the constructed nature of meaning, suggests that the historian's re-creations 'are at best just patchy waxworks' (127).

13 David's experience is reminiscent of Longinus's description of the effects of the rhetorical sublime. According to Longinus, whose treatment of the sublime was translated into English in 1652 and became the source of all discussions of the topic, when the 'soul is raised by true sublimity, it gains a proud step upwards, it is filled with joy and exultation, as though itself had produced what it hears' (qtd. in Boulton, xlv).

14 Patrick's response to the boy conforms to what Weiskel describes as the 'poet's' sublime. In this case, we are suddenly 'caught up in a word (or any signifying segment) which seems to "contain" so much that there is nothing we cannot "read into" it. The word dissolves into the Word' (26–7).

15 Note that 'transcendence' was associated with the sublime as early as Boileau's translation of Longinus's writings, *Traité du Sublime ou du Merveilleux dans le Discours Traduit du Grec de Longin*, 1674. Toward the end of the preface to the first edition, Boileau emphasizes that the sublime refers to a quality in a work which enables it to elevate, ravish, and transport (442).

16 The reference to 'married' and 'buried' recalls the episode in Thomas's *Intertidal Life* where a radio announcer accidentally condenses the words 'murdered' and 'buried' into 'murried,' which echoes what Alice feels Peter has done to her (85).

17 As Kant explains, the 'mind listens to the voice of reason within itself, which demands totality for all given magnitudes, even for those that we can never apprehend in their entirety but do (in the presence of sense) judge as given in their entirety. Hence reason demands comprehension in *one* intuition, and *exhibition* of all the members of a progressively increasing numerical series, and it exempts from this demand not even the infinite' (Judgement, 111).

18 In his discussion of the mathematical sublime, Kant refers to this process as 'apprehension' as opposed to 'comprehension,' which involves collecting and holding together. According to Kant, the imagination can proceed with the process of 'apprehension' to infinity; but there is 'a maximum in comprehension that it cannot exceed' (*Judgement,* 108)

19 In his discussion of Kant's *Critique of Judgement,* H.W. Cassirer clarifies this distinction between a regulative and inappropriate use of reason: 'Reason misuses the principle of totality. This principle was given to human Reason, not to lead it to imagine that all the conditions of its object are given, but in order to stimulate it to try to find all the conditions of its object. What we are expected to do is to try to discover the totality of conditions, but this does not mean that they are given to us, nor even that we shall ever be able to fulfil Reason's demand. The Idea of a totality is an ideal maximum which can never be attained in the sensible world' (41–2).

20 Kant argues that the 'warrior' and the 'general' are sublime as is 'war ... if it is carried on in an orderly way,' whereas peace 'tends to make prevalent a mere[ly] commercial spirit, and along with it base selfishness, cowardice, and softness, and to debase the way of thinking of that people' (*Judgement,* 122).

7: **Epilogue**

1 For a detailed discussion of the political implications of van Herk's parodic treatment of the western and her unique interpretation of the genre known as the 'northern,' see my essay 'Go North Young Woman: Representations of the Arctic in the Writings of Aritha van Herk,' in the forthcoming book, edited by John Moss, based on the talks presented at the Arctic Narrative Symposium, 21–3, April 1995.

Bibliography

Daphne Marlatt

FICTION

Ana Historic: A Novel. Toronto: Coach House, 1988.
Frames of a Story. Toronto: Ryerson, 1968.
here and there. Lantzville, B.C.: Island Writing Series, 1981.
How Hug a Stone. Winnipeg: Turnstone, 1983.
'In the Month of the Hungry Ghosts.' *Capilano Review* 16–17 (1979): 45–95.
Leaf leaf/s. Los Angeles: Black Sparrow, 1969.
Our Lives. Carrboro, N.C.: Truck, 1975; Lantzville, B.C.: Oolichan, 1980.
Rings. Vancouver: Vancouver Community, 1971.
Steveston. Vancouver: Talonbooks, 1974.
Salvage. Red Deer, Alta.: Red Deer College, 1991.
Selected Writing: Net Work. Ed. and introd. Fred Wah. Vancouver: Talonbooks, 1980.
The Story, She Said. Vancouver: Monthly, 1977.
Touch to My Tongue; Musing with Mothertongue. Edmonton: Longspoon, 1984.
Vancouver Poems. Toronto: Coach House, 1972.
What Matters: Writing 1968–70. Toronto: Coach House, 1980.
Zocalo. Toronto: Coach House, 1977.
and Betsy Warland. *Double Negative.* Charlottetown, P.E.I.: Ragweed/Gynergy, 1988.

ESSAYS

'Changing the Focus.' *Inversions.* Ed. Betsy Warland. Vancouver: Press Gang, 1991.
    127–34.
'Distance and Identity: A Postscript to *Steveston.*' *Line* 3 (1984): 42–4.

Introd. *in the feminine: women and words/les femmes et les mots conference proceedings 1983.* Ed. Ann Dybikowski et. al. Edmonton: Longspoon, 1985. 11–13.

'The Measure of the Sentence.' *Open Letter* 5.3 (1982): 90–2.

'writing in order to be.' *Sp/elles: Poetry by Canadian Women.* Ed. Judith Fitzgerald. Windsor: Black Moss, 1986. 66–7.

INTERVIEWS

'Given This Body: An Interview with Daphne Marlatt.' With George Bowering. *Open Letter* 4th ser. 3 (1979): 32–88.

'An Interview with Daphne Marlatt.' With Brenda Carr. *Beyond Tish* Ed. Douglas Barbour. Special Issue of *West Coast Line* 25.1 (1991): 99–107.

'Keep Witnessing: a review/interview.' With George Bowering. *Open Letter* 3rd ser. 2 (1975): 26–38.

'On *Ana Historic*: An Interview with Daphne Marlatt.' With George Bowering. *Line* 13 (1989): 96–105.

'Sounding a Difference: An Interview with Daphne Marlatt.' With Janice Williamson. *Line* 13 (1989): 49–56.

'Speaking In and Of Each Other.' With Janice Williamson. *FUSE Magazine* Feb.–March 1985: 29.

Susan Swan

FICTION

The Biggest Modern Woman of the World. Toronto: Lester and Orpen Dennys, 1983.

INTERVIEWS

'Susan Swan, Mythmaker.' With Donna Guglielmin. *Canadian Author and Bookman* (Fall 1984): 11–12.

REVIEWS

The Biggest Modern Woman of the World
Buitenhuis, Peter. *Queen's Quarterly* 4 (1985): 844–5.
Guglielmin, Donna. *Canadian Author and Bookman* Summer 1984: 25.
Read, Daphne. *Resources for Feminist Research* 14.2 (1985): 28–9.
Seamon, Roger. 'Show Biz.' *Canadian Literature* 102 (1984): 151–2.
Wilson, Paul. *Books in Canada* April 1984: 30–1.

Audrey Thomas

FICTION

Blown Figures. Vancouver: Talonbooks, 1974; rpt. New York: Knopf, 1975; rpt. New York: Ballantine, 1974.
Intertidal Life. Toronto: Stoddart, 1984.
Ladies and Escorts. Toronto: Stoddart, 1984.
Latakia. Vancouver: Talonbooks, 1979.
Mrs. Blood. Indianapolis: Bobbs-Merrill, 1970.
Munchmeyer and Prospero on the Island. Indianapolis: Bobbs-Merrill, 1971.
Real Mothers. Vancouver: Talonbooks, 1981.
Songs My Mother Taught Me. Vancouver: Talonbooks, 1973.
Ten Green Bottles. Indianapolis: Bobbs-Merrill, 1967; rpt. Ottawa: Oberon, 1977.

ESSAYS

'Basmati Rice: An Essay about Words.' *Canadian Literature* 100 (1984): 312–17.
'A Fine Romance, My Dear, This Is.' *Canadian Literature* 108 (1986): 5–12.
'"My Craft and Sullen Art": The Writers Speak. Is There a Feminine Voice in Literature?' *Atlantis* 4.1 (1978): 152–4.

INTERVIEWS

'Audrey Thomas: A Review/Interview.' With Elizabeth Komisar. *Open Letter* 3rd ser. 3 (1975): 59–64.
Interview. With Alan Twigg. *Strong Voices: Conversations with Fifty Canadian Authors.* Madeira Park, B.C.: Harbour, 1988. 248–53.
Interview. With Pierre Coupey, Gladys Hindmarch, Wendy Pickell, and Bill Schermbrucker. *Capilano Review* 7 (1975): 87–109.
'An Interview with Audrey Thomas.' With Eleanor Wachtel. *Room of One's Own* 10.3–4 (1986): 7–61.
'Songs and Wisdom: An Interview with Audrey Thomas.' With George Bowering. *Open Letter* 4th ser. 3 (1979): 7–31.

REVIEWS

Intertidal Life
Bossanne, Brigitte. *North Dakota Quarterly* 52.3 (1984): 223.
Kareda, Urjo. 'Sense and Sensibility.' *Saturday Night* Jan. 1986: 50–1.

Jane Urquhart

FICTION

Away. Toronto: McClelland and Stewart, 1994.
Changing Heaven. Toronto: McClelland and Stewart, 1990.
Storm Glass. Erin, Ont.: Porcupine's Quill, 1987.
The Whirlpool. Toronto: McClelland and Stewart, 1986, rpt. 1989.

POETRY

I Am Walking in the Garden of His Imaginary Palace. Toronto: Aya P, 1982.
False Shuffles. Victoria: Beach Holme, 1983.
The Little Flowers of Madame de Montespan. Erin, Ont.: Porcupine's Quill, 1982.

INTERVIEWS

'An Interview with Jane Urquhart.' With Geoff Hancock. *Canadian Fiction Magazine* 5.5
(1986): 23–40.

REVIEW

The Whirlpool
van Herk, Aritha. 'the summer before browning died.' *Brick* 31 (1987): 15–17.

Aritha van Herk

FICTION

In Visible Ink: Crypto-frictions. The Writer as Critic Series: III. Edmonton: NeWest, 1991.
Judith. Toronto: McClelland and Stewart, 1978.
No Fixed Address: An Amorous Journey. Toronto: McClelland-Bantam, 1987.
Places Far from Ellesmere: A Geografictione. Red Deer, Alta.: Red Deer College, 1990.
The Tent Peg. Toronto: McClelland and Stewart-Bantam, 1981; rpt. New Canadian Library
N196, 1987.

ESSAYS

Alberta Rebound: Thirty More Stories by Alberta Writers. Ed. and introd. Aritha van Herk.
Edmonton: NeWest, 1990. 1–7.

'Double Crossings: Booking the Lover.' *A Mazing Space.* Neuman 276–86.
A Frozen Tongue. Sydney, Australia, and Mundelstrup: Dangaroo P, 1992.
'A Gentle Circumcision.' *Trace: Prairie Writers on Writing.* Ed. Birk Sproxton. Winnipeg: Turnstone, 1986. 257–68.
'Mapping as Metaphor.' Zietsch der Gesellschaft fur *Kanada Studien* no. 2 (1982): 75–87; rpt. A Frozen Tongue. 54–68.
'Stranded Bestride in Canada.' *World Literature Written in English* 24.1 (1984): 10–16.
'Women Writers and the Prairie: Spies in an Indifferent Landscape.' *Kunapipi* 6.2 (1984): 15–25; rpt. in *A Frozen Tongue.* 139–51.

INTERVIEWS

Interview. With Gyrid Jerve. Oslo, Autumn 1985. *Kunapipi* 8.3 (1986): 68–76.
'Interview with Aritha van Herk.' With Dorothy Jones. *SPAN* 1987: 1–15.
'Kiss of the Spider-Lady: An Interview with Aritha van Herk.' With Hilda Kirkwood. *Canadian Women Studies* 8.3 (1987): 85–9.

REVIEWS

No Fixed Address
Kirkwood, Hilda. 'Travelling Woman.' *Canadian Forum* Aug.–Sept. 1986: 40–1.
Leckie, Barbara. 'Circle Games.' *Canadian Literature* 115 (1987): 278–80
McGoogan, Kenneth. Profile/Rev. *Quill and Quire* 52 (1986): 34.
Scobie, Stephen. 'arachne's progress.' *Brick* Winter 1987: 37–40.

Places Far From Ellesmere
Beer, Ann. 'Thinking Too Precisely on Some Events.' *Border Crossings* Summer 1991: 35–6.
Kirkwood, Hilda. 'Geografictione.' *Canadian Forum* April 1991: 29–30.
Thomas, Joan. *Prairie Fire* 12.2 (1991): 68–70.

The Tent Peg
Godard, Barbara. *Fiddlehead* 132 (1982): 90–5.

General

Abrams, M.H. *Natural Supernaturalism.* New York: Norton, 1971.
Acton, W.H. *The Functions and Disorders of the Reproductive Organs in Childhood, Youth, Adult Age and Advanced Life Considered in Their Physiological, Social, and Moral Relations.* London: J. and A. Churchill, 1875.

Adam, Ian, and Helen Tiffin. *Past the Last Post: Theorizing Post- Colonialism and Post-Modernism*. Calgary, Alta.: U of Calgary P, 1990.

Althusser, Louis. 'Ideology and Ideological State Apparatuses.' *Lenin and Philosophy and Other Essays*. Trans. Ben Brewster. New York: Monthly Review, 1971. 127–86.

Archer, Anne. 'Real Mummies.' *Studies in Canadian Literature* 9 (1984): 214–23.

Ardener, Edwin. '"The Problem" Revisited.' *Perceiving Women*. Ed. Shirley Ardener. London: Malaby, 1975. 19–27.

Ash, Susan. 'Having It Both Ways: Reading Related Short Fiction by Post-Colonial Women Writers.' *SPAN: Journal of the South Pacific Association for Commonwealth Literature and Language Studies* 28 (1989): 40–55.

Ashcroft, Bill, Gareth Griffiths, and Helen Tiffin. *The Empire Writes Back*. London: Routledge, 1989.

Atwood, Margaret. *The Handmaid's Tale*. Toronto: McClelland and Stewart, 1985.

– *The Robber Bride*. Toronto: McClelland and Stewart, 1993.

– *Selected Poems 1966–1984*. Toronto: Oxford UP, 1990. 60.

– *Survival: A Thematic Guide to Canadian Literature*. Toronto: Anansi, 1972.

Auerbach, Nina. Rev. of *The Madwoman in the Attic: The Woman Writer and the Nineteenth-Century Literary Imagination*, by Sandra M. Gilbert and Susan Gubar. *Victorian Studies* 23 (1980): 506.

Bakhtin, Mikhail. 'Discourse in the Novel.' *The Dialogic Imagination: Four Essays*. Austin: U of Texas P, 1981. 259–422.

– *Rabelais and His World*. Trans. Hélène Iswolsky. Bloomington: Indiana UP, 1984.

Banting, Pamela. 'Translation from A to Z: Notes on Daphne Marlatt's *Ana Historic*.' *Beyond Tish*. Ed. Douglas Barbour. Special Issue of *West Coast Line*. 25.1 (1991): 123–9.

'Barnum for President.' *Punch* 29 Sept. 1855: 89.

Bates, Ralph S. *Scientific Societies in the U.S.* Cambridge, Mass.: MIT P, 1965.

Becker, Susanne. 'Ironic Transformations: The Feminine Gothic in Aritha van Herk's *No Fixed Address*.' *Double Talking*. Ed. Linda Hutcheon. Toronto: ECW, 1992. 84–98.

Beer, Gillian. 'Darwin as Gulliver.' Alexander Lectures. University of Toronto. 23 Oct. 1995.

Belsey, Catherine. *Critical Practice*. New York: Methuen, 1980.

Benton, Joel. *Life of Hon. Phineas T. Barnum*. [Philadelphia]: Edgewood, 1891.

Bernal, J.D. *The Scientific and Industrial Revolutions*. Vol. 2 Cambridge, Mass.: MIT P, 1973.

Blakeley, Phyllis R. *Nova Scotia's Two Remarkable Giants*. Windsor, N.S.: Lancelot, 1970.

Bogdan, Robert. *Freak Show: Presenting Human Oddities for Amusement and Profit*. Chicago: U of Chicago P, 1988.

Boileau-Despréaux, Nicholas. *Traité du Sublime ou du Merveilleux dans le Discours Traduit du Grec de Longin*. 1674.

Bossanne, Brigitte G. 'Audrey Thomas and Lewis Carroll: Two Sides of the Looking Glass.' *North Dakota Quarterly* 52.3 (1984): 215–34.

Boulton, J.T. Introd. to *A Philosophical Enquiry ... by Edmund Burke*. xv–cxxvii.

Bowering, George. *Burning Water.* Toronto: New Press, 1980.
– *Caprice: A Novel.* Markham, Ont.: Viking, 1987.
– 'The Site of Blood.' Rev. of *Blown Figures*, by Audrey Thomas. *Canadian Literature* 65 (1975): 86–90.
– 'Snow Red: The Short Stories of Audrey Thomas.' *The Mask in Place: Essays on Fiction in North America.* Winnipeg: Turnstone, 1982. 63–76.
Bowlby, Rachel. *Virginia Woolf: Feminist Destinations.* Oxford and New York: Basil Blackwell, 1988.
Brodribb, Somer. *Nothing Mat(t)ers.* Toronto: James Lorimer and Co., 1992.
Brooks, Peter. *Reading for the Plot.* New York: Knopf, 1984.
Burke, Edmund. *A Philosophical Enquiry into the Origin of Our Ideas of the Sublime and Beautiful.* Ed. and introd. J.T. Boulton. London: Routledge, 1958.
Burr, Anna Robeson. *Weir Mitchell: His Life and Letters.* New York: Duffield, 1930.
Buss, Helen. *Mapping Ourselves: Canadian Women's Autobiography.* Montreal and Kingston: McGill-Queen's UP, 1993.
– 'Women and the Garrison Mentality: Pioneer Women Autobiographers and Their Relation to the Land.' McMullen 123–36.
Butler, Judith. *Gender Trouble: Feminism and the Subversion of Identity.* New York: Routledge, 1990.
– 'Contingent Foundations: Feminism and the Question of 'Postmodernism.'' *Feminists Theorize the Political.* Ed. Judith Butler and Joan W. Scott. New York and London: Routledge, 1992. 3–21.
Carter, Angela. *Nights at the Circus.* London: Chatto and Windus; Hogarth, 1984.
Cassirer, H.W. *A Commentary on Kant's 'Critique of Judgement'.* London: Methuen, 1938.
Chodorow, Nancy. *The Reproduction of Mothering: Psychoanalysis and the Sociology of Gender.* Berkley: U of California P, 1978.
Cixous, Hélène. 'The Laugh of the Medusa.' Trans. Keith Cohen and Paula Cohen. *New French Feminisms: An Anthology.* Ed. and introd. Elaine Marks and Isabelle de Courtivron. New York: Schocken, 1981. 245–64.
Clark, Hillary. 'Living with the Dead: Narrative Memory in Woolf's "A Sketch of the Past" and Marlatt's *How Hug a Stone*.' *Signature* 4 (1990): 1–12.
Clarke, G.N.G. 'Taking possession: The Cartouche as Cultural Text in Eighteenth-Century American Maps.' *Word and Image* 4.2 (1988): 455–74.
Clifford, James. 'On Collecting Art and Culture.' *Out There: Marginalization and Contemporary Cultures.* Cambridge, Mass.: MIT P, 1990.
Coldwell, Joan. 'Memory Organized: The Novels of Audrey Thomas.' *Canadian Literature* 92 (1982): 46–56.
– 'Natural History and *Intertidal Life*.' *Room of One's Own* 10.3–4 (1986): 140–9.
Cooley, Dennis. 'Recursions Excursions and Incursions: Daphne Marlatt Wrestles with the Angel Language.' *Line* 13 (1989): 66–79.

Coward, Rosalind. 'Female Desire: Women's Sexuality Today.' Eagleton 145–8.

Creed, Barbara. 'From Here to Modernity: Feminism and Postmodernism.' *Screen* 28.2 (1987): 47–67.

– 'Horror and the Monstrous-Feminine: An Imaginary Abjection.' *Screen* 27.1 (1986): 44–70.

Cunnington, Cecil W., and Phyllis Cunnington. *Handbook of English Costume in the Nineteenth Century.* London: Faber and Faber, 1959.

Daniels, George. *American Science in the Age of Jackson.* New York: Columbia UP, 1968.

Davey, Frank. 'Alternate Stories: The Short Fiction of Audrey Thomas and Margaret Atwood.' *Canadian Literature* 109 (1986): 5–14.

– 'Atwood Walking Backwards.' *Open Letter* 2nd ser. 5 (1973): 74–84.

– *Post-National Arguments: The Politics of the Anglophone- Canadian Novel since 1967.* Toronto: U of Toronto P, 1993.

– 'Words and Stones in *How Hug a Stone.*' *Line* 13 (1989): 40–6.

Davidson, Arnold E. 'Reading between the Texts in Audrey Thomas's *Munchmeyer and Prospero on the Island.*' *American Review of Canadian Studies* 15.4 (1985): 421–31.

de Lauretis, Teresa. *Alice Doesn't: Feminism, Semiotics, Cinema.* Bloomington: Indiana UP, 1984.

– 'The Essence of the Triangle, or, Taking the Risk of Essentialism Seriously: Feminist Theory in Italy, the U.S., and Britain.' *Differences* 1.2 (1989): 3–37.

– *Technologies of Gender: Essays on Theory, Film, and Fiction.* Bloomington: Indiana UP, 1987.

Deleuze, Gilles and Félix Guattari. *A Thousand Plateaus: Capitalism and Schizophrenia.* Trans. and fwd. Brian Massumi. Minneapolis: U of Minnesota P, 1987.

de Man, Paul. *Blindness and Insight: Essays in the Rhetoric of Contemporary Criticism.* New York: Oxford UP, 1971

– *The Resistance to Theory.* Theory and History of Literature, vol. 33. Minneapolis: U of Minnesota P, 1986.

Derrida, Jacques. 'Signature, Event, Context.' *Margins of Philosophy.* Chicago: U of Chicago P, 1982. 307–30.

– 'Structure, Sign, and Play in the Discourse of the Human Sciences.' *The Structuralist Controversy.* Ed. Richard Macksey and Eugenio Donato. Baltimore and London: Johns Hopkins UP, 1970. 247–65.

Diotte, Robert. 'The Romance of Penelope: Audrey Thomas's Isobel Carpenter Trilogy.' *Canadian Literature* 86 (1980): 60–8.

Douglas, Mary. *Purity and Danger: An Analysis of Concepts of Pollution and Taboo.* London: Routledge, 1966.

Duffey, Eliza B. *The Relations of the Sexes.* 1876; rpt. New York: Arno, 1974.

Eagleton, Mary. *Feminist Literary Theory: A Reader.* Oxford: Basil Blackwell, 1986, rpt. 1987.

Ebert, Teresa. 'The "Difference" of Postmodern Feminism.' *College English* 53.8 (1991): 886–904.

Ehrenreich, Barbara, and Deirdre English. *For Her Own Good: 150 Years of the Experts' Advice to Women*. Garden City, N.Y.: Anchor/Doubleday, 1979.

Empson, William. *Seven Types of Ambiguity*. London: Chatto and Windus, 1930.

Felman, Shoshana. 'Rereading Femininity.' *Yale French Studies* 62 (1981): 19–44.

Ferguson, Frances. 'The Sublime of Edmund Burke, or the Bathos of Experience.' *Glyph* 8 (1981): 62–78.

Fiedler, Leslie. *Freaks: Myths and Images of the Secret Self*. New York: Simon, 1978.

Flax, Jane. 'The End of Innocence.' *Feminists Theorize the Politcal*. Ed. Judith Butler and Joan W. Scott. 445–63.

Fletcher, Angus. *The Prophetic Moment: An Essay on Spenser*. Chicago: Chicago UP, 1971.

Foucault, Michel. *The History of Sexuality Vol. 1: An Introduction*. Trans. Robert Hurley. New York: Random, 1980.

– 'Nietzsche, Genealogy, History.' *Language, Counter-memory, Practice: Selected Essays and Interviews with Michel Foucault*. Ithaca: Cornell UP, 1977. 139–64.

– 'Two Lectures.' *Power/Knowledge: Selected Interviews and Other Writings 1972–1977*. Ed. Colin Gordon. New York: Pantheon, 1980. 78–108.

Fowler, Alistair. *Kinds of Literature: An Introduction to the Theory of Genres and Modes*. Cambridge, Mass.: Harvard UP, 1982.

Fox-Genovese, Elizabeth. 'The Claims of a Common Culture: Gender, Race, Class and the Canon.' *Salmagundi* 72 (1986): 131–43.

Fraser, Wayne. *The Dominion of Women: The Personal and the Political in Canadian Women's Literature*. Westport, Conn.: Greenwood, 1991.

Freud, Sigmund. 'Beyond the Pleasure Principle.' *The Standard Edition of the Complete Psychological Works of Sigmund Freud*. Trans. and ed. James Strachey. 24 vols. London: Hogarth, 1955. 18:7–61.

– 'Femininity.' *The Standard Edition*. 22:112–35.

– 'The "Uncanny."' *The Standard Edition*. 17:218–52.

Frye, Northrop. *Anatomy of Criticism: Four Essays*. Princeton: Princeton UP, 1957.

– *The Bush Garden: Essays on the Canadian Imagination*. Toronto: Anansi, 1971.

– *The Secular Scripture: A Study of the Structure of Romance*. Cambridge, Mass.: Harvard UP, 1976.

Gilbert, Sandra M., and Susan Gubar. *The Madwoman in the Attic: The Woman Writer and the Nineteenth-Century Literary Imagination*. New Haven and London: Yale UP, 1979.

Gilligan, Carol. *In a Different Voice: Psychological Theory and Women's Development*. Cambridge, Mass.: Harvard UP, 1993.

Godard, Barbara. *Audrey Thomas and Her Works*. Toronto: ECW, 1989.

– '"Body I": Daphne Marlatt's Feminist Poetics.' *American Review of Canadian Studies* 25.4 (1985): 486–96.

Griffen, Susan. *Woman and Nature: The Roaring Inside Her*. New York: Harper and Row, 1978.

– 'The Way of All Ideology.' *Signs* 7.3 (1982): 641–60.

Grosz, Elizabeth. 'Inscriptions and Body-Maps: Representations and the Corporeal.' *Feminine Masculine and Representation*. Terry Threadgold and Ann Granny-Francis. North Sydney, Australia: Allen, 1990. 62–74.

– 'A Thousand Tiny Sexes: Feminism and Rhizomatics.' Unpub. paper presented at the Deleuze and Guattari Conference at Trent University, 15–17 May 1992.

Grove, Frederick Philip. *In Search of Myself*. 1946. Toronto: McClelland and Stewart, 1974.

– *Settlers of the Marsh*. 1925. Toronto: McClelland and Stewart, 1992.

Haller, John S., Jr, and Robin Haller. *The Physician and Sexuality in Victorian America*. Urbana: U of Illinois P, 1974.

Halmi, N.A. 'From Hierarchy to Opposition: Allegory and the Sublime.' *Comparative Literature* 44.4 (1992): 337–60.

Haraway, Donna. 'A Manifesto for Cyborgs: Science, Technology, and Socialist Feminism in the 1980s.' Nicholson 190–233.

Harpham, Geoffrey Galt. *On the Grotesque: Strategies of Contradiction in Art and Literature*. Princeton: Princeton UP, 1982.

Hart, Kevin. 'Maps of Deconstruction.' *Meanjin* 45.1 (1986): 107–17.

Hartsock, Nancy. 'Foucault on Power: A Theory for Women?' Nicholson. 157–75.

Heffernan, Teresa. 'Tracing the Travesty: Constructing the Female Subject in Susan Swan's *The Biggest Modern Woman of the World*.' *Canadian Literature* 13.3 (1992): 24–37.

Hekman, Susan. *Gender and Knowledge: Elements of a Postmodern Feminism*. Boston: Northeastern UP, 1992.

Hertz, Neil. 'The Notion of Blockage in the Literature of the Sublime.' *The End of the Line*. New York: Columbia, 1985. 40–60.

Hoy, David Couzens. 'Foucault: Modern or Postmodern?' *After Foucault: Humanistic Knowledge, Postmodern Challenges*. Ed. Jonathan Arac. London: Rutgers UP, 1988. 12–41.

Howells, Coral Ann. 'Inheritance and Instablility: Audrey Thomas's Real Mothers.' *Recherches Anglaises et Nord-Americaines* 20 (1987): 157–62.

– 'No Sense of an Ending: *Real Mothers*.' *Room of One's Own* 10.3–4 (1986): 111–23.

– 'No Transcendental Image: Canadianness in Contemporary Women's Fictions in English.' *British Journal of Canadian Studies* 6.3 (1991): 110–17.

– *Private and Fictional Words*. London: Methuen, 1987.

Huggan, Graham. 'Decolonizing the Map.' Adam 125–38.

– *Territorial Disputes: Maps and Mapping Strategies in Contemporary Canadian and Australian Fiction*. Toronto: University of Toronto P, 1994.

Hutcheon, Linda. *The Canadian Postmodern: A Study of Contemporary English-Canadian Fiction*. Toronto: Oxford UP, 1988.

– 'The Politics of Representation.' *Signature* 1 (1989): 23–44.

– *A Theory of Parody: The Teachings of Twentieth-Century Art Forms*. London: Methuen, 1985.

Huyssen, Andreas. *Marking Time in a Culture of Amnesia*. New York: Routledge, 1995.

Hyde, Lewis. *The Gift: Imagination and the Erotic Life of Property*. New York: Random, 1979.

Irigaray, Luce. *This Sex Which Is Not One.* Trans. Catherine Porter. Ithaca: Cornell UP, 1985.

Irvine, Lorna. 'Sailing the Oceans of the World.' *New Quarterly* 7.1–2 (1987): 284–93.

– *Sub/version: Canadian Fictions by Women.* Toronto: ECW, 1986.

Jameson, Fredric. Foreword. *The Postmodern Condition: A Report on Knowledge,* By Lyotard. vii–xxi.

– 'Postmodernism, or the Cultural Logic of Late Capitalism.' *New Left Review* 146 (1984): 53–92.

Jenkins, Dominic. Personal Interview. 13 Oct. 1993.

Jentsche, E. 'Zur Psychologie des Unheimlichen.' *Psychiat.- Neurol. Wschr.* 8 (1906): 195.

Jones, Dorothy. '"A Kingdom and a Place of Exile": Women Writers and the World of Nature.' *World Literature Written in English* 24.2 (1984): 257–73.

– 'Restoring the Temples: The Fiction of Aritha van Herk.' *Kunapipi* 16.1 (1994): 416–31.

Kamboureli, Smaro. 'The Biggest Modern Woman in the World: Canada as the Absent Spouse.' *Australian Canadian Studies: A Journal for the Humanities and Social Sciences* 6.1 (1988): 103–10.

Kant, Immanuel. *Critique of Judgement.* 1790. Trans. and introd. Werner S. Pluhar. Indianapolis: Hacket, 1987.

– *Critique of Pure Reason.* Trans. and introd. Norman Kemp Smith. 2nd ed. London: Macmillan, 1933.

Kayser, Wolfgang. *The Grotesque in Art and Literature.* Trans. Ulrich Weisstein. Bloomington: Indiana UP, 1963.

Keith, WJ. *Canadian Literature in English.* London: Longman, 1985.

Keitner, Wendy. 'Real Mothers Don't Write Books: A Study of the Penelope-Calypso Motif in the Fiction of Audrey Thomas and Marian Engel.' *Present Tense: A Critical Anthology.* Ed. and introd. John Moss. The Canadian Novel, No. 4. Toronto: NC, 1985. 185–204.

Keitner, Wendy, and Phyllis Gottlieb. 'Narrative Technique and the Central Female Character in the Novels of Audrey Thomas.' *World Literature Written in English* 21.2 (1982): 364–73.

Keller, Evelyn Fox. 'Feminism and Science.' *Signs* 7.3 (1982): 589–602.

– 'Making Gender Visible in Pursuit of Nature's Secrets.' *Feminist Studies/Critical Studies.* Ed. Teresa de Lauretis. Bloomington: Indiana UP, 1986. 67–77.

– *Reflections on Gender and Science.* New Haven: Yale UP, 1985.

Kolodny, Annette. *The Lay of the Land: Metaphors as Experience and History in American Life and Letters.* Chapel Hill: U of North Carolina P, 1975.

Kreisel, Henry. 'The Broken Globe.' *The Best Modern Canadian Short Stories.* Ed. Ivon Owen and Morris Wolfe Edmonton: Hurtig, 1978. 50–8.

Kristeva, Julia. *Revolution of Poetic Language.* New York: Columbia UP, 1984.

Kroetsch, Robert. 'The Fear of Women in Prairie Fiction: An Erotics of Space.' *Essays on Saskatchewan Writing.* Ed. E.F. Dyck. Regina: Saskatchewan Writers' Guild, 1986. 97–108.

– *Gone Indian.* Toronto: New Press, 1973; rpt Toronto: Theytus, 1981.

– 'Kingdom of the Male Virgin.' Rev. of *Petrigo's Calgary*, by Walter Petrigo. *NeWest Review* 1.4 (1975): 1.
– 'Unhiding the Hidden: Recent Canadian Fiction.' *Journal of Canadian Fiction* 3.3 (1974): 43–5.

Lacan, Jacques. *Écrits: A Selection*. Trans. Alan Sheridan. New York: Norton, 1977.

Laderoute, Bette, ed. 'Swan: Four Generations of Swans Dislike Her Book.' People Sec. *Maclean's* 17 Sept. 1984: 64.

Laurence, Margaret. *A Bird in the House*. Toronto: McClelland and Stewart, 1974.

Lecker, Robert. *Making It Real: The Canonization of English-Canadian Literature*. Concord, Ont.: Anansi, 1995.

Lee, Dennis. 'Cadence, Country, Silence: Writing in Colonial Space.' *Open Letter*. 2.6 (1973): 34–53.

Lerner, Gerda. *The Creation of Patriarchy*. New York: Oxford UP, 1986.

Light, Alison. '"Returning to Manderly" – Romance Fiction, Female Sexuality and Class.' Eagleton 140–5.

Lorde, Audry. 'The Master's Tools Will Never Dismantle the Master's House.' *This Bridge Called My Back: Writings By Radical Women of Color*. Ed. Cherrie Moraga and Gloria Anzaldua. New York: Kitchen Table, 1981. 98–101.

Lyotard, Jean-François. *The Postmodern Condition: A Report on Knowledge*. Trans. Geoff Bennington and Brian Massumi. Theory and History of Literature, vol. 10. Minneapolis: U of Minnesota P, 1984.
– 'The Sublime and the Avant-Garde.' *The Lyotard Reader*. Ed. Andrew Benjamin. Oxford: Basil Blackwell, 1989.

McCombs, Judith, ed and introd. *Critical Essays on Margaret Awood*. Boston: G.K. Hall, 1988.

McCourt, Edward. *The Canadian West in Fiction*. Revised ed. Toronto: Ryerson, 1970.

McGee, Thomas D'Arcy. 'The Mental Outfit of the New Dominion.' *Montreal Gazette* 1867; rpt. *The Evolution of Canadian Literature in English: Beginnings to 1867*. Ed. Mary Jane Edwards. Toronto: Holt, 1973. 254–64.

MacLaren, I.S. 'A Charting of the Van Herk Papers.' *The Aritha van Herk Papers: First Accession*. Calgary: U of Calgary P, 1987. xi–xlv.

McMullen, Loraine, ed. *Re(dis)covering our Foremothers: Nineteenth Century Canadian Women Writers*. Ottawa: U of Ottawa P, 1990.

Magri, Countess M. Lavinia. *The Autobiography of Mrs. Tom Thumb: Some of My Life Experiences*. Ed. and intro. A.H. Saxon. Hamden, Conn.: Archon, 1979.

Massumi, Brian. Foreword. *A Thousand Plateaus*, by Gilles Deleuze and Félix Guattari. ix–xv.

Mellor, Anne K. *Romanticism and Gender*. New York: Routledge, 1993.

Mitchell, Juliet. *Women: The Longest Revolution: Essays on Feminism, Literature and Psychoanalysis*. London: Virago, 1984.

Moers, Ellen. *Literary Women*. Garden City, N.Y.: Doubleday, 1976.

Moi, Toril. *Sexual/ Textual Politics*. London and New York: Routledge, 1985.

Monk, Samuel. *The Sublime: A Study of Critical Theories in XVIII-Century England*. New York: MLA, 1935.

Monmonier, Mark. *How to Lie with Maps*. Chicago: U of Chicago P, 1991.

Montiesor, C. *Some Hobby Horses; or, How to Collect Stamps, Coins, Seals, Crests, and Scraps*. London: W.H. Allen and Co., 1890.

Moore, Henrietta L. *Feminism and Anthropology*. Minneapolis: U Minnesota P, 1988.

Mort, Frank. *Dangerous Sexualities: Medico-Moral Politics in England since 1830*. London: Routledge, 1987.

Mulvey, Laura. 'Visual Pleasure and Narrative Cinema.' *Screen* 16.3 (1975): 6–18.

Munro, Alice. 'Meneseteung.' *Friend of My Youth*. Toronto: McClelland and Stewart, 1990; rpt. Penguin, 1991. 50–73.

Murray, Heather. '"Its Image on the Mirror": Canada, Canonicity, the Uncanny.' *Essays on Canadian Writing* 42 (1990): 102–30.

Neuman, Shirley and Smaro Kamboureli, eds. *A Mazing Space: Writing Canadian Women Writing*. Edmonton: Longspoon, 1986.

Nicholson, Linda J, ed. *Feminism/ Postmodernism*. New York: Routledge, 1990.

Nietzsche, Friedrich. *On the Genealogy of Morals and Ecce Homo*. Trans. Walter Kaufmann. New York: Random, 1969.

Northey, Margot. *The Haunted Wilderness: The Gothic and Grotesque in Canadian Fiction*. U of Toronto P, 1976.

Ortner, Sherry. 'Is Female to Male as Nature Is to Culture?' *Women, Culture, and Society*. Ed. Michelle Zimbalist Rosaldo and Louise Lamphere. Stanford: Stanford UP, 1974. 67–88.

Osler, Sir William. *Aequanimitas: With Other Addresses to Medical Students, Nurses and Practitioners of Medicine*. Philadelphia: P. Blakiston's Sons, 1932.

Owens, Craig. 'The Discourse of Others: Feminists and Postmodernism.' *The Anti-Aesthetic: Essays on Postmodern Culture*. Introd. Hall Forester. Seattle: Bay P, 1983. 57–82.

Parker, Patricia. *Inescapable Romance*. Princeton: Princeton UP, 1979.

Patton, Paul. 'Conceptual Politics and the War-Machine in *Mille Plateaux*.' *Substance* 44–5 (1984): 61–80.

Pratt, Viola Whitney. *Canadian Portraits: Osler, Banting, Penfield; Famous Doctors*. Toronto; Vancouver: Clarke, 1956.

Prentice, Chris. 'Re-Writing Their Stories, Renaming Themselves: Post-Colonialism and Feminism in the Fictions of Keri Hulme and Audrey Thomas.' *SPAN* 23 (1986): 68–80.

Rabasa, José. 'Allegories of the Atlas.' *Europe and Its Others*. Ed. Francis Barker et. al. 2 vols. Colchester: U of Essex P, 1985. 2:1–16.

Radhakrishnan, R. 'Ethnic Identity and Post-Structuralist Differance.' *Cultural Critique* 6 (1987): 199–220.

Radway, Janice. 'Women Read the Romance: The Interaction of Text and Context.' Eagleton 128–34.

Rich, Adrienne. 'Compulsory Heterosexuality and Lesbian Existence.' *Blood, Bread, and Poetry: Selected Prose 1979–1985.* New York: Norton, 1986. 23–71.

– 'When We Dead Awaken: Writing as Re-Vision.' *On Lies, Secrets and Silence: Selected Prose 1966–1978.* New York: Norton, 1979. 33–49.

Ricou, Laurie. 'Phyllis Webb, Daphne Marlatt and Similitude.' Neuman 205–15.

– *Vertical Man Horizontal World: Man and Landscape in Canadian Prairie Fiction.* Vancouver: U British Columbia P, 1973.

Riley, Denise. 'Does Sex Have a History? "Women"and Feminism.' *New Formations* 1 (1987): 133–45.

Robinson, Sally. *Engendering the Subject: Gender and Self- Representation in Contemporary Women's Fiction.* New York: SUNY P, 1991.

Ruskin, John. *Sesame and Lilies.* 5th ed. Kent: George Allen, 1882.

Russ, Joanna. 'Somebody's Trying to Kill Me and I Think It's My Husband: The Modern Gothic.' *Journal of Popular Culture* 6.4 (1973): 1:666–91.

Said, Edward. *Beginnings: Intention and Method.* New York: Basic, 1975.

Salutin, Rick. 'Americans and Their Cheerful Self-Absorption.' *Globe and Mail.* 6 Oct. 1995: C1.

Saxon, A.H. *P.T. Barnum: The Legend and the Man.* New York: Columbia UP, 1989.

Scott, Gail. 'A Feminist at the Carnival.' *Language in Her Eye: Writing and Gender, Views by Canadian Women Writing in English.* Ed. Libby Scheier, Sarah Sheard, and Eleanor Wachtel. Toronto: Coach House, 1990. 241–55.

– *Spaces Like Stairs.* Toronto: Women's Press, 1989.

Shakespeare, William. *Hamlet, Prince of Denmark. The Riverside Shakespeare.* 2 vols. Boston: Houghton Mifflin Co., 1974. 2:1135–97.

Showalter, Elaine. 'Feminist Criticism in the Wilderness.' *Critical Inquiry* 8.2 (1981): 179–205.

– *A Literature of Their Own: British Women Novelists from Brontë to Lessing.* London: Virago, 1978.

Silverman, Kaja. *The Subject of Semiotics.* New York: Oxford UP, 1983.

Slemon, Stephen. 'Modernism's Last Post.' Adams 1–11.

Slotkin, Richard. *Regeneration through Violence.* Middleton, Conn.: Wesleyan UP, 1973.

Smith, A.L. 'Are Modern School Methods in Keeping with Physiological Knowlege?' *Bulletin of American Academy of Medicine,* 6 (1905).

Snitow, Ann Barr. 'Mass Market Romance: Pornography for Women is Different.' Eagleton 134–40.

Söderlind, Sylvia. *Margin/ Alias: Language and Colonization in Canadian and Quebecoise Fiction.* Toronto: U of Toronto P, 1991.

Spencer, Herbert. *The Study of Sociology.* New York: 1896.

Spenser, Edmund. *Books I and II of The Faerie Queene, The Mutability Cantos and Selections from the Minor Poetry.* Ed. Robert Kellogg and Oliver Steele. Indianapolis: Bobbs-Merrill, 1965.

Staines, David. *Beyond the Provinces: Literary Canada at Century's End.* Toronto: U of Toronto P, 1995.

Stewart, Susan. *Nonsense: Aspects of Intertextuality in Folklore and Literature.* Baltimore: Johns Hopkins UP, 1978.

– *On Longing: Narratives of the Miniature, the Gigantic, the Souvenir, the Collection.* Durham: Duke UP, 1993.

Stouk, David. *Major Canadian Authors: A Critical Introduction.* Lincoln: U of Nebraska P, 1984.

Swan-Ryan, Linda. 'A Swan Song.' Letter. *Maclean's* 29 Oct. 1984: 8.

Theweleit, Klaus. *Women, Floods, Bodies, History.* Vol. 1 of *Male Phantasies.* 2 vols. Minnisota: U of Minnisota P, 1987.

Tolstoy, Leo. *Anna Karenin.* Trans. and introd. Rosemary Edmonds. London: Penguin, 1978.

Tostevin, Lola Lemire. 'Daphne Marlatt: Writing in the Space That Is Her Mother's Face.' *Line* 13 (1989): 32–9.

Vinaver, Eugene. *The Rise of Romance.* New York: Oxford UP, 1971.

Vogt, Carl. *Lectures on Man, His Place in Creation, and in the History of the Earth.* London: Longman, 1864.

Wachtel, Eleanor. 'The Guts of Mrs. Blood.' *Books in Canada* Nov. 1979: 3–6.

Waugh, Patricia. *Feminine Fictions: Revisiting the Postmodern.* London: Routledge, 1989.

Weedon, Chris. *Feminist Practice and Poststructuralist Theory.* Oxford: Basil Blackwell, 1987.

Weir, Lorraine. 'Toward A Feminist Hermeneutics: Jay Macpherson's *Welcoming Disaster.*' *Gynocritics.* Ed. Barbara Godard. Toronto: ECW, 1987. 59–70.

Weiskel, Thomas. *The Romantic Sublime: Studies in the Structure and Psychology of Transcendence.* Baltimore: Johns Hopkins UP, 1976.

White, Hayden. 'The Value of Narrativity in the Representation of Reality.' *Critical Inquiry* 7.1 (1980): 5–27.

Wiebe, Rudy. 'Passage by Land.' *The Narrative Voice: Short Stories and Reflections by Canadian Authors.* Ed. John Metcalf. Toronto: McGraw-Hill Ryerson, 1972. 257–60.

Wilson, Ethel. *The Swamp Angel.* Toronto: Macmillan, 1954.

Winterson, Jeanette. *Sexing the Cherry.* London: Vintage, 1989.

Wittgenstein, Ludwig. *Philosophical Investigations.* Oxford: Basil Blackwell, 1968.

Wittig, Monique. *Les Guérillères.* Boston: Beacon, 1969.

– 'The Straight Mind.' *Feminist Issues* 1 (1980): 106–7.

Wood-Allen, Mary. *Marriage; Its Duties and Privileges.* 1901. Introd. Shiela M. Rothman. Farmingdale, N.Y.: Dabor Social Science Publications, 1978.

Woolf, Virginia. *A Room of One's Own.* London: Granada, 1982.

– 'Professions for Women.' *The Death of the Moth.* London: Hogarth, 1942. 149–54.

– *Three Guineas.* Middlesex: Penguin, 1978.

Zabus, Chantal. 'A Calibanic Tempest in Anglophone and Francophone New World Writing.' *Canadian Literature* 104 (1985): 40–5.

Index